MY TWENTIETH CENTURY

CENTURY

Fragments of Memory

Bina Garncarska-Kadary

Translated from Hebrew by Rebecca Wolpe

TABLE OF CONTENTS

NOTES TO
THE ENGLISH EDITION

This edition is a translation of the Hebrew edition, published in 2008 in Israel by Moreshet Publishing House.

Translating names and places from Hebrew to English presented the usual challenge. In this edition, we have tried to preserve all the names as my mother, the author, kept in her memory: places in Poland are usually spelled in Polish (e.g., Końskie, Łódź), while sites in Soviet Russia are spelled in English.

The family names, often in Yiddish, are usually spelled phonetically using the English alphabet (Shlojme, Rojza, etc.). In addition, the book includes an index of names and places to assist readers in finding possible references to their relatives whom my mother encountered in her life.

The book contains several references to time-related events, like something that happened "two weeks ago," "he is today an IDF officer," or similar. However, since my mother passed away in March 2005, the reader is advised to assume end of 2004 as a time reference for such timeline referrals.

Victor Kadary

PREFACE

I never expected to reach the age of eighty-three. I have finished all my projects and completed all my work. I no longer have the desire to embark on new enterprises. And yet, my children and grandchildren seem to expect something from me; they expect me to say or do something. I feel that I am disappointing them. If I have anything left to tell them, especially my granddaughters, it is my personal memories. They concern a century that is now drawing to its close. They touch, in one way or another, on the events that I experienced or in which I was directly involved. In the time left to me, I will try to devote myself to collecting the fragments of my memories.

The twentieth century was my century. Indeed, this is my opportunity to try to look at the events of that century from a personal perspective. I do not profess to write about the history of that century but about my life and the historical events that affected it, about the surroundings in which I was raised and about the people I knew.

I was born before the cannons of World War I had cooled, as Poland, after almost 150 years of servitude, was liberating itself. It was still fighting for its borders in the east and in the west. To "relieve the tension," during the victory parades held in cities and towns, the regiments of its liberating army commanded by General

Haller conducted pogroms against the Jews, whom they despoiled, beat, robbed. They left marks also on the town of my birth. I was told about this when I grew up.

Germany came out of the war defeated and humiliated. In Great Russia, the Tsar was dethroned. I was two months old when the famous October Revolution took place in Russia, shocking the world.

These events did not herald good things, and the persecution of the Jews and the pogroms that occurred at the start of Poland's liberation were a sign of things to come in liberated Poland. They would accompany me in the coming years, with all the contrasts and contradictions they entailed. World War I left a deep imprint on the lives of my parents and on the narrow world of my childhood. From a more economic perspective—the results of this war laid the basis for the slaughter of World War II. The end of this war almost coincided with the close of the first half of the twentieth century. This was a black jubilee, when civilization and culture reached an all-time low: Stalinism, Fascism, and Nazism; the Holocaust; Hiroshima, Majdanek, Sobibor, and Auschwitz. And my generation, of which only physically and mentally damaged remnants remained, would carry this cursed century with it to the end of its days, leaving open wounds also for the next generation.

Yet, in the twentieth century, we also reached new heights in the development of technology. It was a century of amazing developments in science, it was the century of hi-tech and the internet, which opened new channels of communication between individuals and between continents, the century in which man reached the moon and came close to reaching other planets . . . but . . .

The twentieth century took humanity to the lowest possible level. From this point onward, we see fewer philosophers, fewer humanists, and fewer pedagogues deserving of the name. By contrast, rape, murder, and war have increased. Kosovo, Uganda, and other disasters on the Africa; the radical fanaticism of Judaism and Islam; and in our country of Israel the worrying changes in demography (I do not mean the Arabs specifically) and the increasing nationalism, both directed internally and toward our close neighbors in the Middle East—all this is suffocating. It is hard to live in this modern world, a century during which my son had to go through three cruel wars, in which my daughter, a humanist from her birth, cannot find herself in society. . . . Life has become emptier and cheaper; it is materialistic and cruel. In the twentieth century, children come to school with knives in their pencil cases.

⟩⟨ ⟩⟨

Memory is selective. One usually remembers things that are engraved on the soul, and with the passing of the years, personal experiences become murkier, foggy, and take on different forms, yet some of them are stuck like thorns in our memories. I am aware that different people perceive the same events differently, that each one remembers things or people in a completely unique light. With the passing of the years, we tend to idealize certain things, in particular the people we loved, while less pleasant experiences become foggier, or we forget them entirely. Not long ago I had a chance to speak to my cousin who is the same age as me (he lives in Paris and he came to visit me). His opinions about the people and relatives that inhabit my memories differ completely to mine. He sees events and other things that happened to us in our childhood and in later periods in a completely different light.

With all these reservations in mind, I will try to collect the scraps of my memories and describe the events of my long life as I remember and perceive them.

PART 1

Between the Wars

CHAPTER 1
CHILDHOOD

My Parents' Legacy

I was born in Końskie (Yiddish: Koinsk), the district capital of the Kielce region in Central Poland, an average town with more than 20,000 residents, around 60 percent of whom were Jews. Końskie, an elegant town full of green vegetation, lies within a massive expanse of pine forests. Apart from two or three western industrialized sub-districts, the Kielce region was largely agricultural, although its sandy earth, like the agriculture and the residents, was poor and weak. The Jewish community in Końskie, which was among the oldest in Poland, was like hundreds of other Jewish communities. Indeed, similar to most of the Jewish communities in the surroundings, it was poor and religious, and most Jews were followers of various Hasidic Rebbes.

Within the Kielce region, Końskie was unique. It had a long tradition as an industrial town. Due to its location on the northern edge of the old industrial district (Zagłębie Staropolskie), the soil in the close surroundings was rich with iron lead. Some of the oldest foundries in Poland, dating back to the fifteenth century, were established in the town and its surroundings, and, from the seventeenth century, the owner of the lands, Count Jan Małachowski, built metal workshops and forges. The Jews played no part in this industry but there were more opportunities for trade, which was then entirely controlled by the Jews, than in other poor towns in Poland. Jews distributed the products made in Końskie throughout Poland and Jewish merchants played a prominent role in the area. The town also served as a trade junction of Poland. The developments at the end of the eighteenth century changed the face of the town. As other centers of industry and trade developed, together with the railways, Końskie became a poor provincial town, far from the axes of development. Almost one hundred years passed before, at the end of the nineteenth century, with the construction of the railway to Końskie (in 1885), the Jews renewed the tradition of this industrial town. They established innovative industrial factories, both large and medium sized, and these provided livelihoods for thousands of families in the impoverished surroundings.

I do not intend to discuss here in detail the history of this town, which I left almost as a child (I wrote an article about it in Gal-Ed, no. 18, and in the memorial book about the town Końskie by Zarys Dziejów, Czech 1998. However, many decades after I left, on a hurried visit years ago, I understood that despite the vicissitudes of fate, I carry the memories of this town, my roots in it, and my longing for it, as well as the complexes related to it, very deep inside me. I suddenly understood that a significant part of my being— the good and also the bad parts of me—comes from my home and from the cultural atmosphere of the town.

I know almost nothing about my distant ancestors. I saw my paternal grandfather, Elijah Szarfharc, father of my father Beresh (Dov), once in my early childhood. He came from Lublin, my father's native city, in which he studied in the famous yeshiva, and my grandfather, if I am not mistaken, was a teacher there. I remember my grandfather Elijah as a saintly figure: wearing a shtreimel, a satin kaftan, with a well-kept sage's beard, his back bent over, and walking with a stick. Every now and again, my father reminded us children that we should be proud of our lineage. His was a family of rabbis, great scholars, and well-to-do merchants, but I barely knew them.

My father himself was a scholar of the Torah and the Talmud, and before WWI, he was also well-to-do. He was a wood merchant and he had other business interests as well. I knew that my mother was his second wife. From later stories that my father told, I discovered that he divorced his first wife, despite his great love for her, at the recommendation of his rabbi, because she could not give him children, and mainly because she did not give him a son. Before the divorce, so he told us, he bought his wife a new black dress, and himself a kaftan, and put the quarries he owned in the area of Szydłowiec in her name. And then he looked for a wife who could promise him children.

I do not know much about the origins of my mother, Sarah Rivka, née Rosenfarb, apart from the fact that all the Rosenfarbs, her brothers and sisters, were religious. Sara'le (Ahuva)—the daughter of my oldest brother, Moshe, and the only one who keeps the religious traditions—relates that my mother, her grandmother, had an exceptional lineage that could be traced back to the fourteenth or sixteenth centuries and that she descended from a great rabbi, Simcha Bunim of Peshischa, who composed a number of halakhic works and tikkunim, and who was also rabbi of Prague (Czechoslovakia). I admit that I do not know anything about this. My ignorance in this regard results from the fact that I left home at a young age, and apart from that, I do not attribute any importance whatsoever to lineage.

My mother was a young and beautiful widow. In our town, they called her Di sheyne Rifkele (The beautiful little Rivka). Apparently, a marriage broker suggested the match between my parents, and they married in 1910 or 1911. Each one came to the marriage canopy with memories and experiences from the past, because my mother too, a widow aged twenty-five, nurtured in her heart the memory of the good life she had with her first husband, who died very young. She already had three children, the youngest of them, Shoshana (originally Roza-Raizel), was two or three years old, the middle son, David, five or six and Moshe, the eldest. This match, as I remember, was not the most successful. Each one frequently remembered their past happiness, to the extent that their marriage was paved with crises, leaving in my heart grievances against my father.

Apart from "her" three children, my mother brought to the marriage the dowry of an agricultural farm with livestock. However, from my perspective, this was ancient history. Indeed, I was born at the end of the war, when nothing was left of my parents' wealth. The only sign of it left in our dilapidated house was the fabric hat that belonged to my big sister Shoshana and the stories about a goat. According to the story, Shoshana wore this hat when she took the goat out to graze. This goat was the only animal that remained in our home for any length of time, because it provided milk for the children. I do not remember the goat either.

As I said, the war impoverished our parents. Like most of the residents of Końskie, both worked hard, but my mother worked harder: first of all, my father had to make time to study Torah. Second, my mother endeavored to make sure that our father would not feel the burden of his stepchildren. My mother bore him six children, meaning that in total she had nine children. After the Shoah, only me and my sister Chaya Esther, of blessed memory, who immigrated to Mandatory Palestine in 1938, remained. Of my mother's three children from her first marriage, my brother Moshe, my mother's firstborn, survived the death camps, and my beloved sister Shoshana, of blessed memory, wandered with me and her family through Russia during the war. Now, only I remain among the living.

Fate mocked my father, who so wanted a son to say Kaddish for him. The first three children that my mother bore him were girls. The first, Goldie, I do not remember, because she died as a child. The second, Esther, lived her whole life with a complex that my father did not love her because she should have been a boy (in fact, my father was very fond of her, discerning in her the "male" rational way of thinking). I, the third daughter (and the second to remain alive), felt the same, and I have my own complexes too. Only the two children who came after me, Meir, and two and a half years later Isaiah (Shayale), made my father happy. The last baby, another girl, went to heaven at the age of one month, almost immediately after my mother died.

Between each child there was an age gap of two and a half to three years. Our mother apparently breastfed us for a long time so that she would not fall pregnant too frequently. All my father's children looked like him. All were beautiful, all had blonde curls and blue eyes, all, that is, apart from me. I looked like my mother and my sister Shoshana—with brown eyes and brown hair.

The first flashes of memory, which are stored somewhere in my brain, are foggy. I was apparently around three years old. At home there was extraordinary activity: as I discovered later, the family was preparing to perform the ceremony for the redemption of the son for my father's firstborn son, my brother Meir. I remember clearly that I was sick, that I had fits of whooping cough, and that in the morning my father took me for a "walk" to cross a certain river that was supposed to cure my whooping cough. This was apparently near the village of Rogów, not far from the town. I remember an image: my father crossing a wooden bridge, carrying me in his arms. There, on the other side of the river, we sat for a little while, until dogs approached, barking menacingly, and I started to cry. We returned home. That evening there were a lot of people in our home. In the room the men prayed and in the kitchen the women were busy with refreshments. It's funny—at the time, I was still sleeping in a crib.

In my next flash of memory, Meir is three years old. My father wrapped him in a prayer shawl, took him in his arms, grasped my hand (I was two and a half years older than him), and brought us to the Kheyder. I was the only girl who learned in the Kheyder, and, together with the rest of the small children, I repeated after the "Rebbe"—the melamed or teacher of small children—"Kometz alef – o" to a special tune. The classroom was crowded. Children sat on all three sides of the long and simple table, in a U shape, and the teacher sat at its head. In the small kitchen, which, I believe, had no door or anything else to separate it, his wife cooked the meals. By contrast, the courtyard was spacious, albeit without any greenery or trees. There we played during the breaks. I do not remember how long I learned at that Kheyder, and I wonder why I, and only I, and not any of my father's other daughters, spent time there. Apparently, I was tasked with looking after little Meir, my father's only son. I stopped going to the Kheyder when the next baby, Shayele, was born. I had to look after him.

And indeed, I looked after little Shayele. I spent all day with him at home. To avoid boredom, my mother brought a friend for me. Her name was Bina Ketzale. Not only did we share the same first name, but we were the same age (I was given two names, Bina and Yehudit—the latter is pronounced in Yiddish Yides, and therefore I did not like my second name). The Ketzale family lived in an attic in a house not far from our home. Bina's father was a teacher of young children. His Kheyder was in the same attic in which they lived. We were then in a difficult financial situation. Yet apparently there is no bottom to the depths of hardship, and there is always someone worse off than you, because the Ketzale family was in more desperate straits than we were. Bina spent every day with us, from morning until night. We ate together what my mother left for us. My relationship with Bina Ketzale was broken off when I was about six, when we moved to a new apartment on 3 Maja Street. I met her again in first grade, but there was a certain distance between us. Because, due to circumstances that I will describe later, I learned in first grade for only two weeks; I never saw her again. Many years later, I heard that she had left the town at a young age, and since then I never saw her.

Interestingly, I do not remember anything from that period (about two years). Why was Esther not with me? What was she doing? I also do not remember Shoshana clearly. Later, I learned that Esther was a good and talented girl. From a young age she helped my mother with her work, and apparently Shoshana was also busy with my mother's "business."

At that time, for a short while, we had a hut in an empty lot in which my mother sold wood for heating, or, more accurately, cheap wood chips that fell when the wood was processed for construction purposes—my father's business. She sold the chips on credit because the customers were poor. Getting the customers to pay their debts was one of the most difficult challenges. More often than not, people manipulated my mother's good heart, bought more and more and could not pay their debts. Her daughters, Shoshana and in particular Esther, ran from one debtor to another, back and forth, asking for payments, and they returned empty handed. Apparently, this was the reason that the business closed. Afterward, my mother sold the chips wholesale, meaning that she sold the entire contents of the wagon that came from the city, this too on credit.

The first years of my life were the years of crisis that followed the war. We lived then (apparently until 1923) on Jatkowa (Butchers') Street, in an apartment that had one room and a kitchen, opposite the synagogue and ritual bath. Half of the kitchen was taken up by a Russian oven. The building had one floor and was derelict. In the summer, rain dripped into our apartment; in the winter it was very cold. To explain how much we suffered from the cold, I will only note that the water in the cups for ritual hand washing, which always stood ready in my parents' room, turned to ice during the winter nights. Some of the potatoes bought for the winter were contaminated by frost and had a bad taste even after they were cooked. Therefore, Shoshana, my grown-up sister, would grate them, add a bit of flour, and make dumplings. I was very little and, apparently, I suffered from the cold more than others, because I can see in my mind an image of my father sitting me on the kitchen table and wrapping bandages around my toes, which were afflicted by the cold. And because I was not pampered, I still have a memento of this, which in my old age bothers me more than in the past: one toe on each foot is crooked and hurts.

Behind our house was a field that the owner of the house also owned. Apparently, we were not particularly desired tenants, and he wanted to get rid of us and pull the house down. One night, the owner took off the roof and the ceiling started to fall in. We had to run from the house with our belongings. The only refuge, apparently, was the small synagogue (Shtibl) in which my father prayed: the prayer house used by the followers of the Rebbe of Skierniewice. By this time Shoshana was no longer with us—she had moved temporarily to live with her uncle—and we were four young children: the youngest, Shayale, was maybe one. I, his care-giver, was five or six.

For a few months, until my parents found a suitable place to live, we lived in the synagogue. It was made up of a large hall with two large windows. While we were there, two sheets were made into a divider and we lived beyond the divider during prayers. We, the children, could go out only through the window on our side. Afterward, we moved to an apartment in the center of town, on 3 Maja Street, the main street of our town. This apartment was in a reasonable state (compared to that on Butchers' Street).

This apartment too had one room and a kitchen, but both were spacious. For the first time, we had electricity. The room served as a dining room, as my father's study, for work and Torah study, and as my parents' bedroom. The kitchen provided the children with a place to sleep and spend their time. We had a "normal" cook-ing stove made of china tiles and a tiled oven on the wall, which in the winter heated the two rooms. Our economic situation also improved.

I have already said that I know almost nothing about our family history. I knew more or less about my father's close family. I knew those that lived in Końskie better. I knew that my father had a few brothers and one sister who remained in Vinnytsia in the Ukraine and could not return to Poland.

After the October Revolution, in the early 1920s, my father still received very sad letters from her about what was happening there. Later, all contact was lost. Regarding my father's brothers, I knew that his oldest brother, Uncle Shlomo, left for America (I only had any contact with him after World War II via Esther, because he visited Israel and knew about us. When Victor, my son, became very ill at the age of seven, he sent us a package of antibiotics and vitamins, and from Esther we received a crate of oranges.); I saw Uncle Itzhak once, when I was little, when he came to visit us. And Uncle Aharon, who lived with his family in Przedbórz, I visited once for a week during the summer vacation after my first year of study. Of this visit I remember the River Pilica, its clear waters and the green shore, where I loved to spend time. My stepmother's mother lived in his neighborhood. I will mention this family later.

My relatives from my father's side were spread through all the towns of Poland, and there were one or two families from my father's side in Końskie. I was quite close to one of them, the Kirshenbaum family, who lived on Warszawska Street. More than once, I found refuge from my stepmother with my aunt, Sara, and when my father returned and came to look for me, he received a good tongue lashing from her. The other was the Szarfharc family (the third I do not remember). These two families were well-to-do, respected members of the Jewish community, like my father. My visits to another family from my father's side are bound up with special memories. This was a very wealthy family, in the terms of my childhood, of course. This family had a tradition: on the eve of

Passover they distributed to the entire Szarfharc tribe in the town Charoset for the Seder night. I was the one who was sent to bring it. I remember another visit to this family, connected with the festival of Purim, on which we sent Mishloach manot to relatives. Every year I took to every family a tray of fruits and sweets and I received something similar in return. However, I felt uncomfortable when I went to this family. I brought them a modest offering and in return received a basket full of delights.

My mother, from the Rosenfarb family, also descended from a family of good lineage. Sara'le, the daughter of my oldest brother, Moshe, of blessed memory, takes great pride in this. I still remember my maternal grandmother Hannah: old, with a covering on her head. Whenever she visited us, she brought sweets in her large pocket for us. She died when I was four or five years old. Not long ago, I learned that she was born in Końskie in 1840 (she was apparently about 80 when she died). The Rosenfarb family had many branches in our town: my mother's brothers and three sisters; she was the youngest of them. There were a few families of Rosenfarbs, Miedzigórskis, and others, aunts and uncles and cousins. Among the three Rosenfarb families were two of mother's sisters, who were also born Rosenfarb. It seems that matches were made within the families to preserve the lineage, or so Sara'le, my brother's daughter, the family's Rebbetzin, explains. Apart from these, there was the Miedzigórski family and other relatives.

All our relatives in Końskie led religious lives, guided by the Torah. However, most of the children did not follow the path of their parents in terms of religious observance (I must make a special emphasis: I distinguish between the customs of the home—morality, honesty, etc.—and religious traditions). Among my many cousins, in particular on my mother's side, there were indeed a few ritual slaughterers, teachers of young children, and those who kept the commandments. However, even when I was still living at home, some were members of the Bund, Communists, Zionists, etc.

Life in our home was very clearly delineated: ours was an ultra-orthodox religious home; there were many strict prohibitions that were not to be transgressed. On the Sabbath, for example, it was forbidden to comb our hair, to turn on a light, to do any work, even the slightest. After the afternoon nap on the Sabbath, we went with my mother to visit aunts and uncles, my mother's sisters. Every Sabbath we went to a different family.

Aunt Feyge and Uncle Yosef Meir Rosenfarb lived on Berek Joselewicz Street. Uncle Yosef Meir, who was a Torah genius, was known as "Aby dalej" (incorrect Polish for "Continue, continue"), a term that he used in his trade with Polish customers in his shop. He was always dressed carelessly, with a large red handkerchief poking out of the pocket of his kaftan. They had three or four daughters and two sons. The oldest daughter, Mirele, was married, but at the beginning of her thirties she developed cancer and died. Aunt Feyge, the sister older than my mother, and Yosef Meir ran, I believe, the most religious home in the entire extended family. Their two youngest daughters, who were around our age, meaning my sister Esther and me, did not study in the general school, and I doubt whether they studied at all. At Pesach, Aunt Feyge always honored us with "Bubele" (a kind of fried potato pancake), which she fried for us in the frying pan. It seems that they had some difficulty making a livelihood from their shop that sold building materials and chemicals in Pocztów, the industrial center of Końskie. Their apartment was at the end of a large courtyard and behind it was a large grove in which we, the children, played children's games. Their oldest daughter was, as I said, married, and an age gap of quite a few years divided between myself and their son Abraham.

Abraham was a Communist and spent a lot of time in prison (the Communist movement was illegal in Poland and its members were persecuted). In Końskie, they made jokes on his account, saying his straw mattress in the prison only got to rest on rare occasions, because he was rarely outside the prison walls. He left the Communist Party before the war broke out, spent the war in the Soviet Union, enlisted in the Polish army that was established there, and returned with it to Poland. On the ruins of the Łódź Ghetto, he met Heniek, my husband, who was also among the first who arrived there. Shoshana and I, who were still in Kostroma, in the Soviet Union, received from them the first news about the destruction of our family in Końskie and Łódź. Through him Heniek met Moshe, our brother, and informed us that he had survived the death camps and was waiting for our arrival. Abraham established a family, left for Canada, and died there.

Aunt Frida, whose family lived in a spacious house in the center of town, on 3 Maja Street, opposite the church and the trade center, had a few sons, not all of whom I remember, and only one daughter, Dora. Her youngest son, born in her old age, was called Chaim. On our visits to Aunt Frida, we had to stay quiet, because my aunt lay in bed in her room, sick with TB. We, the children, were not allowed to go near her. She would ask to see us from afar and talk with us, the little girls, a bit. Her husband, Uncle Kadish, provided the family's meager income from a clothing store that he ran in Pocztów. Her only daughter, Dora, who was then fifteen years old, looked after her sick mother and took care of the house. The other children (among the boys I remember only Aharon and Chaim), included teachers of young children in the surrounding shtetls, and only one of them, as Chaim, my youngest cousin in this family, told me not long ago, was wealthy. When my mother, Frida's younger and beloved sister, died, they kept it a secret from sickly Aunt Frida for some time. However, one day, when my aunt felt a little better and left her house, a woman approached her to express her condolences for the loss of her sister, my mother. The sudden news came as a real shock, and my aunt fainted from grief. Shortly afterward, she died too. Before she died, Aunt Frida told me that in her last conversation with my mother, Rivkale, she had complained that her grueling life was coming to an end. And my mother, apparently trying to distract her from thoughts of death, answered that no one could know which of them would die first, because "sometimes a whole, strong pot breaks and a cracked pot lasts a long time" (My mother was a strong woman. She was never sick; she never even had a headache.).

Years after I left home, after the war, I found only a few remaining members of the entire extended family that lived in Końskie. I found Avraham Rosenfarb, whom I mentioned, Aharon, Dorka, and Chaim Miedzigórski. Before the war, Dora (Dorka) was a devoted Communist, and in her wake, Chaim also became a Communist. I found them in Łódź. Dorka and I became close and were good friends, despite the age gap. Chaim, who was my age, was in love with me before the war (we were then around sixteen years old), but I was a girl both physically and emotionally and I understood very little. And really, I could not fall in love with Chaim, because he was my complete opposite. After the war, he lived with his family in Łódź and then settled in Paris. He and his wife worked hard in the business they established. His two daughters, wealthy and educated, also live in Paris. Only his son, Yoel, who became religious, moved to Israel.

I remember the home of my aunt Feyge Mirele Rosenfarb, an older woman, bent over, who lived on Pocztów Street and had a stall in Pocztów. She had two daughters, Blume and Shprintze, and later I also knew their older brother, Abraham, who was living in Łódź during my childhood in Końskie. These two daughters were a lot older than me. The younger, Shprintze, was a friend of Shoshana and was the same age as her, meaning nine years older than me. I loved to go up the shaky wooden steps to their attic home. They lived in a one-room apartment, always well looked after and very impoverished (according to my mother, their father, my mother's brother, whom I did not know, was a saintly man, a scribe of holy writings; he had died long before). The atmosphere was very bright. Aunt Feyge Mirele's attic home was immortalized by her granddaughter, Abraham's daughter, Chava Rosenfarb, the Yiddish writer (she won the Itzik Manger Prize in Israel), in her work *Bociany*.

Chava Rosenfarb was younger than me by about five years, a pretty significant gap for silly teenagers. Despite this, a few years before the outbreak of World War II, we became very close and our friendship continues to this day. She immortalized her father, Abraham (whom she loved very profoundly), in her book *Letters to Abrasha*. All members of Abraham's home were Bundists, and Chava was educated in the spirit of Bundist-Socialism in a school run by Di Tsentrale Yidishe Shul-Organizatsye (Central Yiddish School Organization), TSYSHO. By the age of eight, she was publishing her poems in the children's literary supplement of the Folkstsaytung. During the Nazi occupation, she was among the members of the resistance in the Łódź Ghetto, and afterward she was sent with her family to the death camp of Auschwitz and other camps. Her father perished in the Holocaust. Chava, her mother, and her younger sister survived and were liberated by the British army. She lives in Canada. Among her important works are a trilogy that was translated into English as *The Tree of Life*, in which Chava immortalized Jewish Łódź before the war, and mainly life in the ghetto.

Based on what I have described until now, the reader can understand that we belonged to a group of families in the town and lived within a very well-defined, that is orthodox- religious, world. The Jewish religion is total. The halakhah professes to outline a defined way of life and to give answers to every possible question, from the most simple things—beginning with the question of which shoe to put on first when you wake up in the morning (the one on the left, of course) or whether it is permitted to use gloves that a non-Jew left in a Jewish home—to the stringent issues of kosher food, matters concerning the most intimate relations, and questions about the heavens and the galaxy. I spoke about my aunts, uncles, and cousins. This was my entire world in Końskie. It was forbidden for us, the girls, to have friends or meet with girls or a family that was not of our status, meaning those who were part of the "masses," as my father defined them.

Status was extremely important among the Jews. When I think about our past, it seems to me that in this period the Jews had not only social criteria—rich and poor—but other criteria that were perhaps more important: lineage, origins, scholarship. It seems to me that like the Polish nobility, noble origins still ruled, even when a noble family lost its fortune, and its sons, when they became poor farmers, working "the land with gloves," remained proud of their noble roots. Likewise, for Jews, the "lineage" of a good home distinguished between groups of people. The rich also treated us, the children of good yet poor homes whose fathers were respected and esteemed, with respect and honor, even though we were not of the same socioeconomic level. We were ashamed of our poverty and they, the rich, apparently did not feel comfortable in our company. Therefore, we suffered from double isolation. Indeed, there is a well-known saying: "Although there is no shame in being poor, it's also not a great honor" (I remember my mother saying in Yiddish: "Pinch your cheek to add a bit of color to your face and lift up your head high"). Therefore, at home we learned to preserve our honor. The financial difficulties were a private matter, something we did not share outside. I remember that in school, during the long break, they gave out fresh rolls and a cup of warm milk to poor children. I was in third grade when the teacher added my name to the list of poor children and came to me with a roll and milk. I turned red with shame, stammered something, and ran away. The shame that I felt at being considered a poor girl was difficult to swallow. I did not want to receive this gift, although most days I came to school on an empty stomach. However, this was not due to a lack of bread at home but rather the lack of time to make myself a sandwich.

While my mother was alive, I remember that although there was not always expensive meat on the Sabbath table, but only cheap cuts, the family always ranked welcoming guests as above everything else: Father would bring a poor guest or a yeshiva boy home from the synagogue for a Sabbath meal. On Fridays, my mother made an entire meal for a widower who lived with his daughter opposite us.

The Sukkah that Father built for the festival of Sukkot was the only one in our courtyard. By this point, we lived in a new apartment and Father built the Sukkah so that one of its sides was formed by the outside wall of the kitchen with the window in it. Thus, it was possible to serve the meal through the window to those sitting in the Sukkah. We, the children, decorated it. It was spacious because the neighbors also used it on the first days of the festival. Apart from this, Father slept in it at night and studied the Talmud in it by day. The boys, Moshe and David, who were already working in Łódź, always came home for Pesach and Sukkot. It is hard for me to forget one meal during Sukkot, maybe it was the last festival during which my mother was still alive.

The two boys, Moshe and David, arrived from Łódź. Together with Meir and my father, who was dressed in his silk kaftan, his shtreimel on his head, they went to the synagogue. My mother was glowing with happiness and followed them with her eyes. The entire family was at home. She was especially proud of her sons, Moshe and David. Mother and Shoshana made the meal, but they knew that there would not be enough fish and meat for everyone, and they wanted to ensure that no one in the Sukkah would suspect that this was the case. Mother explained to us, the girls who stayed at home, that we would get only a little of the festive dishes. I remember the portion of meat that we, the women, ate on that Sukkot evening. Each one received on a soup spoon a piece of meat, crumbled up so it would at least fill the spoon. I do not think my mother got even a spoonful of meat. We were not hungry; the festive atmosphere and the presence of all the family filled us with joy.

Thus, on the one hand, we tried to hide our poverty, while, on the other hand, one of the most important mitzvot in our home was welcoming guests; we learned to give to others and not to demand for ourselves—these were things that we, the children, learned from our parents. Remnants of this, without reference to religion and the commandments, which is not something that you can find simply anywhere today, remain with me, and I even passed them on to my children.

There was a special atmosphere in our home when preparing for Sabbaths and festivals. Not only did we thoroughly clean the house before the Sabbath (from the age of ten, I scrubbed and cleaned the wooden floors on Thursdays before running to school). We baked homemade challah, the cholent with the kugel inside, which we took to the bakery and brought home the next day for lunch, when Father, with his shtreimel and Sabbath kaftan, accompanied by Meir and David, returned from the synagogue—these were special experiences for us girls. On Sabbath afternoons, I took a kettle to a woman who had a special container that kept water warm the entire day, bringing water for the afternoon tea. After the meal we all had to have a rest. These were two hours of complete rest. We, the girls, could read books, but only in Polish, which we borrowed from the school library. My father believed that secular books in Yiddish led people to deviate from the straight and narrow (there was a grain of truth in that. . .). And, needless to say, the preparations for Pesach were a special experience for us children, but all this was while my mother was still alive.

If my memory does not fail me, on the festival of Shavuot it is forbidden to eat meat dishes. Yet, every year on Shavuot, my father had a special celebration that allowed him to eat a meat meal: he was the "Torah bridegroom" because he finished learning all the holy books (the Pentateuch with various commentaries, the Mishnah, Talmud, and all the rest).

The qualities and morals that I learned in our home—humility, extreme honesty, modesty, which over the years became my characteristics—did not make my long life easy. Though I have lived in the secular world for a long time, I passed on some of these qualities to my children as an inheritance.

One event that happened in my childhood explains, maybe in part, the legacy that I have carried with me my entire life. I do not think that these were qualities connected only to the religious world. This is the story.

In my childhood, when my parents or one of my big sisters were at home and I had a chance to play outside, I ran to my favorite place, the avenue that we called "Za Dworem," which was in fact called Zamkowa Avenue (Castle Avenue). The castle that belonged to the town's landowners, built in the time of Count Jan Małachowski in the seventeenth century, was located there. In the 1870s, it passed to the noble Tarnowski family, who lived in it also during the interwar period. These two noble families, the owners of Końskie and its surrounding lands, were some of the most important barons, and for more than 400 years, they were involved in the state and spiritual life of Poland. They were politicians, intellectuals, scientists—they left their mark on the character of the town, making it a town one could both love and yearn for. The palace was a large complex, built in Renaissance style. I never saw all of it.

Castle Avenue was wide, planted on both sides with evergreen trees: poplars, chestnut trees, maple trees, and linden trees. On one side of the avenue, you could see only one side of the palace, bordered by a beautiful fence that was made of truly artistic, delicate metalwork, supported by a low stone wall. As a child, I wondered at the beauty of this fence: large arched windows, a cultivated garden, islands of colorful flower beds, a garden shed, between the trees, statues here and there, and a water fountain and a bench. On rare occasions, you could see in the distance a young woman walking or sitting, reading a book. However, usually it was quiet. Opposite the castle, on the other side of the avenue, there was a space planted with linden trees, which also belonged to the owners of the castle and was called Pod Orłem, meaning under the eagle—the symbol of Poland is a white eagle wearing a crown on its head. All the royal and local ceremonies were held here, all the military and Scouts' parades. All week, the entire length of the avenue was empty. However, on Sabbath afternoons, it would fill up with young people out for walks.

The appearance of the avenue changed with the seasons. In the winter, the snow in the avenue was so white that you had to squint when you looked at it. In the spring, the trees blossomed with flowers in all colors of the rainbow, and when the petals fell to the floor, the ground looked like a colored carpet. The chestnut trees, which ripened later, still stood naked, and only buds were beginning to appear on them. They had a bitter smell. In the summer, the trees filled the avenue with special smells of ripeness. In the fall, I loved to walk between the trees that were now many shades of yellow, to hear the rustling of the dry leaves under my feet, and to gather the chestnuts that fell from the trees and shed their spiky shells. Then, they were especially bright and shiny.

One fall day, I was then around the age of five or less, I found something shiny, beautiful, and quite heavy among the autumn leaves. I picked it up and put it in my pocket, running home to show my mother. Both my parents were at home. Mother went to Father and both of them were shocked at what I had found. They asked me where and how I found it. It turned out to be a pure gold cigarette case. My parents looked at it for a while, Father weighed it in his hands, and wondered at its beauty and weight. And what happened afterward will be engraved on my mind and heart as long as I live: they decided that they had to find the owner and give it back to him.

We lived, as I described before, in a house that my mother desperately wanted to leave. The case I found was worth a fortune in today's terms. However, my parents did not even for a moment consider keeping it. Over a few Sabbaths, my father announced in the central synagogue that a golden case had been found and called for the owner to come and get it. One day, a beautiful carriage stopped by our house and Mr. Hochberg, the owner of the largest steel factory in Końskie, climbed out of it. He took the case, thanked my father, and gave me thirty groshen, saying to me, "Buy yourself a ribbon for your hair." I do not remember if I bought a ribbon or not, but I remember well my parents' sigh of relief after he left. Even as a child, I understood that the decision my parents made was difficult but steadfast.

The case of the golden cigarette case accompanied me my entire life and stood by me during the difficult tests that I endured.

I will mention a minor incident that caused me great embarrassment and earned me a lesson in morality from my father that lasted for hours.

I was around ten years old, and by this point I had a stepmother. It was Friday, and on Fridays I could not go to school, because I had to help her. She sent me to the grocery store to buy flour. The owner of the store, like many others in the town, treated me with affection yet with pity. She gave me the flour, stuck a sweet in my hand, and said, "Eat it on the way and don't tell your mother."

I did as I was told. However, when I got home, my stepmother demanded the change, and I did not have any. The cries that I had stolen a few groshen, the curses that all the town could hear, caused my father, who was then sitting in the next room and learning a page of the Talmud, to come immediately to the kitchen and ask what I had stolen. I was silent, because I understood, to my deep anguish, that instead of the sweet that I had eaten, I should have received change. I felt terrible guilt, because it was forbidden to hide the sweet that the woman gave me. I remained silent, but my father's wife explained to him that his daughter was a thief. Father took my hand and led me to the grocery store to investigate the matter. The owner of the shop reproached him for justifying his wife's atrocious and humiliating treatment of his orphaned daughter.

"Yes, I gave her a sweet, but she did not know that it was instead of the change."

However, I already knew that I was guilty of not telling anyone that I got a sweet. In my eyes, this episode assumed the dimensions of a catastrophe. I imagined I would receive a fair punishment from my father. However, when we left the shop, Father did not lead me home but to the bench in the public garden in the center of which stood the memorial to Tadeusz Kościuszko, and he began to explain to me that I needed to behave honestly. Since then more than seventy years have passed, but I have never forgotten that warmhearted and compassionate conversation with my father. He probably never knew how much I thanked him for it.

I have given only two examples of the inheritance that I received from my childhood home.

My childhood was divided into two parts: before my mother's death and after my father brought home his new wife. In truth, my childhood ended suddenly in the fatal winter of 1925, when I was eight years old. Esther was already in third or fourth grade in the state-run elementary school, and I, after almost a year of battling, had started to learn in first grade. I managed to learn the letters A and B and make them from plasticine. I had a whole two weeks as a first-grade student. In the third week, I fell ill with scarlet fever and infected all the children in my family. My mother, who had given birth only a few weeks before, also fell ill because of all her running around chasing after a livelihood and looking after sick children, and she died eight days later. It seems that she contracted a kidney infection and severe general poisoning (uremia). After a short time, the two-month-old baby, whom Father had given to a wetnurse in a nearby village, also died. The wetnurse came a few weeks later with the dead baby and said she had fallen from the cradle. In that winter, after spending a few months on his death-bed, my little brother, Shayele, whom I loved most of all because I had looked after him, also died, at the age of five. (While sick with scarlet fever, without suitable treatment, he contracted a kidney infection and uremia.) In that difficult winter, I did not understand the meaning of my mother's death, but the coming years taught me to value her.

Time has blurred my memories of my mother's face. However, bits of her essence, her movements, certain situations, dresses and articles of clothing, all these I remember to this day. I loved to put on some of her dresses, the really beautiful ones (made of velvet, taffeta, and silk, apparently from better times) and dress up in that fatal winter after her death. Yet the clearest picture, which always accompanies me, is my mother, always busy, always running somewhere, coming home to nurse the baby. While she was nursing, she would stroke and caress the boy or girl sitting next to her. I can never forget those stolen moments of indulgence. I missed them for many years after her death. She worked harder than anyone. She left us in the prime of her life, in her forties.

Apparently, I was a weak and sickly child because that was my nickname at home: "Di tsebrokhene." I was weak and sickly in comparison to beautiful Esther, with her golden curls and blue eyes, who was fast and especially talented, or Shoshana, who was similar to my mother. However, as such I received special indulgences. My sisters told me, although I do not remember it, that my mother devoted more of her time to me, that every morning I would find by my bed some kind of surprise (a pekele-pakunek). Years later, I asked my sisters why I got my nickname. They either did not remember or did not want to tell me, but they explained that I was sickly, anemic, and apparently because of this they called me the tsebrokhene.

If the disasters that fell upon our family in that winter were not enough, Shoshana too had to leave home. Her uncle from her father's side, Yaakov Zilberszpic, took her from our home almost by force immediately after the week of mourning (shiva) for my mother was complete. Our pleas and cries, as well as those of Shoshana, did nothing to help. Father also opposed her departure. Indeed, he had raised her from the age of two. The uncle's demands and his behavior (he grabbed everything that came to hand, he even took a bulb out of a lamp) left us questioning whether he had only good intentions and wanted to protect the orphaned Shoshana. Before our mother's death, Shoshana had been working for him for a number of years. Shoshana was the oldest of us, around seventeen. The rest of the children were little. After her, Esther, around eleven, was the oldest.

Shoshana was like a mother to me and a beloved friend until her last days (she died in Haifa in 1993, may her memory be a blessing), despite the age gap between us—nine years. She lived for a short time with Uncle Yaakov, sewing shirts for his shop, as she had done in the years before Mother's death, and she looked after his house. Although the conditions were difficult there, she would still come home to us and help Esther, who suddenly had to manage our home and deal with two children smaller than her. Every Thursday or Friday, Shoshana came, helped to clean the house and manage the affairs, and helped us younger ones to wash our hair, especially me.

After a while, Shoshana left her uncle, rented a one-room apartment not far from us, and was freer to help us. The only furnishings in this room were a single iron bed, a sewing machine, and two chairs; on the side of the door, next to the washing things, stood a primus, on which she cooked her meals. She taught me, among many things, to eat tomatoes. In those days, Jews also started eating tomatoes. Until then, I had seen them only in the windows of the Poles who later became my teachers and lived not far from us. In their windows, the tomatoes ripened in the sun. They were beautiful and I wanted to taste them. I bought for myself half a kilo of tomatoes for five groshen (where I got the money, I will relate later), and on the spot, I bit into one of them. The juice and the taste were so strange and odd that I felt sick and ran to one of the courtyards to throw up. I threw the rest of the tomatoes away and did not want to eat them again, although they became popular in the homes of Jews in our town. Shoshana, who was concerned about my health, made me sandwiches—pieces of bread with slices of tomato and onion and bits of salted fish—and commanded me to eat them. I tried it and it was very tasty. That was how I started eating tomatoes.

I loved to run to Shoshana and stay to sleep with her. We slept together in her narrow bed and we warmed each other up. I got another nickname as a result: "Kh'drey mikh" (I turn around). Until this day, I toss and turn before going to sleep, meaning that I do not fall asleep immediately and easily but rather try to find a comfortable position. However, sharing a narrow bed during winter was very uncomfortable as any movement disturbed the other occupant, causing the blanket to be pulled, etc. And then Shoshana asked me, "Bina, vos tist du?" And I answered, "Ikh drey mikh."

Shoshana also taught me a kind of "profession" in which I engaged from the age of ten, and with the money I earned, I bought notebooks, writing tools, and secondhand textbooks. It is worthwhile describing in a few words this "profession," for posterity, because a few generations have passed since then and people know nothing about it. In those days, manufacturers began making silk stockings for women. The fashion of these stockings came to Końskie, and Shoshana too, who was already nineteen, wore them. They were cumbersome, thick but shiny, and relatively expensive. However, because they were made by a kind of knitting, the stitches came loose. It was possible to return the "stitches" using a knitting needle. My Shoshana taught me to do this. Girls and women brought me their damaged stockings and I received a few groshen for fixing them.

A short time after Father brought his wife from Przedbórz, Shoshana left Końskie and moved to Łódź, and a year later, Esther followed her. Meir likewise felt uncomfortable at home and slept in the Beit Midrash and afterward in the yeshiva in Końskie. After I too left the house, he moved to a yeshiva in Łódź. I remained alone at home with a stepmother. And so, I will briefly describe my father's third wife.

Feygele—My Father's Third Wife

Immediately after the year of mourning my mother was over, match-makers started to visit our house urging Father not to remain alone with three small orphans. Apart from that, they said, a religious man like my father needs to keep the commandment "to be fruit-ful and multiply," and he had no wife. Among the candidates was a woman (who had never been married) around the age of thirty-five, twenty years younger than my father. He tried to consult with Esther, his daughter, whose wisdom he respected. He justified his possible choice with the fact that the woman was an orphan, from a poor home, who herself worked hard. Therefore, so he thought, she would be good to us and we would not be alone. Esther did not want to say a word to Father. She was angry at him and thought that he was too enthusiastic about marrying this virgin. The wed-ding took place in Przedbórz (in the province of Końskie).

And thus, one fine day, we ran outside to welcome our father's bride. A simple carriage with a railing like a ladder on the sides stopped by our house, and from it descended a whole gamut of women's clothing. First of all, high-heeled shoes, followed by lots of underskirts with lace, and a wide skirt. A small woman looked out at us with curiosity in her little black eyes: the bones of her face stood out and black frizzy hair protruded from under her colorful kerchief.

Afterward, they took down from the carriage a large wooden trunk containing her entire dowry (her personal effects). She had apparently collected these effects during her years serving rich people in the large city. From that day on, I remembered my mother more and more, and I missed her.

She was a virgin of thirty-five years old (in those days, women of that age were considered "old maids"), twenty years younger than my father, illiterate, and very superstitious. Her life had, apparently, been hard. As a servant in rich people's homes, she was terrorized and exploited by her mistresses, the housewives. From the moment she married my father, she was so happy and proud that the happiness radiated from her. Finally, she herself was a housewife. She brought presents for us, the children: she took out from her trunk, with great performance, a small bag that she gave to Esther. She brought me a ball. And for Meir, what did she bring Meir? I think the ball was for both of us.

Did the significance of her appearance penetrate my consciousness? I do not think so, because immediately after receiving the ball, I remember, Meir and I ran off to play with it. There was a corner in our courtyard with a bit of greenery and an empty white wall (the external wall of the inn, the front of which was on Berek Joselewicz Street), and there the children who lived in the courtyard played with balls. However, the next day the two presents disappeared. It was as though they had never existed. They were lost. Afterward, we found out that she passed on the "presents" to the children of her sister who lived in Radoszyce, a town close to Końskie.

As the days passed, I learned a lot more about this woman. Among other things, she was to a certain degree mentally disturbed. At night, she would get up in her sleep, screaming terribly that the house was burning down, that murderers wanted to kill her, or that robbers had attacked her, etc. She would go out into the courtyard crying inconsolably, and it was difficult to stop her and bring her back inside, because she fought back physically, as though she were fighting demons. People came out of their homes and looked, until Father (or, if he was not at home, someone else) managed to grab her and bring her back to bed. Then she went back to sleep. The next day she neither remembered nor believed the story.

Years later, in a moment of weakness, my father told me that Uncle Aharon, his brother (who was a ritual slaughterer in the town of Przedbórz, her hometown), knew the widow and her daughter Feyge (Tzipora) well. They lived in his neighborhood. All the town knew her. After they made the match with my father, he traveled to Uncle Aharon and asked him about her, seeking his advice. However, Uncle Aharon did not say a bad word about her. Afterward, he justified this to my father, saying that her mother, the old woman, came to him and begged him to take pity on her orphan daughter who had never been married (at the age of thirty-four) and not ruin the match. Had he told my father the truth, he would be responsible for ruining her prospects, and his conscience would have pained him. So, my uncle stayed silent when my father asked for his opinion. The wrong he did to us, the little orphans, stayed on his conscience.

She knew how to cook and bake and loved to make all kinds of dishes. She loved her cooking like a cherished art. When she made, for example, meat balls, for which people then used a wooden board and a special knife, she loved to sing while chopping the meat, hitting her hip with her other hand to the beat of the tune. In particular she loved to make dishes for the Sabbath, when my father came home. She started preparing for this already on Thursday (in the evening she went to the ritual bath), and the next day the entire day was devoted to a festival in the kitchen (on this day I could not go to school, because I had to be at her service). She baked challah and sweet pastries, cooked special traditional dishes for the Sabbath, not to mention cholent. She stood in the kitchen and felt herself to be a real housewife (Yaakov Leshinsky, writer, Socialist, and historian, says, in one of his books, that when he visited Bobruisk in Byelorussia, the inhabitants there ate chicken soup with lokshen that tasted and smelled the same as it did in every Jewish town in Galicia). He was right. My stepmother learned to cook in the homes of rich Jews. Consequently, she often complained that she could not demonstrate the full range of her culinary talents now that she herself was a housewife, because her husband did not bring her enough money to do so.

I became a real Cinderella. I do not want to talk about this period of my childhood under the rule of my stepmother. However, the trials of childhood accompany a person until the end of her days, and they have an immense effect on her character. They had, without doubt, an irreversible effect on the formation of my personality, my complexes, my nature—both positive, if I have such things in me, and also negative.

A year after my father married his third wife, she gave birth. The labor was especially difficult. Her pains and her cries, which reached up to the heart of the heavens, continued for a few days. The courtyard was full of people, in particular women, and they said that Rivkale (my mother) was taking her revenge. Esther, my sister, stood by the oven, watching the pot of hot water. Father approached her, asking her to forgive our stepmother for all the sins that she had committed toward her and pray for her. I, who sat in a corner of the kitchen, heard Esther refuse outright: "No. No, I cannot forgive her," she answered. In the end, they took her to the hospital in Łódź where she had a cesarean section and gave birth to a baby girl. (The baby died after a short while. But the event was wiped from my memory and I do not remember when or why.)

A short while after this, Esther left home, without even finishing her last year of studies, and went to Łódź. Meir, my little brother, joined the most radical group of the Hasidim and lived in their Beit Midrash and yeshiva, almost never coming home (he did not even consider our father pious enough). And my father spent the entire week (apart from Friday and the Sabbath) in the forests and villages making a living. Only I remained at home with my father's wife and the baby.

As I already said, my father was a wood merchant. Considering his expertise in this field, he presumably learned the profession from his ancestors. I was amazed by his knowledge of mathematics and logarithms, thanks to which he had a rare ability to assess plots of forest: he could calculate exactly how many cubic meters of wood for construction could be obtained from every plot. He would buy from farmers plots of forest intended for deforestation. Immediately, they were processed by carpenters, and carters took the processed wood to a sawmill or its destination. When my mother was alive, the carters brought the leftover chips to her and my mother sold them as wood for heating. In the years after her death, the chips served only to heat our house, and the remainder were given to the farmers who worked in the forest. When Father returned on weekends, instead of resting quietly and studying a page of the Talmud, some incident always awaited him, with me at its center.

My father did not know much about the full daily routine at home. My days did not always pass peacefully, meaning without screams. I, quiet but rebellious by nature, ran away from home whenever the relations with my stepmother reached an exploding point. I ran from the screams and curses, which the entire town could hear. (She had an extremely rich range of curses. It is a shame I did not then have the sense of humor to write them down, for indeed these were examples of real Jewish folklore used by porters and carters.)

When my father returned from his weekly travels, his wife welcomed him with yelling and thousands of complaints and curses, in which she was an expert, all about me. Usually my father was silent, but sometimes he tried to defend me. Sometimes he also punished me because, wanting to spare him my complaints, I remained silent. For that reason, my grievance against my father built up in my heart for his silence and failure to respond. In particular, I was hurt when I was punished. Sometimes, I even ran away when he was at home. Once I ran away before candle lighting on Friday night and hid in the ruined Russian church on the corner beyond Kazanowska Street (our house was on a corner, opposite the church). I cried bitterly about my terrible life. I hated my father then, as well as the entire world. When Father finally found me, he sat down next to me and cried together with me.

My father, who was one of the respected men of the town and community, known for his wisdom and honesty, who was approached by girls and their parents, particularly orphan girls, for advice about matches, dowries, etc., had become a topic of town gossip because of this woman.

I loved him, but I also amassed a lot of grievances against him. There were times when I hated him so much that I did not know what to do. I just wanted to die. There were Sabbath nights when I lay awake and did not close my eyes, because, after our terrible arguments, I heard, coming through the door, which was not well sealed, her cries of happiness as she jumped into my father's bed. I was a young girl, and I did not understand anything about what was happening in there. However, as a girl, I felt terror. These things cannot but leave emotional scars, scars that have remained with me all my life. Only years later, when my father perished in the death camp, did I understand his tragedy. However, my scars have not healed. This is also the reason, apparently, that I could not return others' love. Despite my grievances against him and the moments I wanted to die because of him, I admired him greatly. It is difficult to explain the depth of the scars on my soul from that terrible childhood.

I have no doubt that my father loved me, as he did all his children. In moments of grace, I shared unforgettable experiences with him. Sometimes, in the school holidays, when my father felt my despair, he took me on his wanderings in the villages and forests. These were the happiest days of my childhood, the almost (apart from school) only rays of light after my mother's death. We walked, holding hands, through the fields and forests around Końskie, and I remember this happiness with longing to this day. The region of Końskie was blessed, among other things, with the largest expanses of forest in Central Poland. Of its area, 75 percent, today 55 percent, was covered with forest. In this magical way, my father told me about the world God created, about His grace and His concern for every living thing, about how He watches over the innocent and honest. He believed in this completely. Sometimes, when we sat under a tree in the forest to rest, around us a range of vegetation—ferns, blueberries, moss—he told me that the Holy One, Blessed be He, controls all the vegetation, that in every bush and leaf there are divine sparks and everything grows according to His will. I remember part of a song we learned in school, named "the prayer of the blueberry," which seemed to confirm what my father said. I thought to myself: Indeed the God of both the Jews and Christians is one and the same, a universal God. Father told me also about things that happened during his various wanderings. And here is one of the many stories:

One night, he was making his way to a village that he needed to reach at dawn. While walking through an open field, a snowstorm began, and a strong wind blew. My father lost his way. When walking alone, he always recited Psalms, and he did so too on that stormy night. However, the storm caused him to err, and he did not know where he was. He kept going until he had no strength left, then he sat down in the open field and almost fell asleep and froze. With the remainder of his strength, he prayed and managed to say "Shema Yisrael" and. . . a miracle happened. An old man (according to his description, it was certainly the prophet Elijah) approached him and asked my father where he was trying to go. And then he discovered that he was at the entrance to the village. My father was sure that this was a miracle from heaven. I too believed it.

When we arrived early in the morning at a village, coming to a home owned by a woodchopper or carter, his wife would be waiting for us. Together with her husband, we sat at a simple wooden table and the woman brought us a large bowl full of warm cooked potatoes, butter, and mugs of cultured milk. And thus, together with the family of peasants, we ate the tasty potatoes.

At the age of eleven, I started to learn to sew, taught by a woman who herself was a seamstress. I went to her in the afternoon, after school, after I had finished my tasks at home. I must write a few words about this seamstress. Although I do not remember her name, her poor house served, for more than two years, as a refuge for me, a place of protection against my stepmother. She, and no one else, knew my despair and she tried to help me when I was sick or in pain. She herself was ill-fated, a victim of the radical traditions of the small town. She had a baby, and, when he was a few months old, they discovered that he was blind. When I started to work with her, her husband was serving in the army. Because he was extremely religious, he did not eat the food from the military kitchen and his wife sent him packages of food from home. She apparently could not manage to keep this up routinely and sometimes he went hungry. The Polish soldiers pestered and tormented him. He came home mentally unstable, and after a while, he died. Her home was made up of one room, which one entered from the courtyard. In this small room was a stove for cooking, a few cooking utensils on shelves, a bed, a cradle for the baby, and, of course, a sewing machine. There were days when I came to her straight from school because I was scared to go home. Despite her terrible poverty, she knew that I was hungry and always gave me something to eat. One day, I got an ulcer on my chest. It hurt terribly, but I was embarrassed to tell anyone, especially my father. I was still a girl, twelve years old. The seamstress sensed my distress and started to interrogate me about what was wrong until I told her my secret and showed her. Then she dealt with it like a loving mother. Her memory holds a warm place in my heart to this day.

The seamstress' husband was a victim of fanaticism, the companion of religion and piety. He was not the only one. Here is another story that is engraved on my memory. On the corner of 3 Maja Street and Kazanowska Street, opposite the corner house in which were we lived, next to the Russian orthodox church that was built at the beginning of the nineteenth century, and around which were camped units of the Russian army, there was a small house inhabited by an old widow and her beautiful, blonde daughter. The family was very poor. On the pavement between the house and the church there was a well of water that served the surrounding area. From this well, I too, aged ten or twelve, filled two buckets of water and carried them home, until the barrel of water at home was full. The problem was in the winter. A mountain of ice built up around the pump, and only in the middle of it was a kind of carved-out hole, into which went the bucket. Standing on the ice hill, it was possible to pump water and take out the full bucket from the hole. This was a pretty difficult task for me. More than once I slipped and the water spilled, and I had to start all over again. Sometimes, someone else who came to the pump would help me pull the bucket out. Sometimes the girl who lived in the house next to the pump would come out to help me. I was always amazed by her beauty. One day, a rumor spread that set on fire the entire Jewish community: this girl had run away with a young Pole. They married in the Catholic church in Końskie. The poor old widow remained alone. An invisible wall of silence and isolation arose around her. In the first days after the event, students of the Batei Midrash and yeshiva, as well as children, crowded around the old woman's house. They shouted and threw stones, breaking the windows and tormenting her for many days.

Longing for School

In March 2002, in honor of the publication of the Polish edition of my book, *Żydowska ludność pracująca w Polsce 1918–1939* (The Jewish Working Population in Poland between the Two World Wars 1918–1939), in Warsaw, I gave a lecture about it to an audience of people interested in the history of Polish Jewry. My son Victor accompanied me. He had assisted me immensely in the entire process of my work, from beginning to end. At that moment, I felt a great deal of satisfaction: this was the fruit of several years' work (and in the meantime two of my books had been published in Hebrew). I felt that I had made a modest contribution to perpetuating the memory of my generation, which perished in Poland and no longer exists. And another thing: at that event, I remembered what the headmistress of the state elementary school in Końskie, the talented teacher Pani Halina Sadowska, said to me when we parted so many years before. It was June 30, 1932, the last day of the school year. For me, this would be the last day of studying. I was finishing school, and it was a sad day for me. Around 11 a.m., after we received our graduation certificates, the classroom emptied, as did the entire school. The summer vacation had started. Only I remained in my spot, sitting on my bench. It was hard for me to leave forever the walls of the school building, knowing that I would not be able to continue the studies I so loved. I also did not want to go home and listen to my stepmother's screams. I sat in my place and cried. At some point, I apparently fell asleep. I suddenly woke up when someone turned on the light. In the doorway stood my father and the headmistress, who had also taught me a few subjects in the previous two years. This was a very strange sight: my father—in his long black kaftan with a yarmulke on his head—and the respected, authoritative headmistress, with a golden cross at her neck. It was already late at night. The first thing that went through my mind was that these two were not meeting for the first time and that the relations between them seemed permeated by mutual respect. I did not know that my father had ever taken an interest in my studies and met with the respected headmistresses. I knew that my father was proud of my studies and of the fact that I learned French (in his business he had regular contact with the noble families in the area, who spoke French). Both the headmistress and my father understood my despair without the need for words. I did not open my mouth. (By the way, the discipline and the behavior toward teachers, especially the headmistress, were radically different in my time to what they are today.) Teacher Sadowska sat next to me and tried to encourage me. Even though we had never had a conversation outside the classroom, it was not difficult to discern how dedicated I was to my studies. She apparently also knew about the situation at home. Therefore, among other things, she said to me that she was sure that in the end I would find my way in life, that my strong will would light up my path also in education. She kissed me. My father and I left the school. To this day, I do not know how my father found the headmistress, who had long since gone home, and how he brought her to the school.

When I stood in front of the audience in Warsaw, in March 2002, I thought about the last words the headmistress said to me back then. I did not forget.

I missed the state elementary school in Końskie for many years, even though I have now spent many years studying, at different times and at different levels. When I left Końskie and was already working in Łódź, every year on September 1, I went out before 8 a.m. to watch with nostalgia as the students walked past carrying their school bags.

I started learning in school in third grade because, as I mentioned, I stopped going to school in first grade after two weeks. This was the difficult year during which the plague of scarlet fever in our home claimed my mother and two children. Esther and I did not return to school that year. In the spring, Father brought a private tutor who prepared Esther, two and half years older than me, for a test for grade 5 or 7, and me for grade 3.

The state school for girls in which we studied was then the only one in our town (beyond the fence there was a school for boys). In the first year, we even learned in shifts because there were not enough classrooms: one week we learned in the mornings and the next week in the evenings. The school was located at the eastern edge of the town, and the only thing beyond it was the hospital building (which was built during the war, in 1916, as a hospital for epidemic diseases, when the plague of typhus broke out in the town. After the war it was expanded and became the general hospital). In its clinic, we, the students, underwent regular checks. The nurse, who was officially called a hygienist and was a nurse in the hospital, checked the hygiene of the students once every two weeks or once a month.

I always arrived last, running into class together with the ringing of the bell. Gasping for breath, I would sit down on the first bench, in my set place, because I was the smallest in the class. The classrooms were large and each room had two big windows. From the moment I sat down, all my worries and tiredness dissipated. I lived every moment of the lessons like I was in another world. I was in a magical world in which I learned something new every hour.

Jewish and Polish children learned together in our school. Apart from one student, Żylińska, who was hostile toward me and anti-Semitic, I do not remember any antagonism from any other Polish student. Also, apart from one teacher, we did not hear anti-Semitic comments from the teachers. The exception was Mrs. Mierzanowska, who taught us French. As you entered the long corridor of the school, you could immediately tell which class she was teaching at the time. She had a strange custom—she would hit the table with a pencil case or whatever else came to hand and shout:

"Jewish girls, quiet, go to Pocztów (the center of Jewish shops and trade) to sell onions, not here." It was irrelevant that the Jewish girls were sitting in complete silence. She had an impulse that made her vent her anti-Semitic anger. And yet, looking back over time, it is possible to say that the relations between Poles and Jews were correct if not warm.

We Jewish girls accounted for almost half the children in the class. Jews and Poles sat next to each other on the same bench. Yet there was an invisible line dividing us. We were two groups, each one with different traditions and cultural baggage. On the wall, above the blackboard, was a cross. The studies started when the teacher entered the room, at which point we rose and sang a song praising the Creator of the world who had given us a new day. The Poles made the sign of the cross, the Jewish girls did not. Religious lessons were conducted separately. The Poles studied with a priest, and the Jews had a Jewish teacher, his name was Halberstadt. He told us biblical legends and taught us by rote Psalm 137, "By the Rivers of Babylon," in the translation by the Polish poet Ujejski.

We felt the different cultural traditions in our daily life at school. For example, Jewish students could not belong to the Scouts youth group, and we Jewish girls were so envious. The Jewish girls usually did not take part in national and state festivities, local or of the Polish nation, even though in school I became a great patriot, feeling great love for this country and its heroic past. I once experienced an unusual and moving experience in this regard. I was very good at reciting poetry (in this period, reciting was accepted as a way of reading poetry). Almost every religious studies lesson started with the teacher or students requesting that I recite the psalm "By the Rivers of Babylon," which until this day I remember in Polish translation.

Our school was named after the heroine of the Polish insurrection against the Russian conqueror that took place in January 1831, Emilia Plater. Every year, prior to the day commemorating the rebellion, the school planned a show that it staged for the entire town. It included singing and plays on topics connected to that day. But we, the Jewish girls, took part only as spectators. About a month before this day, when I was in fifth grade, the headmistress, Mrs. Sadowska, who also taught modern Polish literature and history (she taught me these topics in sixth and seventh grades), came into the classroom in the middle of a lesson. Her appearance always caused a small commotion. We rose to our feet, but she asked us to sit and finish the lesson, because she wanted to examine a few of the girls for the performance. She started reading the list of students according to the alphabet, and every student had to recite for her part of a poem, among others the "The Death of Colonel" (Emilia Plater) by Adam Mickiewicz, among others. She asked only the Polish girls and passed over the Jewish students. When she had almost reached the end of the list, the Jewish girls, especially one called Neuman, asked that she let Bina Szarfharc recite part of the poem. And thus, I was the last to recite it, after the bell rang, signaling the end of the lesson. I passed the test.

We prepared for the festive evening for a month. It was held in the firefighters' hall, the largest hall in our town, where all events and shows took place. For this festival, I wore a dark blue dress with a white collar, like all the students, but it was not mine, because mine was already old and too short for me. Rather, it belonged to my friend, Hanka Krokh (I will come back to her later). The hall was full; in the first rows sat the mayor and his wife, the wives of doctors and all the important people in our town. When I appeared on stage, a murmur passed through the hall like the waves of the sea hitting the shore. From the first rows, I could hear people muttering, "Look, look, it's a little Jew girl." My embarrassment reached such a height that I gave it my all so that I would not be humiliated as the little Jewish girl. When I finished, I received wild and extended applause.

I had a few friends in school. I remember my friend Eyger, who was an excellent student. Sometimes I went to her house.

Her parents treated me with great warmth and sometimes gave us homemade cookies. There was some competition between us, but always in good spirits. She was better than me, because she read a lot of books, and I did not have time for that. She had a wild and rich imagination that I did not possess, and a rich Polish that I loved to hear. In sixth grade, our teacher for Polish language and literature, as I mentioned, was the headmistress. For homework, she asked us to write a story entitled "The view beyond my window." This was apparently at the beginning of the school year and it was just at the time that we, the Jews, celebrated Sukkot. During the festival, I was ill, lying in bed.

My bed was a complicated but "ingenious" contraption. By day it was a large kitchen table that stood by the window. It was closed from all sides and looked like kitchen furniture. In the evening, when the top was opened and we moved the front forward, it became a wide and comfortable bed. When Esther still lived at home, we slept in it together. Afterward, I slept there alone. Because I could only do my homework after my stepmother went to bed, I sat late at night in this bed, took down the surface of the table, and did my homework.

On that festival, as I said, I stayed in bed and did not need to get up early in the morning. Father was at home, and, as on every Sabbath and festival, he got up at five in the morning and studied a page of the Talmud to a special tune, a melody that has accompanied me throughout all the twists and turns of my life. It was, apparently, the intermediate days of the festival (Chol Hamoed), and I lay in bed looking at the view beyond my window. The view was entirely unromantic. There was not a tree or a flower or even a bit of green in sight. Our yard faced the parallel road, Berek Joselewicz Street. In front of my window there were a few storerooms in which the residents stored coal and wood for heating and all kinds of objects and junk. In the middle of the yard was a kind of stone channel that ran its entire length. This filled up with water when it rained, and from both sides there were stones covered in lime (for sanitation purposes). This was the view outside my window, and I wrote about all this in my story, including my father's melody, which I heard in the background while writing.

When I came to school, the girls read out aloud to each other what they had written. I heard stories about fabulous views, gardens with birds chirping, flowers, etc. The most beautiful of all was by my friend Eyger. I did not want to show anyone what I had written, and I debated whether to hand in my story. However, the headmistress took my notebook. The next day, the teacher brought the notebooks to class. I felt a sense of fear and panic when she called me to stand in the middle of the class and read out my story. I read quietly, and I decided to defend my story defiantly. However, there was no need for this. To my surprise, the teacher chose such a realistic story as the most beautiful and afterward it appeared in the school's "wall newspaper."

My best friend was Hanka Krokh, whom I mentioned before. We became friends when her family moved to Końskie from another town. She joined us in fifth grade. Our friendship continued from then and also afterward in Łódź, and it was cut off by the war. I searched for her after the war but found no trace of her. A smiling and slightly overweight girl, she had light blonde curls, two dimples in her cheeks, and blue eyes—she was beautiful. She was different to me in every way. But one thing brought us together almost immediately—we were both orphans. She had lost her mother a few years after I lost mine. As an only daughter, Hanka was pampered. She also came from a wealthy family and did not lack for anything. Even her stepmother was different from mine—a learned woman who fought for Hanka's heart. However, as much as the stepmother sought to draw closer to her, Hanka felt her foreignness and pushed her away. Orphans are, apparently, particularly sensitive and can discern the nuances of false love from true love. Apart from this, she, like me, listened at times behind closed doors to her father and his wife talking about her. We sat and cried together for many hours.

Fate forced me to leave home and Końskie at the age of fourteen. I had to grow up quickly and face a new life. However, in the meantime, to improve my dismal mood—after my father found me in the closed school—he arranged for me and my little brother Meir a two-week vacation in a village with a Polish family, a simple peasant family, the head of which worked for my father. This was the first holiday in my life. What a pleasure it was to run barefoot through fields and forest. Together with the family's children, we picked wildflowers, mushrooms, and blueberries. It was during the harvest, and we ran after the harvesters. I wondered at how their expert hands wielded the scythes through rows upon rows of ripe produce in the field. We drank warm milk straight after the cow was milked and we slept in the attic on fragrant straw. It was a shame it was over so quickly.

After I finished my studies, there was nothing left for me in Końskie. I was about to go to Łódź. I needed to wait until Esther would come home for the festival of Sukkot and coordinate with her how I would join her. Until she came, I returned to the seamstress and worked for her.

I returned to Końskie twice after the war: in 1950 and in 1994. On my first visit, I was a newspaper reporter, investigating a story. I arrived in the evening at the local hotel and early in the morning I left to visit places connected to my childhood and my home. I did not want to see them with the eyes of a stranger; I wanted to be alone with my memories, while the residents of the town still slept. First of all, I hurried to see the house that was once ours. We lived then, as I mentioned, on 3 Maja Street in a courtyard that connected to the parallel, Berek Joselewicz Street. At both ends of the yard there were two big gates and by them were the frontmost homes. I felt great disappointment. In my time, the entrance was from 3 Maja Street. On the left side there were two apartments in which lived two Jewish families, our neighbors, and on the right side was Yaakov Zumer's bakery. On the front, facing the street, there was a shop for baked goods, and behind it was the Zumer family's apartment, which bordered our apartment. Now I found a stone house of three stories, gray, ugly, and closed. Because, as I noted, the building and yard were on a corner, I ran to the other side, via Kazanowska Street, to Berek Joselewicz Street. There I still found an entrance to the yard.

At the gate once lived a widow, whose daughter, Chava, went out early in the morning every day to the nearby village with large containers to bring fresh milk, and her mother sold it to Jewish women in the area. Twice a week, after she returned with the milk and before I went to school, I taught Chava, large and strong, illiterate but with a heart of gold, to read and write. I also taught her boyfriend, her future husband, in the afternoon. I myself was then in fifth grade. I found the lessons for this young man, a shoemaker, very difficult. It was hard for him to grasp things, and I was tired, because my day always began at 5 a.m., when my stepmother woke me with screams and then herself went back to bed. I had only five hours of sleep and therefore I was not always completely awake during the lessons I gave to the young man. However, he pretended not to notice, and, apparently, I was the cheapest teacher in the town.

Then, on my visit to the town in 1950, I stood in this courtyard and searched for my childhood. Everything was strange and odd. Only a few details reminded me of my former life. Here the empty wall in the corner next to the gate still exists. Once there was a bit of grass next to it, and the children played there with a ball. This wall was part of the inn, which still existed in 1950. I stood there, and, against my will, tears ran down my cheeks. A woman came out of the opposite house. I told her that my family used to live here. She thought that I came to demand something from her and started to shout. Her husband, a tough man, came out as well, and the two of them started to tell me that they had lived there more than thirty years and nothing had changed since then, and I would find nothing here.

The visit to my childhood home took me to the cemetery to look for my mother's grave. I could find the short way through the fields with my eyes closed, because almost every day I had visited my mother on my way home from school. But when I got there, I thought I had made a mistake. Before me was an open field, next to which a herd of sheep was grazing. At some distance beyond the field there was a building that was once the ceramics workshop belonging to M. Levin (his daughter-in-law, Dr. Sabina Levin, is a colleague of mine at Tel Aviv University). At that exact moment, the workers arrived for work. The workshop was now in the possession of the state. I asked one of them where the Jewish cemetery was.

Here, he told me. You are standing on it.

I started to walk around on shaking legs. I felt bumps under the surface, as though I were treading on graves. Suddenly I saw in the middle of the field a massive black stone. I approached it and recognized it. It was the tombstone of the mother of the Kronenblum family, a large and rich family in Końskie that had manufactured steel and metal for a few generations, who was buried there. My mother was buried in the second row after this grave, as though in the shadow of the black marble. I always sat next to the marble when I came to visit my mother. Now I stood next to the marble and thought that at any rate wealth leaves behind a perpetual memory. I was wrong. The Nazis simply did not manage to take it; either it was too heavy, or they were not interested in it. However, after the war, the locals succeeded in uprooting it from its place.

The wheels of history are sometimes surprising. In 1994, when I was in Poland to search for documents in the Polish archives in Krakow, Warsaw, and Lublin for my research, Gideon, the youngest son of my sister Esther, of blessed memory, who lived with his family in London, came to join me. While I was in Poland, he wanted me to take him to visit the birthplaces of his parents, who were no longer alive (his father was born in Kalisz). At the time, my colleague and dear friend, Dr. Aryeh Gelbard, of blessed memory, who was also researching in the Warsaw archives and originated from Kalisz, was with me in Poland.

We rented a car and traveled to Kalisz. Kalisz is a beautiful city. The house in which Aryeh's parents lived was in a beautiful and well-cared-for boulevard, through the middle of which runs a river. We looked for the house in which Gideon's father spent his childhood—Gideon himself was born in Israel, a native Israeli (sabra). We did not find his grandparents' home. Likewise, in the local council and its archive we found no record of his family. We had to trust Dr. Gelbard, who pointed out one of the houses. We took a couple of pictures. We spent the night in a hotel in Kalisz. There, Gideon came to me and we had a heart-to-heart conversation: this was the first time that he heard from me details about his mother, about our childhood and our home, things that he had not known until then. We talked until late at night, and, in the morning, we made the long drive to Końskie. We passed through fields, forests, and many villages, and I had a chance to see the great changes in the landscape: we did not see poor rural homes with straw roofs but rather new homes with tiles and orderly surroundings.

Końskie of 1994 had grown and become more beautiful. Now it had around 30,000 residents. When we arrived, we parked the car in the center of town, where Pocztów, the Jewish trade center, was once located. When we got out of the car, a young man approached us and asked if we knew Polish. Thus, we got to know the wonderful man, Marian Chochowski, and to this day I am in touch with him. He was a child when the ghetto was established in Końskie. He was a devout Christian. His father perished in Auschwitz. Why? He did not want to say. This very modest man, who to this day, for some reason of his own, is engaged in collecting every piece of information about the destruction of the Jews of Końskie, gave us pictures that the Germans or other amateur photographers took in that period and explained about them. I had in my possession pictures of the synagogue that the Germans destroyed and Pocztów that was also destroyed. He told us the story of the Jewish cemetery. We visited it. It had become a. . . horse farm. There is no longer any sign of the marble Kronenblum tomb. We stood there in shock. We looked at the place that had once been fenced in by a wall of trees around 400 years old. Now only one corner remained that recalled the fence of the cemetery. In one of the letters that I got from Chochowski later, he told me that since we visited, every year, when the Poles mark the "day of souls" (Zaduszki, a remnant of pagan customs), he comes to this corner and lights a memorial candle for the Jewish victims of Końskie.

Something strange happened in Końskie in 1994. I felt suddenly like sixty years had not passed since I left the town. I ran as though chased by a demon from Aunt Feyge's house to that of Aunt Frida, to that of Uncle Yaakov. In every street I had relatives. Those houses are still standing. The windows were open, the curtains moving in the light breeze, like then. I only needed to wait a bit and my cousin Chava would come out of the house, or Dorka, or Shprintze would emerge from the house on Pocztowa Street, and my cousin Feyge- Mirele. I was as though bewitched—all the images of my childhood returned and came alive. Here, in this house with the large yard, I walked together with little Meir every morning to Kheyder. And in the house at the intersection between Nowy Świat and Cmentarna Streets, my aunt and uncle, Rabbi Szarfharc, lived with their family. And there, opposite, still stands the ruined house in which, eighty years ago, my grandmother Hannah had lived. The illusion that my family members were living in these houses just as they had long ago was so strong that I was disappointed when strangers emerged from them.

There are no longer any Jews living in Końskie.

CHAPTER 2
ŁÓDŹ

The Łódź Reality

My father was in a dark mood. On the one hand, he knew that he could not keep me at home any longer, and on the other his heart grieved that he was going to lose his last daughter, who was about to fly the nest, and his influence over her. Meir had already left and was studying in an ultra-orthodox yeshiva in Łódź. Until the last moment, he tried to stop me from leaving him. Father tried to persuade me that I was still a child, that in Łódź, God forbid, I would be infected by Communism and rot in prison like my cousin Dorka Miedzigórski or the son of Aunt Feyge, Avraham Rosenfarb. And I, pious and pure in my faith, I too was scared. But I believed that the Holy One, blessed be He, would help me to keep my faith.

On a rainy day at the beginning of November 1932, having parted from my mother in the cemetery the day before, my father accompanied me to the train station. I bid him farewell with a heavy heart and boarded the train for Łódź. This was my first journey. I sat alone, bundled up, in the train. The journey took a long time. I had hours to think and remember. Indeed, I was about to start a new life. What awaited me, what was I leaving behind, what would I miss? I thought about my parents, about my mother.

I would no longer run to school every morning, I would not visit my mother in the cemetery, as I had done almost every day after school. On my visits, I would tell my mother about everything that was bothering me, and ask for her help. These visits ostensibly strengthened me, helping me to feel less alone. I would miss these two places—my mother's grave and school. I would miss the long conversations with my father during our shared wanderings. And I would miss our green town, the boulevards, and its forests. I was full of curiosity and apprehension about the future.

I prayed to God asking Him to guard my faith, to ensure that I not stray from the straight path, to help me.

Shoshana and Esther, as I said, were already living in Łódź. Likewise, my two big brothers from my mother, Moshe and David Zilberszpic, had also been there for a long time. My brothers already had families. Shoshana was likewise married. I made her a present with my own hands, sending it with Esther, who attended her wedding—a box made of glass and the sides held with a colorful ribbon, and on the decorated glass door I drew in oil paints rich grass and a stork walking on it. Everyone liked this present, and Shoshana kept it until the war, until it got lost together with everything else.

Now I was joining them. I would work with Esther, who had remained in the city after Shoshana's wedding and had not returned to Końskie.

After long hours of travel, the train finally stopped at the station Łódź Fabryczna.

I do not remember the moment I arrived in Łódź and who was waiting for me; apparently it was Esther. I found myself in Shoshana's home. She and her husband lived at 24 Pomorska Street, where they had a grocer's shop, and beyond the wall of the shop was their one-room dwelling. In the corner opposite the entrance to the shop was the back entrance to the courtyard and there they made for themselves a dark little kitchen. The room that was beyond this wall had, apparently, previously been part of the shop, because a display window covered the entire wall.

After the warm embraces of Shoshana, who had become more beautiful, I met her husband Moshe, a strawberry blond with happy blue eyes and dimples in his chin. He gave the impression that he was a carefree man who was head over heels in love with his wife. From him I heard for the first time the words, "Bina, smile." He lifted up my chin and added, "Lift up your head and look straight at the world."

I heard such remarks afterward for at least two years, my first two years in Łódź. I really did not know how to laugh then; I did not know about simple, healthy, human laughter. I heard such remarks afterward from many people. I heard it even when I was in prison in 1937, during the daily half-hour walk around the yard in the Piotrków Trybunalski prison, when we walked in a single file (gęsiego) at a fixed distance from each other. Professor Halina Weiss was always behind me, murmuring in my ear, together with her history or literature lessons, "Bina, lift up your head."

Esther had changed a lot. There was not a lot left of the glowing blonde girl with golden curls. Her long hair had darkened, it was now a light brown color, and was combed with a middle parting into two round plaits that covered her ears (sometimes she did one plait that she wound around her head). Her blue eyes, Father's eyes, were full of worry.

That same day, Esther and I went to the apartment that we were to share as our living and working quarters. I did not know then that a great financial crisis was underway in the country and in the entire world. I looked around me: tall, gray, ugly buildings, covered with soot, without any greenery or trees. People, so many people, hurrying to work. From afar, as though at every end of the city, I saw tall chimneys that rose into the heights spilling out thick black smoke that covered the skies of the city. After green Końskie, covered in forest and fields, Łódź appeared depressing. Over time I got used to it and even loved this sooty city.

Łódź was built quickly and cheaply in the nineteenth century as a textile manufacturing city. It was the "Manchester of Poland." The Germans, who in the first half of the nineteenth century established the textile industry in this city with the support of money from the Polish royalty, did not worry about building spacious houses with green gardens for the workers. From the second half of that century onward, when Łódź had already developed, with the massive involvement of Jewish industrialists and merchants, they built cheap, multistory houses for the Jewish workers.

And so, we entered a courtyard in the form of a "well," meaning a small yard that was surrounded on all sides by buildings of four stories. The sun reached only the uppermost floor. Our living space was in a roof apartment with "Aunt" Yocheved (I do not know whose aunt she was). It was a one-room apartment with a large kitchen that belonged to an old couple without children who ran a stall in the market in Bałuty (the poor Jewish neighborhood in Łódź). The owners of the apartment left in the morning and returned in the evening (he apparently sat all day in the Beit Midrash next to the stall). "Aunt" Yocheved, a woman of wide dimensions, controlled the house and her husband. She locked their room with a key when they left the house, and I never saw its contents.

We rented a corner in the kitchen of their apartment. A narrow iron bed stood alongside the wall and next to it two sewing machines for the two of us, two chairs, and a small table next to the window. This was all our furniture. Because I was small, my relatives found a chair that would enable my feet to reach the pedals of the sewing machine and operate it. Thus began the epic of my life in Łódź.

We, Esther and I, did a piece work at home (chałupniczki). We received from a company packages of cut-up fabric and sewed shirts. By day we sewed shirts and by night we did the finishing, meaning we sewed on the buttons and folded the shirts nicely. After finishing the entire package, we returned it to the owners and got new ones.

The first shock that I had was on the evening of my first Sabbath in Łódź. We were invited to Shoshana's home for the Friday night meal. It was already late, after candle lighting time, when Esther let out her plaits and began to comb her beautiful long hair. I let out a soft cry, "What are you doing? It's already the Sabbath!"

For a moment she was alarmed, but then she answered me in a very authoritative and decisive way: "You're too little to give me lectures."

This statement silenced me and determined the relations between us for a long time, which was rather painful for me. However, on that first Sabbath, I had to withstand another challenge, even more difficult. Indeed, for me it assumed the dimensions of a catastrophe.

When we reached Shoshana's house, we found the couple busy cleaning the house and cooking dinner. I found myself facing a way of life that deeply shocked me. I ran out into the street and cried. They left me alone. They wanted me to go through this shock; there was no other way. Esther helped them to prepare for the Sabbath. When they finished, Shoshana came to me and sat next to me in the entrance to the courtyard. She was very serious and tried to justify herself. She told me:

"The lives of people who work all week, including Friday until the Sabbath comes in, mean that it is necessary to accept a different way of life. We have no choice. Only after closing the shop, can we do the necessary household chores and cook something. Łódź is not Końskie; there life proceeds at a different pace, there other unwritten laws apply. I am sorry that you have had many disappointments of this kind, but you must work in Łódź; you have no choice but to get used to this reality."

She led me to her home. The table was set for a Sabbath meal, like at home. Shoshana lit the candles, Moshe made Kiddush over wine with a special melody, and after the meal sang Sabbath songs in a nice tenor voice. Afterward, I found out that he helped the chazan in the synagogue with festival prayers.

So, with embarrassment and emotional despair, my life in the new reality began. This despair also affected my relationship with Esther: she treated me like a little girl who cannot understand anything, a burden on her. Another kind of despair resulted from the relations with my brothers from my mother's side. The mutual relations between Esther and I, on the one hand, and David and Moshe, on the other, were multilayered. They made me feel embarrassed, and I think the same was true for Esther, although perhaps because of different reasons. Among other things, the big siblings (meaning my brothers and Shoshana) arranged that on Sabbath eves Esther and I would take turns eating alternately with David and with Shoshana. Eating at David's home, even once in two weeks, was difficult for me. I think it was even harder for Esther. Esther was Father's daughter. She was like him in both appearance and character. She always reacted with exaggerated anger whenever someone made a non-complimentary comment about our father, jumping to his defense. Perhaps because of this, Esther made a clear distinction between us and them, and she was angry with me that I did not want to understand that we had a better lineage from Father's side than they did from their father. May Esther forgive me—her intentions were good, but I rebelled against this. I loved Shoshana most, and familial lineage did not arouse in me any special feelings. Although I was still very religious, more than her, I had a deeper connection with Shoshana than I did with Esther, yet Esther saw Shoshana only as a half-sister. I think that my character was more like Mother's. With all my esteem and love for my father, I nurtured in my heart a lot of grievances toward him and I did not believe him a saint, especially due to his attitude to my mother and to David, not to mention the period in which I lived with his new wife. Therefore, I felt uncomfortable, embarrassed, but I also understood to a certain extent my brothers' comments about my father.

I already mentioned that our Moshe (Shoshana's husband was also called Moshe, so we called our brother Moshe "our Moshe" and our brother-in-law "Shoshana's Moshe") was fourteen years older than me. When I was born, he was apparently no longer living at home, but he came to visit our mother twice a year for Passover and Sukkot. He always brought us, the little children, presents. Thus, he remained in my memory—a big yet distant brother. We did not grow up together and had no shared experiences. When he left home and why, I do not know. I knew him very little. I know only that at first he lived with his uncle on his father's side in Radom and there learned a trade, making cigarette papers; afterward he moved to Łódź. Sometimes it was difficult for me to think that he left home in his youth because of our father.

The story of my relations with David was different. I remember him from my childhood. He was very attached to our mother; he loved her and admired her especially. I do not remember why he was considered lazy at home (apparently, my father thought him lazy because he was not particularly devoted to Torah study). Much later it became evident that David was the most organized, the most industrious, and the only one of all our family to be successful in industry and finance, in fact employing and supporting almost the entire family. But in his presence, I felt great embarrassment.

It was hard for him at home. There was always tension between him and my father: because of the relations between Father and Mother, which were not always good, and mainly, so I think, because he was not so enthusiastic about Torah study, and my father accorded study, especially Torah study, great value. It was customary in our house that on Sabbath eve after the meal my father would examine the boys about what they had learned that week. David studied at the Talmud Torah (or Beit Midrash); at that time, he was the only one studying Torah (apart from my father) because Meir was still young. These tests were a real nightmare for him, and especially for Mother. David was not a Torah genius, however my father treated him with great severity. Once, after the evening meal, with the Sabbath candles and an oil lamp burning on the table (in the old apartment we did not have electricity), my father apparently pushed David too hard during his examination, causing him to fall from his chair. As a result, the candles fell, together with the candlesticks, the oil spilled, and the table went up in flames. Fortunately, the Sabbath gentile lived nearby, and she prevented the whole house from burning down. A short while afterward, David left home and joined Moshe, our big brother. He was then around thirteen years old.

In truth, I should note that David was not the only one to receive blows from father. During my childhood, blows were one of the accepted educational methods. Indeed, there were different levels of blows in accordance with the "crime" committed by the child and the severity of the punishment. With regard to the case described above, such a thing was forbidden because David was my father's stepson, and Father knew it was forbidden to hit an orphan. It is sad that it happened. It could be that my father's gloomy mood at the time was affected by the difficult economic situation, which it seemed would go on forever. He never raised a hand against Shoshana, apparently because he raised her and was attached to her. I, by contrast, received blows from him.

I remember very well the last good measure of blows that I received from my father. In truth, I deserved it. It was in that terrible winter, after my mother's death. We were neglected children, all of us having suffered from scarlet fever. After Shayele's death, I became wild. I think that I did not understand then the extent of the disaster that had occurred. Esther, a child herself, could not control us. I fought with Meir (father's "saint"). He hit me with his fist in my nose and it started to bleed, and I pushed him with my foot and tore his tzitzit. When Father returned and saw Meir crying and his tzitzit torn, he beat us both. But I got more blows because I was bigger than Meir. The blows left me in bed for a few days, and father walked around in an even more terrible mood because of it. However, getting blows from one's father is not like getting them from a stepfather. I learned this well on my own flesh when I was an orphan living with my stepmother. These are fragile and very painful situations; I am not talking about physical pain but rather emotions. One who has not experienced it cannot understand.

My sister Esther developed a sense of responsibility for others under her supervision, but she lacked psychological understanding of the person she was caring for; in this case, me. With exaggerated seriousness, she took it upon herself to look after me, her little sister. Touchingly, she tried to save me from too much physical exertion. Knowing that I suffered from terrible migraines (which began when my stepmother woke me up early every morning with screams), Esther endeavored to let me sleep a little later than her. She herself had "normal" headaches due to malnutrition and the hard work, which was too much for us. When I got up at seven in the morning, Esther was already sitting at her sewing machine with a compress on her head. The sadness gave me a heavy heart. I did not know what to do or how to change our difficult situation. I felt guilty that I had fallen upon her, adding to her burden. This feeling intensified because there was no openness and direct and honest dialogue between us. She constantly treated me like a little girl.

The situation was unbearable. We worked from dawn until late at night (I worked a little less) but made only pennies, using them to buy bread and skimmed sour milk (the cream had been skimmed off it). When the owner of the house came home in the evening, she lit the brick oven and cooked something. Then we could drink hot tea. In the winter it was so cold in that attic that our fingers and toes bloated. And when, in the evening, the cooking stove heated up and the heating was also on, the whole apartment grew hot, and on more than one occasion, our fingers became cracked and covered in wounds (the traces of which can be seen to this day). By contrast, in the summer the attic was so hot and suffocating that it was hard to breathe.

The difficult living conditions, Esther's exaggerated concern, while she herself was exhausted, all this became unbearable for me. I felt that I was too much of a burden on her shoulders, while she continued to see me as the little sister, unable to understand anything yet under her supervision and care. Although we loved each other, and although we were both living in the same terrible situation, sleeping in the same narrow bed, and the age gap between us was not so big, we lacked the conditions, or we did not know how, to break the barrier and develop a more intimate emotional bond. I blamed myself for failing to break the ice and initiate an open and fundamental dialogue. I did not find the right time for this and did not know how to begin.

Shoshana, as I said, was nine years older than me, and Esther only two and a half. Shoshana was my sister on my mother's side, while Esther was my full sister. However, I did not feel any kind of distance from Shoshana. With her, I could talk and converse for hours about everything (maybe because I recognized her authority as my big sister). Until the day of her death, we were so close that my husband Heniek was jealous. The situation with Esther led both of us to seek a refuge for our feelings and interests in different places. And thus, as time passed, I started to try to escape from under the wings of my sister Esther. However, before doing so, I needed to go through several stages of self-recognition or understanding the meaning of our life. This was a rather lengthy process.

In the meantime, there were changes in our close family in Łódź. Moshe, our oldest brother, lived quite far from us together with his wife Yitche, their small daughter, and Yitche's parents. When her parents died, her brother and sister remained in their parents' house, and Moshe and his family moved to live at 5 or 7 Pomorska Street, not far from Shoshana. I liked Yitche and their daughter Rivka (Rita) a lot. I often took her for a walk on Sabbaths and holidays.

Shoshana was about to give birth to her son, Naftali (today a retired IDF officer and an engineer, he lives in Haifa). Their grocery store did not make them enough money, and apart from that, there was no room for a child's bed for the newborn baby in their small room. The couple decided to get rid of the shop and they rented an apartment not far away, at 20 Pomorska Street (on the corner of Solna Street). Moshe, Shoshana's husband, started working in a weaving factory and she started making gloves for David. Their new apartment was only one large room, which one entered directly from the stairwell (on the third floor). Apart from a large window, they had a balcony with half-glazed doors. The window and balcony faced Solna Street. In October 1933, Naftali was born; together with him and his mother, we endured a lot of wanderings and experiences.

David experienced the most significant changes. As I already mentioned, in my parents' home he was considered lazy, although I do not remember why. David married a poor girl, Chava (we called her Eva) Zork, in Łódź. If I am not mistaken, she was from Zduńska Wola and came to live with her aunt and uncle in Łódź. They had a weaving factory, and Eva became like a daughter to them. The aunt and uncle gave her a modest dowry. David and Eva rented a small one-room apartment on Solna street and started to work from home. David, it seems, had acquired expertise in making gloves. They bought a small gas oven for cooking and baking and in this oven they "ironed" the gloves (or gave them the desired shape) on special molds. Very quickly they became independent. They bought merchandise: a cutter, cut out cotton, and silk gloves.

Seamstresses sewed them, and workers and the couple themselves added the finishing touches. They worked very hard.

When I arrived in Łódź, they already had an assistant, someone that David had brought from Końskie. She was my age, from a family of lower standing: in our city it was forbidden for me to know about her existence. She worked for David and Eva until the outbreak of the war. She grew up in their home and she was very loyal to them. Her name was Rella. They called her the Shikse because she did not look Jewish. As she grew up in their home, she developed into a rather beautiful young woman. She had blonde hair, a small nose, and a special smile. For a short period in my life, I shared a bed with her in the kitchen of David's apartment, and she was even higher than me in rank. (Our paths crossed a number of times: in Russia, in Warsaw, and also in Holon. Two years ago, I discovered she had died. She left two children, both well educated. The son, as she told me, was a successful surgeon in Haifa and the daughter was also successful.) However, then, in the apartment on Solna street, a double bed took up all of David and Eva's room. They did not even have a little cupboard but a few pegs on the wall and hangers to hang up clothes. In the corner stood the oven, next to which was a small table on which they "dressed" the gloves onto the molds. These were then placed on a special rack and placed in the oven (two years later I also worked at this, but in different living conditions). The wide bed served as a work-table. On it, they paired the gloves, and every dozen pairs were packed in the firm's packaging, put into special cartoons, and sent off to who knows where.

Rella ate at their table and received a monthly wage. She worked, together with Eva and David, from dawn until dusk. She slept on the floor at the foot of the bed. In these conditions, with hard work, David and Eva amassed an initial, small sum of capital. When Eva got pregnant, they moved to a spacious apartment with three rooms and a kitchen on Schodnia Street, the name of which was later changed to Józef Piłsudski Street (the name of the leader of liberated Poland, who died in 1935, and to this day is considered one of the greatest Polish heroes). One room in the new apartment became the workshop, and a few hired hands worked there, among them Eva's sister, Estherke, and a Polish cutter. After some time, David expanded his living space by adjoining another apartment on the same floor. A door was made in the wall dividing the two apartments. With the development of the factory, they employed about a dozen workers, among them some family members, our brother Moshe, who replaced the Polish cutter (who cut the material), Shoshana, who took piece work home, and more. Most of the work was given to people who took it to their homes.

David's family expanded. Three years after his first son, Naftali, was born, his wife bore a daughter, Sara (named after my mother, Sarah Rivka). They all perished in the death camps.

These changes afterward also affected the relationships in the family. All the brothers and sisters of our family now lived in a radius of a few streets, close to one another, and David became the richest one in the family.

At around the same time, it was agreed, without asking me, that on Sabbath evenings Esther and I would take turns going to Shoshana and David alternately and separately. Whenever it was my turn to go to David for Friday night, I felt very uncomfortable. In addition to feeling awkward with David, his wife Eva did not radiate warm and familial feelings, as, for example, Yitche, our Moshe's wife, did. She did not reveal any particular enthusiasm for me.

I should note that after the changes our family underwent, there were also alterations in our (mine and Esther's) living and working arrangements. For some time, we still worked together in "Aunt" Yocheved's attic. The winter passed and summer came. We made enough money for bread and "skimmed" milk. It was a hot, suffocating summer. We sewed canvas overalls. Our hands could not lift the rough and heavy canvas to the sewing machine. From the distance of time, I see an almost surreal picture: Esther, a cold compress on her head and drops of sweat running down her face; me, fighting with the tough canvas and failing to get the needle of the sewing machine through it. . . both of us, breathing heavily and singing. Oh, we sang. All the songs by Itzik Manger, Shulman, and other songs that I don't know who wrote them, we sang and sang, until we had no breath left:

"It may be that I will never reach my aim / it may be that my ship will never come to shore / life is better in a dream, clearer in a dream / in a dream the sky is bluer than blue. . . ."

We poured all our frustration into our singing. With no need for words, in these moments we were as close as sisters can be, emotionally, and our hearts overflowed with pity for one another. In difficult or intimate moments, we sang. Another picture is engraved on my memory: it was the end of April 1937. I lived with Shoshana, Esther was already on hakhshara, it was almost midnight. Moshe and the baby were asleep in the room and the door to the room was closed. I was helping Shoshana to finish some work and we hummed quietly, not wanting to wake up the sleepers:

Już północ wybiła na miejskim zegarze
Więźniowie dawno już śpią
Lecz jeden z nich nie śpi I wciąż o czymś marzy,
On widzi wolność za mgłą. . .

"The wall clock has already struck midnight/ the prisoners are already sleeping for some time / only one does not sleep and dreams of something / he sees the freedom beyond the darkness."

This was a song sung by prisoners dreaming of freedom. Suddenly, in the middle of the song, someone knocked on the door. When I opened it, a policeman entered, accompanied by the building's watchman, and, after a short search, I was arrested.

(To this day, sometimes, when I sit next to the little electric sewing machine to sew or fix something, I automatically start to hum, like I did then.)

Yet, then, when the two of us sat next to the sewing machines, operating them with our feet, together with the bitter singing, resentment built up inside me. I felt that if I could release Esther from the burden of making a living for both of us, then perhaps each one of us would find for herself a slightly less difficult way of life—otherwise, both of us would be lost. Suddenly, in the middle of this singing, I decided to fight. I rebelled. I got up from my seat and stated that I was not prepared to suffer any more or to be a burden to her. I left the sewing machine with the heavy canvas and ran to the city, looking for any kind of work. I spent a whole day running around and looking for advertisements in shop windows and in the newspaper. Nothing. As you can imagine, I did not find anything. Indeed, these were years of severe economic crisis. However, my rebellion led to changes in our lives.

After I went out and left Esther alone, she went to cry and complain to Shoshana, who was always a rock for both of us. Shoshana understood our situation and saw that it was necessary to do something. She called our sister-in-law, Yitche. After consultations, about which I had no idea, just as I had no idea about the decisions made, we moved in with Shoshana. Esther agreed to this on the condition that we would pay our way. She arrived at an agreement with our brother-in-law Moshe concerning a weekly or monthly sum of money, and we made these payments regularly (afterward, Esther alone and sometimes I myself, when I lived with them), without Shoshana knowing.

I already mentioned that the couple lived with their small son Naftali in an apartment at 20 Pomorska Street, which was made up of one spacious room. How would we live there together with them? Moshe, the man of the house, had hands of gold. He could build and do anything cheerfully and with grace. He put up dividers in the spacious room: one, the width of the entire room, made a small front space in the apartment and a living room. Along the length of this front part, he put up another divider, which made a partially lit corner for a kitchen (daylight entered from two sources: the entrance to the second part of the room and that to the kitchen), where there was a tap with running water, a sink, a cooking stove, and the rest of the kitchen utensils. All that was left of the front space became a corridor, along the length of which, close to the wall between the entrance wall and the big divider, was our wooden bed (for me and Esther). Next to it were our two sewing machines, and close to them was a way to the "living room" or the bedroom and the rest of the apartment.

In the meantime, we continued sewing the cursed canvas. However, after a few days, David appeared. He looked at the room, looked around, and looked at me now and again, and I saw that he wanted to say something but felt uncomfortable. He had a good heart, and I think he wanted to help us. However, David knew well that both of us were proud, perhaps too proud. We did not want pity, and we certainly would not take handouts. Moreover, it seemed to me that Esther and Shoshana knew that I was the cause of the embarrassment. David started murmuring that he wanted me to look after his little Naftali, that is his son (both the boys, the sons of Shoshana and David, were called Naftali, after their father), and come to live with him. I burst out crying and David ran out of the house.

After he left, as though by coincidence, Yitche, my sister-in-law, appeared. We all loved Yitche, who was a good soul, overflowing with warmth, a woman with authority and great persuasive abilities. The three women set about persuading me. In the end, I went to live with David.

Releasing Esther from the burden of responsibility for me caused real changes in her life. Finally, she began to think about herself and take an interest in her own development. She went to an embroidery course and began to work in this profession. She worked less, slept more, her headaches disappeared completely, and she once again became a young woman, beautiful and intelligent. Under the influence of her friend Chava, she joined the Zionist Youth Organization "Gordonia." There, all her beautiful qualities—her willingness to contribute, her responsibility, her generous heart, and so on—flourished. Also, her day-to-day behavior changed entirely. After some time, she had a boyfriend, with whom she was in a hakhshara group in the area of Sosnowiec (Sosnovitz), and together they planned to immigrate to the Land of Israel. Because they only had one certificate allowing immigration to the Land of Israel, they decided that Esther would go first and her fiancé (whose name I do not remember) would follow. In fall 1938, we accompanied her to the train station in Łódź for the long journey to the Land of Israel. My father even came to Łódź to part from his daughter, and did not think, so it seemed to me, that they would ever meet again. Her fiancé waited for a certificate, but it never came. The war broke out and he suffered the same fate as the rest of the Jews of Poland. He perished in the death camps.

In 1956, when, after eighteen years of separation, I met Esther at the airport in Lod, we fell into each other's arms and cried for a long time. Next to her stood Shoshana. I had missed her and all the family so much. I arrived then as a tourist with my two children, Victor, who was twelve, and Hania, who was six.

My Esther. When I met her again, I understood how much I loved her and how dear she was to me. Next to her stood her handsome and beloved husband and their two sons, around the ages of my own children. Esther had people to look after and care for with all her soul and unending devotion. When I looked at her, I saw in her thin face and body that she too had gone through

difficult years. She was among the pioneers who established kib-
butzim in Israel, and the life and work there were then too hard
for her. During the war, Shlomo, her husband, fought in the Jewish
Brigade in the British army. At the same time, Esther gave birth to
her first son in the hospital on Mount Scopus. The difficult conditions in Jerusalem at that time and in the hospital led to the death
of the baby after a few days, and Esther left the hospital very sick.
Shlomo returned as a decorated soldier from the war and afterward fought in Israel's War of Independence, when the kibbutz,
which was in the suburbs of Jerusalem, was battling for its existence. Esther's physical condition declined, and she could not work
hard. Not wanting to be a burden on the kibbutz, they decided to
leave; of course, they left with nothing. Shlomo was offered good
jobs, but he rejected the offers and preferred physical labor. The
couple were very similar to one another in their honesty and truth-
fulness, and I understood this well. Esther and I grew up together
in the same home and absorbed the very same values.

On that visit, in 1956, as a tourist, I felt that Esther was happy
with her small family and modest life; indeed, this was the period
of austerity in Israel. We looked at one another and declared, with
humor and a certain degree of satisfaction, after eighteen years,
that genetically we were sisters too: we had the same distortions
in our bones. We discovered that both of us, for example, lacked
molars and we had the same prominent bones in our feet.

Esther felt herself, even after eighteen years, "my big sister,"
something that made us both laugh. I was then quite a well-known
journalist and I had managed to get a higher education, but to
Esther I was sometimes still the same little sister who does not
understand anything (Do you know the bible?). We had conversations that were a little bit funny, but they aroused associations
and memories. To tell the truth, we both complained that fate
did not allow us to follow each other's emotional and spiritual
development. We felt that there were chasms between us due to

the many years of separation. Shlomo, who was more open than Esther, understood this. He was a very wise and warm man; he also foresaw the fate of my family in Poland. However, no one foresaw that only three years after saying goodbye, we would hear of his death. He died of a heart attack at the age of fifty, leaving behind a widow of forty-five with two children, Dov and Gideon. Until the end of her days, Esther mourned her husband. She succeeded in becoming a teacher and was greatly loved by her pupils. She raised her sons and fought with all her might to ensure they would get a higher education. She died at the age of sixty-eight, by which time both her sons had become psychologists and could fend for themselves. She did not live to meet her grandchildren.

Returning to the 1930s, I worked for David for about two years. At first, as I said, I slept with Rella in the bed in the kitchen, behind a curtain. After their apartment was expanded by the addition of another three rooms, I got a folding bed and slept alone in a work room. This change was very important for me because in the evenings, after work, I could read books until late at night. I looked after David's Naftali, who was three or four years old. I fed him, took him for walks, played with him, and read him children's books. Apart from this, I ran errands as a messenger girl: I took cardboard packages full of merchandise to the post office or brought them to shops, or they sent me to bring something from the shop, and I ran to do so. Sometimes, I also worked in the workshop. I loved that more than anything else. In short, I was the Friday girl, doing all the jobs (apart from the maid's work). In that period, gloves with embroidered muslin cuffs were in fashion, and they were embroidered by a man named Yaga. As the person who brought him the work and took back the products, I got to know him quite well. His young wife was very pretty, but you could feel the tension between them. Yaga seemed like an absent-minded man, a philosopher or an actor. His head was crowned with long blonde hair, and he was a good person to talk to.

Yaga was indeed an actor in the Yiddish theater in Łódź. He was not part of an established or permanent theater but part of a group of actors that every so often managed to put on plays in the Łódź theater. Each one of them worked in a different place to make a living, but every evening and every Sabbath they met and worked on texts and plays. I was then a young woman who had just begun to blossom. Yaga tried to persuade me to take part in these meetings with the actors, and sometimes I went along. Once I went on a trip with all the actors. It was a trip to a forest in the city's suburbs. What is mainly etched into my memory were the relations between Yaga and his beautiful wife. In the midst of a seemingly carefree conversation, his wife suddenly had a panic attack. This was the first time in my life I had seen such a thing. She started shaking, her breathing became labored, and she let out strange noises. Yaga got her to stand up, hugged her, and while embracing and stroking her, he took her for a walk. When they came back, she was fine. When they left, the others told me that Yaga was a homo-sexual, and thus I met a homosexual for the first time in my life.

The improved nutrition, walking with the child in the park, and the less exhausting work—as a result of all these factors, I began to develop and grow physically. David watched me with strange looks, and I did not know why. Later, when an argument broke out between us, he told me that since I had grown, every time I came into the room he saw our mother, whom he loved so much. I became like my mother.

My relationship with him was not open like that between a sis-ter and brother. Something separated us. I already wrote about this. It seems that the source of David's complexes was the relation-ship with my father, and thus my relationship with the couple (also his wife Eva) was not good. On more than one occasion David came to my room at night and turned out the light, saying that it was not healthy to read late at night and I needed to get up early in the morning. I always saw in my mind's eye that same Sabbath eve when Father caused him to fall to the floor. It seems that he had told Eva about this, because she treated me, or so I felt, with obvious distance. These mutual relations were in no small part my fault. One of my many issues was a certain embarrassment, an inability to achieve normal employer-worker relations. This sometimes resulted in my silence, when I felt that the employer was not fair toward me and I rebelled internally. Sometimes I felt embarrassed and could not respond because of feelings of inferiority, even toward people on whom I depended to some extent or another, although in terms of knowledge and professionalism I was not inferior to them. These complexes made life difficult also in my scientific career. Sometimes they were expressed in stubborn silence, sometimes the embarrassment was covered by exaggerated self-confidence, or outbursts of anger, after which I felt deep regret.

I caused David no small amount of anguish. In the period that I spent with him, I went through a process of pretty dramatic development: from a girl so religious that I even denied the existing world order to a devotee of another religion—Communism. However, David and Eva also influenced this process of secularization to a certain extent.

They were not really religious. David even had a period of enthusiasm for the Socialist movement. However, as a couple, they agreed to keep, at least for the sake of show, the main principles of tradition. When their business grew, David made connections with merchants from the religious circles to which Eva's aunt and uncle, who were very religious, belonged. These circles had their own synagogue and David began to attend services there. The way of life at home was secular, but David would sometimes go to this synagogue on Sabbaths and festivals. He dressed in the fashion of the progressive Jews (he did not wear a kaftan but a three-quarter length jacket, without a head covering). I followed with curiosity this double life (I should emphasize that this was characteristic of many Polish Jews in that period at all levels of Jewish society, apart from the orthodox). However, providing it did not affect me personally, I did not care. I was still very religious.

The last day of Sukkot is Simchat Torah. This day is particularly joyous for Jews. In synagogues people dance, sing, and drink, praise the Holy one, blessed be He, for giving the Torah to His chosen people; afterward the rejoicing passed to the private homes of the synagogue goers. This time, David invited the group to his home. The celebratory meal was perfect. They drank a lot of beer, danced, and ate and drank. At some point, David came to me and tried to give me money so I would run to buy beer. I refused and answered that I would not touch money on the festival and would not buy anything. Instead, he sent Rella (or the maid) and did not speak to me. This time I stood up for myself, but the double standard vis-à-vis religion, in comparison to my upbringing, bothered me. Indeed, Shoshana and her husband behaved in the same way, and they were Jews and people that I loved, but at least they did not try to cheat the Holy one, blessed be He. In this environment and in these conditions, I increasingly found myself asking the Creator of the world: "Do You see and remain silent?" Over time, the questions multiplied. And, as usual at this age, if you look for answers, you find them. Life helped me to find them.

After around two years, I was still working for David. Then something else happened and I was dismissed from my job. It was my fault this time. I was no longer that same innocent girl from Końskie. I had learned a lot about life. Here is what happened:

On the last Yom Kippur when I was working for David, David and Eva went to synagogue, as was the custom of the Jews who fast and pray to the Holy one, blessed be He, in the synagogues for an entire day. David took his religious paraphernalia and Eva her prayer book. I remained at home with Naftali, who was four or five. This was a period in which David had already expanded his business. His home, which was combined with the workshop, had two entrances (it included six or seven rooms). At ten or eleven in the morning, a few of my friends arrived with a loaf of bread and sausage (not kosher) and we had a meal, together with little Naftali, which made him happy. After the food, I tidied everything away, so that there would be no signs of our "wild behavior," and a little while later we heard Naftali's parents coming home for a break. My friends hurried to go out of one entrance, and David and Eva came in from the other. The couple also ate a rich meal, and afterward they rested a bit. When they returned to the synagogue, they took Naftali with them. When they came back, another storm broke over my head. Eva's uncle had put Naftali on his knee and asked him what he did that day. And he told him that he had fun, because. . . etc. David had to fire me, because Eva's family and she herself could not bear to have me in the house any longer. I was sad that I had caused trouble for David, and I believe that he was also sorry that he had to fire me.

In the first days of the war, when I decided to flee to the Soviet Union, I went to say goodbye to David and his family. I received from them a warm sweater (I left it somewhere on the roads of the Ukraine). David parted from me with tears. He asked me to forget all the misunderstandings between us, and I too, with tears in my eyes, asked for his forgiveness. We both felt that this was our last parting. David and his family, they had two children—Naftali and a little girl, Sara— who perished in the death camps.

After I was dismissed from my position with David, I went to live with Shoshana. Esther was already at that stage with the hakhshara group near Sosnowiec. I looked for work in textile or confection workshops, or anywhere else. However, Jews were not accepted to work, even when the factory owner was Jewish. I thus made a living by taking home piece work. Among other things, I took home linen tablecloths from a wholesale merchant; I tied fringes around the edges, and for this they paid me five groshen for every dozen heavy tablecloths. With strenuous work from morning to night, I could make one zloty. Everyone who came to visit Shoshana's house helped me. These tablecloths had to be spread on the table. Everyone (male and female) who came in the evening—because in Shoshana's home there was always a good atmosphere (she told me once, many years later and in different conditions, that when she was among my friends, she herself felt young, and she loved them)—talked, laughed, argued about politics, and meanwhile tied fringes.

I also took on other jobs. For a while I looked after the children of wealthy families. One family was from the Jewish intelligentsia—she was a doctor and he a lawyer—with two small children. It was a pleasure to work for them. I worked from the morning until five in the afternoon, when the couple returned from work. It was less nice to work for bourgeois families. Their children were more spoiled and difficult, and the wives very demanding.

With one such woman and her two children, together with the maid, I traveled to Ciechocinek, a well-known health spa in Poland. My contract was for the entire summer. While the mother enjoyed baths and massages, I walked with the children in the beautiful and cultivated parts of Ciechocinek. Once, while I was playing with the children in the park, a young man approached me and sent me regards from someone named Adele, the sister of one of my acquaintances. I knew that she had been released from prison due to her health condition. It became apparent that she was in Ciechocinek, sick with a serious infection of the joints, which she had "acquired" in prison. The young man asked me to visit her and help her however I could. In the evening, after putting the children to bed and doing what was necessary, I went to visit Adele.

She was in a sad condition: in a wheelchair, unable to do things for herself, accompanied by a caregiver. They lived in a small room in which many people gathered in the evenings. There I met interesting people who enriched me with new experiences. My employer was not happy about the fact that I went out every evening, and, fearing that I would exert a bad influence on her children, she dismissed me. I demanded, of course, compensation until the end of the season, and I received it. Thus, I enjoyed another seven days in Ciechocinek with Adele and the interesting people. In the mornings, I helped the caregiver take the patient to treatments and so on, and in the evenings the guests came. Among them was a Ukrainian poet who spoke to me in poetry. He came for treatment in the local clinics, as did others. Once or twice, we went for a walk in the surroundings. Not far from the town, on one of the hills, were the remnants of a castle that was apparently built by King Kazimir the Great in the fourteenth century. When we reached the top of the hill, it began raining heavily and there was a storm with thunder and lightning. I had always loved rain and storms. There, on the top of the hill, the skies flooded us with thunder and lightning—an unforgettable experience.

I enjoyed this holiday for only a short time. When I returned from that walk to Adele's room, a letter from Shoshana and David was waiting for me, asking me to come straight to Czarniecka Góra to look after David's son. Shoshana was waiting for me with the children, both Naftalis, hers and David's.

Czarniecka Góra was a village in the region of Końskie, lying on both banks of the Czarna River. The village was surrounded by pine forests. It was a quiet village, known for its healing qualities due to the forests. We were happy together, Shoshana, the two boys, and I. We bathed and played in the pure river water and on the shore, we walked and sat for hours in the beautiful, unforgettable forests, we collected fresh green pine cones, full of sap. Shoshana steeped them in boiling water and bathed her son, Natush, in the water. This was the prescription given by a doctor to strengthen the child's bones.

Because the town of Końskie was a few kilometers from the village, our nephew Chaim Miedzigórski, Aunt Frida's son, came to visit us. He was my age. We were then sixteen years old. He claimed until the day of his death (he died a few months ago) that I was his first love. I did not sense anything then, and I do not remember. However, he reminded me that I received my first kiss from him. After the war, he lived with his family in Paris. His son Yoel became religious, moved to Israel, married a religious woman, and they live with their children in Kfar Saba.

My father also visited us once in Czarniecka Góra. When Father came, I was with the children on the riverbank and Shoshana was making lunch. Father walked around the small apartment, and as he did so, he saw a book lying on the windowsill. The book, I remember correctly, was André Gide's *Return from the U.S.S.R.* The name of the book aroused my father's suspicions. When I came back, I was pleased to see him, but he received me with an angry face. The conversation between us, caused by the book, was difficult. I should remind you that my father's only sister, Aunt Brenda, was stuck in the Ukraine during the revolution and could not return. Her letters from the beginning of the 1920s were full of terror. She wrote that her sons hung on the walls of her home pictures of Lenin and the other leaders of the revolution, that she was afraid of them and had to hide her religious objects from her sons. My father, like all religious Jews, hated the Soviet regime due to its war on religious, mainly Jewish, tradition. My father again warned me against Communism.

What my father said to me then with a sadness that I had not seen in him for a long time, I remember well. These were words, I dare to state (because I dealt with the topic for many years) that expressed the helplessness of religious fathers who lost their control over their children because they were unable to provide for them and ensure their future. My father said to me then, "I can no longer direct your path. You make your own living. I pray that God will reside in your heart. Do not go down the path of Communism. . . . "

Only a few years later, I would see him crying in the courthouse as I stood trial.

CHAPTER 3

ON THE INEVITABLE PATH

Finding Myself

Hanka Krokh, my school friend from Końskie, had been living with her family in Łódź for around a year. We had kept in touch, corresponding by letter, and when I arrived in Łódź she looked for me. One day, she came to Shoshana's home and asked after me. That evening we met, and from that point onward we became closer than we had ever been in Końskie. I worked until late at night, so we could not meet on weekdays. However, we met in Shoshana and Moshe's apartment every Sabbath afternoon, when the couple went out to take a walk and enjoy themselves, and I, the aunt and babysitter, stayed at home with little Naftali. These hours in Shoshana's home were my private time. There, every Sabbath and holiday, I met with Hanka and another two girls, her friends, who became my friends too. Together we became a "quartet" of young women who were quite well-known in certain circles. Let me introduce these young women.

Helka Goldberg lived with her widowed mother and her unemployed brother on Śródmiejska Street. She was small and thin, with black eyes and black curls. The pleasant lines of her face and her prominent chin testified to a strong and decisive character.

She was serious, but she also knew how to laugh and have a good time, like all young women her age. Hella worked in a clothing factory, supported her small family, and was already a member of the professional "Needleworkers" union, one of the oldest professional unions among the Jews of Łódź. Guta (I do not remember her surname) worked as an assistant to a clerk who worked for someone. Guta did not stand out in particular. Likewise, there was nothing striking about her appearance. She was just a Jewish girl with dark hair, a Jewish nose, intelligent and quick-witted, a young woman who read a lot of books, something I had been unable to do.

Hanka Krokh, my school friend, stood out among us in many ways, in particular her appearance. She was tall, erect, blonde, pale, and chubby, with two dimples in her pale face and blue eyes full of light and joy. She was very beautiful. The only daughter of her beloved father, whose second wife, wanting to win her over, spoiled both her and her husband. Hanka had time to read books and was the most developed of us in terms of literary knowledge. Hanka did not need to work. She was still trying to find her place in Łódź. In contrast to Helka, whose family often suffered from great poverty, and me, the homes of Guta and in particular Hanka were relatively wealthy. All of them, together with their families, apparently perished in Auschwitz, with the rest of the Jews of the Łódź Ghetto.

Many of my memories and thoughts are connected to my blessed and intimate friendship with these young women. They helped me to find myself within the difficult whirlpool into which I had fallen in Łódź. It was to a great extent thanks to them that my thirst for books, knowledge, and study awakened. All three were more developed than me, both physically and spiritually, in particular Hanka, but also Helka.

Our first meetings were typical of silly teenage girls. Laughingly, we compared chest sizes (I had almost no chest whatsoever at this stage), we measured the lengths of our noses (here mine stood out), our hips, etc. Hanka, who was the most physically developed of us and also the prettiest, told us every time about her secret love for the young neighbor who lived opposite her window, etc. All this chatter was natural, apparently, for girls in the first stages of their female awakening. For me, it was all so new and magical that I was happy to be a girl with them, even though I was still so innocent and shy. I learned to laugh and to be a bit silly.

Slowly, our interests expanded. We talked about books we had read, causing me to sign up for the M. Grosser Library. The library belonged to the Kultur-lige, and I later discovered it was the workers' library of the Bund Party. This was the largest and cheapest public library in Łódź. However, at that time, I was not able to read a lot, and this contributed to my distress.

On one occasion, my friends came and invited me to go to the cinema. However, the Sabbath had not yet ended. I still obeyed the commandments as much as I could and would not touch money on the Sabbath. They showed me the tickets that they had already purchased, telling me that I would pay them back on a weekday. Shoshana, who was home, encouraged me to go. For the first time, I accepted such a compromise and did not think that I was perhaps committing a sin. I went with them and saw a movie for the first time in my life. I remember the movie, *Oczy Czarne*, to this day; even though it was not particularly worthy of being remembered, it made a strong impression on me. Since then and to this day, films move me to the point of tears, even kitschy romances, not to mention really good movies. In 1935, when I read Victor Hugo's *Les Miserables*, which also moved me greatly, they were showing the movie of this book in Łódź. What can I say? I went to the cinema alone because I did not want anyone to share my experience. I came back shaking, with a 40-degree fever (it was, I think, during the time that I was living with and working for David, my brother).

Our Sabbath afternoons, and our "quartet" in general, began to change. Almost without noticing, it became a study group for furthering our education. At first, we chose writers who were popular then: André Merlo, Henry Barbois, Maxim Gorky, Lev Tolstoy, Dostoyevsky, and other classics of French, Russian, and, of course, Polish literature. We would at first survey the content of the book and then discuss the characters of the heroes, we argued about the nature of the social milieu depicted in one book or another, about the writer's main idea, etc. The literature and these discussions widened our horizons and helped us to become accustomed to reality and life in the world around us. But that was not enough. We were united by a thirst for knowledge. We began to take an interest in Socialist utopians such as François-Noël Babeuf, Saint-Simon, and I do not remember when I started reading and discussing the teachings of Darwin, we studied the theories of Karl Johann Kautsky (even though we did not really understand him then), and we tried to understand something of *Das Kapital* by Karl Marx. *The Communist Manifesto* by Marx and Friedrich Engels in fact spoke to us greatly. I do not know how much we, the girls, understood of all the teachings in these works. I should also emphasize that what I have described in this small section was for us a long and rather difficult process. My time for reading was limited. Perhaps because of the disparity between my reading ambitions and the lack of suitable conditions, I became moody and impatient.

The Young Communist League in Poland (Komunistyczny Związek Młodzieży Polski, KZMP)

As I mentioned, Esther joined the Zionist youth movement Gordonia, apparently in 1933. This was not a Socialist movement, but it espoused the idea of work and a just society. Esther also wanted me to join, but she herself did not try to talk me into it. Instead, she sent a friend's younger sister to me, who took me along to meetings of the movement. I sat there. The young men and women danced a hora, sang, and flirted a bit.

With the emotional baggage I brought from home and my long work hours, which were beyond my strength, I felt strange in this group of largely spoiled young men and women. My assessment was certainly subjective. Without doubt, Gordonia educated youth to immigrate to the Land of Israel, although for the most part they came from bourgeois or petit bourgeois homes. I only went for a few days or weeks and I felt like an unwanted guest. Esther belonged to a more advanced group of veteran members. She already had a goal, a destination: leaving for the Land of Israel. I watched her efforts to become acclimatized to this environment and her success; she even changed her daily behavior, her speech. She became an interesting, intelligent girl, loved by the young men and women there. I do not know if I could have changed so much.

It is possible that I was more attached to our land. Also, the connection with my friends and our study gave me something else at which to grasp. I loved Polish literature and culture. Until today I remember by rote many poems by Adam Mickiewicz and Juliusz Słowacki. Perhaps the school I so loved influenced me, and I loved my country. By contrast, in my consciousness, the Land of Israel and Jerusalem were connected to the Jewish religion. My father prayed toward Jerusalem; on festivals, people blessed their friends, saying, "Next year in Jerusalem." I saw the Land of Israel as the remnant of an earlier period, mainly a religious custom, maintained for two thousand years by the faith of generations. I saw my roots as belonging to the country in which I was born, where my mother, grandmother, and forefathers were buried: Poland, a land in which Jews and Poles had lived together for more than a thousand years. Apart from that, I believe that among the Jewish youth the choice of destination was often coincidental and spontaneous. I myself am a good example of this.

And yet, for weeks or months, I was a member of Gordonia. In honor of May 1, 1934, all the organizations that were part of the Zionist Labor organization and their youth movements arranged their own parade in Łódź. Our route was different to that of the central demonstration by the general workers. Through Zawadzka and Żeromskiego Streets we reached the "Green Market" Square. There I heard speeches that did not really appeal to me, and the parade dispersed.

On the way home, I had to cross the main street, Piotrkowska. When I reached it, I found masses of people blocking access to the street, and along it was marching a demonstration organized by the Polish Socialist Party (PPS), with its professional unions, together with the Bund and the Jewish professional unions. This was a parade of more than 100,000 people, carrying signs in Polish and Yiddish, and many red flags; they sang and shouted slogans. Alongside the demonstrators were their own security guards: heavyset workers.

I stood amid the masses cheering for them and looked at them with mixed, ambivalent feelings. This was a parade of strength, of the masses rejoicing in their strength. Suddenly, someone shouted at me, and a figure emerged from between the lines, grabbed my hand, and drew me into the parade. I found myself among members of the Labor Party, among them Chaim, my cousin. And thus, without meaning to, I found myself in a parade of workers, in the midst of what was apparently the Communist youth group. Together with them I sang Socialist marching songs (God forbid).

The next day they threw me out of my group in Gordonia. Chaim Miedzigórski, my cousin, was then an "active" member in the Pioneer Movement (a Communist Scouts organization) and maybe even in the youth organization of the Communist Party (KZMP). His sister, Dorka Miedzigórski, was already a party activist and leader of (KPP) the Polish Communist Party for the entire Radom area. She spent more time in Polish prisons than she did outside them. (She was the bad example with which my father tried to scare me into abandoning my plan to go to Łódź.) Chaim, her little brother, was a short, powerfully built young man. I once had the opportunity to hear him speaking before the Jewish professional union at 9 Ogrodowa Street in Łódź. He spoke to dozens of striking sock weavers and glove makers who worked in wretched Jewish workshops.

Our Chaimke cried from the stage: "All the world is watching our battle, the workers fighting for our future. . . behind us, supporting us, is the entire Polish and global proletariat, and the entire mighty Soviet Union. . ."

Needless to say, no political or economic factor had an interest in the strike of a few dozen Jewish workers, apart from the few dozen owners of the workshops, who themselves barely made a living.

I mention my cousin Chaim (may he forgive me, I heard that he passed away in Paris, at the age of eighty-six), because I suspect, to this day, that he was behind the unexpected visit that my friends and I received.

The meetings of the "quartet," my three friends and I, who met every Sabbath afternoon in Shoshana's apartment, as I noted, became more and more like a study group: together we attended lectures at the Open University; together, at home, we learned the basics of autodidactism. Once, on one of the Sabbaths, while we were sitting in Shoshana's apartment immersed in an active discussion, someone knocked on the door. A young man appeared. He was around our age, tall and blonde, with an open and trustworthy face. He apologized for bursting into the home of people he did not know and introduced himself:

"My name is Arthur. Someone told me about your group. Would you let me join? Perhaps I could contribute something from my experience. . . "

My friends were enchanted by him at first glance. After a discussion, and after he responded to our request and told us about himself, we welcomed him with open arms. In hindsight, it turned out that he had not told us the whole truth, but he also had not lied. He told us that there was an anti-Fascist organization, and he was a member of it, and he asked not only to join our group but also to talk to us, among other things, about the aims of the movement and perhaps to guide our interests to new horizons.

To this day, I have a warm relationship with Arthur and his wife Roza. They have remained some of my best and closest friends. They live in Stockholm, and two years ago I spent a week with them there.

I believe that his visit did us good. Arthur also did not regret getting to know us, because he met four pretty girls, all rather intelligent and thirsty for knowledge. We argued with him stubbornly, and read Karl Marx and Kautsky again. Arthur was an idealist, open hearted, and straight as a ruler. After all the things fate had thrown at us, Arthur remained a cheerful and open person, just as he was in his youth. Fate did not treat the hero of our youth kindly. He has now sunk deep into a terrible illness—Alzheimer's.

When Arthur came to us, we were not completely cut off from the reality and the social and political situation in Poland and the surroundings. The rise of Hitler to power in Germany shocked the Socialist movement and humanist intellectual circles in Europe. A group of French writers, among them Romain Rolland, André Gide, Henri Barbusse, and André Malraux, in that period left a permanent mark on humanistic thought in France and progressive circles in all Europe. At their initiative, "The League for the Defense of Human and Citizen's Rights" was established in France. I am not sure what happened first: the summit of the representatives of the Socialist left wing from Italy, England, and France, which took place in Paris, I believe, in 1934, which decided to establish the anti-Fascist "Popular Front," or the seventh summit of the Comintern (Communist International), which took place at the beginning of 1935 (I will return to the Comintern later).

At any event, the two organizations that were established at the Parisian summit—The League for the Defense of Human and Citizen's Rights and the Popular Front—became popular in Europe, particularly among the Jewish youth in Poland, which felt suffocated and isolated. The Socialist newspapers and journals and those of the left (the legal ones) published, among other things, articles by French writers, and we read them with great interest. In that same period, as Fascism was spreading throughout Europe and following the alliance that had been forged between Nazi Germany and Poland in 1934, Poland quickly descended into a murderous anti-Semitic chasm. The Jews, in particular the Jewish youth, felt that they were in a civil and political trap. The European and American immigration policies vis-à-vis Polish Jews, and England's mandatory policy in particular, led to a deep crisis among all sectors of the Zionist youth in Poland. As a result, the Jewish youth became increasingly attracted to the Socialist and Communist movements. Only many years later did we understand that the guiding hand of the entire anti-Fascist movement was in Moscow.

In 1934, French writers with whom I was familiar arrived in Poland for the first time, on their way to visit the Soviet Union. In 1935, they visited Łódź, among other places. I remember the reception given for these French writers by the masses of supporters at the Łódź train station. Many accompanied them to the gates of the city's prison, where they visited the political prisoners and investigated the conditions in which they were imprisoned.

Therefore, when, one day, Arthur invited us to join the anti-Fascist movement in the battle for human rights and the rights of citizens, we agreed without hesitation. This reality affected me personally and changed my outlook, in no small part because of Arthur. At the time, I was not a Communist but just close to anti-Fascist groups. However, all the signs in heaven and earth seemed to me to suggest that, in the existing situation, the inevitable path would lead me there. And when I became a Communist, I devoted myself to the new ideology heart and soul, and I was willing to sacrifice myself more than my friends. Thanks to Arthur, our group expanded, and we increasingly met new people, mainly young people who worked hard and lived in poverty, just like me. The openness and warmheartedness that existed between us had a positive effect on me. Finally, I felt liberated, I learned to laugh. I felt like I was one of them.

I took my first steps in the field of organized politics, together with my friends, in the semi-legal circles of the anti-Fascist movement. We collected money for political prisoners, joined demonstrations against Fascism and anti-Semitism, bought and read with diligence the left-wing newspapers and journals, etc.

One day, apparently at the end of 1935 or the beginning of 1936, when Arthur visited us, I noticed that he was embarrassed about something. He asked for our forgiveness because until now he had not been completely frank with us. He told us that in addition to being an activist in the anti-Fascist front, he was also a member of the city's council of Communist youth—the KZMP in Łódź. He invited us to join this organization, but not before explaining to us the idealism of the Communist movement, which was embodied by the Soviet Union. Likewise, he warned us that in Poland the Communist movement was illegal, that its members were persecuted and sometimes served prison sentences. This did not surprise me, because my father had already warned me about it.

One must believe in the Communist ideology, and I became a devoted believer with all my heart. I began to receive and read illegal literature describing the Soviet Union as the only country in the world ruled by the proletariat. There are no exploiters or exploited there, no unemployment, no poor and rich; education and higher education are free of charge for all citizens, regardless of race, religion, or nation; everyone is equal before the most democratic constitution in the world. How could I doubt Arthur's words and what we read in hundreds of articles and books about the Soviet Union? Certainly. I believed, and my friends and I accepted everything with fervor. Indeed, there could be no ideals more lofty than these.

Arthur too believed, just like me.

Arthur came to us straight from the meeting at which they discussed the decisions made by the Sixth Congress of the Communist Youth International (KIM, Komunisticheskii Internatsional molodiozhy) at the beginning of 1936, and following it the sensational decisions of the Central Committee of the KZMP, which loosened the iron discipline of the KZMP and made it necessary to organize new foundations.

He was upset because he did not agree with these decisions. I do not remember what exactly he disagreed with; I do not even remember to what extent I understood the meaning of these changes, as decided by the KIM, and why he opposed them. Yet, while emphasizing his opposition, he imparted to us the decisions of the Central Committee of the KZMP in their original wording (it is worth mentioning that more than 80 percent of the members of this youth organization were Jewish young men and women).

My life changed dramatically. As I had been devoted in my faith to the Holy one, blessed be He, now I immersed myself in a new religion, Communism. I was devoted to it body and soul. My membership in the Communist Youth organization was short lived, because at the end of 1937 or beginning of 1938 the KPP was disbanded by the Comintern. Although I was only a member of the KZMP for two years, it became my way of life for many years.

After a short time, the "institution" or our group of girls broke up and each one of us was sent to positions and other groups in the framework of the Communist youth movement. Arthur disappeared for a long while because he was arrested and sent to an administrative prison camp in Bereza Kartuska (to which Communists and extreme nationalists, members of the Falanga

[National Radical Camp] were sent without trial and for an unlimited period).

The first task I was given—me, a brand-new recruit to this movement but ready for battle, without understanding why and how—was political activity on one of the most dangerous fronts: among the Polish army, no less! It sounds pathetic, especially once it became clear to me that the young woman who was active in this role before me was caught and sentenced to ten years of imprisonment.

This was a difficult and "hot" period in the Communist movement. In Russia, collectivization and the purges were underway. While millions were dying of hunger, the seventh summit of the Comintern gathered in Moscow in the months of July–August 1935, and after it, the KIM, in 1936. These radically changed the tactics of the national Communist parties. This change was expected, because in the west, changes were underway too. After the rise of Hitler and his Nazi Party to power, the Social Democratic and Communist parties blamed each other for the defeat in Germany, where these two movements were the largest and strongest: indeed, the battle between them enabled the Nazis to grab power.

We must remember that, according to the previous Congress, the sixth, of the Comintern, which took place in summer 1928 (which served Stalin's internal party policy at that time), Communist parties in various countries were required to fight against the Social Democratic and other non-Communist workers' movements, which were considered the most dangerous enemies of the Soviet Union. (In Poland, for example, the KPP managed a dirty battle against the PPS, which was referred to as "social-Fascist," "revisionist," "the servant of the bourgeois," and so on, and also against the left-wing Jewish parties, such as the Bund and in particular Poalei Zion Left, which was subject to particularly wild incitement by the Communists.)

In light of the new political situation in Europe and the fermentation in the left-wing movements, the slogans were inverted at the seventh congress. The seventh congress publicized new slogans regarding the Social Democratic movements: the establishment of "popular anti-Fascist fronts," and a "united front of Social Democratic workers against Fascism," albeit without "revisionist leaders," in all the countries. Subsequently, instructions regarding the destruction of these fronts also arrived.

All this I discovered later, after the war and after the death of Stalin. However, then, in 1936, new recruits to this youth movement in Poland had no idea what was going on behind the scenes in the Soviet Union. The anti-Fascist front was popular, and we felt ourselves warriors on the front lines.

Looking back, after so many years and experiences, this activity looks like a dangerous child's game. However, then I found myself in a select group, separated from all the members of the organization due to the need for secrecy, given an important and sensitive mission on the "military front." I remember a few pictures and people that I should mention in connection with this activity.

I was partnered with an older man known as Stach (a real Pole, whom I had not met before in the movement). I did not know his real name, although I visited him at home (which was apparently not his permanent residence) frequently. He lived in a one-room apartment with his Jewish girlfriend, who was called, if I am not mistaken, Rozka. In my presence, he took her in his arms, embraced her, and kissed her; sometimes I was present, not of my free will, when he bathed her. The metal tub was placed in the middle of the room and there was an entire ceremony surrounding it. Although I was a member of this revolutionary movement, such open relations were not to my taste at all. I remained all my life largely puritanical with regard to intimate relations.

Apart from me, there was also another Jewish young man, Rivak (Reuben), under Stach's command, and together we met in

Stach's home. The main thing: through Stach I made contact with a Polish soldier. The soldier's family lived in the industrial pro- letarian quarter of Chojny, a suburb of Łódź. I was to meet this soldier, masquerading as his "fiancée," every Sunday morning next to the barracks, when the soldiers were allowed out and their fian- cées waited for them at the entrance. I accompanied him home through the fields and at the same time imparted to him orally all the news and party decisions. He, for his part, reported to me on the situation in his unit. Presumably, over time, I would have been asked to give him pamphlets and other illegal propaganda materials. However, I did not reach this stage. "My" soldier was from a working family. I accompanied him to his home, which was warm, simple, and sympathetic. The contrasts between my Jewish surroundings and this Polish workers' family were so great that I could not absorb them. They made me feel great embarrassment but at the same time also enchanted me. Once I came to "my" soldier's house around Christmas time. His parents, who maybe thought I was his girlfriend, invited me to join them for the festive meal, but I refused, afraid that I would not know how to behave properly.

The activists in the military field were, as I noted, a select group in the Communist youth organization. This was a closed group, isolated from all the rest due to the need for secrecy. It was forbidden for them to be in touch with other members. Our con- tact was Stach. We gathered in his home or another place and he directed our activities. Our behavior outside, in the city's streets, was also special. For example, when I needed to meet Rivak, who was also active in this field, he took my arm, or I took his, and we walked arm in arm as though we were out for a walk on the street. Sometimes this caused misunderstandings when people saw us walking arm in arm in the streets of Łódź. Even worse, once, when Rivak and I were going to a meeting, walking along arm in arm, my little brother Meir, a very fanatical yeshiva student, came walking toward us. He was so shocked that he sent my father a worried letter, telling him that his daughter was going off the rails.

My worried father came to Łódź to see what was happening. He calmed down a little after conversations with my sister Shoshana and my big brothers (Esther was then in the hakhshara group near Sosnowiec), when he was persuaded that Rivak and other friends were visitors to Shoshana's home (I then lived with her), that they were solid young men and good friends. (Even while my father was staying with Shoshana, at times someone knocked on her door, put his head in, and when he saw my father, an older man with a beard, ran away. My father saw this and thought about the changing times, and the fact that apparently, he would not need to worry about a dowry for his daughters.)

When my father left, I accompanied him to the train station. On the way, we had a serious conversation. My father once again emphasized:

"I have no right to demand anything from you because you have left my authority and are living and standing on your own two feet. I cannot make promises about your future, and for that I am sorry. I can do nothing but ask that you walk a straight and correct path. Choose for yourself one young man from those that come to visit you—Shoshana promises that they are all good boys—and marry him. Then I will be calm, and I will happily give you my blessing."

I tried to persuade my father that the morality he taught me was anchored deep inside my heart and was part of my essence, although I understood it differently, perhaps in a wider context. Apart from that, I told him that I had left home not only with morality and tradition but also with a burden of pain, hurt, and severe complexes. This burden was what bothered me, made me afraid to develop more intimate relations with any boy. Even if outwardly my friendship with these good friends was seen in a different light, none of them wanted to get close to me. I told him that with all the love and respect I felt for him, he also knew that he was not free of sin toward my departed mother and myself. My father remained silent. We parted with heavy hearts.

Presumably, the leadership of the KZMP, which was made up mainly of Jewish Communists, knew better about what was happening in Moscow (there, members of the Central Committee of the KPP were already being arrested). It is not impossible that they wanted to put an end to the authorities' persecution and the young men and women who fell victim, giving them some freedom of action and an opportunity to enjoy a normal cultural life.

Today, this is the only way I can interpret the decision to dismantle the "military front" in which I was involved, and to instruct young men and women in the Communist movement to join the existing Democratic and Socialist movements and establish new ones. Ostensibly, the intention was to convert more people who were members of these movements, but in fact no one asked for or demanded anything.

As a result of these new initiatives, a youth organization was established by the Jewish People's Party, the Folkspartei.

The Folkspartei Youth Movement

Following the dismantlement of the military activities, Stach disappeared. I waited for a new contact. One day, I received instructions to meet someone on the corner of a certain street; he would put me in contact with new activists. The man would be recognizable by his traditional Jewish dress.

On the corner of the street was a young man wearing a long kaftan. His head was bare, he was of medium height, blonde, and around my age. I approached him and he put out his hand and said, "My name is Heniek." He looked at me seriously, surveyed me carefully with his light blue eyes, and seemed confused. I noticed he was a bit hesitant and not a big talker. I also lacked self-confidence. We barely spoke as he led me to our destination. He told me only that he was taking me to a youth center. Heniek became my husband, friend, and the father of my children.

The center on Piotrkowska Street belonged to the Folkspartei. The youth organization of this party was established by a group of Communists in Warsaw, apparently at the instruction of the Central Committee of the KZMP. In truth, there was already, in 1936, an atmosphere of confusion and unclarity in the Communist movement in Poland. Presumably, the leadership of the Folkspartei had no idea who these young people were who came up with the initiative of establishing a youth organization for this small party. However, it did not lose anything by doing so, but rather gained.

The Łódź branch of this movement had a center with two large, connected rooms, a few tables, a lot of chairs, and many new faces. In the middle of one of the rooms was a ping-pong table. I was welcomed with a wide smile by Mr. Unikowski, the head of the Łódź branch of the Folkists. He came every evening and ensured order, arranged various events, and apparently was happy to spend time with young people. Two years later, this same man was a witness for the defense when I was tried for Communist activities. Now, he welcomed me in a friendly manner as I became a member of this youth organization, and, after a few standard sentences, he wished me luck and enjoyment in the center and left me with my chaperone.

Heniek took me to the corner of the other room, where a large group of young people I did not know was sitting. We introduced ourselves. Some of them became good friends of mine for many years. Apart from Heniek, who fell in love with me "at first sight," I will mention Shlomo Pront, Alter Wieluński, Heniek Birenzweig, and others. Not all of them belonged to the KZMP, but all of them held views that were close to the left. It became clear that being in the Folkist movement was a good decision, and it was possible to play a really active role in it.

The Folkspartei was established in 1906 in the Jewish Pale of Settlement in Russia. Among its founders and thinkers was the historian Shimon Dubnow. It was a liberal, Yiddish-supporting movement. After the October Revolution in Russia and the liberation of Poland in 1917, this party was established in Poland under the leadership of Noach (Nojach) Pryłucki (Prilutski, 1892–1941), a journalist and social activist, a scholar of Yiddish and its culture. He was murdered by the Nazis. The party advocated freedom of conscience, was active in disseminating culture and Yiddish, negated the Zionist idea as a solution to the Jewish problem in the diaspora, and in the economic field it was a mouthpiece for craftsmen and small merchants, supporting them. The party established a central network of Jewish craftsmen and supported the battle against the many decrees issued by the authorities to restrict Jews' freedom of employment. In the 1930s, the party shrank. The establishment of the youth movement refreshed it.

In this youth organization we were active in various fields, in particular cultural activities. We organized lectures on a range of topics; there were also evening courses on different levels for those who wanted to complete their education (Shlomo Pront was a teacher by profession). We established a sports group for light athletics and football (it's funny, but they chose me as the secretary of this group). After a short while, we founded a drama club, a choir, and a circle for artistic group reading (declamations), in which I myself participated. The life and soul of this group was Max Szarfharc. I got to know him only in the Folkist center, but I knew of his existence before. In Łódź there were two brothers— David and Max Szarfharc—who were distant relatives of mine. Both were older than me and both were Communists, but David, the older brother, was an active Communist. I knew him and his family well (the two brothers survived the war in the Soviet Union, and both came to Israel with their families after 1956 and 1967). Not long ago I found Max's name in a book published in Poland by Pawel Spodenkiewicz, *Zaginiona dzielnica: Łódź żydowska - ludzie i miejsca* (Łódź, 1999), which in translation means The Forgotten Quarter—Jewish Łódź, People and Places. The mention of his name was to a certain extent connected with my activities in the Folkist youth movement at that same time.

Among the testimonies about Chanoch Cohen (Henekh Kohn), a musician and composer who was then famous in Łódź and all of Poland, there is also an interview with Max Szarfharc, who was himself an enthusiastic actor. Reminiscing about Kohn, Max mentions the artistic studio that he established in the Folkspartei center in 1936. This musician composed melodies for choirs and artistic reading and also wrote the music that accompanied the skits and plays performed by the studio under Max's management. He writes:

"Why were we active among the Folkists? Because the Communists had no place under the Polish sun, and there was no other possibility for such activity. The studio was active until the outbreak of the war. This was a studio of amateurs: we were all amateurs, no one received a penny. This was how it was before the war. There was no bread, but we paid membership fees for the movement. . . . Evenings of singing and performances were a great success and Henekh Kohn was our composer." (pp. 111–112)

The Folkist youth movement expanded and absorbed young men and women of all kinds. All those looking for a place to enjoy themselves in the evenings, those that the framework of our cultural activities suited them, they came and joined this youth group.

Although a group of members of the KZMP was formally behind the group, this did not have any great significance. To this secret group belonged, apart from me, Heniek, Shlomo, Felix Weingut-Warzyński, a certain Neufield, an educated man, who contributed much to the cultural activities, and someone who was dressed traditionally, with a beard (I do not remember his name), an intelligent and sharp-witted man. The meetings took place usually once or twice a month in private homes. (Once the meeting of this circle was held in an apartment on the second floor on Pomorska Street. The young man in Hasidic dress was late, but suddenly he came into the room, his shirt open, half dressed, the rest of his clothes in his hands, completely confused. By mistake he had gone into an apartment on the first floor, which, it turned out, was a brothel, and he had barely managed to escape.) At these meetings we surveyed the general political situation in the world and the country as well as our activities in the youth organization. I should add that I do not remember that there was anything illegal at these meetings or anything connected to revolution. We simply felt more proud of our work.

After the Polish Communist Party and all its organizations were disbanded, we continued our work in the Folkist youth movement. In summer 1938, there was a national conference of the youth movement in Warsaw. I was among the members of the delegation sent by the Łódź branch. We spent three or four days in Warsaw. The conference was attended by the highest echelons of the Folkspartei and its youth organization.

I do not remember much about the discussions at the conference, apart from some personal experiences. We slept on pingpong tables and on the floor of the club at the party center. I saw Warsaw for the first time in my life, and it made a deep impression on me. It was a beautiful city. The squares, the streets planted with greenery, with trees on both sides, the architectural beauty of the tall buildings, the wide boulevards, the regal Łazienki park—all this, in comparison to sooty and dirty Łódź, seriously impressed me. I felt unkind toward Łódź, to which I had become accustomed. Warsaw of 1938 was reduced to rubble and ruins in the war.

In Warsaw we had another surprise. One evening, all the attendees of the conference were invited to the Polish National Theater for a production of Ucieczka Absalona (The Escape of Abshalom). The National Theater immediately conquered my heart. First, the theater itself—the interior design was especially beautiful. The colorful chandeliers, the rows of chairs ascending in a half circle, covered in red velvet—all this made such a strong impression on me that to this day I see them in front of my eyes just as they were then. The Łódź theater was so simple. In truth, it was a building that served for all kinds of big conferences and also plays, and we, my friends and I, did not miss any good play that was showing there. However, the impression that the National Theater in Warsaw made on me, as well as the play itself—the sets, the costumes from the period of King David, the dramatic content, based on the known bible story—I remember it all to this day.

In those years, my life became richer and more intense. I had a group of friends (male and female) with whom I met not only at the center of the organization but also on Sabbaths and on other occasions. Together with some of them, I attended lectures at the Open University. Among them was my close friend from childhood, Hanka Krokh, and also Heniek Garncarski, Shlamek Pront, Heniek Birenzweig, Alter Wieluński, among others. I did not like all of them to the same extent. Some joined us because they liked our group and wanted to join our trips into nature on Sabbaths and festivals.

My personal relationships with boys were complicated. I remained neutral and independent, and I did not allow any of them a reason to get too close. They saw me as a young woman with whom they could share their most personal secrets, because I was not a gossip, I had a sense of humor, and I knew how to joke about myself, although always within certain boundaries. They saw me as an idealist and a daring young woman with principles. Apparently, that is what I was, because a good number of boys and girls younger than me saw me as some kind of symbol. Only years later, when we met again, did they tell me that.

However, in my personal life, I was not at all daring or decisive. My weak point was my relations with the young men who tried to get close to me, beyond friendship. I must emphasize that my generation was much more restrained and moralistic in relations between the sexes than today's generation is. However, I, who carried from my home an exaggerated puritanism with severe complexes, was restrained and even fearful of intimate relations. I sometimes covered this fear with exaggerated self-confidence. However, I cut off contact with every young man who tried to create more intimate relations with me. I made a rule for myself at the beginning of my social contacts with young men and I kept it for many years: I never agreed that a boy would give me a present or pay for me when we went as a group to the cinema or the theater. For a long time, I endeavored not to spend time with someone alone. On the one hand, I cannot say that the boys were standing in line to kiss me. Some of them told me openly that they would not want a wife who was so independent and complicated. I agreed with them. On the other hand, I cannot deny that I lacked admirers and those who tried to court me. More than once I had to cut off contact with a good friend, and it was hard for me to see his suffering. One of them stood out in particular.

I had a friend named Mietek. He worked in a large textile workshop "Widzewska Manufaktura." All my unemployed friends were jealous of his job in this large factory, although few knew how hard it was for him. I sometimes visited his parents' home in Bałuty (the poor Jewish neighborhood; together with a few additional roads, it became the Jewish Ghetto under the Nazis.) His was a special house. The father, with a beard and head covering, was sick with TB and always lying in bed. Mietek was the only one in the family earning an income. He had another little brother, maybe eight years old. Mietek was a Communist who was active in the technical field, meaning he copied and distributed propaganda leaflets and booklets—illegal literature. This was dangerous work. His mother, a religious woman, would often pass on packages of this literature "under her sweater" (A wide colorful covering woven from wool with fringes that simple older women wore instead of a coat. It was called a draka.) in order to make things easier for her son and protect him. It is hard for me not to remember his mother with pity. In this poor household, she was mother to everyone who came to visit her son, taking care of them. Usually, these were members of the underground. She did not ask questions. She gave her son's guests hot soup, removed their shoes and darned their socks, etc. She was the mother of all the persecuted, Maxim Gorky's Mother.

When I was still in the anti-Fascist group, they would sometimes arrange evenings of singing and refreshments, and even dancing, at someone's home, collecting contributions from the attendees to help political prisoners. Among other things, New Year's Eve served this purpose. I had a good time every year at the home of someone who organized this event. After midnight we went out to walk the streets of the city, which was then, for the most part, covered in the first snow. Such a night was beautiful and unusual in Poland. Usually, the first snow already covered the streets in white; here and there sellers sold colorful balloons, and on the corners of the street stood people with baskets of hot bagels, calling out loudly to passersby to buy them.

Once I spent such a night with a group that included Mietek. After midnight, I walked the streets with a few other friends. It was a cold night, and snow and rain fell, mixing together. The hour was late, it was long after midnight. On one corner stood a child with a basket of hot bagels. It was Mietek's little brother. He stopped next to him and so did we. Mietek turned red with embarrassment, but he gathered himself together and told us that at home they needed the pennies from selling these bagels. He took the basket from his brother and told him to run home. In the basket there were a lot of bagels and we bought them. Mietek went with us, carrying the basket for quite a long way, parted from us and went home.

Mietek loved me. At the time, I was working for a family, taking care of their two children. When I went out with the children for a walk in the public park, Mietek would often suddenly appear, as though by coincidence, and explain that he was working the second shift that day. Finally, I had to have an honest conversation with him, telling him that I would "never" get married. This was hard for both of us. Mietek suffered greatly. It was hard for me. I blamed myself for not severing the connection with him long before, and it was also a shame that I lost a cheerful and good friend. I loved his poor home. The connection with him was severed and I do not know what happened to him.

Some suffered less or not at all. It usually left me embarrassed.

I did not imagine that I would awaken in Rivak (Reuben), with whom I was active in the military cell, any feelings toward me. He was a pleasant and large young man; I did not discern in him any special qualities and not even a particularly developed intelligence. Yet he was full of humor and good tempered. I was a young girl, around eighteen years old. We were active on the "military front" and we met only when there was a consultation at Stach's house. I worked then for David, my brother. I was still clumsy, in terms of dress and also in my personal relations.

One day, at the end of December, as I left David's house on an errand, I found Rivak standing next to the gate. He was embarrassed and said that he had been standing there for a long time hoping that perhaps I would come out. He asked me to go out with him for New Year's Eve to the party that his sisters were arranging in their home. I was shocked. Why me? I asked. He replied that I was his best friend. I did not know his family and I did not know what group would be going to this party. I did not have anything to wear, and I did not know how to dance. I told him all of this, and I added that I did not want to and could not attend this private event. Rivak took me to my sister Shoshana (where he had been previously) and they both persuaded me to go. In the evening he came to take me. I wore a sweater (that I had made) and a simple skirt—the clothes I had—and he promised that in this clothing I would indeed be worthy to be his friend that evening. I went with him. I felt very uncomfortable there, because all the group were dressed in festive clothes, ball gowns, and inquisitive eyes surveyed me from head to toe. . . . in my life I have never felt less suited to an event. After midnight, Rivak accompanied me home and opened his heart to me. I responded by completely rejecting him and I was angry with him for inviting me to the party. However, because we needed on occasion to meet for our secret political activity, I asked that we remain friends. And so it was.

With the end of the activities of the military cell, I had no further contact with Rivak. I only met him once more. He told me that he had a girlfriend, and they were going to get married, "But I will never forget you." We laughed, and I did not believe him. He perished, with his family, under the Nazis.

However, let us return and try to bring back to life a few personalities from that period during which I belonged to the Folkist movement. There I had good friends as well as acquaintances with whom my path crossed again years later.

Here is Shlamek Pront, a handsome young man, with dark skin, a racial Jew. By profession he was a teacher at the Jewish elementary school. He grew up without parents—they died when he was a child— and he was raised by his three sisters and oldest brother. They arrived in Łódź from Sosnowiec and all of them lived together in an apartment that had two rooms and a kitchen. I believe that they had a tailoring workshop and all of them worked there apart from Shlamek, the youngest. This family, which lived in poverty, made sure that their youngest brother received an education and a higher education. The house was always open in the evenings and filled with friends.

Many girls fell in love with him, and for a short while I too felt that way about him. However, watching how the other girls behaved with him, especially one of them whom I did not know at all, I was disgusted. He treated these girls with indifference, but he never put an end to their behavior. Shlamek used to visit us (at Shoshana's house) in the afternoons and spend time with us until other friends arrived, among them, of course, Heniek, and together we went to the youth center. In the youth organization, Shlamek taught young people who lacked a basic education and also gave lectures in the field of political economics and philosophy to a wider forum. One girl, who apparently followed him until she found out that he was spending time at our house, approached me on the street, presented herself as a friend of Shlamek's from Sosnowiec, and asked me to let her come to my home to meet him. My female curiosity won out and I agreed. From then on, we witnessed embarrassing scenes of love sickness. The girl suffered, without doubt. They apparently had had a romance back in Sosnowiec. However, Shlamek was surprised by her appearance and was not happy to see her. He was angry with me for bringing her, and even stopped coming to visit for a while. I breathed freely. Shlamek had a beautiful tenor voice and often, when we went out hiking on Sabbaths, Alter Wieluński would play his balalaika and Shlamek would sing Yiddish, Polish, Hasidic songs, etc. in his tenor voice, and we would all sing with them.

The war put an end to these pleasures. Our group dispersed. Only a few remained alive and among these were some who were emotionally damaged. When I was in Simferopol, the capital of the Crimea, I was in contact with a few friends spread throughout Russia. A few of these fled from the forests of Siberia and the Urals and even came to Simferopol. They found there a haven—a beautiful city, fantastic climate, work, and decent living conditions.

When I was in Simferopol, one day I received a letter from Shlamek Pront. It was a sad letter. They, meaning he and his family, were in the forests of the Urals, around Magnitogorsk, working at cutting down trees. His oldest sister, Adzia, had a work accident: a tree fell on her and she lost a foot. They fled from there to the Ukraine. It was hard for them. Shlamek was depressed. When he found out that I was in Simferopol, he wanted to come to me, but he did not have money. In my neighborhood lived a couple of my friends, refugees from Poland (I will come back to them later), and together we sent him money so that he could come to us. He did not make it. The Germans invaded the Soviet Union and I lost contact with him. After the war, Shlamek returned to Poland and visited us. I already had a family and a small son. Subsequently, he was among the frequent visitors to our house, and we remained good friends throughout the years. Heniek, my husband, and I were always happy to spend time with him. In the years 1967–1968 all our friends again dispersed. Shlamek and his Polish wife came to Israel, but she could not acclimate and they left for Stockholm, Sweden. He died of cancer more than 20 years ago.

The most colorful figure among our friends was Alter Wieluński, of medium height, thin, blond. A few hairs covered his rounded scalp. From under his high forehead peered out blue eyes, one of which went left and the other right. He had a pale face, covered in red stains, and a sharp chin. His head was the shape of a big pear. In short—he was not exactly Apollo. Alter lived with his mother. When he was a baby, his father went out to buy cigarettes and never came back. This was during World War I. Years later, Alter discovered that his father was living in Paris, had changed his name a little to make it sound French, established another family, and was very wealthy. Out of consideration for his mother, Alter never contacted him.

The mother and son lived in a small attic room that was always sparkling clean on Pieprzowa Street (in Yiddish it was called Feffer Gas, Pepper Street, and it is obvious why). This street was at the center of Bałuty, the poor quarter of the Jewish workers. Pieprzowa Street had a bad name. It was a street of thieves, prostitutes, and the underworld. However, this world had its own rules. Here not only was no one hurt, but rather there was solidarity and help was given to the needy. On this street they spoke with a special Jewish dialect. Alter was a tailor, but he rarely worked. (Who wanted to come to Pieprzowa Street to order clothes or even have them repaired?) I never knew whether he and his mother had a meal to eat. Alter was chronically unemployed. His mother was sometimes invited to help at events organized by rich families.

It is possible to understand, therefore, that Alter had a lot of free time. He often suffered, apparently, from the shame of hunger. In contrast, he read a lot of books. He was a walking encyclopedia, a philosopher, poet, and dreamer. While his external appearance was not the most beautiful, he had a lot of internal beauty and a big heart. He fell in love with beautiful girls who did not return his affections, of course. Alter was in love with my friend, Hanka Krokh. He spoke about her in the poems he wrote and composed a song that he sang to his balalaika. He had enough self-awareness and wisdom to joke about himself and his one-sided love affairs. And he also laughed together with the object of his affections at that time, Hanka, with her blonde hair, pale, laughing face, and two dimples—both of them laughed and sang together the songs he wrote for her. We all sang his songs together, accompanied by Shlamek's tenor and Alter's bala-laika. I remember to this day a verse from one of his songs, a lullaby, about the future of a child in the Jewish state. . . . in Birobidzhan. Alter's Yiddish, rich and spiced with the dialect of Pieprzowa Street and hand gestures, was a pictorial and juicy language.

Alter was an exceptional friend. When I was found innocent and released from prison, my friends, without my knowledge, arranged a surprise for my birthday: they collected money, and Alter bought fabric and sewed me a skirt and tight-fitting sweater vest (how he did it without taking my measurements remained his secret). The clothing suited me well. Every time I wore it, it warmed my heart to think of all my friends, especially Alter.

During the war, Alter was in Soviet Russia. Somehow, he found out that I was in Simferopol. And one day he appeared with his wife, whom I had never met. They began to work there, but the relations between the couple were unstable and their shouting matches could be heard from afar. I asked Alter how they had come to be together and he told me the following story: when we left the city, he did not want to leave his mother, who was already sick, and apart from that he did not have a penny to leave her or suitable clothing. His mother died, but he did not leave. Then a young woman from the neighborhood appeared and asked him to go east with her, to the Soviet Union, and, as he added in his joking tongue, she had both money and a warm blanket. Thus, the relationship of the war years began, a connection that made him miserable. In June 1941, when the German army invaded Russia, Simferopol was bombed on the first night of the invasion. On the following day, masses of refugees left the city, including Alter and his wife. After that, I lost all trace of him.

Years passed, it was already the beginning of the 1960s. A young man appeared at our home with a note in his hand bearing our address and introduced himself as Wieluński, Alter's son. This young man, a sympathetic boy, had arrived in Poland for the first time at the express request of his sick father, who asked him to go to Łódź, find us, and visit us. He looked for Pieprzowa Street (which no longer exists because the entire Jewish Ghetto was destroyed and in its place a new neighborhood with ugly multi story buildings was built) and found out that we were living in Warsaw, thus he came to us. Alter's son told us the story of his father's life in Canada. Alter divorced the woman I knew, married again, and with this second wife had his son. Shortly after the son returned to Canada, he wrote to us that his father had died.

I see him, the young Alter, able to laugh at himself, in love with my beautiful Hanka; Alter the troubadour, the people's philosopher, the typical representative of the Jewish proletariat in Poland between the wars.

Another story is that of Felek (Felix) Warzyski (originally Weingut). I have a story to tell about him as well. However, this is something completely different. He was never my friend, although he was always around our shared friends. He was a member of the circle of the KZMP and was active in the youth organization of which I was a member. Our paths crossed frequently. He was of less-than-medium height, with wide shoulders, very short curly hair. Felek had a cold disposition, he was cynical and treated everyone and everything with cynicism, even his wife. He was an intelligent young man, with a high school education, who lived with his divorced mother; his father was in Warsaw and was rather rich. Felek was always wandering around unemployed, but he did not lack money, because his father provided for him. Close to the outbreak of the war he was working as a clerk in a textile factory that I also worked in as a spool tender. Felek had a rather rich choice of jokes and he told them with a poker face. Everyone burst out laughing and enjoyed them and he enjoyed it too. The group loved this clown. However, when the jokes repeated themselves, they became less funny. That did not bother him. Before the war he sometimes visited our house (meaning, the home of Shoshana and Moshe). I got to know him in the Folkist youth movement. There he spent time with Dina, a blonde girl who talked a lot, a gossip. She knew at least half of the inhabitants of Łódź and always knew everything better than anyone else. Felek humiliated her in front of everyone. And the more he did so, the more she stuck to him. During the war, in Russia, I found out that she had in fact married him.

My Shoshana did not want to hear about this couple in Russia. Why? She told me a story about a chance meeting with Felek and Dina somewhere on the roads of the war in Central Asia, in the desert. The entire family—little Naftali, Shoshana, and Moshe—sat, surrounded by all their belongings and their meager posses-sions, with no idea where to go after they had been driven out of Simferopol. They were hungry and had no water to drink. Suddenly, Dina and Felek appeared, burdened down with food and bottles and wine, sat next to the family, ate, drank, and joked on my account, when they found out that I was on the front. Shoshana emphasized with concern that she had no information about where I was and maybe I was already dead, and they laughed, cynically, saying that I always was an idiot.

After the war, Shoshana and her family left Łódź, and, together with our brother Moshe, who survived the horror of the concentration camps, left Poland. Via Germany, they made their way to the Land of Israel. We met the couple again. Felek started to work together with Heniek in the same office. When we moved to Warsaw, we found them there, with a baby named Celina. Fate destined it that we would live for close to twenty years as neighbors: we at 9 Rakowiecka Street, on the corner of Sandomierska, and they on Sandomierska, three houses away from us. Our house was open to all the friends who remained alive and returned from Russia. Almost all of them worked in various jobs, and the Warzyński couple knew how to get by. At these meetings, Felek and Dina often joined us. He continued to tell the same jokes that had already gotten old. In his last years, he lived in Stockholm. Dina died a few years ago. When I was in Stockholm two years ago, he called me, but we did not meet.

And there was a good friend in our group whose original name was Heniek Birenzweig (who after the war adopted the name Żytomirski, the name of the hometown of his wife Pola, Zhytomyr, in the Ukraine). He was a warm hearted friend. You could always rely on him. A simple young man, whose entire education was from the Kheyder and the street, and afterward the youth movement. After the war, Heniek and Pola joined our circle of friends, and they were always happy, always ready to help. They live with their children in Stockholm, and we are in touch by telephone. There were among us young women—Hanka, Dinka, Sara, and others that over time found themselves partners.

However, I must go back to the beginning of 1937.

Prison

One night at the end of April 1937, at midnight, as I already mentioned, I was sitting with my sister Shoshana, finishing the day's work and singing quietly. Moshe, her husband, was asleep because he needed to get up early for work, and their son, Naftali, four years old, was sleeping in his little bed. Suddenly, we heard heavy knocks on the door and into the apartment came the building's watchman and with him a policeman and another man in civilian clothes. They searched the entire house, took out and confiscated all my newspapers and journals (all legal), and ordered me to go with them. I was in shock. I had not engaged in underground activities for a long time. I put on my coat and we went out into the night. Soon, I found myself in a dark, stinking room, and the heavy door was closed behind me. This was the police's holding cell. I felt around in the dark, looking for a place to sit, and I found that the room was full of sleeping people. I lowered myself down on bent knees in an empty spot by the wall and waited for dawn.

In the dawn light, I discerned many strange, half-dressed women lying on beds made of boards and on the floor. Slowly they awakened and I found that I was indeed in the company of strange women: each one of them began to remove the heavy makeup from her face and prepare themselves for something. They looked at me and saw that I was a rookie. They began, therefore, to teach me what would happen: shortly they would bring breakfast, then we would go for medical checks with a doctor. If you were healthy, you could go free, and if they found something, to the hospital.

Why, I asked, do I need to be checked by the doctor? And I asked other silly questions, until the women understood that I was not part of their group, and then they announced, "Apparently, you are a political." I too understood what kind of group I was dealing with.

The room emptied and I remained alone for a few days and nights. During the day I was interrogated by the police and at night the cell filled anew with prostitutes caught on the streets without documents stating that they had been checked by a doctor (the authorities were concerned for the health of the "male public").

The interrogations did not clarify to me why I had been arrested. It seems that they wanted me to tell them why. The investigator showed me lots of "incriminating evidence" that they had confiscated during their search: newspapers and journals, albeit well-known as left wing, yet legal. They could not show me any document or anything else illegal. The unpleasant investigation continued for three or four days, during which every second sentence that the investigators said involved the words "Jew-Communist, Jewess," threats, etc.

Eventually, I was transferred to the prison on Kilińskiego Street (the corner of Narutowicza), one of the prisons for political prisoners in Łódź. They put me in the holding cell before May 1, and therefore I thought that they had arrested me as a preventive measure because someone had informed on me. There were around thirty women in the cell, most of them "veterans" who had spent many years in various prisons. Every new victim who was brought to the cell caused rejoicing. When I arrived in the cell, a special festive evening was arranged in my honor. I had to relate in detail the circumstances under which I was arrested and why, and also to provide a survey of the news from the free world. I was the youngest prisoner among all the women in the cell and it was my first time in prison. This was an infrequent opportunity for the "veterans" to tell a rookie how life once was, at the beginning of the 1920s, in prison. It was almost a lost Garden of Eden: there were packages of chocolate up to the ceiling, butter, halva, and luxuries aplenty. The veteran prisoners heard the stories for the hundredth time. Every time that the storyteller added her own inventions to the tale, all the other prisoners demonstrated that they already knew the story by rote. At the welcome for a new prisoner, they sang the entire repertoire of political prisoners' songs.

May 1 arrived. We celebrated it in all the cells in the prison in Łódź with the same ritual. There was constant communication between the cells and between the men's and women's wings. In every cell a speech was given about the history of this festival and its significance, we sang songs, I recited the poems by Władysław Broniewski ("Łódź," *"No pasaran!" "May 1,"* and others) and people told stories from memory. At a time determined in advance, all the prisoners, male and female, stood close to the barred windows and sang "The Internationale." The song, which was heard in all corners of the prison, caused me to shiver. It was not the same song that I heard at festive gatherings. This was the hymn of prisoners, of those calling for people to go to the barricades; it was a song of revolution.

In the week after May 1, the cell slowly emptied and I remained with a few women, some of whom had been sentenced, others awaiting trial. After a short time, they transferred me to the prison in Piotrków Trybunalski. This was a fortress built when the Russian Tsars ruled Poland. There was a different atmosphere there, one of permanence.

I arrived in the new prison. After only a few moments, a guard led me through a long, damp corridor to cell no. 13. She pushed me inside and closed the door after me. I stood for a few moments next to the door. I looked around me and a strange feeling took hold of me. I saw a row of women, all their faces the same color—gray like dust. I was then nineteen years old and a blossoming young woman. The first thought that passed through my mind was that in a short time I would look like them, like dust. It seemed that at the same moment the prisoners in the cell were also shocked to see me, a flower amid the dust. They did not move a muscle. However, the initial feeling passed quickly, both for me and for them, and they welcomed me warmly and cheerfully. There were twelve women (I was the thirteenth) in this cell, all of whom had been sentenced to five, ten, or fifteen years in prison. Apart from one Ukrainian, they were all Jews.

After a few days in the new prison, I received the first letter from my sister Esther. The letter clarified a few important things, first and foremost, the reason for my arrest.

Here is the story. Esther was, as I already mentioned, in a hakh-shara group near Sosnowiec. One of the members of this group made purchases in a grocery store and among the banknotes he used one was a forgery. The authorities were called, and the police conducted a search of the residence in which the group lived. There, instead of fake money, they found a different "trea-sure"—my letters to my sister Esther. What was likely to threaten the peace of the country in the things I wrote to my sister Esther? Apparently, I wrote to her that I believed the Soviet Union was a Garden of Eden for the global working classes and that the Soviet Union was the solution to the Jewish problem, not Zionism. This crime was the excuse for the raid on my sister Shoshana's home in the middle of the night, for putting me in the cell with the prostitutes, and for my imprisonment without a trial. On the same day, Esther tried to inform me that I should flee, but the guard-ians of the law got to me first. She left the hakhshara group and returned to Łódź to help me. (Not long ago, the couple Dora and Heniek Francuz, to whom I will return later, visited me, and Dora mentioned that on the same night as I was arrested, they also searched the home of my brother, David, for whom I had previ-ously worked.)

In hindsight, I will add something that may seem strange—I have no regrets whatsoever about the year I spent in prison. I had the privilege of sharing a cell with the flowers of the Polish intel-ligentsia: a professor of Polish and European literature, Halina Weiss, a doctor of mathematics, an irritable yet nice woman named Hanka, an expert in general history, Dr. Felicja, and more. Among the twelve women was an expert on the history of the worker's movement, Halina Zand (I will mention her later), and more. I do not remember many names, even their faces have become blurry over the years. However, I remember some of them, those who made a strong impression on me.

Among us was a professor of pedagogy, a woman of around thirty or thirty-five. She was beautiful: tall and dark-skinned, wearing a long, black evening dress embroidered with delicate silver threads, her large, black, and beautiful eyes like those of a Sephardic or ethnic Jew. Her name was Olga. She was a striking beauty. I love to see beautiful people and beautiful things, and in general I enjoy aesthetics, and so I enjoyed looking at her. In addition, she had a deep and penetrating voice, velvety and quiet. She had been sentenced to ten years in prison, and her husband was in the men's wing, serving a similar sentence. Both were members of the Central Committee of the MOPR—the international organization to help political prisoners. They, together with Mrs. Stephania Sempołowska—a woman of noble birth, an author, and a pedagogue, who was known for her educational social activities—organized balls that were attended by the cream of Polish society. There, among other things, they gathered donations to help political prisoners. At one of these balls, while wearing this evening dress, she and her husband were arrested.

There was another prisoner (I do not remember her name) who was the daughter of one of the best-known industrialists in Warsaw. She had already been imprisoned for a long time and was serving a sentence of fifteen years. She was the spokesperson of the commune in our cell vis-à-vis the prison authorities. When they took her to solitary confinement, Olga replaced her. Both were frequently and intermittently taken to solitary confinement. She was a sickly woman, but she did not break. Modestly, quietly, she managed life in our cell.

Almost all the inhabitants of cell no. 13 had a higher education. I was the youngest of them and had only a modest education—elementary school and the little I had taught myself. I had learned a bit in the Workers' (Open) University, albeit chaotically and not in an organized manner. Thus, each one of the residents of the cell was enthusiastic to teach me, and I was the most enthusiastic of all. For me, the days were full of systematic studies, according to a high school program. I felt that my great dream of gaining a high school education might finally come true, and, when I would eventually be released, I would be able to complete my studies and take the external exam. I studied without notebooks or textbooks (sometimes it was possible to find in the prison library a literature or geography textbook). All the studies were conducted orally, and I had to train my memory. So it was also with regard to mathematics. The lessons continued even during our half-hour walks every day in the yard, when we had to walk in single file (gęsiego). Behind me strode Professor Halina Weiss, who, between comments such as "Bina, hold your head up," or "Straighten your back," whispered in my ear the foundational principles of Polish Renaissance literature.

While I was in this prison, the political prisoners conducted an extended and difficult battle against the attempt to demote them to the level of criminal prisoners. They fought to retain the rights of political prisoners. The battle focused mainly on the right to wear civilian clothes, that the prison authorities would recognize the representatives of the cells and the commune, the right to visits without dividers, etc. By contrast, the prison authorities tried to make us wear striped uniforms and set us to work cleaning and doing other prison jobs. This was a difficult, daily struggle that involved constant sacrifice and feelings of hopelessness. The Polish regime was taking great strides toward becoming a Fascist regime.

When I arrived in prison, the decree had already been partially instituted. After an extended hunger strike, every evening after roll call (8 p.m.), each one of us had to put her clothes on a bench in the corridor outside the cell. The authorities gave us nightgowns. We were never sure whether we would find our clothes outside before the morning roll call the next day or, in their place, striped prison clothing. And one day this indeed happened. Our representative demanded our clothes back, of course, and on the spot declared a hunger strike. The same day all the political prisoners in both wings declared such a strike.

The commune was well organized. There was constant communication between the cells and between the men's and women's wings. All the efforts of the prison authorities to put an end to it failed. When something happened in one cell, or a new political prisoner arrived, the news immediately spread to other cells via an announcement (meaning knocking on the wall using a special code developed by the political prisoners). We had to be sure that the guards would not hear the knocking, so one of us kept watch next to the door, warning the person knocking when to stop. Apart from this, news passed also through "grypsy" (notes in tiny writing written on cigarette paper using the lead of a pencil, which the guards must under no circumstances find in the cell or on the prisoner's person). This correspondence was passed on via a secret place in the shared toilets, during the weekly organized visit to the showers, or during the walk in the yard. The male prisoners followed our movements from their small, barred windows. The connection with the free world was usually through lawyers and mainly via the packages received from family members and from the MOPR organization.

To be a representative of the commune vis-à-vis the prison authorities sometimes entailed severe punishments. Usually, during the morning roll call, the cell representative would speak on our behalf and only she could present demands or answer the questions posed by the prison director or his replacement. On more than one occasion the guards battled against a representative of the commune. For example, they turned to us directly and did not allow our representative to speak. We kept silent, and when they used force, we responded that we had a representative and she was authorized to speak on our behalf. Then they implemented sanctions against the cell (for example, not receiving letters, visits, or packages, or suspension of the right to the daily half hour walks in the yard). Intermittently, our representative was sent to solitary confinement for a few days. On the following day, a duty representative took her place. Sometimes, the decrees instituted in that year, 1937, caused hunger strikes. Once we continued for a week and we sent all our food back. In the first days of the hunger strike, we did not change our daily routine. However, toward the end, we lay on our straw mattresses. It never happened that a group in one or two cells declared a hunger strike. Rather, the entire commune did so, as part of a fundamental and radical battle. The commune of the entire prison also decided to end it. This happened on the day that they did not return our clothes and instead we found the striped uniforms. We did not take them but remained in our nightgowns. This was a difficult and uncompromising battle. Elements outside the prison also joined the fight, and strikes were even arranged in some factories, as well as demonstrations campaigning for the rights of political prisoners. Our battle led to a commotion and many political elements became involved. When I went to Łódź for trial, the battle in the Piotrków Trybunalski prison was still at its height, and the political prisoners were wearing nightgowns in the cold cells.

Thirteen women living in a cell the size of one regular room with two small, barred windows near the ceiling—in which we urinated into a lead tank with a lid that was emptied twice a day and we scrubbed it when we were led to the toilet and back— necessitated punctilious attention to personal hygiene and internal discipline. Moreover, so that thirteen women would be able to live and endure together in one cell, it was vital to maintain cleanliness, order, and quiet, and therefore we stuck to a meticulous daily routine. Morning roll call took place at eight in the morning. Before this, we washed and cleaned: each one washed in turn, while the other twelve made comments about her body, accompanied by outbursts of laughter, which always embarrassed me. Thirteen straw mattresses, which at night covered the entire floor of the cell, became one sofa that was constructed carefully and covered with blankets. Some of the blankets were rolled up and served as finishing for the "sofa." Later it gave us a place to sit and rest. All the residents of the cell scrubbed and polished the floorboards once a week using empty bottles. The long, narrow table and the two long benches, and likewise all the tin utensils, were shining and clean. The Ukrainian prisoner, a member of the commune, was responsible for order and routine.

The routine in the cell was maintained punctiliously. After the morning roll call, the political prisoners distributed a warm liquid like coffee and daily portions of bread that tasted like clay, and from this we made ashtrays and other things, because it was impossible to eat it. Usually, the commune lived on the food from the parcels we received. (My Communist friends in the cell were not members of the working classes. For the most part, they were daughters of wealthy, bourgeois families.) There was a similar ritual when they brought the lunch that included soup, in which sometimes a piece of unidentifiable meat floated, and porridge.

Between breakfast and lunch were hours of group or individual learning, with a half-hour break for our walk in the yard. Lunch was followed by an hour of complete silence, during which each one read or was busy with other things. After this rest hour, I again studied until dinner and evening roll call. After the roll call, it was necessary to get ready for the night, to prepare the mattresses, and to arrange our clothes and put them out in the corridor.

At eight they turned off the light, and then began the hours I loved best. Among us were women who could sing and they sang beautiful songs at our request. We sang songs of prisoners dreaming of freedom. The mathematician Hanka knew songs about Chinese subjects, about the wise Buddha, others could tell stories; sometimes one of them retold the contents of a certain book. I learned from them about the cultures of Eastern nations, about the ancient Chinese culture, and also about ancient Greece. Sometimes, in particular during the hunger strike, we dreamed aloud about fantastical food, about tables full of delights, etc. Sometimes each one talked about what she would do on her first day out of prison. Usually, these were stories about her favorite foods. In these hours there was also "correspondence" with the nearby cells. In the late hours of quiet and dark, friends lying on adjacent mattresses whispered intimate secrets and shared confessions of the soul.

As I already mentioned, I was imprisoned in 1937. In this year, the Soviet Union conducted show trials of leading revolutionaries whom Stalin had decided to eliminate. In particular, Stalin treated with great cruelty members of the Central Committee of the Polish Communist Party in Moscow, in the Kremlin (most of them were murdered or sent to camps and their bones scattered in the northern Urals). I remember how our commune responded to these show trials. Gazeta Polska, the official Polish newspaper, wrote at length about the trials, especially about those spicy details that the trials uncovered. In particular, it reported on the trials of the leaders of the Polish Communist Party, who in Poland were considered agents of Moscow, while in the Soviet Union they were accused of spying for Poland and acting as Polish agents. I remember that the guard on duty threw the newspaper at us during our afternoon rest, saying, "Read about your Tukhaczewski (a Polish Communist, who was a commander of the Red Army in the civil war following the October Revolution), about Zarski," or about some trial or another. Afterward, they closed the door noisily and watched through the window in the cell door, curious to see our reactions. Knowing this was the case, we threw the newspaper into a corner with disgust. However, after ensuring that they were not watching us, we read the news in detail, accompanied by comments and responses from the veterans among us, in particular Helka, our Politruk (Russian for political commissar). From all this we understood, without any shred of a doubt, that Gazeta Polska, the mouthpiece of the bourgeois and the Polish landowners, was lying. The thirteen prisoners battling for Communism and the Soviet Union never wavered. They believed, and of course so did I, that there were no mistakes in these show trials. Rather they exemplified the proletarian justice of Soviet law.

I confess that my time in this prison and in the company of intellectuals to a great extent was my basic training in the army of Communism, to which I clung with all my heart and soul. There I learned to view and to assess phenomena through their eyes: anything written by our enemies was a lie, and everything others said about the Soviet Union was the exact opposite of the truth. Not only this, but the Soviet Union and the attitude toward it became a measurement by which I assessed various political situations. At the same time, I must admit that these assessments were for the most part correct within the array of political powers of the 1930s. It is interesting that even the way they assessed the views of other people was not always wrong.

The other residents of the cell did not always view my behavior favorably, and consequently I encountered some problems. One day a new prisoner joined us, a young woman member of the youth organization of the Bund, called the "Tsukunft" (Future). This was a legal organization, like the Bund. However, in the 1930s, not only were the Communists persecuted but also anti-Fascists and Socialists, and members of the Zionist workers' movement, such as Poalei Zion Left. The member of the Tsukunft was the same age as me, and it was only natural that we became friends. Her straw mattress was laid next to mine, and we whispered to each other until late at night about our dreams and other things, sharing our most intimate thoughts.

The commune did not look well on this friendship with the young woman from the Tsukunft. Indeed, like the Bund, the veteran prisoners considered this movement a "social-opportun-ist," even "socio-revisionist," group and they did not look upon it well. In particular, Helka Zand saw my friendship with this young woman as inappropriate. More than one of them spoke to me about it, even angrily. However, I always responded that I saw noth-ing wrong with our friendship, because we did not discuss ideol-ogy or politics. My other friends gave up, but not Helka. She stood in the breach, trying to defend the "pure" ideology and prevent any deviation from it.

Halina Zand was an exceptional woman, both internally and externally: she was less than medium height, with a firm chest, wide shoulders, and narrow hips, blonde, with cold gray eyes, and prominent cheekbones; she looked similar to Arctic peoples. The entire structure of her body was very masculine, as was her voice. I must add that she taught us the history of the WKPB (the Bolshevik Party in Russia), but she never moved beyond the well-known argu-ment between Lenin and his journal, *Iskra*, and the Bund and the anti-Lenin faction in the Social Democratic movement in Russia, which at the summit of 1903 split into Bolsheviks and Mensheviks (Bolsheviks—the majority; Mensheviks—the minority, among them the Bund). Her anger at the Mensheviks, and mainly the Bund, which dared to attack Lenin more than thirty years previ-ously, caused her to draw out the subject eternally and she never managed to even reach the revolution of October 1917.

These lessons were compulsory for all residents of the cell, and it did not matter that the veteran residents had heard them already countless times. Hella played the role of politruk. She also was responsible for the preparations for the festival of November 7, the day celebrating the October Revolution of 1917 in Russia. I experi-enced this festival myself.

I met Helka sometimes in Warsaw after the war. By that time, she had a PhD in history, a degree she had acquired in Moscow. Her doctoral thesis concerned the history of the Communist Party in the Soviet Union. Our meetings with Helka Zand after the war were coincidental, mainly in the street or restaurants. Her attitude to me had not changed. Her arrogance toward me when we bumped into one another testified to the fact that she had not forgotten the "sin" I committed in prison in 1937.

However, we will go back to describing the festivities of November 7 (in the old Russian calendar this was October 25) of that year, 1937, in the Piotrków Trybunalski prison.

The day before November 7, while we were out for our daily walk, our cell was searched. These searches were so thorough that the mattresses were emptied. Eating utensils, underwear, and everything in the cell was thrown on the floor, but everything they found was "kosher." They did not find a single thing. The did not find the "grypsy" for writing that they were looking for, even though they searched me personally, as all members of the cell, because I had hidden them in a fold in my belt, which I held with my hand. When we got back from the walk, we found the cell in chaos, and we spent hours putting it to rights. Considering this, to this day I do not know how the commune leadership in each cell managed to keep a piece of red cloth, making out of it a flag and small ribbons that, in the morning, before the roll call, each one of us placed on the left side of our chest. This was a ceremony that was repeated every May 1 and November 7.

On this day, the prison authorities prepared reinforcements, in accordance with the politics of the regime. That year, it began in the following way: before the morning roll call, the door opened and into the cell came male and female guards with clubs in their hands. We stood silently in a line. First, the female guards fell upon us and violently ripped the red bows from us, hurting our chests. Our representative protested energetically, but then the male guards fell upon us with their clubs. We cried: "Don't hit us!" (nie bić). Our cry was a signal to activate the entire prison, and in the political cells they banged with all their might, crying out: "Don't hit!" Then, male guards entered each and every cell and beat the prisoners. Thus began the festival. Those who were beaten badly and needed medical attention lay on the floor. After breakfast and until lunch (on that day, as punishment, we were not taken out for a walk in the yard) we celebrated in each cell in almost the same way: a speech about the international significance of the October Revolution and the existence of the Soviet Union. This speech was given by Olga. After the speech, the veteran residents reminisced about the celebrations of this day in various Polish prisons. There were also stories about class wars in different countries and how this festival is celebrated in the Soviet Union (I will relate my own experiences elsewhere).

The main show, in which all the political prisoners as well as people on the street participated, occurred in the evening. At a set time, all the prisoners stood by the small, barred windows, one of them waved through the window the small red flag (a piece of cloth) and everyone sang the song of the revolution "To the barricades, working people!" and The Internationale. The song was heard in the entire prison and on the neighboring streets, and admittedly it was very moving and made a great impression. While we were still singing, the cell doors opened, and the guards began to beat us and tried to take down those standing on the tables and waving the red cloth. The Internationale drifted out from the window (the windows, as I mentioned, were high, directly under the ceiling, and instead of bars there were glass rungs, closed halfway, like in a shutter), mingling with the shouts of "Nie bić!" (Don't beat us!) that people in the street could hear. The crowd also began to shout "Nie bić!". . . . This event was very moving, but we received a lot of blows (even now, when writing these memoirs, I feel shivers). Afterward, in every cell, despite the murderous blows, we sang and recited revolutionary songs. Thus ended the festival commemorating the October Revolution in the Piotrków Trybunalski prison in 1937.

There can be no denying it; this event made a great, unforgettable impression on me.

One day, I was called to a meeting. A lawyer arrived, bringing me news of my family and informing me that he would represent me at my trial, a date for which had been set, in the Łódź municipal court. We talked about my defense. He already knew that all the material they confiscated from me on the night of my arrest contained nothing suspicious. We decided, at my request, that the line of defense would be my activities in an anti-Fascist movement. I was a bit shocked. The date of the trial was approaching.

At the beginning of spring 1938, the trial took place. Parting from my friends in the cell was difficult. Despite the difficult battles for the rights of the political prisoners and in spite of the small misunderstandings between myself and Helka, my relations with them were good. Apart from Helka, all the women loved me and spoiled me. I learned a lot from them, I had hoped that the knowledge I had acquired in prison would constitute a basis for my continued efforts to gain a more organized education.

At night, they took me to the prison on Mikolaja Kopernika Street in Łódź. Again, I found myself in a cell full of prostitutes. The next morning, they took me to the courtroom for the trial. When I found myself in the seat of the accused, I felt terrible. I surveyed those present in the packed courtroom. Among the many strangers, I saw all my friends from the Folkist movement, at their head Mr. Unikowski. All my close family was present (only my two big brothers, Moshe and David, were not there). However, my eyes focused on my poor father, who sat in silence, tears falling onto his beard. I felt a stab to my heart. Next to him was Meir, mumbling Psalms, on his right was Esther, more worried than ever, and next to her Shoshana and all the rest of my relatives. After my arrest, Esther had left her hakhshara group and returned to Łódź, where she worked for David and endeavored to send me parcels in prison.

I understood nothing when the judge quickly mumbled his way through the prosecution letter. The general prosecutor demanded a sentence of three years' imprisonment. My lawyer argued that I was innocent. Finally, I was given permission to speak in my own defense. I repeated the same things that I had said during the police interrogation. I spoke about my anti-Fascist activities in the Folkist youth movement. I emphasized that I believed the ruling authorities were also battling against Fascism, and thus this was legal activity. My words were verified by the only witness in the case, Mr. Unikowski, who pleasantly surprised me. The judge declared me innocent of all charges.

My trial and defense in the Łódź court became famous. The day after my release, the mouthpiece of the PPS in Łódź, Życie Robotnicze, published a large article with an interesting title: "It's Possible to Be Anti-Fascist and Not Be a Communist!" However, this too was not the entire truth. I left prison more of an idealist than I was when I entered.

After the judgment, all the family waited for me to be released and go out to them. This did not happen. Following great efforts by my lawyer, I was allowed to meet Esther in private, from behind bars. Afterward, they took me back to the prison to complete all the bureaucracy and only then was I released. Outside, in Kopernika Street, my father, Meir, and Esther were waiting. They rented a cab (dorożka), and we drove home, meaning, like always, to Shoshana's house. The entire journey, my father sat sad and silent. My heart went out to him. Meir told me that he and our father had prayed and lit candles for my release. He himself, so he told me, visited our mother's grave every day, lighting candles there and begging her to intervene with God on my behalf. Meir was sure that I was released because of these prayers.

Now, in my old age, I bow my head in submission before the ashes of my father, who did not receive a Jewish burial, to tell him with great sorrow that all the ideology in which I believed was not worth one of his tears. To reach this conclusion, I needed to endure numerous disappointments, and, more than anything, to gain knowledge and life experience.

Looking back, it seems to me that my ideological extremism was the result of my character and the conditions in which I, a girl from the provinces, with a pure heart and open to new ideas, came to live in a difficult city in insufferable conditions. In such circumstances, I sought to grasp at a belief in a better future, otherwise there was no meaning to life. Therefore, I was bewitched by the Communist ideology and the beliefs it represented: its catchphrases about social justice without divides of race and religion, about international solidarity, etc. I should mention that in these years such ideas were almost the only ones standing in the face of the Fascist threat and the Nazi racism that spread through Europe, including to Poland. This racism had a murderous anti-Semitic character. Łódź was patrolled by groups of members of the Falange (the youth of the radical nationalist camp) holding whips, and they were encouraged to beat Jews. Around us, in the small towns, pogroms took place, and in institutions for higher education there were riots against Jewish students, and ghetto benches were instituted, not to mention the ban on trade with Jews and Jewish workers and the increasingly explicit anti-Jewish policy of the ruling authorities. All these led to a feeling of hopelessness among the young generation of Jews, who searched for straws at which they could grasp, something to believe in and to guide them.

In this situation, the Communist utopia seemed like a source of hope and a ray of light for masses of Jewish youth. We saw the Soviet Union as the promised land. We found out only many years later what really happened in "the promised land."

Not long ago, I read *Strzępy Rodzinnej Sagi* (Shreds of a Family Saga) by Celina Budzynska. I knew the author personally; she was a unique person. The book was fascinating, like the author herself. She experienced all the stages of ideological development and all the stages of painful disappointment. She returned from the North Pole, from the Gulag. Of course, I cannot compare myself and my story to hers, although it seems to me that quoting a few lines from her book explains the faith in the Communist idea among my generation:

"The Communists in Poland loved this land, fought for a better future for the working class in Poland and for all its population, without distinction between origin or religion. Blinded by the vision of the revolution, they believed without any doubt whatsoever in the land of the October Revolution, which was building a Socialist society. From here derived their deep dedication to the Soviet Union, which gradually became a blind belief, an idealization of all that happened there." (p. 443)

The Last Years Before the War—Heniek

After my acquittal and release from prison, I found myself in a sad situation. I had no work and no roof over my head. I could not go back to living with Shoshana, because Moshe's mother, Shoshana's mother-in-law, had moved in with them (I moved back in with them in 1939, when her mother-in-law remarried and moved out).

I rented a corner in an attic kitchen on Pomorska Street from a single woman, in return for ten zlotys per month. The house was not far from Shoshana's home. Again, my old friends and acquaintances appeared, and I found their concern touching: they helped me to find work and with their aid I also returned to the Folkist Youth Movement, however KPP and its youth movement (KZMP) no longer existed.

Through connections, I got a job looking after the children of a family with two sons, three and five years old. The family was nice and sympathetic. Both parents were members of the working intelligentsia: she was a doctor and he, I believe, a teacher. They knew that I had been in prison and had been acquitted. I returned and registered for the people's university, and I dedicated the rest of my free time to various activities and pleasure.

We were all together again. However, a lot had changed. A year in teenage friendships is a long time. In the meantime, couples had emerged in the group. We had all become much more serious and realistic, although we still went on hikes on Saturdays and Sundays, again singing songs accompanied by Alter's balalaika. However, something had changed in the atmosphere of our "togetherness." My friends were more realistic, more individualistic. They no longer dreamed of global revolution but of finding some happiness for themselves. Young men also started crowding around me.

Indeed, two boys went out of their way to win my heart. Both were close friends of mine since 1936— Heniek and Shlamek. I already mentioned Shlamek elsewhere. He was the opposite of Heniek in every way. Shlamek was every girl's dream. His external appearance captured hearts: he was tall, dark skinned, always wearing a white shirt with a "Słowacki" collar, golf trousers, and a leather belt. After I got out of prison, he again started coming to visit me frequently, and he always encountered Heniek. Heniek was a dreamer. He was head over heels in love with me and did nothing to hide it, while Shlamek, who also demonstrated his feelings toward me, was much more reserved and waited for my feelings to ripen. Heniek was very proactive, and in his efforts to win my heart he even recruited the help of Alter, who shared with me horrible rumors about Shlamek. When I found out, I cut off relations with them. However, because this also involved cutting off connections with the organization and my social activities, it was not long before intercessors came to me and asked me to come back. I endeavored not to stay alone with either of them. Yet Heniek was stubborn (in our almost sixty years together, he never ceased to be so).

According to the rule I set for myself, I did not allow any of the boys to invite me or pay for me. This rule applied also to Heniek.

I do not mean only an invitation to the theater or a movie, but also small things. For example, when I parted from the group in the evening, he always drew out our parting because he suddenly had something important to tell me. And thus, he accompanied me home and, consequently, did not manage to get to his house before the gate closed, that is, before 11 p.m.. In return for opening the gate, he had to pay ten or twenty groshen—I returned this money to him and he accepted it in silence.

He was romantic, sensitive, and gentle. He treated me as though with silk gloves. He knew about my hesitation regarding the opposite sex and tried to understand it. Heniek was born and spent his childhood in Przyrów, a small town in the Częstochowa district. After his Bar Mitzvah, he thought himself mature enough to decide his own path in life. One morning, without the knowledge of his parents, he got on a wagon going to Częstochowa, there he went to a yeshiva and asked the head of the yeshiva to take him on as a student. The head of the yeshiva invited his father to speak with him; in short, Heniek became a student at the yeshiva. At the age of thirteen or fourteen, he studied the laws of ritual purity, marriage, and divorce, without knowing what this was all about. It was completely forbidden to look at women, yet yeshiva students were also prone to the evil inclination. From his window he saw in the house opposite a girl, and she was his first love. He never met her face to face, and certainly she did not know about his existence or his dreams about her. In his words, I was his first, and apparently only, real love. I met him when he was still wearing traditional clothes, although he was already a Communist.

I must admit that Heniek, although he was a sworn Communist and despite all the disruptions in our lives, remained until the end of his life a yeshiva student in his behavior and mentality. This applied also to our daily life and intimate relations and mainly to his honesty and his desire to avoid anything and everything connected with injustice, which was deeply imprinted on him. In this sense, we made an understanding and supportive partnership.

In the spring of 1938, we were still big children, innocent dreamers, with no worries, albeit without a penny to our names. Sometimes Heniek came to me in the evening with a bag of sandwiches and we ate them together. Often these sandwiches were the main meal that I ate that day, but he did not know that. Afterward, I again got work looking after the children of a family, and again I distanced myself from him. However, Heniek looked for me and endeavored to spend more and more time with me. Maybe already then he dreamed about our life together.

In the meantime, Heniek endeavored to persuade his brother, Alter—who, together with a partner, had a small factory that made short cotton socks—to take me on as a spool tender at the spooling machine (szpularka), which contained twenty-four spools. Usually, people worked there for many hours per day. I was given a half day's work, meaning eight hours daily. Heniek warned me not to mention the eight hours, because among the partners this smelled of revolution: "An eight-hour workday" was still a slogan of the Socialist left, only realized in large factories in which Jews had no foothold. Five brothers worked there. According to age order they were: Fitl, Alter, Shmuel, Heniek, and the youngest, Mendel (Mundek). Apart from Alter, all worked in one line by the primitive manual machines that stood along the wall, making socks. Alter was a partner in the factory, and, according to Heniek, it was like something out of a story by Shalom Aleichem: "The partner had money and a beautiful wife, and Alter—the initiative and the brains." Alter was exceptional in his family: he revealed a business instinct already as a child, when he was studying in Kheyder. He knew how to play a game with buttons against other children and earn a groshen or a pretty button. Alter's partner was rather ugly, and he apparently knew about Alter's affair with his wife and kept quiet.

But I will return to the factory in which I worked together with Heniek and most of his family. The four brothers worked along a long wall. Opposite it stood the spooling machine with twenty-four spools, at which I worked. Heniek taught me how to tie the threads, which were constantly tearing. This knot, the speed at which it was made, and its quality—I became such an expert in tying it that no other spooler could compete with me when I worked in other places.

For an hour's work, I was paid fifteen groshen, meaning that I made 1 zloty or 1.20 zlotys for an eight-hour day. From this salary I had to pay rent (for the corner in the kitchen), support myself, and provide for myself as much as possible a cultural life. I preferred this work to looking after the children of bourgeois families. Once a week, I allowed myself a hot meal in a workers' restaurant that belonged, I believe, to the Socialist professional unions. Although the work was hard and dirty, I felt freer and, no less importantly, I learned a new industrial profession.

I must briefly describe the appearance of the "factory" that was partially owned by Alter, and the working conditions therein. More than 80 percent of all Jewish workers worked, like me, in tiny factories of this kind and other similar workshops. Therefore, this description is something of a historical testimony.

The factory was located on Północna Street, which, during the Nazi occupation, became the street bordering the Łódź Ghetto. There was a yard—a rather large "well"— in the corner of which was a public toilet, meaning, one that served all the residents (more than forty families) and people who happened to come into the yard. There was no running water there, and every few weeks it was necessary to empty the contents of the toilet. In the corner apartment adjacent to this toilet, on the ground floor, was the factory run by Alter and his partner. It was made up of one room with two large windows located exactly next to the public toilet. Needless to say, it was impossible to open a window due to the stink emanating from there. Through the dark window, covered in a thick layer of dust, it was possible to see who went in and out, and even some images that I would rather not remember.

Working in a textile factory, even a small one such as this, without a special machine for removing the dust that accumulated from the threads of the spool and weaving, meant that the dust built up, covering kerchiefs and aprons, sticking to the walls and windows. We breathed it into our lungs. The air was suffocating. The room was never cleaned, and the floorboards were red. On this floor, next to the spooling machine, there was always a pile of cotton threads. On this pile, the four brothers who worked there sat to eat their breakfast.

The brothers knew that Heniek was interested in me, but they did not give me any special treatment. Only Shmuel sometimes tried to flirt with me a bit. Often, their father, Mordechai Garncarski, appeared in the factory. The father was religious, but the sons, although some of them still dressed in the traditional manner, did not, apparently, keep the commandments. If my memory does not deceive me, Heniek was the first to buy a Western suit and after him Shmulik, who was two years older than him. When their father came, he followed me, sometimes asking me a question, as though he wanted to know who I was.

Although his father apparently knew of Heniek's intentions, I was never invited to their home. I visited this home twice or three times: once or twice a meeting of our KZMP nest was held in Heniek's home, and once I visited the house when Heniek was sick. His mother, Rachel, hid in the kitchen every time I came, and I did not see her. They had one daughter and another small child who was maybe four years old. He was a strange child. All Heniek's brothers, like him, received a religious education. None of them went to a general school (only Heniek and Mundek acquired an education after the war). However, according to Heniek, at home they argued more about Schopenhauer, Spinoza, and Darwin than about questions in the Talmud. Each one of them was a "philosopher" and a home-grown poet, in particular the oldest, Fitl. Perhaps in suitable conditions he would have become a poet. However, he was murdered, like all the rest of the Garncarski family, by the Nazis. Only those who fled to Russia (Heniek, Shmulik, and Mundek) were saved. Heniek also wrote poems that he put in the drawer, but Mundek was a real writer and some of his poems and his prose were published. Some appeared in the journal *Po Prostu*, where he worked in the literary section. I'll come back to Mundek later.

I should have been ready, or at least felt, that Heniek would soon come to me to propose marriage. However, when, on the evening before May 1, 1938, he came to me and with great excitement offered me his love, I burst out crying and fled to the home of Moshe and Yitche (where I was sleeping for a few weeks in case the authorities would try to arrest me before May 1). I cannot explain my behavior other than saying that I fled due to the same fear of intimacy that had pursued me for many years. I cried all night. How could I explain my fears to Heniek? Indeed, of all my friends and acquaintances, he was the most devoted and constant. He was my best friend. That night I saw in front of my eyes very specific images from my childhood, and I could not make a decision.

The next morning, I went to a May 1 demonstration organized by the PPS, the Bund, and the Polish and Jewish professional Socialist unions of Łódź (the Communist Party no longer existed; it had been disbanded according to the Moscow order). This demonstration involved more than 100,000 people, and it was the last legal demonstration before the Nazi invasion. The procession set out from the gathering point in Widzew Square (close to the Widzewski Manufacturing Factory), turned to the main street, Piotrkowska, and went through the Pieradzkiego alley. When a large group of a few thousand young Jews in the procession reached this corner, a unit of policemen on horseback crossed it and encircled this part of the procession. They pushed us into the alley with their horses and clubs and there they behaved with terrible violence. I was among the hundreds hurt and wounded.

With the remainder of my strength, I got home, making my way through alleys and side streets. Shoshana looked after me and put me to bed. In the meantime, news of the massacre spread like wildfire among the lines of the mass procession, accompanied by cries and calls for a protest against the police and those who dispatched them, meaning the authorities. This reached the ears of my friends, who were spread among their professional unions. After the demonstration, Heniek arrived, and immediately after him Shlamek and the rest of the friends who had attended the demonstration and heard that I was among the wounded. I was in bed for a few days.

In the fall of that year, 1938, Esther received a certificate and left for Palestine. My father came from Końskie to part from his oldest daughter. Among those who accompanied her to the train station when she left for Warsaw were, apart from family members, Esther's fiancé, who had been promised a certificate in the next round (I already mentioned that he perished together with all the Jews of the Łódź Ghetto) and also Heniek. It seems that Esther or Shoshana hinted to my father that Heniek was a serious boyfriend, and thus Father had an opportunity to talk to him and get to know him. A few hours after Esther left, I accompanied Father to the train station on his way back to Końskie. This was the last time I spoke with my father. He talked to me about Heniek, who had made a good impression on him, and hinted that he would be happy if I were to marry him. I promised him that if and when I would decide to get married, it would be with Heniek.

I should note that after Heniek and I left for Soviet Russia during the war, Heniek's father, Mordechai Garncarski visited Shoshana (I don't know how he got her address—I thought that he knew nothing about me). He wanted to know if we had been married properly. He did not know that I still refused to be together with Heniek. But again, I have run forward with my story.

Changing Work Conditions

In the last years before the war, Poland experienced an economic upturn. However, the situation of the Jews, apart from a few hundred large industrialists and merchants, was terrible. Jews were not given jobs in state and municipal institutions and industry during the entire interwar period. The increasing anti-Semitism, the attacks on Jews, the wild campaign against Jewish traders and craftsmen, and the ban on Jewish workers, when even the gates of the large workshops owned by Jews were closed to them, all these intensified in particular in the years 1936–1939, causing the distress of the Jews to reach new heights. The Jewish social and economic organizations, which fought to help ease the distress of the Jewish masses, managed here and there to break the ban on Jewish workers in Jewish-owned factories.

In these hard times, in an atmosphere permeated by mutual aid within the Jewish community, Jewish factory owners were more willing to give jobs to Jews than they had been in the past, despite the opposition of the Polish workers they employed. In this last battle, there were some successes. I also won in this respect, with the help of Yitche, my sister-in-law, who was a nurse by profession. Among other things, she gave massages to family members of one of the textile industrialists. Thanks to her I was given work as a spool tender in a large factory that made knitwear and tricot, in the firm "Kanal and Zbar," whose factory was located at the edge of Kościuszko (or Wólczańska) Boulevard, near the industrial area in Chojny.

It is hard to describe the feeling of happiness when I was told that I was to report the next morning for work in this factory. I was going to move from a stinking, dirty hole like Alter's factory to work in a large, real factory among hundreds of other workers, and the conditions, thus I hoped, would be totally different. Yitche advised me to wear clothes that would suit me. Although her suggestion seemed strange to me, because I had a very modest selection of clothes, I wore that morning a simple flowery cotton dress of two parts that was called a "chałupka," a popular outfit worn by village girls on festive occasions. Thus, I reported to the manager of the department I was to work in. He had apparently already received instructions regarding me. He examined me from all sides, asked questions about my professional knowledge, and ordered me to report that same day for the second shift (I believe that this was from 2 p.m. until 10 p.m.).

The first day at work in the new factory ended miserably. The noise of the machines, my tension, and my desire to prove my professionalism resulted in a serious migraine—I had suffered from migraines since childhood—accompanied by vomiting. I had to stop working. I was the only Jewish woman in the unit. The Polish spooler tenders that worked on another spooling machine, who did not know me, helped me, sending me home and promising that they would try to ensure the unit head would not find out. I despaired. I did not believe the promises of my new work colleagues. I was afraid that I would not get another chance to work in this factory. However, the next morning I reported for work and it was as though no one knew or had heard what happened the previous day. I worked in this factory until the Germans entered the city.

In the department stood lines of large, round mechanical knitting machines, and not far from them stood, also in a line, about ten spooling machines, each one with twenty-six spools. The noise was immense, but over time I got used to it. Not long passed before I learned that the workers at the knitting machines were fighting among themselves over my spooling, because the knot that Heniek had taught me in Alter's factory did not make holes and did not tear. An acquaintance of mine worked in the administration of the factory at that time, the only other Jew in the whole factory, Felek Weingut, whom I already mentioned. He attended the management meeting of all the departments, and he heard that the knitters praised my work, the work of the only Jewish woman in the department.

The working conditions were completely different to those I had known previously. For the first time, I had social benefits like all workers, including belonging to a health provider. During work there was a break of half an hour for breakfast, in which we went to the dining hall, where there was hot tea and coffee. Each one brought her own food from home. We sat by a long table with simple benches. There I got to know my work colleagues, who treated me well, and I also felt some degree of respect toward them.

Indeed, in Łódź there was a sad tradition, the roots of which went back to the nineteenth century, when the Germans established the first textile factories in the city. They and their technical staff, from the master to the official and the engineer, treated workers from the nearby villages like subjects who were under their control. Cases of rape were frequent, and the workers were treated as though they were there to satisfy the desires of their superiors. In the 1890s, against this background, turbulent strikes broke out in Łódź. Later, in the 1920s and 1930s, although the rape of female workers was usually a thing of the past, with unemployment chronic and the area impoverished, the desire to please one's superiors created certain practices, a certain culture in the relations between the female workers and their male superiors, or just those stronger than them, the men in the department. For the first time in my life, I witnessed these relations, which I did not want to see or know about. I was even afraid to leave my spool for a moment to bring raw material (piles of threads) when my stock ran out. However, over time my work colleagues learned to treat me with respect.

In economic terms, for the first time in my life I had room to breathe. I made 28–30 zlotys per week (instead of 7 zlotys when I worked for Alter and his partner). I started to dress a bit like a real woman. I bought myself a winter coat with a small fur collar (I covered a severely wounded soldier with it somewhere in the fields of Ukraine in 1941. He died on my knees, and I left it with the dead body.), I wore high-heeled shoes and even a fashionable hat.

By this time, Heniek had become a regular fixture in our home, meaning the home of Shoshana and Moshe, when I returned to live with them. He very much wanted us to live together. However, we lacked two things. First of all, we did not have the means to rent an apartment that would be more or less suitable. Perhaps, if I had wanted it too, the family would have helped us marry and take our first steps. However, second, and perhaps mainly, I still had not reconciled myself to the idea. Also, the political situation was foggy and unknown. On the horizon were frightening clouds that threatened our lives. They dictated our fate in the near future.

From the moment that Poland signed a non aggression pact with Nazi Germany in 1934, the "flirtation" between the Polish and German governments deepened. The Poles saw Germany as an ally in the final solution of the Jewish problem according to Hitler's *Mein Kampf*—anti-Semitism blinded most of the Polish population. Chamberlain's Munich agreement of 1938 and the annexation of Austria and Czechoslovakia to Germany increased the threat that the swastika posed to Europe. However, for Poland, this was the right time to make territorial demands and annex Silesia, beyond the River Zaolzie (October 1938), the river that had served until then as the border between Poland and Czechoslovakia. The Germans "generously" agreed. Likewise, the battle over Klaipeda, Lithuania's port on the Baltic Sea, which was beyond Poland's borders, ended in success. The intoxication and impassioned patriotism flooded Poland to such an extent that the Polish government even managed to hide the fact that, in the same month as Zaolzie was annexed to Poland, on October 28, 1938, Ribbentrop, the German foreign minister, presented to the Polish government an ultimatum regarding the annexation of the free city of Gdansk, the port city on the Baltic Sea. In addition, the Polish government had to agree to the building of a railway in Polish Pomerania, which was intended to improve Germany's connection with Royal Prussia (Prusy Królewskie).

It was not necessary to be left wing to see that all of Poland was proceeding toward a catastrophe, not only its Jews. You only needed to have your eyes open and think rationally. I should add that the Polish Communists had no idea that the dissolution of their party in Poland, according to the Moscow order and the physical annihilation of all the leadership, was intended to "clear the ground" for a secret agreement between the foreign ministers of Russia and Germany, Molotov and Ribbentrop. According to this agreement, as is known, upon the German invasion of Poland, Soviet Russia took over Eastern Poland as far as the Bug (meaning Western Ukraine, White Russia, and Lithuania).

At the same time, the Polish government was discussing various anti-Semitic laws, and to improve the mood of the Polish nation, the prime minister, General Sławoj-Składkowski, instructed that all the public toilets should be painted one color (therefore they were called "Sławojki"). All this was around half a year before the German invasion.

The German minority in Poland, which had a significant presence in Łódź, was in close communication with the German consulate in Warsaw and conducted hostile activities against Poland almost openly. They prepared bases for the arrival of the first groups of messengers on motorcycles. They were also the ones who signaled to the German air force and marked the strategic locations for the air strikes. After the invasion, they received documents stating that they were Volksdeutsche and became the main assistants of the invaders.

The panic began only a month before the invasion. There arrived an order to dig trenches around Łódź, and we too participated in this. Every day, after work, all my friends and I reported to dig in the northern suburbs of the city. There were masses of people; not everyone even received a shovel, and it was necessary to swap from time to time. Gypsy fortune tellers wandered around. Despite my heretical beliefs, hidden within me, it seems, was some kind of superstition, and I asked a gypsy woman to tell my fortune for a few groshen. It was not difficult for her to see the future for a young Jewish woman under the Nazi occupation. Nevertheless, I remember her words. She told me that a long road awaited me, twisted and difficult, but that I would remain alive and that at the end of the road I would again meet the young man who was with me, and we would establish a family.

PART 2

The Vicissitudes of the War

CHAPTER 4

TOWARD THE UNKNOWN

Fleeing East

September 1, 1939, was a Friday. It was a beautiful day in Łódź: the skies were blue, and the rays of the autumnal sun seemed to try to soften, if only a little, the tension hovering over the city. The atmosphere was also somewhat festive. It was the first day of the school year. As in previous years, on my walk to work, I felt sadness at the fact that I had not been able to complete my studies and a sense of longing. I was already grown up, and I had been supporting myself for some time. As I said, I worked in a textile factory that was far from my home. I loved walking to work.

On Fridays, on the way home from work, late in the evening, the streets were usually quiet; the shops were already closed, the Sabbath approaching. However, on that Friday evening, I felt a sense of agitation, nervousness, and anxious activity. People were crowding around notice boards. A new notice had just been put up. I approached. The new, large notice announced a general call for recruitment. The war had broken out. I was not surprised. For a few months, we had lived in an atmosphere of impending war and the expectation that Hitler's troops would invade Poland. As I noted, for a few weeks we had already all been digging trenches around the city.

After the Sabbath, we heard the first sirens and artillery explosions in Łódź. The bombardment continued all Sunday—day and night. That evening, we heard the call on the radio: all men able to bear arms were to leave the city and make their way to the highway in the direction of Warsaw. They would be given weapons and become part of the Polish army that sought to push back the invaders.

Oh, that night. The city was enveloped in darkness; it was forbidden to light a lamp. Suddenly, the roads were full of people. Groups upon groups, masses of people, filled the streets and alleys. The stream of people on Pomorska Street, where we lived, grew constantly. The men went out, accompanied by their wives and children. Afterward came the turn of entire families, their possessions loaded onto handcarts or children's carriages, and those who went on foot—everyone was going, leaving the city. These were mainly Jewish families. I too accompanied Heniek to the city boundary, where we parted. My brother-in-law and brothers also left Łódź. When daylight arrived, it was quiet, suffocatingly so, a silence that heralded bad news. There were no more bombardments. We heard explosions far away. In the afternoon, a rumor suddenly spread that the call for the men to leave the city was a trick: the road to Warsaw, which was full of people, had been bombed, leaving thousands dead and wounded.

Wagons full of the dead and wounded began to arrive. The dead were taken straight to the cemetery and the wounded to the hospitals, which filled up quickly. We searched, together with masses of others, for our loved ones among the dead in the cemeteries. Here and there someone burst out crying after finding their relative among the murdered. We searched, along with others, for our loved ones in the hospitals. We received our first taste of war. In the evening, we went home with hope in our hearts that they were alive.

My brother-in-law, Moshe, and my brother returned the next day. Heniek followed after three days. They told us about the hell they had encountered on the road to Warsaw, because the Germans had already taken control of this highway. How did Heniek nevertheless manage to return? He told us that amid the horror, a Polish man stood some distance from the road and invited people to follow him. Heniek, together with others, followed him and found himself in the Grabski family's castle. This was a multi-branched family with several brothers and sisters, among them Władysław Dominik Grabski, who was minister of the treasury in the 1920s. Almost the entire family was affiliated or close to the national camp (Narodowa Demokracja Party), but when they saw the horrors perpetrated by the Nazis, they changed their attitude to Jews. Heniek spent two days in the castle, and he told us that the owners welcomed him and dozens of other Jews, and about the conversations between them. After two days, when there was relative quiet, they returned home through the forests.

Poland was the first victim of the Third Reich's Blitzkrieg, as prepared by Hitler. The Polish army, which numbered almost one million soldiers armed with old weapons, was encircled by an army of a million soldiers, ready and mechanized, with 1,200 Luftwaffe (air force) planes, which managed to conquer a country of 34 million residents within a dozen days. Only Warsaw held out with great bravery for almost a month, falling on September 27. A large part of the Polish army, which was ready to defend Poland's eastern borders, was encircled by the Soviet army; according to the Molotov–Ribbentrop Pact, Russia conquered Western Ukraine, the western part of White Russia (Byelorussia), and Lithuania. After the war, a rumor circulated regarding a mass grave of hundreds of Polish officers who were murdered in Katyń by the Soviet army on Stalin's orders, but the first time we heard of this was from Radio Free Europe.

The terrible days of the German occupation ensued. The Polish government and some branches of the bureaucracy fled in the very first days of the war. A government-in-exile was established in London, although it was not recognized by the German and Russian invaders. The Allies' declarations regarding their support of free Poland and their opposition to the occupation did not do much to help. For the three and a half million Jews, residents of Poland for more than a thousand years, this was no comfort. Our fates were in the hands of the Nazis.

Łódź was among the first large cities conquered by the Germans. However, three days after the night of the bombardment, the city was quiet, frighteningly so. There were no authorities, no officials; everyone had fled. We, the Jewish residents of the city, waited in fear for what was to come. On Tuesday, they arrived. German troops marched to the thunder of drums, with much noise and tumult. The Jews closed themselves in their homes, however we heard all too well this victory march.

As I mentioned, we lived at 20 Pomorska Street, not far from Freedom Square. The welcome reception for the victors was held there. Their first act was to tear down the memorial to Tadeusz Kościuszko and destroy it. To further defile and humili-ate the memory of this freedom fighter in the eyes of the residents, dozens, even hundreds, of kegs of beer were brought and distrib-uted to the masses. The masses drank until they were intoxicated, standing on the remains of the destroyed memorial, while the vic-tors regaled in their glory.

It should not be forgotten that Łódź was home to one of the highest concentrations of Germans in Poland since the nineteenth century, and they accounted for around 10 percent of the city's population. The Jews amounted to around one third (according to the 1931 census) of the population. At the beginning of the nineteenth century, the Polish kingdom invited German weavers to Łódź, offering them preferential conditions and investing great sums, and they began to develop the textile industry. As a result of the condition dictated by the Germans and stipulated in their agreements with the Polish authorities, Jews were not permitted in the new Łódź. This condition was maintained meticulously until the 1850s. The textile industry they built was tiny compared to that built by the Jews of Łódź in the 1870s and 1880s. At the end of the nineteenth century, the Jews of Łódź owned 80 percent of this industry. Now, after more than a hundred years, the Germans were the owners of the city. They prepared the city to welcome the occupiers, and, upon the arrival of the Nazis, all the German residents of the city received them with victory cries and became Volksdeutsche. Only one family of German origin refused to accept the status of Volksdeutsche; they were executed on the spot, apart from the eldest son, who managed to flee. This was the Birman family, among the largest textile manufacturers in Łódź. The city of Łódź was annexed to the Third Reich and renamed Litzmannstadt.

The following day, when I went to work, I noticed that some workers who had previously been members of the professional Socialist unions now wore an armband bearing a swastika and had been promoted to managerial status. After two days of insufferable tension in the factory, I requested a few days' leave, claiming that I needed to travel home to see my sick father. I left the factory without my apron and my last pay packet. I knew that I would not be able to bear the new atmosphere there.

The windows of the shops on Piotrkowska and Pomorska Streets, which were owned by Germans, were already decorated with swastikas and large pictures of the Führer, Hitler.

A state of emergency was declared. It was forbidden to be in the streets, on the balconies of buildings, or to look out of windows from six in the evening until six in the morning. The patrols shot without warning at anyone who dared to approach the window or balcony. Every day brought new decrees (Verordnungen). Expropriation of food and the imposition of supervision on produce—for example, on flour for the bakeries—immediately created long lines of people waiting for bread, and there was only enough for those at the front of the line. The distress motivated many to take risks and leave a little before the end of the curfew hours, hoping to be first in line.

On Pomorska Street, almost opposite the house in which we lived, there was a bakery. One day I stood, together with my sister Shoshana, in front of the closed gate of their courtyard, waiting for the moment it would open and it would be possible to run in and grab the first place in the line for bread. It was still a few moments before six. We peeked through the small opening and saw that a few people were already standing in a line crowded near the gate. Suddenly, a military patrol of motorcycles arrived and, within one second, with a burst of gunfire, all the people fell down. We, my sister and I, were eyewitnesses. We were horrified. We ran home and went out onto the balcony (now it was allowed) to see what was happening. The sight was even more awful. Other people ran to stand in the line. They dragged the dead, according to the orders of the patrol, to the courtyard and on that very same spot, on the fresh blood that had just been spilled, other people stood in the line waiting for bread.

This was only the beginning.

Afterward, some things started to seem normal: the killing, the long lines for food products, hunting Jews and pulling them out of lines, sometimes by local "orderlies." Despite the dangers, the need to obtain bread and the most essential food items forced us young people to go out and stand in lines, risking our lives, and sometimes we even managed to bring home a loaf of bread. The humiliations and the killings became daily occurrences. Very quickly, notices appeared announcing the imposition of the yellow star, and after a few weeks we were informed about the establishment of a ghetto in Łódź.

Every individual and every family searched for a means of salvation. We were so afraid of what was to come, yet no one imagined what would happen.

We, the young people, thought about fleeing. We wanted to escape and to try to cross the border with the Soviet Union. Each one had his own difficult decisions to make. Heniek and I decided to take our chances and leave. Our families were still not ready to go with us, but we wanted at least to go with our good friends. This became complicated, because it involved terrible deliberations. For example, Alter Wieluński did not want to leave his old mother; apart from that, he did not have a penny for the journey. Shlomo Pront lived with his three sisters and a brother, and they did not want to be separated. And so too others. Hanka Krokh was very close to her father and would not leave without him. I too did not have a penny or suitable clothing for the approaching winter. Yet Heniek succeeded in raising some money for the journey. We packed some personal effects, almost like we were going for a picnic (toiletries, a towel, and some clean underwear), and the difficult moment arrived. It was time to bid our families farewell.

I begged Shoshana and Moshe to join us, but it was hard for them to leave their well-cared-for home and their few belongings. It was also difficult for me to insist, because I did not know what awaited us on the way or there, in the Soviet Union. They were afraid that their only son, six-year-old Naftali, would not survive the unknown future and journey. I knew that I would not be able to persuade my brothers to join me. Therefore, I went to bid them farewell. David, with whom relations were strained due to our family history and the tension during the period that I had worked for him, welcomed me warmly, as did my sister-in-law, Chava. They gave me a warm blue sweater for the journey, and David burst out in bitter tears, as though he knew that this would be our last meeting and our last farewell. From Moshe, my oldest brother, I parted in sadness, and Yitche, my sister-in-law, could not hold back her tears. I did not have the opportunity to go to Końskie to bid goodbye to Father and Meir. It was dangerous to travel by train. Indeed, they threw Jews out of the carriages, and I did not have money to pay for a private vehicle.

We left. It was already forbidden for Jews to travel by train or other public transport, so we looked for a wagon that would take us part of the way, at least to Warsaw. While looking for a wagon, we encountered some other young men and women who were looking for a wagon for the same purpose. Some of them knew Heniek. We decided to travel together.

There were seven of us—four men and three women—all more or less of the same age. Among the men, apart from Heniek, was a man named Adam. I later discovered that he was of German origin but was a Polish citizen from Łódź. He was accompanied by a very beautiful young Jewish woman. Both had previously been members of the Communist youth movement, as were all those traveling with us. There was also a tailor (I do not remember his name). The women were all seamstresses or worked in other professions. The youngest was Lazar Dizenhaus.

A few words about him. From the entire group, we made friends with this Lazar, and we corresponded with him until his tragic death in the Polish army, after the liberation of Poland. Lazar Dizenhaus was around nineteen when we met him. He was full of ideological enthusiasm and thirst for life. When we were already in Białystok, he volunteered to go to Donbass, on the River Don, to work in the coal mines. He wanted to work in the most dangerous places, doing the most difficult work. While I was in Bobruisk and in other places in the Soviet Union, I received letters that he sent to me from there. He also corresponded with Heniek. He returned to Poland with the Polish army that was established in Soviet Russia, the Kościuszko army. He discovered that no one from his family had survived. After he was murdered by a Polish nationalist group that opposed the new regime, we received an official notice from the army that he had fallen as a hero. Our address was the only one that they found on his person after his death.

We left Łódź, feeling that should we manage to cross the border into Russia, we would open a new page in our lives. However, we did not know how and with what this new page would be filled.

We left Łódź behind us, and the wagon rolled slowly down the road leading to Warsaw. We had a long way to go. Suddenly, a German motorcycle patrol was advancing on us. We were immediately filled with fear. It stopped by the wagon. The Germans asked us where we are going. We replied that we were returning home to Białystok (some of us had documents, which it was possible to buy). Afterward, they checked the horse and the straps of the bridle and declared that they were rubbing against the skin of the horse's neck. As punishment for this, they dealt the wagon driver a strong blow, causing him to fall to the ground. The young men with us were ordered to get out of the wagon and run on foot, because they were making the burden too heavy for the horse. We, the three women, remained sitting in the wagon and the Germans suddenly became gentlemen, ordering the wagon driver not to touch us in any untoward way. In the meantime, our men were running in front of us. On the side of the road was a forest. I thought that they should flee to the forest, but they did not. The Germans sat on their motorcycles and we feared that they were about to shoot our friends. However, they rode off. Our friends returned to us. Now, the wagon driver, fearing more blows, no longer wanted to take us. He wanted to return to us some of the money we had paid in advance. He turned his wagon back. We were still not far from Łódź, and from there we continued on foot.

I will not describe the rest of the nightmarish journey to Warsaw. At the last moment before curfew, we arrived at an address that one of the young men with us had been given. We went into an apartment on the ground floor. It was dark, and it was forbidden to turn on a light. The room was full of people. Each one of us grabbed a place to sit on the floor and waited until six in the morning, when we were permitted to go out and continue on our way. In the meantime, the woman who lived there gave us some tea. We drank and, with words of thanks, parted from her.

Our goal was to continue east. We went most of the way on foot, and I will not describe all our adventures. The small town beyond the border was Małkinia (in the Białystok region), and the city itself had already been conquered by the Soviets. On the way to this town, we met frightened people returning. They told us that the Germans were slaughtering Jews who tried to cross the border. We decided to circumvent the town and steal across "the green border." People told us that in a nearby village there was a family that helped people cross the border. We reached the forest and, in return for money, a farmer promised to help us cross the border by night.

When the sun set, we set out and entered a seemingly infinite forest. I will not forget the night we spent in that forest. It was so dark that we could not see each other, and it was forbidden to shout; so we advanced slowly. The forest became thicker and thicker. The darkness around us caused us to see things. The trees took on various forms. Once they seemed like threatening people approaching us, later they looked like dangerous animals. Sometimes it seemed to me that instead of the forest and the trees, evil soldiers of hell were attacking me; the branches became murderous swords trying to cut me down. Every time someone trod on tree roots or a branch, the fear intensified.

Suddenly, we understood we were alone—our guide had disappeared. The fear increased. We gathered close, held hands, and decided to hold out and not move until dawn. It rained all night, and under the trees heavy, thick drops fell. Finally, dawn arrived, and we began to discern the vegetation in the forest, to distinguish between the massive trees and bushes and the carpet of vegetation. We looked for a path, some route that would take us out of the forest. We found a narrow path and started to walk east. To find our direction we used the forest trees, the northern sides of which were largely covered with moss. We had no idea for how many hours we walked or what time it was when we approached the edge of the forest, because whoever had possessed a watch had lost it on the way to the local collaborators. They "helped" us to dispose of our excess baggage. From one person they took a watch, from another a shirt or towel, from another a bit of soap—everything had a value, and everything was taken from us.

In the afternoon, we arrived at the edge of the forest. Not far from the line of the forest was a wide road. We had still not reached it but looked at it from afar. And then we heard soldiers' footsteps and saw a unit of German soldiers, apparently the border patrol. They passed us and we understood that we were at the German border. We thought that after they passed, we would be able to run across the road to the other side of the border without them seeing us. We were wrong. The moment our feet hit the road we heard from every side "Halt! Hande hoch!" Only now did we see that every few dozen meters were lookout points where the German patrols were stationed.

That's it, it's all over. They put us in a line, holding automatic rifles, fingers on the trigger. . . .

What happened in the next few seconds was unbelievable. In that same second before the trigger was pulled, there was a cry from afar. We saw a soldier on horseback in uniform crying out, "Halt! Halt!" He whispered something to "our" soldier and that one barked an order at us to follow the soldier on horseback. We reached a farmer's cabin, outside which were a few soldiers who led us to the adjacent room. There sat an elderly general with thinning white hair. He looked like an Austrian officer from the army of Kaiser Franz Josef. He asked us a few questions: where we came from, where we were going, who we were, etc. Each one of us answered separately; each one identified himself, presenting his identification documents and his work records. The General was so surprised that he checked our work records from all sides.

"You are workers? Jewish workers?" He was shocked. It seemed that until now he had believed that every Jew was at least a Rothschild.

He ordered us to sit and told his soldier to bring us coffee and something to eat. After a few moments, we received real hot coffee, with milk, and fresh white bread with jam. We had not eaten such luxuries for a long time. In the meantime, the general asked each one of us where we worked, where we were going, etc. All of us said that we wanted to go home: to Białystok. After we had eaten, drunk, and were satisfied, he called his soldier and told him to lead us over the Soviet border and made him responsible for our safety. That was it. Thus, we were saved, and we arrived at the Soviet border.

After the unexpected meeting with the Germans on the Białystok border, we felt trepidation at our first meeting with a Soviet soldier. The first impression I got was funny. He was wearing a hat like none I had ever seen before. Afterward, I found out it was called a budyonovka (named after the soldiers of the legendary marshal Budyonny), with a red star on its visor, and he had slanted eyes. As I have already emphasized, I was a young, enthusiastic idealist. Although I did not know what the Soviet regime looked like in reality, in my imagination, the Soviet Union embodied the dream of a global workers' homeland. And, moreover, in my thoughts, the Soviet man was a fervent Communist just like me, because this was a country in which there was no place for evil or injustice.

Therefore, I was pleased to meet a Soviet soldier, and I saw this Mongolian soldier as a symbol of freedom. To my surprise, this symbol behaved strangely and was very unfriendly. He tried to explain to us, but we did not understand a single word, and I laughed. Finally, he got angry and started to push us back toward the border. We refused. Then he got even more angry and shouted: "Pashol von!" (Go away!) I understood this expression (I sometimes heard it from my father). Likewise, his hand movements made it clear that it was forbidden to continue onward; we needed to go back. We finally understood that he was planning to send us back to the Germans. However, we could not believe that he really meant it. We started to fight with him. At the same time, we heard from afar people singing The Internationale. The soldier ran toward this noise.

I looked around me. In the field was a young girl grazing her sheep. I approached her and sat next to her. I found myself away from my group. I prayed that they too would disappear, that they would do something. I must admit that for a moment the idea of leaving the group and staying with the girl passed through my mind. However, the soldier returned, and Heniek called me to come back. The soldier also called me. I had to go back. We were in a difficult situation. The sound of The Internationale came closer and closer. A mass of men, women, and children had broken through the border and was approaching us. We also started to sing, and we mixed in with these people. We found out that they had been waiting for more than two weeks at the border without a permit to enter the Soviet Union. Our situation improved. We were no longer alone. The soldiers gathered all of us in one place and an officer came out to us. After long discussions, we were given permission to travel to Białystok.

When I saw Białystok for the first time in my life, the city made a strange impression on me: it was a large refugee camp, mainly inhabited by Jews fleeing from Nazi-occupied Poland, in a sea of red flags. We had reached a city captured by the Red Army. Masses of soldiers walked the streets. The city was in chaos. We searched among the refugees for familiar faces. Someone told us that a refugee center was operating in the city. We went there. It was crowded. However, in the tumult there was some kind of order. We found a few acquaintances, received the address of a house in which we could stay for the time being and coupons for the public kitchen. We spent the night in a large house, which was full of people. We lay widthwise on a double bed like sardines in a can, all our group—seven people—under one blanket. We spent a few days in Białystok. However, apart from the general impression of chaos, preparations for the municipal elections, and lots of red flags, I do not remember much.

In Białystok we had two pieces of good luck: many of the refugees intended to go back to Poland in order to bring their relatives. One of these was my acquaintance, Shlomo Pacanowski, who knew my family well because he had worked for my brother, David. I asked him to visit my sister Shoshana, to tell her about my situation, and to ask her to come to Białystok with her husband and child. I had no hope that my father and three brothers with their families would be prepared to come to the Soviet Union. Pacanowski did as I asked. He visited my family, and indeed, my sister and her family arrived, although only after a few months did I find out they were in Russia and had been sent to the Urals. Later, we managed to reunite. This was my first great piece of good luck. (I met Pacanowski and his wife again three years later, in a completely different situation. I will return to it later.)

My second piece of good luck was that there, in Białystok, some friends and acquaintances of mine and Heniek's were active in the refugee center, and they received a license to prepare a list of various professionals for work in Russia. In this way we were included in a group that registered for work in Bobruisk, near Minsk, in Byelorussia. We were lucky, Heniek and I, because apparently we were in the only or the last group of refugees that managed to register for work. These lists were cancelled afterward. Thanks to our voluntary registration for work, we were not sent to the Urals or Siberia, as, among others, Shoshana and her family were, and many of us were given the opportunity to work in our profession.

Bobruisk

Bobruisk—a regional capital on the River Berezina. In the period of my stay, the city had 80,000 residents, the great majority Jewish. The city had wood, food, textile, and metal industries. These were small factories, for the most part. Only the wood factory (Lesozavod), located on the river, was a large factory, but it was far from the city.

We arrived by train in the first days of November. Only days later, we participated for the first time in the celebrations of the twenty-second anniversary of the October Revolution (November 7). We were a group of around twenty refugees, mostly young men and women who shared the same outlook, meaning members of the left-wing youth movements in Poland, most former members of the KZMP. We were surprised to find masses of people waiting for us at the train station in the suburbs of the city, in the early morning cold of the beginning of November. A welcoming ceremony was held, complete with speeches and signs, of which we could not understand a word, apparently for the purposes of internal Soviet propaganda. Later we found out that these people had been taken from their night shift jobs to the ceremony to welcome the "victims of capitalist Fascism" in Poland.

After the strange ceremony, the masses of people were taken back on buses. Afterward, each one of us received a workplace and living place as secondary tenants with various families. Some of us were taken to the workers' dormitories for workers of Lesozavod. Heniek and I were given work at a cooperative, a textile factory named "Vosemnadtstogo parts'iezda." I was given work in my profession, as a spool tender. Heniek worked in the same factory, at an overlock machine, a job in which he had experience.

In the first days, I lived with a Russian family. The husband was an officer in the Red Army who served also as the political instructor (politruk) in our factory. His cheerful and sympathetic wife was in advanced pregnancy and they lived in two tiny rooms with a cooking area. While living with this young couple, I learned my first words in Russian; not without some embarrassing misunderstandings on my part. The officer, for example, explained to me that I needed to come to the factory at a certain time: "Ladna?" (Ok?). I went red. Why was he telling me that I am beautiful (which is what this means in Polish)? I did not know that this word, like kharasho, asks you to confirm agreement: Did you understand? Similar things happened frequently. This lieutenant-politruk also understood Polish. He spoke with me in Russian and I answered in Polish. I told him my life story, at his request, and he was especially interested in the Communist youth movement, about which he was hearing for the first time. This was apparently the first time that he had heard about life in Poland, and he had no reason not to believe me. He and his wife liked me, but after a while I had to move because his wife was about to give birth.

Thus, I was moved to a young Jewish family with one child that lived in an apartment with one room and a kitchen. They added a bed for me in the kitchen. Everything then looked new and promising. Apart from the fear for our relatives, who had remained under the Nazi occupation in Poland, Heniek and I were satisfied. We had work, we knew how to work, and discipline was already in our blood. People around us treated us nicely. What else could we ask for from fate during a war?

Quickly, and without knowing anything about norms, the fixed amount of daily output became "Stachanovite." We worked in three shifts. I should mention and describe a little the environment and the people, which are engraved on my memory.

Our cooperative, the textile factory, was located in a large, enclosed area. We entered and left through a closed gate, at which those arriving and mainly those leaving underwent an inspection. In the same area there was another factory, a cooperative for the production of clothing; there, a few months later, Shoshana would find work. In that same yard, next to the factory, there was a dining hall, and what remains in my memory is a cup of "kisiel," a kind of watery, sour fruit pudding, for dessert, which accompanied every lunch. I hated it.

We worked, as I said, in three shifts. In each shift there were a few dozen workers. There were few men: if my memory is not mistaken, there were, apart from Heniek, only two other men. One was a mechanic, who was raised and educated in an orphanage, and therefore had received a fair portion of brainwashing. He was an incorrigible Soviet patriot. He praised the machines, stroking them and saying: "These are our Soviet technology; there is nothing like them in the world. . . . " The machine I worked at was almost brand new, but its technology was like something from the nineteenth century. I had worked in similar factories in Łódź; I knew the machines and I could compare them. The second man was the head of the supply department, a Jew, who sought to draw close to us (Heniek and I). He was also apparently the one who really managed matters in the factory.

All the managers of the cooperative were Jews. By contrast, the workers were non-Jews, born there and in the surrounding area. The manager of the cooperative and the chairwoman was Comrade Zifina. She was an example of social promotion, Soviet style. She belonged to the old guard of the revolutionaries (which somehow still survived in the Jewish surroundings), barely knew how to read the annual report of the factory's activities, which was written by the head of the supply department. She was a woman of about sixty years old or more. She guarded the property of the factory like a chicken guarding her chicks. Yet it is difficult to say to what extent she knew about the real economic state of the factory. The annual reports, which she could barely understand, were promising (remember the reports by Lasik Roitschwantz, the rabbit breeder, hero of Iliya Ehrenburg's novel?). Comrade Zifina was a woman with a good heart, never did wrong to a soul, and apparently was very honest. She was old and lonely.

The manager of the department was a Jewish woman. She was energetic, professional, with a Jewish heart. She did not want to see how some of the spool tenders cheated her when weighing the cotton, and she saved me from a trial. She may have even saved my life.

In those years in the Soviet Union there was a law against those who were late or did not show up for work (protiv letushchikom i progulschchikom). This was a cruel law, because being ten minutes late to work, or missing one day's work without a doctor's certificate, caused the worker to be put on trial. The punishment was often exile to a work camp. I was among the most disciplined. Once it happened that I was due to be at my machine at 6 a.m., but I woke up late and ran to work in panic (I had a good excuse—I suffered from bad migraines). When I reached the factory, I found that the clock said exactly six. The work manager, a warm hearted

Jewish woman, and Heniek were more scared than I was. The manager came running toward me, calling out:

"How do you feel? How is your migraine? At least you are not late."

Heniek was as white as chalk from worry. Both had decided, as I found out, that she would move the clock back, because I was already about twenty minutes late. This could have cost the manager her life (not to mention what could have happened to me).

After my first day working in the factory, when I left, I stood at the gate and the guards tried to search my person. I was in shock. I shouted, "Get your hands off me, I won't let myself be searched!" I caused a disturbance, and the guards called their superior. When the superior arrived, I explained to him that I am a proud worker from Łódź and I know about workers' rights. At the end of the nineteenth century there were strikes in Łódź regarding this, and since then, female workers did not have to undergo body searches. "And here, in the homeland of the workers, surely it is impossible for such things to happen." After conversations with the management and "my" young officer, who was the politruk in our factory, I won the battle. Since then and until the end of my work, I was not searched.

Life in the town was pretty simple and monotonous. We lacked small, everyday things like a needle to sew a button on a shirt, like socks; instead of toilet paper we used newspapers (which was not nice or hygienic); instead of a paper or a plastic bag to wrap salted fish, bread, and other things, we used newspaper. Newspapers served many purposes. The most popular newspaper was the daily *Pravda*. At first, I was surprised that people were so excited to read this important and central paper. It took me a while to understand the real, more prosaic, motivations. This was the biggest newspaper in terms of size, and it was useful for wrapping things. We lacked many basic products, and this was explained by the extended war with the "great power" Finland. Nonetheless, the Soviet citizens considered 1939 a good year in terms of the provision of food.

However, I was not pampered, I did not complain about the lack. There was a rich choice of bread (later, I would dream of the bread we ate in Bobruisk).

We were a rather large group of young men and women, most refugees from Łódź. We had our own life. We met at the workers' club next to the wood-processing factory (Lesozavod), where a large group of our friends worked.

The factory was a few kilometers from the city. The work in the factory was difficult. It was mostly outside, on the bank of the river, where the temperature dropped to minus 30 degrees in winter. Also, the food there was not as good as the food we were given in our cooperative.

By contrast, I liked the workers' dormitories next to the factory. I even envied the workers that lived in them. The rooms were small, but each room had two residents, while I lived with a family with children and had no privacy or a corner of my own. No one who worked in the city had his own room. There were shared facilities, including laundry, toilets, kitchen, and so on, for every floor. On every floor there was a Red Corner (Krasnyi ugolok), where it was possible to sit and read. There were books and journals, it was nice to sit there, to prepare lessons, to learn. To learn. . .

This factory, which employed thousands of workers, had a permanent elementary-level night school for workers. At our request, they also opened a Russian language course for us, the refugees, with the possibility of also opening high-school-level studies. A few times a week, Heniek and I walked many kilometers from the center of the city to this school. The teacher, a Jewish woman, was interested in our lives in Poland. During our breaks we sang songs in Yiddish and she melted with joy. We sang about the heroes of the Spanish Civil War, about which she knew nothing (we did not know then that this was dangerous for us in the Soviet Union) and other songs in Yiddish.

I will never forget these evenings, in particular the way to school and back in the winter. We wondered at the beauty all around us.

Imagine the picture: an unending expanse of white snow with a tint of yellow and dark blue from the sky and moon that were reflected in it. Here and there a lone white tree struggled in the wind and cold. In the distance, lights twinkled from low houses under roofs heaped with white snow, almost melting into the white surface of the land. Here and there, from inside, as though from within the snow, a light twinkled from windows and smoke rose from chimneys. You see something similar in pictures on Christmas cards, but here everything was real, infinite, and amazingly, breathtakingly beautiful. We absorbed the magical beauty of our surroundings. I, wearing my thin coat and summer shoes in which I had left Łódź, sunk into the snow up to my knees. When I got home, my socks and shoes were wet. I had to dry them on the Russian oven. At 6 a.m. I had to be standing at the machine in the factory. Yet this was an unforgettable experience and I never thought of missing it. In particular, when I was twenty and beside me was a besotted young man who warmed my frozen hands.

At the evening meetings in the factory's club, we had political arguments; sometimes they were heated. Things occurred that I only understood a long time afterward. Adam, the young man of German origin from Łódź that I already mentioned, who left Łódź together with us, disappeared one day and no one heard from him again. We thought he had fled, but his girlfriend denied it, saying it was impossible. Her suspicion was apparently correct, and naturally she was worried and nervous. The arguments concerning Adam's disappearance became more and more heated. In the air hovered the question: What is happening? No one could understand or guess what we found out years later.

In that winter of 1939, we discovered additional sides of life in the Soviet Union that horrified us innocents. Among us, the refugees from Łódź, were a pair of friends. The man's name was Lastman. He was known by his underground name Murzyn (Negro) and many knew him in Łódź as a Communist in his heart and soul. In Łódź there were legends about his bravery, his good qualities, etc. His girlfriend was called Jadzia. I met them only in Bobruisk. Just as Murzyn was short, dark skinned like an Ethiopian, with glimmering black eyes and curly black hair, so his girlfriend was the complete opposite: tall, blonde, pale-skinned, with blue eyes. She was beautiful and he, one could say, the opposite.

Murzyn was a baker by profession, an expert in making pastries. In Bobruisk he was given work in a factory that baked sweet butter rolls. Once, after he had been working there a while, he came to us perturbed by something. He told us about the strange behavior in his bakery. One day, before finishing work, the workers came to him with a large sack full of sugar and a decent-sized package of butter, telling him this was his share. He asked what and why. In response, he was told that one doesn't ask such stupid questions. Murzyn did not want to take the good things and said he did not deserve it. Quickly, he began to understand what was happening in the bakery underneath his nose.

What happened in the bakery was pretty simple: a certain amount of butter and sugar was allocated for one series of sweet butter rolls according to the standard recipe. The bakers put into the baked goods only half the amount of these products and divided the other half themselves (certainly not equally). Here I should add that these ingredients could not be found in state-run shops, and on the black market their prices were so high that few could afford them.

Murzyn came to us and asked for our advice: How should he fight the bribery and theft? What idealists we were then! As refugees from Łódź, with paragraph 38 written on our IDs, we still did not know that this paragraph meant that we were untrustworthy. We decided to fight the evil in the Soviet Union. We collected money to fund Murzyn's journey to Minsk (the capital of Byelorussia) to enable him to reach at least the head secretary of the Central Committee of the Communist Party in White Russia (KPSB) and tell him what was happening under his watch. Murzyn did indeed reach the secretary, who received him warmly and cheerfully and talked to him at length. Regarding the matter itself, he admitted that the system was helpless and there was no chance they would be able to fight effectively against the bribery and theft, as long as there were not enough civilian customers coming to the state-run shops every day. Until that happened, they had to agree to the existence of the black market.

The head secretary of the KPSB was no fool.

Murzyn came back to Bobruisk and told us everything. He failed to change anything, but he lost his workplace. Murzyn's case was a warning for me. Whoever was able and did not want to get dirty and enter into moral decline needed to avoid any work connected with corruption. This was not an easy path. Murzyn also chose a more difficult life, to the dissatisfaction of his girlfriend.

After some time, I had the pleasure of hosting the couple in Simferopol (the capital of the Crimean Peninsula). He had to leave Bobruisk because no bakery would employ him. At first, he came alone, rented space with a family, and found some kind of work (I don't remember where). When Jadzia arrived, she lived with me, until they found a suitable place for them to live together. I had the opportunity to get to know them up close and see their less flattering side. I was then living with an old Jewish woman who had, as I found out, a rather rich food supply (jars of butter and oil, jams, confitures, etc.), because this good-hearted woman was always waiting for the arrival of her only son, an officer in the Red Army. I lived with her for quite a while and even I had no idea about her stock of jars. I never thought to take an interest in it. Jadzia was apparently hungry. The times were hard. I shared with her what I ate, but evidently this was not enough for her. One day the old lady showed me her empty jars. It was hard for me to hear her complaints and listen to her detail how hard she had worked to obtain this store, which was disappearing. This was not the only incident.

One day, when I came home from work, I went to take out my books and notebooks and run to school (I will talk about my studies elsewhere). However, the drawer was empty. Jadzia admitted that she had sold my books because she needed money. "You," she said, "you do not need to learn when others don't have money." I asked her if her husband knew about this, and she burst out laughing.

I was sorry that I spoke to Murzyn about his wife's actions. These things hastened her departure from my apartment. I was sorry that I lost a connection with a good friend. I do not feel any hatred toward her. The conditions were indeed difficult, but I did not understand why she did not work. In Simferopol anyone could find work. Apparently, what her husband made was not sufficient.

To end the story of Murzyn and Jadzia briefly, I think that this couple underwent some kind of crisis. When the war between Russia and Germany broke out in June 1941, both of them fled Simferopol together with the rest of the population and institutions. Murzyn came to bid me goodbye. I never saw him again. I know that he joined the Kościuszko Polish Army and died in a tank together with all its crew, to avoid falling into the hands of the Germans. I was told that The Internationale was heard coming from the burning tank. Such a death suited Murzyn, who was pure to the end. At least he was saved from disappointments and emotional crises such as the ones we went through later.

After a few years, my husband Heniek showed me a letter he had received from Jadzia. She had written it while in Simferopol. In it, she claimed I was having an affair with her husband. Murzyn and I had no idea about it. Heniek himself did not take it seriously.

Jadzia appeared one more time at our home in Łódź after the war. She tried to avoid reminding me of what happened in Simferopol. And I, by my silence, responded with good will. She married someone else, lived in Sweden, and tried to help me. I have had no contact with her for about thirty years.

Again I have jumped forward. I will go back to my experiences in Bobruisk.

In life, nothing comes free. Even pleasant experiences and moments of spiritual elevation. The walk to Lesovozavod, many kilometers there and back in snow that reached our knees, and without suitable clothing, led to an infection of my thigh tendon (sciatica) which caused me terrible pain. The doctor did not want to give me a medical certificate to let me off work for even one day. There are no external signs of this illness. "Maybe you are faking?" he declared.

Therefore, I went to work. The work at the spooling machine with its twenty-six or thirty-six spools, between which I was constantly moving, tying knots in the torn threads, was difficult enough for a healthy spool tender. However, I was really sick, and I was suffering. With all my strength I tried not to faint from the pain. However, when the workday was over, I could not walk home. Heniek took me straight to the cinema that was a few paces from our workplace.

In Soviet Russia all the public buildings were grandiose. The shops were expensive and comfortable, albeit empty, and in the large and ostentatious display windows of the butchers' shops, for example, were beautiful sausages of all kinds, fresh, red cuts of beef and pork. However, they were fake, they were not edible. Cinemas were comfortable, the anteroom was spacious, and it had armchairs for the public and a band that made the waiting pleasant, as well as a food stand. Most of the Soviet movies were political and were intended for brainwashing, but there were also good films. For us, at that moment, the movies were not necessary; rather, I needed to sit and rest, to gather strength so that I would somehow be able to make it home. Once, Heniek took me there, sat me in the armchair, and went to buy something from the food stand. A man standing next to him expressed his sympathy that he had a disabled wife.

Personal experiences of a different kind are tied up with Bobruisk. In 1939–1940, the law of a five-day workweek was still in force, and the sixth day was a rest day. That means, we worked

166

on Sabbaths and festivals if this day was included in our five days of work. However, it also happened that we did not work on the Sabbath. Then we walked around the city a bit, between the Jewish alleys. Here it was like the revolution had changed nothing. From a one-story wooden house, especially in the summer, when the windows were open, I heard on Sabbath mornings a tune so familiar that it hurt, making me stop in my tracks. This was the tune of reading from the Talmud, a tune with which I grew up in my parents' home. I woke to this tune on Sabbath mornings and went to sleep listening to my father singing it. I stood for a long time on the spot and longing choked me. I thought in my heart about the secret it held. Indeed, Końskie was thousands of kilometers from Bobruisk; the Jews from these two towns had never met. And yet, despite everything, despite all the upheavals and the change of regimes, here, in the faraway Jewish town, I heard the same tune, the same cadence of studying the Talmud that I heard when my father sat and learned a page of the Talmud. I saw before me images from my childhood. Even the smells, the smells of the Sabbath, were the same as those of my childhood in Końskie.

One day in the spring of 1940, my sister Shoshana appeared. I knew that she, her husband, and her young son were somewhere in Siberia. I had managed to make contact with them. Shoshana's letters were sad, and I tried without success to get them out of there. And now she stood in front of me. My happiness knew no bounds. Finally, we would be together. However, after the embraces and kisses, she announced that she had only come for a few hours to see me and take her leave, because Moshe and her son, together with a group of a few other people who had fled Siberia, were waiting for her in Minsk and they planned to go back to Poland. She told me that in this group were Alter and Ethel Goldberg, the brother and sister of Yitche, our sister-in-law.

I was shocked. Shoshana, as I noted, was a mother and a big sister to me, the person closest to me, the person I loved best. Esther was in Palestine; my relatives and loved ones—father and the rest of the family—were living under the Nazi occupation. I could not let Shoshana and her family leave. I had a deep feeling that if I let her go, I would never see her again. I gathered all my resources and thinking power. I used Heniek and other good people. I went with her to the clothing factory that was in the same area as our factory, and there they immediately invited her to work for them. I invited her to the dining hall of the factory (which was shared with the workers of Shveiprom, the sewing industry), and they gave her lunch. I bought her an excellent ice cream, etc. We tried to show her that it was possible to get by in Bobruisk, to make a life there. We did somersaults to show her the town in a more positive light than it really deserved. I knew then that if I would succeed in delaying her for a day or two, her husband and son would join her. The main thing—I managed to persuade her, and she did not return to Minsk. After two days, my brother-in-law Moshe and little Naftali, to whom I was so close, arrived. And after that, they stayed with me. The rest of the group returned to Poland and were murdered by the Nazis.

We were together again. We rented a room from "Aunt" Zenia, a woman of Polish origin whose husband had disappeared (like many others) without a trace. She lived with her only son, who became a small-time thief. Zenia never told us about her husband.

At the beginning of my stay in Bobruisk, I still had a connection with my father in Poland. I even sent them two modest food packages and received letters from them. These letters were sad. My brother Meir was caught by the Germans and taken for work to Majdanek. He returned home because this extermination camp was still under construction. My father wrote that Meir returned bloated and sick. Meir managed to marry. His last letter was long and heartbreaking. He confessed to me that he had wasted his life in an ultra-orthodox yeshiva instead of learning about life. He was sorry that he had not wanted to listen to us, because then maybe he would have been able to save himself. This was a difficult confession for a young man, twenty years old, who knew for sure that the world was now closed to him, and maybe also his life was over. This was followed by a long silence. We received no news about what had happened in Poland or to the Jews during all the years of the war.

Separation from Heniek—Simferopol

Naftali was the main reason that his parents fled Siberia. He was their only son, and my sister was willing to sacrifice her life for her loved ones. The doctors advised them to move to the southern Soviet Union, where the air was warm and healthier and should benefit him. They decided to try to move to Crimea. It was decided that Moshe, my brother-in-law, would travel to Simferopol, the capital of Crimea, and look for work there. He left in September 1940. From his first letters it was clear that life was easier; it was possible to make a living there. He began working and looked for a suitable apartment for his family. Shoshana started to prepare for the journey.

And what about me?

I did not want to part with Shoshana and her family. I had other personal motives too when I decided to accompany them to Simferopol.

I was then already twenty-three years old, and my personal life was still complicated: I was confused, burdened with complexes, like in the past. I had not matured over the years. Heniek was my closest friend, but was that enough to build a family? In addition, we were both innocent, and in terms of sexual relations we were really childish. We tried to live together, but we did not know how to manage it. And the conditions! We found a room, a closed balcony that was an addition to an original apartment. Only one wall, which was the external wall of the kitchen belonging to the apartment, was not covered in ice. The cooperative at which we both worked gave us a straw mattress and a thin blanket. At night we covered ourselves with all our poor clothes and froze. The only furniture in the room was a narrow iron bed and a kitchen table. That was it. In these conditions, I got the infection in the tendon, sciatica, that I mentioned.

After a month or two of living "together," when Shoshana's family arrived, I went to live with them and Heniek returned to his former residence. In the evenings, he sat in our home until late at night, even when I was already asleep, and Moshe had to ask him to leave. So it was every evening. I felt that I had to put an end to it, at least for the time being. I knew that he loved me with a first, impassioned love. But could I return his love? Apart from all the difficulties involved in this, I had a clear personal goal: I wanted to exploit the opportunities of free studies in night schools, which were common in the Soviet Union. Heniek, by contrast, was not enthusiastic about studying.

After a conversation with Heniek that was far from simple, in which I asked him to understand and told him that I wanted to maintain our friendship, we decided to keep in touch by letter, hoping that time would work its magic. I accompanied him to the train. He left Bobruisk with sadness in his eyes. Heniek went to Ivanovo-Voznesensk (in the central region of Russia). Shoshana, Naftali, and I waited for Moshe to call for us to come to Simferopol.

The winter of 1940 was harsh. In Bobruisk the temperatures dropped to minus 30–35 degrees. Bobruisk was covered in a thick layer of snow and frost. The window panes of the houses were decorated with wonderful pictures, frost pictures. When the weak sun briefly broke through the heavy clouds and spread its rays of light, the frost pictures on the window panes were tinted yellow and became fairytale scenes. In my imagination, I saw a magical and wonderfully beautiful world.

In those days, the long-awaited letter from Moshe arrived, asking us to come to Simferopol. We packed our few belongings in a few sacks and brought them to the Bobruisk train station. There, after an inspection, it was necessary to write our address on the packed sacks. Our hands were frozen, and we could barely fill out the forms. We got on the train. Finally, we set off.

During the journey from north to south through infinite expanses, which took a few days, we went from frost to blooming spring. It is hard for me to remember anything about the landscapes that fled past like a movie, in particular because, for the first part of the journey, the windows of the train were covered with a thick layer of frost. However, near the city of Dnipropetrovsk (in Southern Ukraine, on the Dnieper River) the frost on the train windows began to melt slowly. We opened the windows, and, after a few more hours traveling, a pre-spring wind blew into the wagon. It was unbelievable: two or three days previously, we had left the harsh winter of minus 30 degrees, and now it was almost spring. At the train station in Dnipropetrovsk, women with baskets entered and sold fresh, springtime apples. With every additional hour of travel, our wonder at the changes in nature increased.

When we arrived in Simferopol, we were met not only by Moshe but by the blossoming spring of the Crimean Peninsula in all its beauty. In January! The city was immersed in green and sunlight. After Bobruisk, it seemed like Eden. Instead of going to see the apartment that Moshe had arranged for us, and without thinking very much, we set out to explore this wonderful city. This was Simferopol—the south-western showcase of the Soviet Union.

Moshe had arranged a nice, private apartment (meaning, without other tenants) that was made up of one room and a small kitchenette. Leading up to the entrance were a few stairs, and before them a yard in which stood a few lemon trees, and under them a bench. In the evening, the yard came to life. There, in Crimea, the yards played a significant role in the lives of family and neighbors. Life was open. I found a place to live in the same courtyard, in the home of an old Jewish woman who lived alone in an organized, beautiful apartment. I lived on a large balcony, all closed in with colored glass. This woman, as I already mentioned, had an only son, an officer in the Red Army. She was very proud of him, but the entire time I lived in the apartment, I never met him. She was in a good situation. I believe that in comparison to the standard of living in Bobruisk and in other cities in Byelorussia or the Urals, life in Simferopol was much easier and better. And this was not only in Simferopol, but, as I saw in the war, also in the southern Caucasus.

Simferopol, the capital of the Crimean Peninsula, was populated by many national minorities, but the Tartars constituted the majority. Apart from them, there were Russians, Ukrainians, Tajiks, Jews, and other minorities. In the 1930s, the city's population was around 40,000 people, among them about 20 percent were Jews (in the entire Crimean Peninsula there were around 17,500 Jews). In the city there were no large industrial factories. The main industry was food processing, canned goods, wines (in the city and the surroundings there were vineyards and orchards). A few metal factories made the machines and equipment for the local industry. There were small factories making clothing, confections, etc. At the same time, there was no problem finding work. There was a factory for clothing and underwear, "the sewing industry" (Shveiprom), which had a few departments spread throughout the city. We went there looking for work.

Shoshana was accepted to work in the underwear department. When I came to the factory office to ask for work, I was taken to a manager named Portnoy. This Jew looked at me and asked:

"My girl, do you know how to work?"

I replied that I had been working since the age of twelve, and among the professions I had learned, I had also been a seamstress. He took my hands, turned them over to look at both sides, and declared:

"These beautiful hands have never worked. Here we do not lie."

I could do nothing but smile. At that moment, distant pictures from my childhood flooded my memory: when I was between the ages of ten and thirteen, living in my hometown of Końskie. I suddenly remembered one Thursday.

My normal days began at five in the morning. By eight, meaning, before I ran to school, I had to make my bed, which was quite complicated, bring five buckets of water from the well—the water pump at the corner of the road—to fill the barrel, bring wood, and start the fire in the oven (and twice a week, as I mentioned, I gave a lesson in reading and writing to the neighborhood's dairy woman). In addition, on Thursdays I had to polish and clean the wooden floors, and after all this, had to run to school. In the afternoon, I ran to the seamstress who was teaching me to sew. And one Thursday in June, while polishing the floor in the room in which my father's wife was still sleeping, I did not notice that in a corner, under the children's chair, was a clay pan full of cucumbers together with water and pickling agents, covered by a large stone. The brush that I was using touched the pot, the stone fell, and the contents began to spill. Silently, so as not to wake my stepmother, I moved the contents from the broken pot to another one, I finished cleaning the floors and ran to the dairy woman to give the lesson. She noticed that I was red and scared and asked me what had happened. After I told her, the girl, who knew what would happen when the woman woke, advised me to forget about the lesson and run to school. So I did. After school, in my great fear, I did not go home but straight to the seamstress who was teaching me to sew. She lived at the edge of a large courtyard. The seamstress gave me something to eat, and I started to work. I knew that hell awaited me at home. However, my stepmother did not wait for me to come home. After a while, I heard her screams in the courtyard. She could not reach me, because there were young people and children in the yard who blocked her way and sent her away.

"My hands have never worked?"

The water pump close to our house was beyond the corner, quite a distance from our house. The buckets were almost the same height as me, and their handles cut into the skin on my hands, especially in the winter, until I bled. Not to mention how Esther and I fought to work, in Łódź, while living with "Aunt" Yocheved, when our hands were bloated from the cold.

I did not tell Mr. Portnoy these stories. However, I asked him to give me a chance to prove myself. He agreed and sent me to the dress department.

In truth, I had never sewn dresses and I was scared. I was always scared when I started working in a new place, but now my fear had a basis. In addition, two young women, refugees from Poland, worked in this department. On my first day, they took me for lunch break and began to fire questions at me which I could not answer, because I had never sewed dresses.

"If you've never sewn dresses, you can't work with us. You have a problem," they declared.

My fear increased. However, it seemed that these girls wanted to show off in front of me and scare me, and therefore they told me about their jobs in the exclusive firms in Warsaw, etc. The fear accompanied me in my work in the first days, but after the first week they were ashamed to look me in the eye.

In the dress department there were two types of production: dresses made to order, which were sewn in the atelier, where a few experienced seamstresses worked, and dresses for mass consumption (readymade). These two girls worked in the latter with around another ten women, and I also had to work there. The work manager, an authoritative Russian woman, received piles of material cut into parts and divided the work between the seamstresses so that each one sewed a certain part (in a conveyor belt system). Eventually, without knowing or intending it, I caused a rise in the daily norms and output. To a certain extent, this hurt not only the two girls from Poland but all the seamstresses, and the one who had previously been a Stachanovite. There was no need to make a particular effort in Soviet Russia in order to be a Stachanovite. The output was low in comparison to Poland because there were no incentives to really work.

The celebrations of May 1 that I saw in Simferopol were unique. As I mentioned, in this city there were a lot of national minorities.

I stood among them watching the parade, at the side of the main road. The weather was wonderful. On both sides of the street, trees blossomed in a range of colors, as though merging with the colors of the parade that passed, people walking and dancing down the middle of the street, and everything seemed like masses of colorful flowers from which red flags protruded. Each national group was dressed in traditional colorful clothing, decorated with garlands of flowers, and with their own dancers. This was a beautiful and unique sight. I saw such a parade only once in my life, in Simferopol.

I kept in touch with Heniek by letter. We wrote frequently, each of us describing his or her life in the new place. I also wrote to some of my friends from Łódź who were spread out in various places in the Soviet Union. Some of them came to me after I wrote to them about the pleasant climate and the possibility of making a living in the city. Thus, Murzyn and his wife arrived, as I mentioned earlier, as well as Alter Wieluński and his wife, and Moshe Boim, a large, strange young man, an acquaintance of Alter, who came to me with a large horsemeat sausage and, on the spot, with complete decisiveness, wanted me to go with him to the ZAKS (the office in which civil marriages were conducted). I opened the door and asked him to leave, together with his horsemeat sausage. During the war and the terrible hunger, people ate only horsemeat sausages.

I met Moshe Boim in Łódź, I think in 1947, at the train station. He was accompanied by a Russian and a woman and I invited them to visit. He sat in our home for many hours and told us about his life after Simferopol. He was in prison and was sent to forced labor camps and liberated only a few weeks before we met. Why? Because someone was quicker than him (and ran to inform the authorities about something that someone said).

I think that in the south of the Soviet Union, including Crimea, among the various national minorities, the oppression and persecution of minorities by the Soviet regime were felt less strongly, as we felt during the war and after it. For example, although I was a refugee and my ID papers contained paragraph 38, which marked me as untrustworthy, I was approached and asked to join the Communist Youth Movement Komsomol. There, in Simferopol, it was important for them, the members of the Communist Party in the factory, that an excellent worker should belong to their ranks. I responded positively and became a member of the Komsomol. This was later. When the war broke out and most of the members of the municipal Komsomol joined the army, I too asked to volunteer and approached the municipal committee of the Komsomol to ask for its support. The general secretary of the organization sat alone; the rooms were empty. She asked me to come to work with her until the situation would become clear. She recommended me to the Recruitment Office, and I worked with her for a few weeks, until it was necessary to evacuate the office and the head secretary.

The most important event in my life in Simferopol was that I registered for high school evening classes immediately upon arrival. This was the best year for me in the Soviet Union. I passed the exam for ninth grade; according to the system then in place in the Soviet Union, ten classes were needed for a matriculation certificate. I was the first to come to class, and the teacher asked me to sit in a certain place. There was another young man who looked older than me. He welcomed me in Polish and introduced himself: his name was Yosef Goldberg. He also intended to study rapidly and take the matriculation exams at an accelerated pace, so we decided to take extra classes together with private teachers. One teacher for math and physics, while we studied the rest of the subjects with another teacher. I studied very intensively, and I almost managed to realize my dream of gaining a high school certificate.

CHAPTER 5
IN THE PATH OF THE WAR

From Perekop to the Kerch Strait

Our Shveiprom sewing factory organized a three-day trip to Alushta to reward the best workers (Stachanovites). It was June 17 or 18, 1941. Approximately one hundred people, mainly women, went on the trip. Around a dozen people were chosen from each department, among them also Shoshana, who was one of the excellent workers in the undergarments department.

I did not know anything then about the beauty of Crimea beyond Simferopol. (In the near future I would get to know all of it on foot). Alushta lies on the southeast side of the Crimean Peninsula, a little higher than Yalta, a well-known holiday resort on the shore of the Black Sea. Alushta's advantage is its special location. It lies on the cliffs of the Crimean Mountains, which are also the seashore. When you stand on the edge of the cliff, you feel its height above sea level. From here—a massive rock wall; from there—somewhere in the depths, the waves of the sea rise up and crest. On the south horizon before you is the endless sea; when you turn around, before you is a chain of mountains that is breathtaking in its beauty. We arrived in the evening, so Shoshana and I encountered these sights only the next morning, wondering about them over the coming days. On the night we arrived, we saw only the tip of the mountain on which we stood, on it a wide flat field full of white tents that had been prepared for us. There was also a restaurant, in which we ate dinner, and afterward there was music and dancing. Shoshana and I were given a tent and went to rest.

I slept, and I was woken by Shoshana calling me, as though in panic. She was outside the tent. It was still almost dark. When I left the tent, my heart stopped beating. We held hands and looked at the sun rising as its first rays appeared gradually over the tops of the trees and spread out, touching the horizon of the sea under us and made everything turn red—the trees, the tips of the mountains, the sea. The Black Sea. We discovered the secret behind the name of this sea: the rocks of the mountain and the low trees are reflected in the sea's surface in dark colors, almost black. Slowly, the sun rose and revealed to us the magical sight. We stood in silence, caught up in amazement. For the three days that we stayed in Alushta, we were in a euphoria of wonder at the sunrises and sunsets and the wonderful views. We went on hikes in the surroundings, and we forgot all the sorrows in the world, including the Germans and the war.

We returned to Simferopol late at night. I was tired and very emotional. I went to bed and immediately fell into a deep sleep. I was woken the next day by a noise in the courtyard. People were talking, arguing. I did not try to find the cause of the noise. I got dressed and went to work. On the way, I noticed that people were very excited about something, stopping next to loudspeakers to hear announcements. I did not see or hear anything, as if I was still sleeping, or as if I was still in magical Alushta. I only woke up when I got to work and saw the fear in the eyes of the workers, all crowding together, and the crying women.

I discovered that on the night of our return, June 22, 1941, German planes had bombed Simferopol, and I slept through it, sleeping the sleep of the righteous. At eight in the morning, we heard Molotov's speech, which informed us that German forces had invaded all along the Soviet border.

None of the residents of Simferopol could understand the meaning of the German Blitzkrieg. Only those who had experienced it, the refugees from Poland, like me, knew the truth. The Nazi army was chasing me. There was nowhere left to flee. I had to decide what to do.

In the meeting of all the workers that day, Comrade Portnoy, the head of the cooperative, gave a speech. He brought with him a large map and hung it on the wall. With complete certainty, he showed those present, like a great strategist, how the Red Army would defeat the Nazi Hydra on German soil within a few days. This was a concept well-known from the big placards showing a burly Soviet soldier, accompanied by an extract from a popular song: "If war will break out tomorrow" (Iesli zavtra voina, iesli zavtra pakhod). This song was sung at processions, we heard it on the loudspeakers in the streets and blasting from the "plates" in every home.[1]

I do not intend to describe the development of the war, because the facts are known. In the first days of the war, Simferopol wore many faces. The Jews panicked, and many of them planned to evacuate. They were among the first to leave the city, together with the Russian officials and the factories with their workers, institutions of the regime and the Party, and most of the Russian population. The authorities encouraged the evacuation and helped the evacuees with transportation. By contrast, among the Tartars and the Tajiks, there were differences of opinion. Many were even happy to see the Germans' arrival.

I decided not to flee anymore and instead to volunteer for the army, to fight the Germans in the lines of the Red Army. I should note that in Simferopol, apart from work and general studies, I took nursing courses. My dream was to learn medicine.

---

1 The "plates" replaced the forbidden radio receivers.

Until now, I had managed to a certain extent to get by in Soviet Russia. However, now, with paragraph 38 in my ID, I did not have much hope of being accepted into the army. I decided to seek help from my connections. As I already mentioned, in those days I helped the general secretary of the municipal committee of the Komsomol. I approached her, and she promised to help me. She called someone and the Recruitment Office accepted me on her recommendation. However, before leaving, I needed to take a crash course on practical work in the battlefield.

The city was in a state of chaos: buses, trucks, and pick-up trucks filled with people and soldiers left every day. Shoshana and her family again intended to leave, without knowing where they would go. Again, they prepared the sacks with their possessions. They begged me to go with them. It was hard for us to part. I helped them get into the truck, and we parted with tears, not knowing if we would ever meet again. I waited for my call-up papers. Our courtyard had almost entirely emptied. I moved into Shoshana and Moshe's old apartment for the meantime. My classes in school stopped, but the nursing courses took on new form and content. A group of nineteen girls of recruitment age, I among them, all intending to join the army, prepared to work in the conditions of the battlefield and war. We studied for twelve hours every day, and we also studied in the city hospital.

In those days, which were full of tension, something personal happened that one could see as quite romantic. However, I will mention it from a different perspective. As I said, the city was very quiet. It was evening, I was sitting at home, and suddenly someone knocked on my door. At the entrance stood my colleague from my high school class, with whom I had studied with private teachers for the matriculation exams, Goldberg. At the beginning of our acquaintance, he had tried to flirt with me quite aggressively, and with similar aggression he received a negative response. Since then, we had barely spoken, and we had not met outside of lessons.

As I noted, he was a few years older than me, good looking, blond (blonds always followed me), his enthusiastic face with its large, Jewish nose expressed self-confidence. In those days, full of tension while I was waiting for recruitment, I rarely thought about school. And my dreams of a matriculation certificate had gone up in smoke. I had completely forgotten about Goldberg's existence. Now, he stood before me in the doorway, and before I could say a word, he beat me to it:

"I know that you won't let me in. Let's go out. I want to talk to you."

I went out, and we sat on the bench in the courtyard. He was serious and worried. He asked me to run away from the city with him because the Germans were approaching Crimea. He tried to persuade me that he always had serious intentions toward me, that I had misunderstood him. He spoke seriously:

"Now, I want us to go together. I knew that we were meant for each other from the first moment we met."

Who knows? Had I not been waiting for my call-up papers and been intent on going to the army, perhaps I would have responded positively. When I told him that I was waiting to be called up and that my documents were already there, he was shocked. He was really scared. He described to me what happened to girls in the army, how they were treated, and he said that I, with my dissenting approach, would suffer terribly. Apart from that, he emphasized another two points that could be dangerous for me: as a Jew and a refugee, my superiors would treat me with suspicion, and I would suffer doubly.

I, sure of myself to an exaggerated extent in these matters, did not want to hear his warnings. He came a few more times and tried to persuade me to go with him. Eventually, he disappeared. I never saw him again. However, I must admit that all his warnings about how they would treat me in the army were correct and wise, perhaps even more than that.

A few days passed and I received a notice to report immediately to the Recruitment Office. I took a few personal things, a bundle of letters and pictures, and reported for duty. There, another seventeen girls were waiting to go with me. They gave me the documents for all the girls, put us on a truck, and we set off. We traveled north to Perekop. This was a narrow strip, an isthmus eight kilometers wide, connecting the Crimean Peninsula with the Ukrainian mainland. We reached a certain point in the open country and got off the truck. Someone showed me where the commander was to be found.

The brigade commander, an older man whose hair was streaked with gray, looked at me and asked, "Are they now sending girls to the army? How old are you, little girl?"

I stood to attention and answered, "Twenty-three, sir."

"Don't lie! Are all the other girls so young?"

I gave him the papers. He commanded one of his officers to take us to a certain unit. There, in the field, soldiers were sitting in a circle, and someone was talking to them. The appearance of seventeen young women caused the soldiers to chuckle. They ordered us to join them and sit down. It was a quiet night. The unit commander told us that not far from this place, a few kilometers away, were German army units. Thus, it was necessary to act with caution and be quiet. It was forbidden to light fires. In the morning, they would divide us among various brigades. They told us, the young women, to gather in one place and sleep. We received no equipment. That night, we slept under the open sky. The bags containing our personal effects served as pillows. We gathered around a tree in the field and lay down. I could not sleep. After a short while, it was completely quiet, and then I heard explosions from afar. At some point, I felt that I was alone under the tree; the other women had disappeared. I looked around and saw them enjoying themselves with the soldiers.

In the morning, we were divided among the various brigades. I, together with a few more women, was sent to an infantry brigade.

I do not remember the number, but in some corner of my mind is the number 178. There, each one of us was sent to a different battalion of the same brigade. I found myself in an infantry battalion. I was to open a mobile station to help injured soldiers, to accompany them in battle, to evacuate under fire the injured, and provide first aid. I was to evacuate the severely injured to a field hospital. This was in theory my role as a saninstruktor. The reality was very different.

I did not manage to hold on for long in this battalion. I remember two main encounters. In both I failed. There, in Perekop, the Germans had launched an offensive. The commander of my unit tried to lead his soldiers to liberate a certain point from the Germans. He led us to open country, to a field that had been harvested. Here and there were still lying piles of produce. No tree, bush, or vegetation could serve as camouflage for our soldiers. We were ordered to advance, crawling, to the other side of the field. I crawled along with the soldiers. At a distance of a few hundred meters, I saw open-topped armored vehicles full of German soldiers with machine guns aimed at the crawling soldiers. The latter were armed only with a simple Russian rifle (vintovka). I could see the laughing faces of the Germans. They waited until the first lines were close to them. Suddenly I understood (I, ignorant in matters of warfare) that we were in a trap. All hope was lost: this operation had been planned from the outset without thought. I turned to look back. Far behind us, our commander was hiding under a pile of crops.

Suddenly, the Germans began to shoot with their automatic weapons. Our soldiers understood that they needed to crawl back. Then I was grasped by terrible fear, fear that paralyzed my legs and spread through my entire body and I could not move. I was not scared of death. I was scared of falling into the hands of the Germans; that was what paralyzed me. The soldiers fled. One of them, thinking I was wounded, lifted me up and helped me flee under fire. My shame knew no bounds. The soldier who lifted me up apparently understood my situation and helped me onto the truck together with the wounded and then I gave them first aid.

This was my first baptism by fire. It was strange. Afterward, I was among the only ones in the medical unit who did not flee into a trench during the canon bombings or the air bombardments, when the Germans left barely a meter of land untouched, but ran among the soldiers and commanders providing medical aid. However, then I did not see the faces of the German soldiers. Their proximity was what caused my paralysis. I was afraid of the Germans, apparently this was because of the scenes I had experienced in Łódź and during the flight from occupied Poland. More than once I had to provide first aid to an injured German soldier who was captured. To do so, I had to tell him to his face that I, a Jew, was saving his life.

The second time that I failed was when we arrived in a certain place and, according to my orders, I was to open a first aid station for soldiers in an abandoned house. I did not even manage to unpack the supplies that I had been given before the artillery and air bombardment began, and immediately I was surrounded by masses of injured and severely incapacitated people. I provided first aid, I dressed the wounded, but there were those who needed to be evacuated immediately to a hospital. However, our army began a panicked withdrawal. The entire road was full of trucks and vehicles and soldiers fleeing from the front line. The traffic jam was very long. I despaired. I went out to the road, stood in the middle of it, and amid this chaos, the noise, and the screaming, I too screamed and asked for help for the injured. No one wanted to listen; everyone was thinking about saving his own skin. At a certain point, an officer got out of one of the vehicles with his weapon drawn and stopped two trucks. He ordered the soldiers to get out and help me put my wounded in, to take my sanitary supplies, to put everything on one of the trucks and take them to the field hospital that was supposed to be located at the tenth kilometer. I also got into the truck with the severely wounded. For the first time, I was face to face with the wounded and had no possibility of easing their suffering. One of them was critically wounded in his stomach. When I dressed his wound with military dressing, it sank into his intestines, which were leaking out. He was dying. I held his hand to my chest and cried. Those who were less severely wounded laughed at me. "What kind of brave warrior are you, crying at a dying soldier?" they laughed. My tears spilled down my face unchecked. My soldier shivered with fever and chills. I took off the coat I had brought with me from Łódź and covered him. He murmured some address of his family, which I did not manage to catch, and began to sink into unconsciousness. The hours seemed to go one forever. We traveled for long hours into the night. The traffic jams lasted for kilometers. This was my second, cruel baptism by fire.

When we finally reached the place where the medical unit of the regiment was supposed to be located, I discovered that it was no longer there, having fled in alarm as the entire front had collapsed and a general flight ensued. We continued onward. My soldier became quiet and cold. I knew that he was already dead, but it was hard for me to let him go. Finally, I laid him down. I left my coat over him. We eventually found a first aid station that took the wounded and the dead soldier from me, with the trucks. They sent me off with a receipt in my hand testifying that I had brought in wounded from such and such unit and told me to go back to my unit.

This receipt was the only document I had in my possession and I was still wearing the civilian clothes I had been wearing when I left home. I ran around between tanks, cannons, and soldiers looking for my unit. I asked an officer about my unit, and he told me with certainty that the unit I was looking for was among the first to pull back, that I would not find it there. He suggested that I travel with them. If I found my unit on the way, I would move to it, and if not, I would stay with them, because they did not have a nurse or medic to take care of the wounded. I agreed, because at that time I had no other choice. It became clear that this officer was the staff officer of an artillery battalion. His name was Dvortsky.

When my problems in the army turned out as they did, I often thought that I made a mistake here, that I should have continued searching and found my original unit.

I was in the artillery battalion led by Officer Dvortsky for only a few months, but there I finally received an army uniform and bag for the personal belongings that had survived. There I also passed the difficult months of fighting during the withdrawal from the Crimean Peninsula, through which we passed on foot, and the terrible crossing of the Gulf of Kerch (Kierchenskii zaliv). In this unit, I suffered greatly seeing numerous victims, experienced much emotion and pain, and personally I felt that I played my small, yet important, role in this cruel war.

In the meantime, we were withdrawing from the north to the south of Crimea, where Jewish kolkhozes were still fully active, and in some of them we spent the night. It is worthwhile mentioning that until the war there were more than 80 Jewish kolkhozes were in Crimea, totaling 20,000 souls (a third of the Jews in Crimea). They were focused on two administrative centers: "Freiland" and "Landedorf" (these were the final kernels of the dream of Jewish autonomy in Crimea that blossomed in the 1920s and concluded in the failure of Birobidzhan). When we reached these kolkhozes as an army retreating from the peninsula, we saw their residents in the grip of despair. The fields were cultivated beautifully, there were cattle and other animals, sturdy houses, but the people, including the Jewish residents, were helpless, knowing that in only a few days everything would fall into the hands of the German army. I know that not one of these Jews managed to flee. Crimea was among the first strips of Soviet land conquered by the Nazis.

The Germans pursued us. Our artillery battalion provided defense as the rest of the forces withdrew, and therefore we were the last to pull back. In the midst of artillery battles and air bombardments, we marched toward Kerch, the port city on the strait connecting the Black Sea to the Sea of Azov. Opposite Kerch is the shoreline of the Sea of Azov and the strip of land that goes through the strait and the sea, the spit. There were fishermen's huts there. The narrowest section of the strait is about forty kilometers in length. Those forty kilometers of the strait's waters were covered in the bodies of our soldiers.

Tens of thousands of soldiers, tanks, artillery, and other weapons were concentrated in Kerch. The artillery of my regiment provided cover for the crossing during the constant fighting; for some time, it slowed the advance of the Germans. However, they could not protect the masses of soldiers from air bombardments. In the skies, the Messerschmitts ruled. Two rafts rowed backward and forward between the two banks of the strait, moving horrifyingly slow. The Messerschmitts—the bombers—dropped endless numbers of bombs and fired their automatic weapons at the sea crossing and those waiting for a raft. In this chaos, when a mass of thousands stood facing death, a rumor suddenly spread that there was a wagon full of vodka and yeast in the nearby train station. The masses fell upon this wagon; within minutes, they emptied it entirely. In the hell of death, drunkenness, and the battle for life, the soldiers preferred to die with "mother" vodka. They filled their pockets and bags with bottles of vodka. Even on the rafts, with safety in sight, many of the soldiers were too drunk to hold out in the face of the German bombers and jumped to their deaths.

I continued to fulfil my duty and I dressed wounds, although I had no hope that the wounded would be taken to the other bank. It was impossible to transfer most of the as yet unwounded soldiers. Also, our artillery eventually fell silent. The Germans were now right behind us. When the raft arrived, the masses began to push

forward in an indescribable fashion. I found our political officer
Kishel, and some of the people from our unit, who were rolling a
cannon onto the raft. Only five people reached the safety of the
other side, together with the cannon. All the others remained in
the water, dead.

The survivors reached the empty fishermen's huts on the
shore. The politruk Kishel took me to a room to rest. There was
one bed. When we arrived, wearing our uniforms, we took off only
our boots and lay down to rest.

We were silent. I was deathly tired, but I did not close my eyes.
The images from that shore in Kerch passed before my eyes.
Indeed, I left there most of our soldiers; there were thousands and
thousands more. Among them were certainly many wounded. I
should not have gotten on the raft and left the wounded. I got
up and told the politruk that as long as the raft was still working,
I needed to go back and help the soldiers. Kishel looked at me
strangely, got up, and began to pace the room in annoyance.

"Chert iego znaiet chto eto za dievchonka!" (The devil knows
what kind of girl this is!) he shouted. "You are not going anywhere.
That's an order!" I stayed where I was. The words that the politruk,
Kishel, spoke were engraved on my mind and later I connected
them with other events, which I will describe below.

On the evening of that same terrible day on the Kerch strait,
the rafts stopped sailing. The Germans seized control of Kerch and
the port. Thousands of soldiers and weapons fell into the hands of
the Germans, there were thousands dead and wounded.

Of our entire artillery battalion, thirteen men reached the
shore of the Azov Sea. All the rest were killed or taken prisoner by
the Germans. Our commander, a young officer, was in shock. At
night he had a high fever. In his feverish state, he shouted, "Where
are my soldiers? Where are my artillery batteries?" He got up to run
and look for them. We had to stop him and lay him back down. In
our room, we were all lying on the floor, all thirteen soldiers and

their commanders. I was the only saninstruktor, medic, and it was my duty to take care of the sick commander. I changed the cold compresses on his head, I gave him some medicine to calm him, I stroked him. All this calmed him, and he fell asleep. After he fell asleep, I left him and sat down in a corner at some distance from the rest of those lying on the floor and cried for a long time. The scenes from the Gulf of Kerch accompanied me for a long time.

We found ourselves in Kossa, on the southern shore of the Azov Sea. The next day, and in the coming days, the atmosphere was dejected. However, we had to move. We began a journey on foot northward, through Kuban, the northern strip of the Caucasus, next to which is the land of Krasnodar. We passed through hundreds of kilometers moving north and west, dozens of towns and villages. The closest goal was the town of Maikop in Krasnodar. Northwest lay Ukraine on the banks of the massive River Don, which flowed into the Azov Sea.

We experienced many things on the way. We met masses of soldiers, remnants of various units that survived the war in the Crimea and crossed the Kerch Gulf, and also new recruits from the Caucasus. Due to the logistical conditions, the settlements we encountered on the way were full of soldiers from different units. We endeavored to stay together, but the conditions did not always allow this. Usually, when we arrived at a certain settlement, all the spots were already taken.

Our young officer, who had left at home a wife and small baby, certainly missed his wife and his home. However, after my night watching over him, he treated me with great attention and gentleness. He was an intelligent and sympathetic man. I began to worry about his behavior toward me, because he started to treat me with intimacy: when he returned from a meeting, he gave me his bag, wanted me to take care of him, make him coffee, look after his clothing and other personal belongings. When we arrived at places where there were many military units and had to search for a place to spend the night, when the huts and houses were full to bursting, he looked for me. Once, he grabbed my hand and looked for a place for both of us, until he found a place in one of the houses, under the table. There we lay. He started to stroke me and wonder at my silken skin. I took his hand away gently and told him that I greatly respected him and understood that he missed his wife, but I was sorry, I could not have an affair during the war. So too Officer Dvortzky, whom I mentioned—he adopted me into his unit when I was in the middle of the road looking for my lost unit in the Crimea—started to look at me with the eyes of a man. I distanced myself from him with less gentleness and I went to rest with our soldiers. They treated me with respect and did not dare to touch me.

The remnants of the survivors from the units who fought in Crimea and passed to Kuban had to reach a meeting point with the forces of the Southern Army. For many days we walked through Kuban and Krasnodarskii, through Taman, Sennoy, and many other settlements, the names of which I do not remember, until we reached Maikop. There I had to part from the members of the artillery unit and move to a new unit, to new conditions.

In the Ethnic Minorities (Natzmen) Brigade

Maikop looked like an endless military camp. Not only the units retreating from the Crimean Peninsula had arrived there, but also those from Southern Ukraine, which had already been captured by the Nazis. In Maikop, new divisions were created. There, I finally found people from my first unit, which I had lost in Crimea. One girl, among those with whom I had joined the army in Simferopol, was wearing my golf sweatshirt, a leaving present from David. When I asked them if they had the rest of my possessions—in particular, I hoped to find a small package of pictures and letters—they laughed at me.

There was no way back. I was seconded to a new brigade, an infantry brigade made up of recruits from the national minorities of the Caucasus and Central Asia. If I remember correctly, this was the 172nd Infantry division. It was called the Natsionalnyie Mienshestva (Natzmen) division. This was how the many national minorities of the Southern USSR, the Caucasus, and Central Asia were generally referred to.

The transfer from the artillery unit to the infantry changed my life in the army dramatically. In the artillery unit, I was the only nurse and the only woman. As such, I had problems and experiences of a different sort. I often felt lonely, and amid this loneliness, I had to clear a path for myself independently and ensure that those around me recognized it. This relates in particular to how the young officers treated me. With the artillery soldiers, who were usually intelligent and had a certain level of education, I had an easier life. And, the main thing, in my professional field, I was independent.

In the infantry brigade, everything changed immediately. I was sent to a medical unit that was attached to the brigade headquarters. I advanced with it from Northern Caucasus, through Southern Ukraine, over the Don River, finally reaching somewhere above the western bank of the Volga.

Once, we found ourselves in a ghost town. I saw a beautiful city, untouched by the hand of war. A city full of green, everything was still blooming. Yet there was not a single living soul, neither young nor old, not a cat or a dog. The ghost city had a terrible effect on us. This was the city of Engels. Before the war it was the capital city of the Volga German Autonomous Soviet Socialist Republic on the western bank of the Volga River. Opposite it, across the bridge, on the other bank of the river, was the city of Saratov. In the first days of the war, the Russian Soviet authorities transferred the entire population of this region to an unknown destination.

In my wandering in the paths of the war, Engels was not the only ghost town I saw. After some time, as I passed on foot through the entire length of the Caucasus, I encountered whole regions empty of people. A year or more later, I met in the Urals, on the

River Berezina, Tatars from Crimea, Kalmyks, and Chechens from Northern Caucasus searching through rubbish looking for something edible and dying en masse of hunger and cold.

With the 172nd division, I endured a journey that involved several battles, I experienced days of grief and difficult moments, but also moments of pleasure and excitement. We fought and marched the entire length and breadth of the Ukraine. On the way to somewhere new, in the fields or on the paths, they sometimes let us rest for ten minutes. Deathly tired, behind us the magical landscapes of Ukraine covered with a thick layer of snow, or at night in the blossoming spring crowned with beauty and maddening smells, someone would take out a harmonica and start to play and to sing, and immediately a few people would rise up and dance folk dances with squats, acrobatic dance steps almost like those of a folk dance, and the entire unit would wake up. Or, under the open sky, the tired soldiers would sit around the fire and sing Armenian songs: "My beloved Yerevan" (Yerevan is the capital of Armenia). The Georgians would sing: "My beloved soul, where are you?" or a Russian song full of longing, such as:

Как я люблю глубину твоих ласковых глаз,
Как я хочу к ним прижаться сейчас губами!
Бьется в тесной печурке огонь,
На поленьях смола, как слеза.

(In the dark night, my love, I know you are not sleeping,
And, near a child's crib, you secretly wipe away a tear
Logs burn bright in my cramped little stove,
On the wood, flowing tar, like a tear,
Oh, harmonica play me any song,
About happiness and great joys you shall tell us,
That in the cold of the trench I will be warm,
From the fire of love in my heart.)

The soldiers poured all their longing for their homelands, their homes under vines and orchards, into these songs. The Russian songs that everyone sang, which were written during the war, were full of warmth and longing. And again, someone would take out a harmonica and start to play a rhythmic Russian tune, and our feet would start to dance, until dawn came. There were also days of small satisfaction at the small victories. However, we suffered far more disappointments and defeats in battle.

The time has come, therefore, to describe my unit a little.

In our medical company there were three doctors, two or three doctor's assistants (by training these were somewhere between a doctor and a nurse), three nurses (including me), a few medical assistants, people responsible for supplying food and equipment, for moving equipment, and the rest of the services. There was, of course, a company secretary at the level of officer, a Ukrainian named Telitchko (whom I have not forgotten). The politruks, the secretary of the Komsomol, the doctor's assistant Zorka, and two nurses were Russian. The nurses were Vera Ivanovna, a middle-aged woman who moved to us from another unit, after her husband, a doctor, fell in the war, and a mischievous and somewhat silly girl, Polina, who after a short while became friends with Zorka. A fervent love bloomed between them, although Zorka had a wife and child. There was also a Byelorussian, Sergeant Syomka.

Apart from these, almost the entire company was made up of ethnic minorities: Caucasians, Uzbeks, Tajiks.

The head doctor, an Armenian, was a tall, thin man, fifty or more, his hair was almost entirely gray, and he was quiet and punctilious. The commander of the company, the Polkovnik (colonel), was a Georgian doctor. He was middle aged, short, and fat, with a large stomach. He repeatedly announced that he was not a man of war. Rather, he longed for peace and his beloved practice and patients. He did not understand why he had to play the idiotic role of commander. I was very fond of this Ivan Ivanovich—so everyone called him, without unnecessary manners or ceremony—and he also treated me in the same way. To a certain extent, he protected me, related to me miracles and wonders about his son, and dreamed of a daughter-in-law like me.

The doctor's assistant, Avtik, was Armenian. He wanted me to call him "Avtik Dejan," meaning my beloved. He dreamed, apparently, of traditional Armenian family life: he would sit in his orchard under his vine and his fig tree, and his wife, meaning me, would work and bring him whatever he desired. When I asked him if only women work in their society, he answered me simply, "That's what the woman is for." However, I should note that Avtik treated me with respect, and everything was ostensibly a joke.

There was a ginger-haired sergeant major; it was hard to know his ethnicity, and a supply officer (I forget his name), who was always drunk. His assistant, a certain sergeant from Belarus, was a sympathetic young man, and even when he was drunk, he became happy and likeable. I liked him more than everyone (after Ivan Ivanovich), and there was a period that, to make a point, I became very close to him and he was in on the secret of my plans. The memory of other different characters around me has blurred over time.

Life in the company proceeded on two separate paths. I will try to describe each one separately, as far as I can remember.

As I said, the company was attached to an infantry brigade. Thus, obviously, our main means of transport were our feet. From the town of Maikop in Kuban (after a short while it was captured by the Germans), where I joined the regiment, we went on foot, marching in a great curve through Azov, Bataysk, and other towns and settlements of the Ukraine, and reaching the eastern bank of the Don.

From here onward, the days of relative quiet, which had lasted since we left Kerch, came to an end. As long as the front was far away, we stopped after every hour of marching for a break of ten minutes. When we reached Ukraine, near the front line, there was activity all the time, and our marching changed. Sometimes we were in direct contact with the enemy.

On the western side of the Don was a big city, Rostov-on-Don. We crossed the river and reached the outskirts of the city. The city was under German control and our division liberated it, fighting street battles. I took part in these battles as a nurse. This was a unique experience. During the battles, which occurred in every street and every house, I ran after the soldiers, providing first aid to the wounded and removing them from the line of fire. There were also many wounded among the civilian residents, and I provided them with first aid as far as the conditions allowed. I gathered them in one place in the hope that they would be evacuated with the wounded soldiers. In other parts of the city, my friends were at work, collecting the wounded. The soldiers were evacuated, but the citizens of the city were left to their fate at the hands of the military rule, after we left the city of Rostov and hurried after the Germans to Taganrog. We were unable to keep hold of Taganrog. Following the German counterattack, we were also forced to leave Rostov. The German corps pushed us back across the Don. We tried again to conquer the city on the Don because it was a strategic position of the greatest importance.

Again, therefore, I took part in the battle for Rostov. This time the city was empty of residents. Sometime later, I discovered the fate of the citizens who had fallen into the hands of the Nazis and were liberated by the Red Army: the Soviet authorities saw them as collaborators and sent them to forced labor camps in the Urals and in Siberia.

In July 1941, the Germans began the second stage of the Blitzkrieg to occupy Russia. The German army's aim was to end the war before winter arrived. With the conquest of the port city of Sebastopol on the Black Sea and Rostov-on-Don, Hitler demanded that his army conquer the Caucuses, with its oil reserves, up to

Anatolia. Then he hoped for Russia's surrender. They almost achieved this aim.

Within four months of the Blitzkrieg in 1941, by mid-October, around three million citizens of the Soviet Union came under German rule. In November 1941, there were battles in the north— on the outskirts of Leningrad (Petrograd); in the center—around Moscow; and the south—in Rostov-on-Don. The conquest of this city opened a way for the German corps to the Volga River, to Stalingrad (now Volgograd). Thus, it is obvious why the battle for Rostov was so bitter and cost so many lives.

The terrible strategic situation in which the Soviet Union found itself led to an awareness and panic among the highest echelons in the Kremlin. Stalin declared a state of emergency: "The line of the Volga River must be the last line of the German advance. From here, no further." So his orders stated. The Red Army was reorganized. New uniforms were distributed, and signs of excellence and medals were given out generously. Ilya Ehrenburg, the well-known Jewish Soviet author who served as a military reporter, wrote in his sharp and warm articles about the courage of the Soviet warriors, fanned the hatred of the enemy, and called for a war to the death. He tried to persuade the soldiers that there was no choice other than to stand against the Germans to the death. There would be no surrender, and it was forbidden to be taken captive, which was worse than death.

The Russian people paid a high price in this war because of Stalin's arrogance, because of the purges in the military command, which was left without professional commanders. This resulted in the fact that, during the first days of the German attack, the enemy managed to paralyze the entire Soviet air force, and the skies were left empty for the German planes. One of the Soviet generals, still alive somewhere in a concentration camp, Rokossovsky, sent letters to Stalin in which he asked to die in the battles to defend the homeland. Only in the critical winter of 1941 did Stalin answer his pleas. He indeed became a war hero.

At the same time, there also took place a sharp change in Soviet propaganda. Presumably, this turning point was connected to the alliance between the Soviet Union and the Western Allies in the war against Nazi Germany and their influence on it. In this atmosphere of political compromise and concessions in the authorities' attitude to religions, many churches opened all over Russia and were filled with devotees praying. This resulted in a massive improvement of the population's morale. The media received a particularly free hand to praise the heroic past of the Russian army in defending "the holy Russian motherland." Subsequently, the war was called Vielikaia otechestviennaia voina, "The great war for the homeland." From the dust of Russian history, heroes such as Field Marshal Kutuzov (in the war against Napoleon), Tsar Peter the Great, and certainly Catherine the Second as well as other Russian heroes were dragged up, cleaned, and purified.

The winter of 1941/1942 was one of the harshest winters of the war. In that winter, the Wannsee Conference prepared for the "Final Solution" of the Jewish question. On the Russian front, the German attack was stopped on the River Don. In that winter, our brigade was located somewhere between the Don and the Volga. The regiments of our brigade were stationed along the defensive line between various Ukrainian villages. In each one of them there was an infirmary with a nurse or a doctor's assistant from our company. We were constantly on the front line. Every so often, the Germans attacked our positions and vice versa, and thus we did not stay long in any one place. We progressed slowly forward, amidst battles, and sometimes we retreated. All this, I believe, was in Northeastern Ukraine. However, in that winter there were no large battles and both sides more or less treaded water.

Yet even the local battles left victims, and over time it was necessary to refill the ranks and reorganize. Then we moved to another defensive line and our place was taken by another brigade of the same division. The two neighboring brigades constantly swapped places.

This difficult winter stopped the German progress, determining the fate of the war on the Russian front. I will mention the epic of defense of Leningrad, which was besieged for 17 long months and during which 700,000 people in the besieged city died of hunger. The Russian people suffered from hunger and cold and gathered all their inner strength in that "Great war for the homeland" against the German enemy. America began to send food to hungry, bleeding Russia. Doubtless, without this help there would probably have been many more victims of starvation. However, the sacrifice of the Russian soldiers and their heroism subdued the enemy.

With regard to our company in the ethnic minorities' brigade, which was made up, as I said, of ethnic minorities, it is difficult to speak about heroism. Their heroism was limited to the fact that they held out despite the conditions at the front.

Our forces were constantly positioned opposite the German forces. Sometimes, there was a village between us, sometimes the border passed through a village or a forest. Life was conducted in hastily dug trenches, the height of a soldier, in the most primitive conditions. Not all of them had kerosene ovens (Teplushka). Even when there was an oven, it was only possible to warm one's hands on it a little, because around it everything was covered with snow and ice. The snow served as drinking water and for washing. One raised one's head out of the trench at great risk—German snipers shot at anything that moved. There were also snipers on our side who did the same thing. Even in days of calm without attacks, the bored Germans, who also suffered from the cold, aimed one or two shells at our side, and quickly renewed the fighting.

A soldier from an Armenian or Uzbek village, who came from a hot climate and suffered greatly in his trench, who at any moment was liable to take a shell or a bullet to the head, he did not feel that he was suffering for his homeland. He did not have the same motivation as a Russian soldier. His homeland was Armenia, Georgia, or

Uzbekistan. I learned from them that among these peoples there was significant hatred, and a trivial matter could lead to a knife fight (for example, because the Armenian said that Yerevan is the most beautiful city and the Georgian claimed that Tbilisi is more beautiful). However, all were united by hatred of the Russians.

Therefore, when a soldier of one of these ethnicities stood at night on guard in the terrible cold of minus 30 degrees, fearing that at any moment he was liable to be killed, he looked for a way out. Sometimes, despairing, he went mad. And thus, I learned a new word in the dictionary of war: "striel-Samo," meaning that a soldier had shot himself. Usually, they shot themselves in the hand or foot. Such a soldier preferred to suffer, hoping to be sent to a military hospital and, from there, after recovering, home. However, the reality was far more cruel. When a soldier came to us with a wound in his hand or foot, the doctor checked the wound and immediately dictated to the nurse: ss (striel-samo—self-inflicted). It was not difficult to identify this, because a desperate guy who shot himself from up close left signs of gunpowder. In order to neutralize this, he shot through a wet rag that left a white stain with gunpowder around it. Such a soldier received from the doctor a referral to a military hospital with his diagnosis. The guy did not even know that he had signed his own sentence.

These cases developed into a plague. The head doctor in our division decided to hold a series of lectures among the soldiers and explain to them the fate of those who did this. This indeed helped.

Another misfortune in that winter were frozen hands or feet. We dealt with first- and second-degree frostbite in the company: the poor soldier remained with us for a few days and after treatment returned to his company. Only severe cases of frostbite were taken to the field hospital. Among the cases of frostbite, we also registered instances in which it was self-inflicted. The soldier grew weary of life in the trench, the icy conditions and the constant threat of death. During his nighttime guard duty, the biting wind made it hard to breathe and numbed his senses. In those moments, he longed for the warmth of his homeland and yearned to escape the horrors of war, no matter the cost. He removed the glove from his hand, put his hand into the snow, and when it was wet enough held it in the wind for a few minutes. He immediately got frost-bite: the entire hand was covered with cold blisters (a third-degree burn). These cases too were easily uncovered, and no one envied such a soldier his fate.

I already mentioned that the medical unit attached to the brigade command, which was usually located two or three kilometers from the front line, had a number of first aid stations along the front line. Such a station was manned by a nurse with an assistant and sometimes also a doctor's assistant. When I was at the front station, I was usually accompanied by the doctor's assistant, Zorka. Here, at this frontline station, the soldier received first aid and was sent to our sanitary company, which included doctors. At this station, on the fire lines, in days of relative calm, life started only at night. Only then could we and all the soldiers receive hot food from the field kitchen, together with vodka, the post, and military newspapers. Polina, who missed her lover, Zorka, often came to visit.

The post was an important part of the nighttime experience. I too received letters from Heniek and Shoshana. My sister and her family were in Uzbekistan, somewhere near Samarkand, in the town of Urgut. For me, every letter was worth more than gold and took me to other worlds. It was enough to look at a soldier who received a letter from home to understand how he felt. Seeing how he read the letter was material for a literary pen. Many poems full of longing and suffering were composed on the front. It was worth-while also to look at those who received no letters, those who left behind at home a young wife, a fiancée, an old mother. . . .

At night we had a lot of work to do. The sick and wounded came to us, and the wounded who were brought from the frontline positions during the day received first aid and waited until dark, because it was only possible to send the wounded to the company at night, apart from emergencies or severe injuries that had to be evacuated immediately. Every such attempt led to more wounded because any movement in daylight was seen by the other side and led to an exchange of fire.

According to the orders of the head doctor, and when the conditions at the front allowed it, I had to check the health conditions in the trenches and of the soldiers at the posts. The conditions were terrible, and I could not help much, but here and there I provided first aid on the spot, I asked them not to drink water from the snow without boiling it, which was not always possible, explaining the reason for this, and gave them other such advice.

I arranged every visit to the frontline posts with Zorka, the doctor's assistant, who outranked me. I was also accompanied by the commander of the company that I was visiting. But I almost always found Zorka there, as though by coincidence.

Although I was not always at the front position, I felt better there, despite the dangers it entailed, than in the headquarters, a few kilometers behind the lines. Every so often, I swapped places with another nurse and I returned to our base next to the headquarters. Here, at the base, there were a few people I liked, such as the nurse Vera Ivanovna or the commander Ivan Ivanovich. However, there were also people I did not like especially, and likewise various intrigues were woven around me because I maintained my independence. The conditions in which we lived, among men far from their wives, were not, to put it mildly, sympathetic to me. Usually, we slept in our uniforms in a village house, lying on the floor (more precisely, on the bare earth, which served as the floor), one next to the other. More than once, I woke up at night with a man breathing on top of me. Without making a sound, I rudely pushed him off and went to lie in another free space somewhere else. It happened that they took bets among themselves at my expense or played other crude tricks. Yet none of this was the worst. The troubles started from the moment I joined the 172nd division in Kuban.

"The Flirtation" with the Special Unit

One day, I read in the military newspaper a short piece about the establishment of a Polish military unit that would fight shoulder to shoulder with the Red Army against the Germans. This small report moved me greatly. I read it to those with me in the room, and I added that I was not opposed to joining this unit. Among those present in the room was the ginger-haired sergeant major (I do not remember his name) who by chance was not drunk and he advised me to write to one of the Polish organizations in Moscow. It seemed like a good idea. I did not know about any Polish organization other than that attached to the Comintern (the Communist International), and without thinking too much I wrote them a letter.

At that stage, I did not know some things that were likely to bring trouble upon my head. First, I did not know that the Polish section of the Comintern and almost the entire leadership of the Polish Communist Party had been eliminated. Secondly, I did not know that as the Soviet Union drew closer to the Western Allies in the fight against Germany, the Soviet regime had made a gesture to the West, among other things destroying the Comintern. Certainly, I did not know that because of the tightening ties and the accompanying agreements, a Polish military unit was established according to the agreement with the government-in-exile in London, which Stalin hated. Only after a long time did I find out that this was a military unit under the command of General Anders. This was a temporary Soviet tactic, but General Anders managed to liberate thousands of Poles from forced labor camps in Russia and take them and their families out of the Soviet Union. Meaning that even the Polish military unit, to which I wrote my letter, was apparently already at this stage considered "non-kosher":

What was the fate of my stupid letter?

I do not know to this day whether it was because of the letter I sent or if it had nothing to do with it (although, as I found out, the letter reached Moscow, arriving at a completely legal Polish office), but one fine day, a young, pleasant-looking officer appeared and asked to talk to me. It turned out he knew my life story well: he reminded me that I had been a member of a Communist youth organization, that I was a loyal warrior, and so on. He talked to me in a soft, friendly manner. He explained to me that in this difficult war, all kinds of enemies of the Soviet state were raising their heads, that the enemy sends its people everywhere, meaning, there were enemies also among us, etc. I did not know where he was going with this, and, moving my head, I responded affirmatively, without questioning what he said. And then he told me that, as a former Communist, I had to devote myself to the war against internal enemies. "Certainly," I said. However, I asked what he meant. He did not lose his patience in an effort to ensnare his victim. After long explanations, according to which, when I had a doubt about someone, I should inform him, I agreed. He gave me a document to sign. I signed. I did not know that I had practically signed my own sentence.

The Special Unit (Osobyi otdiel) was the arm of the KGB in the army. From that moment, as I found out afterward, they followed me; or perhaps even long before this meeting they had already been watching me. Perhaps from the moment that I volunteered they were already following me. Only much later did I start to connect things, and among other things single statements, into a bigger picture. For example, the cry of the politruk Kishel while we were still on the Strait of Kerch: "Chert iego znaiet chto eto a dievchonka!" (The devil knows what kind of girl this is!). Were they already following me then? Did they suspect me? I was still too innocent and had faith in the Soviet machinery. As a result, I did not feel a need to hide anything.

I did not give the officer of the Special Unit the material he asked for, and I also did not know that I needed to do so, even if I had nothing to give. In my surroundings, there were no "enemies of the Soviet regime." However, at various times, I was called to this officer, and he asked me about all kinds of people in our company. The questions concerned people in the company command, in particular the head doctor, the Armenian.

The head doctor, an Armenian (whose name I cannot remember), was a quiet man who fulfilled his duty with loyalty and honesty. He was meticulous about himself and those under him. I told the officer of the special unit all this, but he was not happy. At one of the meetings, another officer was present. They wanted to know if the head doctor spoke Armenian. I answered that he did not, but they demanded that I reveal to them that he knew German and they would deal with the rest of the questions. After this meeting—I was prohibited from even mentioning the fact that it had taken place—a red light began to flicker in my subconscious, and I became more aware. After I again failed to satisfy their desires, I was called back for another meeting, and then the voices rose. They threatened me. Indeed, I had signed a document stating that I would bring them information. I answered that I had promised to bring them information if and when I thought that something hostile was underway. However, I did not see any hostile threat in this man. They demanded that I become the doctor's lover in order to acquire his trust, etc. I refused this demand outright.

If so, they told me, someone else will take your place and do what is necessary.

I felt an explicitly threatening tone and it seemed to me that my connection with these people had concluded. In the meantime, a gloomy atmosphere began to hover around me. The party secretary, the Ukrainian Telitchko, treated me with open hostility and made all kinds of comments on my account. I asked the brigade commander to send me to a frontline post. He answered me, speaking in an authoritative tone, that they would send me where they thought it was necessary for me to go, and thus the matter was closed. I was shocked. Until this point, he had treated me with warmth.

In the meantime, the activity in the medical unit continued. One day in the winter of 1942, while I was busy at the base, two men in civilian clothes approached me and asked me to go with them. A few dozen meters from the base were two black cars, and I was ordered to get into one of them. Two men were already sitting inside. We drove toward the nearby forest, which was covered with a thick layer of snow.

I must admit that I was completely innocent then, ignorant of what they were capable of doing to me. However, that same innocence and faith apparently led to a moment of hesitation on their part. They probably only meant to scare me and to wait until I would fall into their net. There were three men in the car, and they attacked me, screaming, threatening, and frightening me: "You signed an agreement with us. You are no longer free." I told them that I was willing to pay for my mistakes, although I had no idea what the price was. It is a good thing that I had no idea about the price and therefore I stood up for myself: I volunteered to fight the Germans, I am not scared to die, etc. Now I cannot reconstruct all the threats they used against me. Eventually, in anger, they screamed: "We will meet again!" They threw me into the snow in the forest and drove away. I never saw them again.

I already mentioned that, with all my rationality, somewhere inside me there is a degree of superstition. On the night before this terrible meeting, I had a dream. We, the three nurses in the company, had a custom: in the morning, Polina, and sometimes I too, would tell Vera Ivanovna about our dreams and she, the expert, would interpret them. I told her about a strange dream: I was alone in a thick forest covered in snow. I had lost my way in the snow and was looking for a way out. Suddenly, I fell into a pit and could not get out of it. I screamed for help. The soldiers came to save me, but while they were approaching me, the ground and the snow sank, and the pit grew larger. Thus, in my dream, the soldiers tried to pull me out but failed. I woke up. Vera Ivanovna interpreted this dream as concerning an illness or another event with an unclear outcome.

After hours stumbling around the forest, I returned to the base. It was as though no one had seen or heard anything. Everything went on as normal. I was forbidden to speak a word about the whole "affair" with the Special Unit. Every so often, I went with Zorka to a front line position or returned to base. These changes were normal and all the nurses in the company changed places. For some reason, I was always at the frontline position with Zorka, and only after some time did I understand why.

Once, the party secretary, Telitchko, and the division's politruk decided, in agreement with the neighboring brigade, that the medical units of the two brigades would hold a Socialist contest (sorevenovanie-sots) over the number of wounded evacuated from the front lines during the battles and the provision of first aid. This was a stupid idea, or it was intended from the outset as a trap for someone.

The members of our unit had to go to the neighboring unit, which was then located on the second line of the front. I was the only woman to go from our unit, because Vera Ivanovna was at a frontline post, and Polina had to stay at the base. Apart from me, Telitchko and our commander, Ivan Ivanovich, went, as well as a few others. We got on a wagon and set off. It was a rather long way. Somewhere, half way, we stopped and went into the cabin of the post at which Vera Ivanovna was working; there we warmed ourselves a bit. There were a few people; I did not pay attention to who was present, and there was a comfortable atmosphere of laughter and clowning around. In the meantime, I took off my military coat and went to relieve myself. When I came back, the group was preparing to set off. I put on my coat and off we went.

The rural house at which we arrived was full of light. In a spacious room were gathered a lot of officers and young women, all in military uniforms. In the kitchen sat the homeowner, she was also a rather young woman.

From the first glance, I understood that the competition was a pretext and a cover up for a cheap celebration. The girls sat on the officers' laps and on the table was a supply of vodka bottles. Our Telitchko very quickly joined the head of the neighboring medical unit, and both began to manage matters at the table.

I knew the commander of the neighboring unit from visits to our unit. He was an older, lusty character. Whenever he visited us, he came close to me with disgusting lustfulness and sweet talk and called me "Binotchka." So too now, after a few moments, he began to approach me. However, my commander, the nice Ivan Ivanovich, took me by the hand and said quietly, "This isn't for you. Come with me." He took me to the homeowner and asked her to let me lie in the bed that stood in the kitchen. She was to be responsible for not letting anyone near me. She promised, but said that another girl would also sleep in the bed. After an exchange, ostensibly regarding the so-called competition, I went to the kitchen and lay down to sleep in my uniform (I took off only my coat and boots).

I was tense and I did not know exactly why. I felt that something was wrong with all this. It seems that my sleep was also tense, because I knew that some other girl was supposed to join me in the bed. However, when I felt someone touch me in the bed, as though stealing in, I woke up in anxiety, sat up, and asked:

"Who is that?"

"It is me, Binotchka," I heard a whisper beside me.

"Please go away immediately, or I will call for help," I replied quietly.

I was shaking all over from fear and nerves. In the room it was pitch black. The blinds were closed, and no ray of light could be seen. Such darkness in such a place, only a few kilometers from the front line in wartime, was completely forbidden, because in the case of an enemy attack they would have slaughtered us all like sheep. I sat in bed, shaking in the darkness, afraid to move. For long moments I was afraid to check whether he was still there or had gone. I did not hear any rustling or other noise. Finally, I dared to move my hand carefully over the bed and check whether he was still sitting next to me. I found that I was alone again. I sat there for a while with black thoughts in my head about the results of that night, on which I had angered the commander. Finally, I lay down again and slept a nervous sleep. Due to my furious emotions, my period came early, and I stained my trousers. I could not ask for a pair of trousers to change into, so I put on my military coat and went into the dining room.

They were all sitting around the table eating breakfast. All eyes shone and faces turned toward me with sly smiles. More than anyone else, this was evident on Telitchko's face. It was not difficult to understand immediately that I had been the subject of a bet among them, and the one interested in victory, the wicked commander, was playing the role of Victor.

A few hours after we returned to our base, I understood that the night of betting on me with the commander of the neighboring unit had already taken wing and spread through our entire unit. Sergeant Simka, who liked me (and perhaps loved me a little, but not seriously, and I did not completely deter him, because to a certain extent he served as cover against the other lads that swarmed around me), came to me in great anger and asked me how I could do such a thing and sleep with that bastard.

I told him all that had happened to me that night and he believed me.

Simka was a simple lad who was raised in an isolated village in Belarus and had quite a lot of good sense. Apart from that, he had personal charm, he knew how to get by in any situation and to help others, was always smiling, always in a good mood, and his eyes laughed with the craftiness of a peasant. We had long talks at night, and sometimes I ran to his hut when it was hard for me to be with Telitchko, Zorka, and their like. Simka did not dare to touch me, and we became good friends. This friendship did not prevent him from openly going to the village with other soldiers "to drink milk," meaning, for women. For a certain period, after we reconquered populated towns and villages from the Germans, before the authorities decided to evacuate the residents, a plague of gonorrhea spread through our unit, as well as through the villages evacuated by the Germans. There was also a plague of large, fat lice, the likes of which I had never seen before.

That night of "Socialist competition" in the neighboring unit had a painful sequel for me. It was a sequel and also the end of my affair with the Special Unit of the KGB. That night, when we got back to the base, I was called to the Special Unit and asked as an opening question:

"Where did you get phosphorus?"

"Phosphorus? What is that?"

I knew that there were watches on which the numbers were lit up with phosphorus. I knew that there was such an element in nature, although I had never seen phosphorus in its natural form. I already mentioned that on the way to the neighboring unit we had stopped at a position in which the nurse Vera Ivanovna was working. There, I took off my coat and went for a moment to relieve myself. At that moment, they claimed, the phosphorus fell out of my coat pocket. This phosphorus served as a signal for German spies. That was what the two officers from the Special Unit told me. A nice story, no?

In short, I was accused of spying for the Germans. It did not matter what I answered, although I must admit that like that attempt in the black car in the forest, so now too, my stupidity was unfathomable. I was horrified that someone had apparently put phosphorus in my pocket or threw it next to my coat, meaning that there was an enemy, a dangerous spy, threatening the Red Army. I believed every word they told me, and apparently in my great horror cried out that the enemy must be found; I would do everything to find him. Presumably, the officers from the Special Unit of the KGB enjoyed this entertaining spectacle. Finally, I was told to go back to my company, not to speak a word of this, and to wait until the matter would be investigated. In the meantime, I was forbidden to leave the base without their knowledge.

To this day I do not know why they did not put me up against a wall and put a bullet in my head. This was wartime and there was an expression "Voina vsio spishet" (war covers everything). This expressed the state of anarchy, and in that spirit terrible things were done.

I spent three months living in indescribable anxiety. During this time, I lost ten kilos. My commander, Ivan Ivanovich, hovered around me in worry. He told me once that he did not understand what was going on with me, but he was worried that something was threatening me. I could not tell him anything. I wrote a farewell letter to Heniek, in which I tried to hint to him that I might die at the hands of a friendly bullet. After more than two years, when I was reunited with Heniek, he told me that he understood the letter and tried in all kinds of ways to help me. But in the meantime, our connection was severed.

During these months of waiting, every time I saw one of the officers from the special department riding on his horse, I ran to him to ask if they had some news for me. Every time I returned rebuked. At one of these accidental meetings, he shouted at me:

"Sit quietly as long as we don't touch you. If there is a need, we will find you."

I did not run after him anymore.

In the spring of 1942, I was working at a frontline first-aid station, of course together with Zorka. The silence around us was tense. Both sides were preparing for the deciding battles. Our position was located in some village and its surroundings. My first-aid position was in a rural house, in the garden. I cannot describe the beauty of the Ukrainian spring: the trees in the garden were covered with flowers of all colors, the smells were intoxicating. Despite the fact that going outside in daylight was dangerous, I could not stop myself from going out and sitting behind the house and enjoying the beauty and the smells. I noticed that Zorka, who always followed me when I visited the soldiers in the trenches, did so now too. When I sat in the garden and read a book or prepared dressings, he followed me with his eyes. One day, when I was sitting in the garden, I received a surprise visit from a lieutenant serving in the neighboring brigade. He was also Jewish. He introduced himself and said that he wanted to make my acquaintance. We talked for a few minutes. At some point he leaned in close to me and whispered: "Be careful." Zorka immediately joined us. We then talked about inconsequential matters and the lieutenant left us.

At night, the post arrived, as always. This time there was a surprise for me: a large package of newspapers and journals in Polish, published by a left-wing Polish group in Moscow, the life and soul of which was the Polish writer, Wanda Wasilewska.

The package of newspapers and journals included a newspaper entitled Wolna Polska (Free Poland) and a journal entitled Nowe Widnokręgi (New Horizons). I was so shocked and excited that I let out a squeal of surprise. Zorka, who was also in the room, noticed and came up to me to ask what I had received. I showed him with great excitement the newspapers, and he, my "advocate," seeing newspapers in a language he did not know, jumped with joy and said:

"Finally! I've caught you!" He grabbed the entire package from my hands and ran off somewhere. I understood where he was going.

Suddenly, I was painfully aware of many things falling into place; Zorka, who was ostensibly friendly to me, worked for the "Special Unit" and had reported my every move from the moment

I had arrived in the division. Who knew what he had reported about me? I felt cold and bitter.

I went to the front lines of the war of my own free will to do my part, giving my all, in the war against a cruel, murderous, Nazi German enemy. Apart from the shell shock I felt in the early days in Crimea, I constantly ran between bursts of shell fire and explosions, serving in the most dangerous places. I did not think about saving my own life, while others hid in the trenches and shelters. And now, it became evident that from my first day in the army they had seen me as an unwanted guest and laid a trap into which they expected me to fall.

I was overcome by terrible tiredness. I had had enough. Enough! All my revolutionary and battle fervor disappeared. From that moment I began to dream of quiet, of being far away from here, from Zorka, from Telitchko, from the "Special Unit," and everything to do with them. I missed Heniek's words of comfort and his cheerfulness, I missed Shoshana's house, I missed little Naftali. . . .

Zorka returned with his head hanging, returning the package of newspapers to me without a word. I too said nothing. Presumably, he was reprimanded by the "Special Unit" for revealing himself to me for no good reason, because these papers were completely legal, albeit in Polish.

After a few days, I was called back to the base.

Our brigade prepared to set off. The period of relative quiet was over. The two sides were getting ready for the decisive battles. Hitler wanted to complete the conquest of Russia in the summer of 1942. Again, the division was reorganized. At that time, apparently in July, our brigade received a command to transfer me to the division headquarters. I did not know what awaited me, but I was pleased—for good or ill —whatever would be, would be.

CHAPTER 6

THE LAST CHAPTER IN THE RED ARMY

In the Nieblagonadiozhnyie (Unit for Untrustworthy Soldiers)

Sergeant Sima accompanied me to the division headquarters in a wagon. It was a long journey. As I mentioned, we were friends; it may have been more than that on his part. We were both wrapped up in our thoughts and we barely spoke. After around two hours of traveling, we took a break. We got down from the wagon to stretch our legs a little. Sima, who had brought provisions for the journey, prepared breakfast for us. We sat down on the grass on the outskirts of the city. At first, we just chatted, until he started to unburden himself of what was weighing on him. He told me things that he had previously kept locked inside himself. This was a Sima I had not met before. The young man I knew was always in a good mood, always cheerful; I thought him flighty, a sympathetic, nice guy. Here, on the outskirts of a Ukrainian city, I discovered another Sima, a man with a bitter heart who left me puzzled as to who he really was.

First, he said bitterly, perhaps I had not taken him seriously. He, however, thought about me with great seriousness. Therefore, he had looked after me and hoped that maybe, if we both survived, we would establish a family. However, here we were, forced to part. He said a lot more than that. He revealed to me that even though I had never shared with him any details of my persecution, he had felt it. Yet he kept silent because he had learned to keep quiet under the Soviet regime. Great bitterness had built up in his heart. He talked about suspicions, derogatory treatment, humiliations, and the evil that he had been subjected to in the Red Army by those slightly above him in status, the Russians.

"Bad people, liars, are in charge in Russia," he said. "You have to be on alert all the time, to watch your tongue and your heart. You must not let a 'non-kosher' word slip out, because immediately, one of your 'friends' will inform on you."

I tried to deny it. I said that he was exaggerating, that not everyone is evil, etc. However, he again burst out bitterly, "You have learned nothing despite what you have been through! You are innocent, too naive. All the regime is like this. There's no escaping it."

I cannot remember all of Sima's words. However, when he revealed to me that, if we had to part, he would search for an opportunity to flee to the German side, I was shocked and astonished. He asked me for my opinion. I was gripped by fear. I asked him to abandon any such thoughts, for his own good, that such a decision would be destructive. However, in my mind, warning bells started to ring. Had Sima also been sent to catch me out, or was this an honest stream of confession to a kindred spirit before parting? I will never know. We got on the wagon and set off. When we arrived, before parting, we made a toast.

It was summer; I believe it was the end of July 1942. I found great activity underway at the division headquarters; everyone was busy, and no one had time even to take an interest in me. The same day, soldiers and officers arrived, as well as female soldiers from other brigades who belonged to this division, having received the same order as me. They too did not know what it meant. At least, I thought, I was not alone. Apparently, something connected us. Who knew what? At the end of that day, they gathered us together and ordered us to wait. Every day, new fighters joined us, and after a few days, we numbered a few hundred. It became evident that this division had become a gathering point for a certain type of soldier from the entire Southern Army, meaning, all the divisions and brigades belonging to it. However, not one of us knew why. Eventually, we found out.

High Commander (General) Stalin had ordered that anyone whose commitment to the good of the country was in the slightest doubt should be removed from all military units involved in battles with the Germans. In other words, those whose loyalty to the state was questionable. I never managed to find out what kind of untrustworthiness this referred to. At any rate, I was included in this category. I was not sorry for it at all, and I did not even worry about what awaited me and all these people.

A military unit was established for the "untrustworthies," and a commander was appointed. We were ordered to join the headquarters of the Southern Army, which should have been located somewhere in the Caucasus. We set out from somewhere between Saratov and Stalingrad. Among us were officers and rookies and a few women from medical units. We were divided into companies, and we set off. Interestingly, although we spent a long time together and endured various adventures, not one face remains in my memory. However, I remember certain situations, sites, and an unforgettable series of places.

I should note that, although to all intents and purposes, we were a military unit, we suffered from a lack of supplies. We went most of the way on foot. Our boots became worn and torn, as did our military uniforms, and there was no possibility of changing them. There were long days when we were hungry; we ate what we found in the fields after the harvest. Here and there someone found a carrot, a pumpkin, a watermelon, or a bunch of grapes. I should add that whoever found something edible was lucky. Whoever found nothing was even hungrier. However, there were kolkhozes on the route of our march that lacked working hands (the men, for the most part, had been conscripted into the army) and they were happy to welcome us for a day or two to help in the fields in return for food and a place to sleep. For city people like me, who had never worked in agriculture, this was hard work, weeding while constantly bent over. After a few hours of such work, I had a bad backache. However, in a kolkhoz, you could take a shower after work, wash your clothes, which would be dry by morning, and sleep on sweet-smelling hay.

You could say that we marched the entire length and breadth of the Caucasus. Only in big cities did we have the opportunity to use any kind of transportation. We went through amazing places: deserts and mountains. In the desert, the climate was almost tropical, while the tips of the mountains were covered in snow. We passed through places that are among the most beautiful on earth. For example, the administrative region then called Stavropolskij krai in the Caucasus. This mountainous region is part of the Caucasus Mountain chain. The views are breathtaking. These are not the highest mountains in the Caucasus, but their tips are always covered in show, as though rising up from the beautiful green slopes. Here and there between the mountains. we found massive waterfalls, pastures, grazing grounds. Between these mountains are villages and towns that boast well-known healing resorts, like the Mineralnye Vody (mineral water), Kislovodsk (oxygen rich water), Pyatigorsk (five mountains), Zheleznovodsk (iron water), Semi-Kolodets (seven wells), and others, the names of which I do not remember. Their names signify their healing properties.

In the nineteenth century, members of the upper echelons of the nobility who dared to speak out against the Tsar's policy were exiled to this area. The locals call one of the mountains around

Pyatigorsk "Kinjal," and, officially, I believe, it is called Lermontov after the lyric poet Mikhail Lermontov. He was the most prominent representative, after Alexander Pushkin, of the Russian and European romanticism of the first half of the nineteenth century. In one of his poems, he pointed out that the autocratic regime of Tsar Nicholas I was morally responsible for Pushkin's death. The poet was punished and sent to serve in the army putting down rebellions in the Caucasus. He lived on the mountain that bears his name in the period of his exile. His poetry from this period is modern and lyrical. He was murdered, like Pushkin before him, in a duel.

These places in the Caucasus were, in the period of the Soviet regime, famous for their beauty. They were known for their special, curative mineral springs. We saw beautiful healing spas, where the most influential figures in Stalin's regime spent their holidays. We made a great curve and went east toward the Caspian Sea. We arrived at the port city of Makhachkala, the capital of Dagestan Republic. There we spent a few days at an army headquarters. We were put up in various private homes, received military supplies, and apparently also the necessary documents to continue our journey to Tbilisi, the capital of Georgia, the headquarters of the Southern Army.

The remnants of my remaining memories from this port city concern its residents and the quiet. Three young women, I among them, were sent to a small, white house on the seashore. A sympathetic old couple lived there. These quiet people welcomed us in good spirits. Before entering, we removed our shoes. Inside, the house was exquisitely clean. The blinds filtered out the burning sun (we were in a post-tropical climate). The couple walked around almost naked, and they suggested that we immediately remove our clothes and leave only our short underwear. They explained to us that in this climate, on the seashore, it is impossible to breathe when wearing clothes. The girls with me took off their clothes, but

I did not want to. To this day, I feel embarrassed at being naked, a feeling I have retained from my childhood home. Apart from that, I was different to the other women due to my white skin. I was embarrassed. However, nothing helped. With laughter and jokes, they removed my clothes. They left only my knickers and bra because I clung to them and refused to take them off.

The young men and women had a great time. They spent a lot of time in the sea, swimming. Others, including me, took care of our feet, which ached after months of walking. Some organized an evening of singing and dancing under the open skies. I could not go into the sea, because I knew that I would get sunburned immediately: I would turn red, and my skin would blister. However, I had to wash my uniform. They told me that it was best to wash the khakis of military uniforms in sea water. I went in, therefore, in the evening, when the sun had already passed its height. Within ten minutes, maybe fifteen, I had washed my clothes and hung them outside. My back was exposed for these ten minutes. After half an hour, my clothes were dry but hard like sheet metal. By contrast, my back was burned and covered in blisters. Early next morning, we received orders to leave. I was forced to wear my hard shirt and backpack and report for duty. The elderly woman gave me a bottle of flaxseed oil, which was supposed to help me. However, my back was entirely covered in wounds. This was the present I received in Makhachkala from the Caspian Sea. This sea, which did not treat me well, I would meet again.

On the way from Makhachkala to Tbilisi, the capital of Georgia, we traveled on a goods train. A few flatbed wagons were allocated to our unit. The journey, long hours in which we were exposed to the burning sun of the Southern Caucasus, was difficult for everyone, me in particular. Under this sun, the wounds on my back caused me to faint from pain. My friends and the young men made me an awning to protect me: they placed a few guns in the four corners of the open wagon and tied a sheet to each of the four corners. They made a canopy and there I sat and healed my wounds with the help of the oil given to me by the good woman in Makhachkala. We arrived in Tbilisi.

The headquarters of the Southern Army or some other head-quarters was located in Tbilisi at the time, I do not know. There, our unit was dismantled and each one sent to his destination. Before we were dispersed, a high-ranking officer spoke to each one of us. In the conversation with me, he offered me work as a nurse in a military hospital. I refused. After the experiences I had undergone in the Soviet army, all I wanted was to be released from the army entirely. I told them that I had family members in Uzbekistan and asked that they help me to reach them, because they needed my help. To my great surprise, they not only agreed, but they even helped me. I received money, the necessary documents, some pro-visions for the journey, and an instruction to report to the military headquarters in Tashkent.

And thus, I continued alone from Tbilisi and could trust only myself. I was happy. First, I wanted to get to know this beautiful city a little. Tbilisi is located in a mountainous region, immersed entirely in green vegetation. The city is built on the side of the mountain on two levels—an upper city and a lower city. In the upper city there are many roads like bridges, from which it is pos-sible to see the lower city. The architecture of Tbilisi, the chang-ing light, in particular in the mornings and evenings, the fresh air—Jerusalem sometimes reminded me of it. In Tbilisi there was no sense that Russia was fighting for its life: in the streets, masses of well-dressed young men walked about, women in silk dresses; in the shops, which were built according to the grandiose Soviet model, you could buy luxuries, not like in Bobruisk, where the sausages and meat in the shop windows were fake and the shops were empty. And not only Bobruisk. During all my wanderings in those years I did not meet anywhere else so many young men with no worries, wearing civilian clothes, and living the quality of life that I saw in Georgia, in particular in Tbilisi. It seems that Stalin, in keeping with his character and methods, showed concern for his homeland and people.

There, in Tbilisi, I was released from the army, although formally I would be released only in Tashkent. I wanted very much to inform my family. I knew that Shoshana and Heniek were worried about me. However, from the time that I left my unit at the front for the unit of untrustworthy soldiers, I lost contact with my relatives, with Heniek, and with Shoshana, and they did not even know whether I was still among the living. Now I could not even tell Shoshana that I was on my way to them. The only thing I remembered was the name of the city they lived in, somewhere in the region of Samarkand.

Yom Kippur in a Bukharian Kolkhoz

From Tbilisi I needed to reach Baku, a port city on the southern shore of the Caspian Sea. Thousands of kilometers separate Tbilisi and Baku, and railway lines are rare. I was forced to walk long distances. On the way, here and there, I caught a ride in a truck or on another vehicle. Here and there I also encountered a train station and found a place on a goods wagon or in a passenger carriage. I passed through undeveloped deserts in Azerbaijan. As I got closer to the area of Baku, the number of oil mining towers increased. The city itself is not interesting, it is even ugly, without planning or cultivation; the only remarkable thing being the mining towers rising up around it. This is an industrial city, with the smell of oil hanging in the air. A place in which the people are irritable and mainly poor.

In Baku I boarded a ship for the opposite shore, Central Asia. The moment I got onto the ship and it weighed anchor and began to sail, I got seasick. I vomited the entire way. The sailors brought me tea and laid me down on a bunk. Every time I lifted my head, I vomited again. I do not know how many days this terrible journey lasted. I could not eat or drink anything, so the sailors brought me chocolate. However, my stomach even refused to accept the chocolate. Nevertheless, everything comes to an end, and eventually we reached the longed-for shore.

I do not remember which port we arrived at. However, when I disembarked I had no doubt that I was in Asia. I was shocked to see how much the landscape before me differed to that of the Caucasus. There, in the Caucasus, despite the different cultures and traditions of the peoples that populate that massive peninsula, you feel, nevertheless, something of a European atmosphere, not to mention the geographical and geological beauty of the region. By contrast, on my first meeting with Central Asia, I saw infinite desert sands, almost completely unpopulated. Communication between the few settlements, if any exists, is by donkey. Also, the customs and way of life in Central Asia are different. Here live on the cruel and blood-soaked legends associated with the period of Genghis Khan.[2]

The boat let us off in the "Turkmen Socialist Republic," most of which is covered by the Karakum desert. The train station is a few kilometers away, in the settlement of Dzhanga, and I made my way on foot. In this entire massive area, until Bukhara, there is only one railway line. If you follow its route on a map, you see that it turns south from Dzhanga through Ashgabat until the border of Turkmenistan (to Dushak) and from there turns again northeast to Bukhara (Uzbekistan).

The train arrived in Dzhanga once every day. When the passengers from the boat arrived at this station, the train was already full of people. The masses waiting at the station (those from the boat, and I among them) added to the overcrowding. Not only were the insides of the carriages full to bursting, but people also

---

2 It is worth reading the beautiful book by Kyrgyz writer Chinghiz Aitmatov, *The Day Lasts More Than a Hundred Years*, which is set in the reality of the Soviet period immersed in legends about these places.

hung from the outside and the train soon looked like grapes stuck to a moving vine, like the trams in Warsaw in the 1950s. I managed to find a place "to sit" on the outside of the train, on the step of one of the carriages. There I got my first taste of the Karakum desert. This infinite desert is characterized by moving sands. When a local person dares to wander from place to place on his donkey, or on rare occasions on a camel, he is covered from head to foot and only his eyes are visible. The donkey, whose head is also covered, carries water and the rest of the necessities that his owner needs in the desert.

After around one hour of traveling on the step of the carriage, it was hard to distinguish me from the desert. I was completely covered with a thick layer of sand. The sand got into all the folds of my skin, my mouth, eyes, and ears, and, with the addition of the burning sun, after a few hours I could not breathe. The hot sand burned my skin. On this long, almost endless journey, the stations were few and far between. At a station I could at least drink water and remove some of the layers of sand, at the very least from my face. Returning to the train, if someone had taken my place on the carriage step, it was possible still to find room "lying down" on the roof of one of the carriages. However, there too it was crowded. There, on the roof, there was a silent war over the possibility of holding onto the chimney from which the compressed air left the carriage. However, this made the journey safer. The roof was arched, making it vital to remain awake constantly. Closing one's eyes could mean rolling off the train's roof. Thus, "sitting" or "lying" after many days and nights, I passed through the Karakum desert and arrived in Bukhara.

I do not remember the city of Bukhara, but only that in a certain Bukharian tea house (chaikhana) I had a chance to wash a little and take the desert off me. I drank herbal tea with Bukharan pitta bread and set out on foot to Tashkent, because there was no train going there.

Around Bukhara I happened upon a kolkhoz. It was already late, evening time. I planned to sleep there. I should add that on this entire long journey, which I made on foot, I was still a soldier in uniform, and therefore people on kolkhozes and even on private farms hosted me generously. This was their civic duty—to provide soldiers with aid. When I reached this Bukharan kolkhoz, the office was closed, and I found no one outside. I walked around for a while, until someone appeared. The bearded man looked like a local. He asked me what I was looking for. I told him that I was making my way back from the front and asked for a place to stay. I asked why the place was closed. He looked at me and unwillingly answered, "Today is Yom Kippur. We do not work on this holiday."

He took me to the office and told me drily that I could sleep on the desk. I asked him if this was a Jewish kolkhoz, adding that I too was Jewish. However, he did not answer me. I think he did not believe me, because he looked rather scared. I must admit that I did not know anything about Bukhara and even less that there were Jewish kolkhozes there; certainly, I did not know that it was Yom Kippur, the holiest day of the year for Jews. I stayed alone in the dark office. I did not think about sleeping, because I was quite shocked by this meeting and the fact that I "had happened" upon a Jewish kolkhoz on this day of the year. I sat on the chair in the dark and my thoughts ran backward—to my close family, my father, my brothers, and sisters. Where were they? How was my father?

Yom Kippur night. How many such nights were etched onto my memory? A white hen, which was supposed to take all the sins that I had committed in the previous year. What sins does a small child commit? I see Mother lighting large candles and quietly murmuring the prayer, tearfully asking the Creator of the world to watch over her home, the health of her family. . . . we, the children, standing around Father. I waited for my turn and then he put his hand on my head and blessed me that I should be inscribed for a good year, a year of health and peace.

The evening of Judgement Day in the home of my stepmother, full of superstitions. Today, the eve of Yom Kippur, she feared me. In the morning, I had visited my mother's grave in the cemetery. Certainly, I had complained to my deceased mother about the wrongs perpetrated by my stepmother. She screams at me, cursing hysterically next to the burning candles. Father does not know what to do. He reminds her, "Stop! It is Judgement Day today." She cannot stop. Perhaps she is waiting for me to ask for her forgiveness. That will not happen. I will never do that, even if my father asks me to do it. However, he does not ask, and I leave because I can no longer listen to her curses.

The years run by. Here is another Yom Kippur eve, in Łódź, in Shoshana's home, on 20 Pomorska Street. Shoshana and Moshe have gone to the synagogue to hear the Kol Nidre prayers, the prayer with the most beautiful melody of all. Moshe helps the chazan this evening, singing with him. A girl of sixteen, alone at home. Little Naftali is asleep in his cradle. She sits by the candles and speaks to the Creator of the world, as though He were sitting by her side, talking to her. This is the monologue of a girl rebelling [against Him]. She does accounting with Him. She thinks that He is completely unfair. She prays to Him, pure in her perfect faith, and asks Him to help her to remain faithful to Him. She has severe complaints. But He is deaf; He does not see or hear the wrongs, the injustice. If so, it is not worthwhile sacrificing her life to this faith in Him, because it is difficult for her to live with her faith alone in this cruel world. And she already has doubts: perhaps He does not exist at all? In her shame, she covers her mouth with her hand, horrified at this terrible thing that she has just said out loud. The conversation with God continues for a long time. She cries bitterly, the doubts eating away at her faith in Him. This is not the first time that she has turned to Him with doubts and questions. Behind her are many nights of tears and questions or rebuke. Is she ready this time to "abandon her faith"?

My monologue to God on that Yom Kippur eve, years before, testifies to the emotional distress of a girl who still believed that the Holy One, blessed be He, listened to prayers and the arguments of a girl on the eve of Judgement Day, next to the burning candles. She waited in vain. Since then, over time, the breaches in her faith continued to grow, until she found another faith, a faith in revolutionary rationalism.

These pictures of past Yom Kippur nights merged in my mind with the other holidays as I sat in the office of a Jewish kolkhoz somewhere in Bukhara. That night, my thoughts and memories turned to my family. What had happened to my father, my sisters, and brothers? When would I ever see them again? Very far from this kolkhoz, over the sea, was my sister Esther, my only full sister who shared both mother and father with me. I cannot remember her without pain and sadness. She remained my father's oldest daughter after my mother died and after Shoshana left home. I loved her very much. She was a beautiful girl, with Father's blue eyes (which I see today in my son, Victor) and long golden curls. Since fall 1938 she had been in Palestine, in a kibbutz.

My Esther, whom I loved and secretly admired for her beauty, for her talents and her ability to make sacrifices for her relatives, for her pure qualities—I could not repay her, let her feel my love and admiration. Despite the difficult conditions in which we lived together, lying on a shared straw mattress, crowded against each other on the cold nights in the attic room when we lived with "Aunt" Yocheved, we did not manage to bond emotionally.

My Esther has now been dead for twenty-one years. Life did not treat her well. She did not live to see the fruits of her labor and her infinite sacrifices for her sons and her grandchildren. May these words be an eternal candle burning in her memory.

On the night of Yom Kippur in the Bukharian Jewish kolkhoz, my thoughts ran to my family. I relived with each one of them the days of my childhood. I remembered a traumatic event that made waves in the town of my birth, and it is connected to Moshe, my oldest brother from my mother's side.

As I already mentioned, in my childhood, Moshe was no longer living at home. He was already working in Łódź. The event that I remembered is connected to his first engagement, when he was around twenty years old. They made a match with a girl from a good and wealthy house in Koluszki or Kalisz (I do not remember which one). We still lived then in our old apartment, on Jatkowa Street. The house was prepared in honor of the intended bride's parents, which was difficult, because we had to borrow a few things from the neighbors. My parents, together with the intended groom and Shoshana, went to the train station to meet the guests. I remained at home with Esther (and maybe my little brother, Meir). Esther was then seven or eight, and I was five. Suddenly, it started pouring. The rain never missed our house, the roof of which had holes that made it like a sieve. In a few moments, the entire house, with the beautifully set table, filled with water. My Esther, so brave, rolled up her sleeves, cleaned and dried the floor, changed the tablecloth, cleaned and dried all the utensils, etc. When the guests arrived, the apartment looked sparkling clean.

Afterward was the return visit. My mother wore her best clothes and looked beautiful, so too my father and Moshe—the intended groom—wore their best clothes and traveled to see the bride in her home, where the engagement took place. They returned full of pride, happiness, and wonder. The bride was beautiful and intelligent: she treated my brother warmly. Moshe praised her beauty and learning; he carried her portrait on his chest. Everything seemed like a fairy tale. Not long afterward, the bride's parents arrived in mourning dress, and with heartbreaking sorrow begged for forgiveness and mercy. It seemed that only days after the engagement the girl ran away with a Polish "sheygetz" and married in a Catholic church. Moshe burned her picture without looking at it. After the festival, he returned to Łódź and to normal life. Our mother never saw her daughter-in-law Yitche, whom we all loved very much, and her granddaughter, Rita (who was named after her, Rivka), both of whom perished in Auschwitz.

Today such an event is not so tragic. We live in an open society and among us there are quite a number of mixed couples in terms of religion and ethnicity. However, it was impossible to even think of this in the Jewish community eighty years ago, in a town with a population that was mainly made up of ultra-orthodox Jews, in a closed society. The parents of the girl mourned her and tore their clothing. For them, this fate was worse than death.

I sat on the chair in the office of the kolkhoz immersed in my thoughts, which turned to Soviet society. Here they do not recognize religion, there is no God in the USSR, and yet in this sea of secularism and persecution of religious people from all religions, I heard in faraway Bobruisk the tune of Talmud study, and here, in the deserts of Central Asia, in Bukhara, at the end of the world, in a Soviet kolkhoz, the Jews celebrated Yom Kippur and fasted. The wonders of faith.

Early in the morning, the same Jew whom I had met the evening before returned to me. He asked me if I needed anything. I thanked him, wished him a good year and that he should be inscribed in the Book of Life, and I set out on my way.

I do not remember how I reached Tashkent. Tashkent is the capital city of Uzbekistan. It made a strange impression on me. This was the first time I saw a large city in Central Asia (I emphasize, this was sixty years ago or more). The streets were almost empty. The houses, mostly one or two floors, merged with the general landscape and the desert surroundings. Only rarely did the windows of the houses face onto the street. I found out that all the windows and balconies of the homes turned into inside courtyards. This, according to the tradition, was to protect the women from the gaze of strange men. Only the buildings of the ruling authorities were four or five stories and they had windows facing onto the street. In the offices, the faces of the local women were covered with a veil, only their black eyes exposed. In the center of the city was a beautiful Muslim mosque that deserved a visit. However, impatient to see my family, I did not look inside but just wondered at its external beauty.

In the streets, as I said, I saw few people. Here and there I saw men crouching, knees bent, in the middle of the street (which was not paved) and I did not know what they were doing. It turned out that this was a way of relieving themselves—they wore special, wide trousers, open at the back, suitable for this. It is still possible to find similar ones among old Bedouins.

The only Russians were working in the army headquarters, which I finally reached, and so it was also in the rest of the state and local offices in Uzbekistan. There I was finally released from the Soviet army. There I received money for a year and a half of military service and also military provisions for the journey: a loaf of bread and a few dried fish (I did not know then what a treasure I would bring for my family). I also received the necessary paperwork regarding my release and a referral to the Interior Ministry with the instruction to issue me a new ID. In this office I received a normal ID (without paragraph 38), and in another office I received a train ticket to Samarkand.

CHAPTER 7

THE GROAN OF THE GREAT SOVIET EMPIRE (FROM SOUTH TO NORTH)

Urgut—Reunion

As a regular citizen, albeit still wearing a uniform that I had not changed for a long time (for lack of other clothes), I traveled by train to Samarkand.

Samarkand, located southwest of Tashkent, was much more interesting, lively, and vibrant than Tashkent. This may have been due to the arrival of masses of refugees from other areas of the Soviet Union occupied by the Germans. I met many Polish families in Samarkand and its environs; they had arrived from forced labor camps and deportations from all parts of the Soviet Union, and they were there to join the units of the Polish army established by General Władysław Anders. There were many Jewish refugees from Poland in Samarkand, a few of whom joined the army of General Anders or joined their families in order to flee through Central Asia.

There were many tea houses in which it was possible to order herbal tea and special pitta bread (Lepyoshki). In the middle of the city was a vibrant market (the entire city gave the impression of being one big market). The refugees and the fleeing Poles and Jews sold everything they had and bought other things. I was, as I said, wearing a Red Army uniform. I wanted to buy something to drink because I had a long journey ahead of me, fifty kilometers by foot to the town of Urgut, where, I knew, Shoshana was living with her family. The money that I had received from the army in Tashkent was in the upper pocket of my army shirt. At some point, as I stood waiting to pay for my drink, I caught two fingers of a hand approaching the pocket with the money. A man, who had stolen from behind me, immediately darted away. This was a warning for me to be more alert. On the way out of the city, I noticed a poster in the windows of an office. It called for people to join groups for work in the Urals. I read the notice with curiosity and continued on my way.

This was not the first time that I had walked fifty kilometers. I was already well practiced in walking such distances, but I hurried to Urgut. I had a feeling that I needed to hurry to my family, that they were waiting for me impatiently. Urgut lies south of Samarkand, isolated from all public transport. I did not see any vehicles on the way.

It was an unpaved road filled with sand and dust. For the first few kilometers, close to Samarkand, I encountered occasional farms and vineyards, or I saw straw mats laid out on the ground. These were covered in sweet grapes, which turned into raisins under the sun's rays. The owners of the vineyards gave me bunches of grapes, I stopped to talk briefly, to rest for a few minutes in the shade, and then continued. It is impossible to describe how important my Red Army uniform was. This uniform, worn by a white person among the peoples of Central Asia, aroused at once respect and fear. I walked through fields and areas about which there is a

Polish saying, "There, where the pepper grows," meaning, the end of the world. Indeed, this was apparently the end of the world: I saw fields of red peppers. I collected fresh and beautiful peppers in the pocket of my army coat as a memento, although later they, together with my uniform, went through disinfection and all that remained of them was red dust.

After walking about eighteen or nineteen kilometers from Samarkand, I encountered the silence of the desert. Occasionally, I could see in the distance a few trees and miserable huts. On the way I met here and there a couple on a donkey. Or, more exactly, because there they say that a donkey is more valuable than a woman, usually the man was riding the donkey and the woman was walking behind it, sometimes even carrying a large part of the baggage, to ease the donkey's burden.

In the evening, I arrived in Urgut, a godforsaken desert town. I started to ask some people for my family's address. They directed me to the police station, saying that they should be able to help me. I arrived at the police station. They indeed knew where my family was. A female worker accompanied me to a large courtyard and told me:

"Call out the name of the woman's husband, and they will appear."

I shouted out, "Moshe! Shoshana! Moshe!" It was almost dark. From the edge of the courtyard, a man appeared from a hut. From afar, he looked drunk, because he approached me on legs that appeared to be failing him, slowly and hesitantly, like he was seeing a ghost. He recognized me even before I saw his face. He fell upon me, embraced so forcefully I thought he would choke me, and murmured:

"Oy, Shoshana will live, oy, oy, Shoshana will live. . . ."

I could not get out of his grasp, but I felt that he was burning with fever. Suddenly, I saw a boy running toward me. Natush (Naftali), the child I had raised together with Shoshana. I felt a lump in my throat. I could not speak. I caught hold of the boy and embraced him, tears falling from my eyes.

"Where is Shoshana?" I asked eventually. Instead of answering, they pulled me into the hut. In the meantime, I had begun to fear for Shoshana's safety. The hut was dark inside. There was no candle, not even a match. We sat down on a hammock bed of some kind. Moshe had a 40-degree fever and was shaking all over. Little Natush, now already nine years old, was the only one able to look after the house and his sick parents. In the dark, I took out the provisions I had received from the army in Tashkent: the loaf of (no longer fresh) bread and the dried fish. . . . these two people—the child and Moshe, who was burning with fever—fell upon the treasure and, in the dark, using a board that served as a kind of table, ate up every last crumb.

Meanwhile, I discovered some information about their situation. I had no doubt that I had arrived just in time. According to how Moshe described Shoshana's condition, she was dying. After they finished eating, I asked to see her. We left Naftali in the hut and Moshe took me to the hospital. On the way, he asked me to wait until he could prepare Shoshana for the news that I was alive. He told me that one of the reasons for Shoshana's condition was the belief that I was no longer alive. Now, my sudden appearance was likely to give her a shock that might lead to her death.

The hospital, a one-story house soaked in gloom, was in a small garden. We approached an open window. I crouched down, and Moshe called out quietly to Shoshana. I heard her weak voice, answering him with a question, asking why he had come so late. Had something happened?

"Yes, Shoshana, I have good news."

"Maybe a letter from Bina, oy, tell me already. . ."

"Yes, Shoshana, she is on her way to us."

Shoshana, impatient and nervous, wanted to know everything immediately. Moshe started to stammer something. I saw that he was in distress. I decided to reveal myself. I got up from my place under the window, jumped up, and as quietly as possible answered that I was already here.

The broken, sick cry from Shoshana alerted the nurse on night duty, who came running into the room in panic. She saw a soldier next to the window and heard the story. She allowed me to come in and see Shoshana. In the pocket of her apron, the nurse had a box of matches, the only one in the entire hospital. She donated one match so that I could see Shoshana. I saw her. I grasped her in my arms. I too almost fainted. I had a terrible feeling. I held in my arms a bag of bones with a spark of life still glowing in it, but at any moment it was liable to go out. We sat on her bed for some time, until the nurse asked me to leave, because the other patients in the room needed to rest. I left her and asked her to hold on a little longer; I would get her out of the hospital. I understood immediately what was wrong with her: dystrophy from hunger. A few years later, I would care for patients in a similar condition in the state hospital in Łódź, survivors of the extermination camp in Auschwitz.

On the way back to the hut, I was plagued by black thoughts. I had arrived five minutes before the last bell. Would I be able to save the soul I loved most in the world, the person closest to me, or was it already too late? Moshe was also sick with a dangerous illness. What could I do? I understood that I had to save my family because, without me, they were lost. In the morning, I would acquaint myself with the conditions and decide what to do.

Somehow, without closing my eyes, I passed the night. Only when dawn arrived did I look around me. I was in a clay hut that Moshe had erected on his own. The other huts in the courtyard, and almost the entire city, were the same. There were no real houses apart from the municipal or state offices. In these huts there were no windows and doors. Moshe's hut had a small hole on one side that served as a window, through which a little light entered, and a big hole for the entrance, which at night was covered with a sheet.

The hut was small. The board bed on which they slept provided them with a place to sit during the day, and Naftali, the child, lay on the "floor," which was sandy earth. That night, I lay next to Naftali.

This child, nine years old, did not go to school. He looked after his sick parents. Early in the morning, he was already busy making something warm to drink, a coffee substitute. This was no simple operation. "The kitchen" was outside the hut: it was made up of four stones, on which it was possible to place a pot or kettle, and in the middle, a place to burn fire. For fuel they used cow dung that was dried on the external walls of every hut in the town. How could one light a fire without electricity or a match? Like our forefathers in the stone age: by rubbing together two stones until a spark appeared that set light to a bit of straw or other material held close to it. Thus, after five or ten minutes of rubbing the stones, Naftali succeeded in lighting the fire. Naftali learned the teachings of our forefathers from Moshe and became an expert. I was familiar with this method because in the army the soldiers lit cigarettes, meaning a handful of tobacco wrapped in a bit of newspaper, in this way. Among the personal equipment of each soldier were two small stones suited to this task and a stick.

There was no food in the house at all. First, it was necessary to go shopping, to make food for them, and to prepare something to keep Shoshana alive. I bought her grapes. As early as possible in the morning, I went to her carrying this package, accompanied by her child.

Shoshana was waiting for me impatiently. I noticed that her eyes filled with light when she saw me with her child. With his help, I took her out to the garden and sat her on a chair in the shade, under a tree. I gave her something light to eat and asked her to eat slowly. All that day I sat with her, and the next day I took her home. I fed her grapes and healthy food. After a week, she could get up on her feet. For Moshe I was able to get hold of some Akrikhin tablets against fever (malaria).

The town was in a terrible state. Moshe worked in metal work between one bout of fever and the next, if he had work. However, there was no work. This was a town condemned to death. It had no agriculture, no economic infrastructure, nothing. The family usually starved. I could imagine how Shoshana had reached this state and been admitted to the hospital. She had starved herself to give a crumb of bread to her husband and child.

The money that I brought from the army would not last for long. I had to find work so that I could keep my family alive. Indeed, I was an army nurse. Shoshana and Moshe thought that this was an excellent profession, that it paid well, and there was as much food as you wanted.

I went to the town administration, presented my documents, and asked for work. They seized me immediately with both hands. There was work. I was given a grandiose position: managing "the war against malaria." This was just right for me. I was "to manage the war" at the special medical station responsible for the surrounding villages. Wonderful. However, how would I help Shoshana and her family? My Shoshana did not worry at all. She was sure that every few days I would come home with sacks of food for the whole family. The next day, a man from the area showed up riding on a donkey, ordered me to sit behind him, and we set off.

I held on for two weeks, a period that I will never forget. I could have disappeared there forever and no one would have even noticed. At the same time, I should emphasize that I did not flee because of the inhuman conditions. I fled for a number of reasons. The first was the question of what help I could really offer to people with malaria in the existing conditions and in my working conditions. The second was the question of to what extent I could help my hungry family in Urgut, for whose good I had agreed to take the job. The third was that others endeavored to ensure I failed.

Therefore, I will describe the conditions in the area and my working conditions.

The area was poor, like the town of Urgut. Passing between the villages, I went through fields of rice growing in water and swarms of mosquitoes buzzed in the air. The fields belonged, apparently, to Soviet farms (Sovhokhim) or to a kolkhoz in the area. Many kilometers separated the villages. In every village, people lay in huts, or under a tree next to the hut, dying of malaria. Flies, mosquitoes, and all kinds of insects covered the sick, who were no longer able to fight them off. People died like flies. In the huts there was no clean water and nothing to eat. The terrible feeling of helplessness weighed on me from the first day that I started touring this rural population.

My role was to go to every village, to find and locate those with malaria, and once a day place an Akrikhin tablet in their mouths (I was not permitted to leave the medicine with the sick people). The reality I encountered upon my arrival at a village led me to conclude that I offered no help to the dying whatsoever. This feeling, that my help was as useful as bleeding the dead, increased from day to day. When I arrived in a place the following day, they showed me how new cemeteries had sprouted up over the course of one day on the edges of the villages, and I found new people dying under the trees. The entire area was sentenced to death. I had not seen an entire area so wracked by poverty and neglect anywhere in the Soviet Union. I would have been more useful had I been able to bring sacks of food to such a village. However, I myself was hungry.

The second reason that led me to flee was the evil tricks played on me by the two Russian nurses in the first-aid station. I returned every day tired, hungry, and feeling completely helpless. I could not help the sick or change anything, and I felt that I had neglected my relatives, who were also hungry. And here, in the station, after an exhausting day during which I had not drunk even a little water, the nurses looked down on me with contempt, left me their left-overs, and I went hungry. But even that I could have forgiven.

Once, the two nurses informed me that they were going to the city and that I should remain in the station. They told me that a sick person was due to arrive and that he was to be given an injection (this was their job) and that the medicine was in the medicine cupboard. They warned me to be careful with the syringe, because breaking it would be considered sabotage. Indeed, it was the only syringe. I did not take their words seriously, because I was pretty experienced in using syringes. However, I did not think to check the syringe in their presence, and it did not occur to me that they had left me with a fractured syringe. This was my mistake: it never occurred to me that it was possible to be so evil. I should remind you that back then we used glass syringes finished with metal. The internal part was also metal.

In the afternoon, the patient arrived. I prepared the medicine, put the syringe in a dish of cold water, and put it on the primus. The moment the water started to heat up, the syringe fell apart. This was a warning sign for me. I understood that the Russian nurses wanted to get rid of me: apparently, I made things uncom-fortable for them in their dealings with the local population. That day I returned to Urgut. I did not even wait for the Russian nurses to return.

In Urgut I found my family hungry again. The little money I had left them had run out entirely. It was necessary to do some-thing to get my family out of Urgut; otherwise, we would all per-ish. I persuaded Shoshana and Moshe that we needed to move to a place where we could find work. The three of us knew how to work and hard-working hands were needed in big cities. But where should we go? Suddenly, I remembered the advertisement I had seen in a shop window on the outskirts of Samarkand. We agreed that I would go back to Samarkand and search for a solution to our problem.

I must admit that at the time, after my release from the Red Army, after surviving the battles on the front and everything I had endured and remaining alive with rich experience, I felt liberated, invulnerable, and at the height of my strength. I had faith in my powers and in my ability to save my relatives, who were dearer to me than anything else. The concern for my remaining relatives in Poland increased my concern for those who were with me and now dependent on me. I was full of energy and ready for sacrifice.

I arrived in Samarkand in the afternoon and found the notice in the same place. I went into the office to find out more details. It turned out that they were signing up people who were willing to volunteer for work in factories located in the Urals. The government promised housing, food, and a salary. The government would also pay for the journey and provide provisions and some money for the way.

All this seemed promising. Even if things would be less rosy there, I thought, at any rate, it had to be better than Urgut. I could not go back on foot fifty kilometers to Urgut to consult with Moshe and Shoshana and then return again to Samarkand. I feared that I would miss the opportunity. Therefore, without consulting anyone, I took upon myself the responsibility and signed up the entire family to work in the Urals, in the town of Berezniki (in the Molotov region, now in Perm).

I left the office gripped with fear at what I had done. I had doubts. Could I determine their fates without asking Shoshana and Moshe? Indeed, they had already been to the Urals and fled from there. Then they were in a work camp in the forests, but who knew what would remain of all the promising guarantees made while recruiting workers? Could I be sure that we would not experience a similar trial? Many doubts ate away at me. Yet, I thought, we are free people. If one factory did not work out, we would look for work in another. The main thing was to get out of Urgut. Anyway, I could not change what was already done. I had left my ID documents in the office and in my hands was only an authorization paper. Indeed, I thought, if the place I had signed up for would prove to be no good, we were free people and could move somewhere else. The vital thing was to get out of Urgut.

I walked around the city a bit. Suddenly, someone grabbed my hand. It was Shlomo Pacanowski, whom I had met in Białystok before he went back to Poland to bring his wife. He was the one who had led to Shoshana and her family coming to Russia. He was pleased to see me. Shlomo had in the past worked for my brother David, and I knew that he was a Communist. Here, in Samarkand, I saw him carrying a prayer shawl and other prayer accessories. He was on his way to synagogue because it was the festival of Sukkot. I asked him whether he had become religious. He laughed and answered that he had not, but this was necessary for his business, because people with whom he did business came to the synagogue. I did not ask him what business he was involved in. I wanted to part from him, because it was late, and I had fifty kilometers to walk back to Urgut. He was not willing to hear of it. He told me that it was already late and that it was dangerous to walk in the area alone at night. He took me to his home.

His wife, I believe her name was Sara, had already returned home from work. They lived in a tiny room, apparently an addition to the neighboring apartment. Along the entire length of the wall was a bed, beside another wall was a kitchen cabinet and next to it was a manually operated machine for making socks. He began to take out of the cupboard jars of sugar, melted butter, jars of fried pig fat, smoked meats, dried fish, all kinds of barley, etc. I was dizzy. I thought of Shoshana starving in their empty hut.

"How do you do it?" I asked.

I did not yet know enough about this way of living in the Soviet Union, a political system that rocked the foundations of human morality.

It was very simple, in his opinion, and the two of them were proud of it. Sara worked in a textile factory. There, she found a dark corner, and, before the end of her shift, she tied around her body bunches of raw cotton strands and brought them home. At home, Shlomo made them into socks using the manually operated machine. Their business bloomed.

I remembered Murzyn and his troubles in the bakery that made sweet rolls in Bobruisk, how he was fired from his job because he did not want to be party to stealing.

Although I knew that Murzyn's case was not rare, I had believed in my heart that nevertheless the Communists from Poland would not be caught up in this moral decline. At any rate, I was far from understanding such tricks, like those of Shlomo and his wife. All my family belonged, apparently, to the strain of innocent, naive people who could not adapt to such an immoral life. With this unpleasant feeling, I wanted to leave them and go back to my relatives, to the simple and purer atmosphere. However, they would not let me go. It was already evening and in Samarkand in the evenings it was dangerous to go out on the streets, so my hosts explained, because you could get a knife in the back. I was forced to spend the night with them.

The three of us lay in the couple's narrow bed and talked almost the entire night. I found out a lot of things I had not known before. I found out only then that the establishment of the Polish army unit on Soviet soil commanded by General Anders (to which I, in my naivety, had wanted to transfer) was the result of the agreement between the Soviet Union and the Polish government-in-exile in London. This flirtation was intended, on the part of the Soviet Union, to keep the Allies happy, in particular the UK and the USA, who were fighting against the Nazi forces to release

Europe and were helping Russia in its war. From the beginning it was known that this agreement would not last for long, because each side had conflicting aims. The Soviet Union, whose aim was to conquer Poland, would eventually need to fight the Polish government-in-exile, while the latter was interested mainly in extracting from the Soviet Union the tens of thousands of Poles who had fallen into captivity or had been exiled to forced labor camps from the eastern territories of Poland, which had been conquered following the famous Molotov–Ribbentrop Pact.

At the same time as Stalin allowed the Polish army under General Anders to leave the borders of the Soviet Union, a different Polish center was established in Moscow, one supportive of the Soviet Union, which saw it as the future savior of Poland from the claws of Nazi occupation. This was the Związek Patriotów Polskich (ZPP, Union of Polish Patriots), which I mentioned already; it sent me the Polish newspapers while I was in the army. Behind this union was the Polish author Wanda Wasilewska, who was close to Stalin, and around her gathered former Communist activists who had immigrated to the Soviet Union during the war (as exiles from Poland). As a result of the union, the Tadeusz Kościuszko Infantry Division was founded, and it fought alongside the Soviet army.

I already mentioned that on my way I met Polish women and children in Tashkent and Samarkand. These women addressed each other as "Pani (Madam) Pułkownikowa," "Pani Generałowa," "Pani Prezesowa," when they stood in the lines for the well or the grocery store. They were moving toward the southern border, following their husbands.

While I was with Shlomo Pacanowski, I found out that in Samarkand there was a Polish diplomatic representation that issued Polish IDs and helped those about to leave the Soviet Union. Among them were also quite a few Jews who declared that they belonged to the Polish nation and received Polish IDs. So too, the

Pacanowskis were now Poles according to the new IDs they had received from the Polish consul (many were killed on the way during battles and no small number were harmed because of the anti-Semitism among the ranks of the Poles).

I did not intend to leave the Soviet Union and I hoped that the way to Poland was shorter from here than via Iran or the Sahara Desert). We argued that night, and, in the morning, I left for Urgut.

Years later, I found out that Shlomo and Sara parted from the Poles in Iran and traveled to Argentina. There they bought a few houses, making a living from the rent. However, they did not enjoy much of their wealth, because one of the tenants murdered Shlomo when he came to ask for payment. May the earth of Argentina be sweet for him.

I returned to Urgut. My family agreed to go to the Urals. In the meantime, we had eaten through the remnants of the money I brought from the army. We were lucky and did not have to wait long. In October 1942, we received a notice that we should prepare to set out. Again, we shoved all our belongings into a few sacks, and one morning a truck arrived that was supposed to take us and a few other families from the town to the train station in Samarkand. Sadly, just before we got on the truck, two people approached us and asked about Moshe Benda, my brother-in-law. They presented to him a conscription order for the labor battalions,[3] and on the spot they took him away. He only managed to embrace Shoshana and the child and part from us.

We remained alone, two sisters and a child. Shoshana was in shock. She almost fainted. Little Naftali clung tightly to his mother, and I embraced her and tried to whisper calming words in her ear. Having no other choice, we got on the truck and left. Shoshana cried the entire way. Until now, Moshe had been her only rock.

---

3 Batalion-stroi (Labor battalions). Men who, for security reasons, were not conscripted into the army, were recruited to these battalions, including most of the Jewish refugees from Poland. The conditions were very harsh.

Now, I needed to play a double role, also taking Moshe's place, because the weak Shoshana was unable to perform any physical work.

The Journey—Berezniki

As I mentioned, I was full of energy and at the height of my physical strength. We reached the train station in Samarkand. On a side track stood freight wagons fitted with benches. This was where we were to live during a long journey that would take weeks, traveling from the south of the Soviet Union to the north, the Urals. Now I needed energy not only to take our belongings from the truck but to run to find a comfortable place for my family in one of the carriages. I left Naftali with his mother and ran back and forth with our baggage to the train. Finally, I arranged for us a place on two benches side by side, I put the sacks in the space between the two benches, took out our bedding, and made a place for Shoshana to rest. It seemed that she had calmed down and felt better and was even pleased that the town of Urgut was behind us. When everything was arranged, the person accompanying us entered our wagon, gave out food, hot tea or coffee to drink, and also a bit of money. Everything looked excellent.

The train set off. We set out for the unknown. Shoshana was very sad. She was thinking about Moshe. We talked mainly about him. Would they ever be together again, or had she been fated to raise her son alone? What awaited us at the end of the line? Mainly, we talked about those we had left behind in Poland. She remembered those who had fled with them to the Urals before, in 1939, and returned to Poland, wondering if perhaps she and Moshe should have returned to Poland, then Moshe would not have been forced to join the labor battalions.

Was she sorry that they were left with me? Although we did not know about the bitter fate of Alter Goldberg and his sister, the brother and sister of our sister-in-law, Yitche, who fled together with Shoshana to the Urals—just as we did not know the fate of all the rest of our family—but in our heart I was sure that by preventing Shoshana and her family from returning to Poland, I had saved their lives. I tried to remind her at least of the horrific acts the Nazis had committed against the Jews before we fled Poland. These memories spoke to her. We tried to be optimistic, but new trials still stood before us.

I do not remember much from that freight wagon, because on one of the first days of the journey, I contracted a high fever. We did not know what to do. Shoshana panicked, fearing that they might take us off the train. She did not want to reveal my illness. In the evening of that day, the fever rose and I lost consciousness. Then she also began to fear for my life. Eventually, the others traveling in our wagon found out, and, fearing that maybe I had typhus, they demanded that I be taken off the train. And thus, at the train station of Eris in Kazakhstan, they took me off the train and put me into the epidemic hospital next to the train station. Despite my high fever, I was conscious enough that I would by no means allow Shoshana and the child to stay in this town without a roof over their heads. I demanded that she continue on with him, and I would join them later. And so it was. However, in the confusion, Shoshana forgot to give me my documents and some money.

In the hospital I lost consciousness. When I woke up, I understood that I was lying in a room full of patients sick with typhus. I had a strange feeling. Around me, in every bed, lay hallucinating women, talking in loud voices about all kinds of things. There were even some who in their hallucinations had sexual experiences. And I too, in my high fever, I lectured to an audience, and every time I had myself saying "товарищи" (tovarishchi—comrades), I woke up. It is interesting that I remember images from my hallucinations. So, for example, I saw many beautiful flowers in a range of colors constantly falling down upon me, until I woke up again. (I had similar experiences and saw similar images in 1959 after an operation to remove my gallbladder; I was bleeding internally and it took me a long time to recover. For many hours I lost consciousness. I was almost in the next world. Then I saw next to me an open coffin, Esther crying, and many flowers around me.)

The fever abated after eight days. The doctor determined that I did not have typhus and there was no reason to keep me in the epidemic hospital. I was released and given half a loaf of black bread for the journey and a certificate saying that I had been taken off freight wagon X that was traveling north. This was the sum total of my possessions and ID: all the documents, including my ID, and all the money we had received for the journey remained with Shoshana.

It is hard for me to say that after my release from the hospital I was healthy. On the contrary, my feet were unsteady, my head spun, and I was very weak. However, I had to get on a train going north. I had no money to buy a train ticket. I knocked on the door of the station manager in Eris, told him my story, and he shouted at me:

"What do you want? You want me to pay for a train ticket to Berezniki from my pocket? Try your luck without a ticket. When you get caught, try and make excuses. . . ."

So I did. When the train going north arrived, I got into a carriage in which there were a lot of soldiers (I too was wearing a uniform). There were soldiers who, like me, had already been released from the army—some having been injured and spent time in military hospitals, some for other health reasons and some, like me, because they were not "trustworthy." In every carriage on the long-distance train, there were another two wooden boards on both sides of the seats. I told the soldiers that I did not have a train ticket and explained the reason for this. I showed them the certificate from the hospital, and they immediately adopted me. I gave them the bread I had, because, in any case, I could not eat anything, and they exchanged it at a station on the way for milk, which they gave to me. They helped me to get up onto the upper board and I lay there for almost the entire journey, because again my fever rose. My soldiers were fantastic. They took care of me for the entire journey. In Russia, where the distances between stations are so great, every station has boiling water (kipyatok). The soldiers brought me hot water to drink when they got out at the stations to stretch their legs.

⚔

At this point, I would like to include a few words in praise of the Russian soldier in particular and the simple people in general. I was not afraid to be with them in the trenches at night, even when they were drunk. You could trust them when you were in trouble. When life at the headquarters of my regiment became difficult, I always ran away to the positions of the simple soldiers or to Sergeant Sima.

As a footnote, I will note what happened, when, in fall 1944, with a two-month-old baby, I had to move from Ivanovo-Voznesensk to Kostroma. I was sent to Kostroma by the ZPP to organize a ZPP branch in the region (Kostromskaia oblast). We moved together with Shoshana and Naftali (my husband Heniek was then some-where in Eastern Poland with the Polish army). Our baggage had increased in the meantime: it was no longer made up of only Shoshana's two or three sacks but also mine, including a tin bath, which was made especially for the baby, an instrument for heating water, Naftali's skis, and more. I did not know how we would get on the train with all these things, through the masses of people waiting for it. When the train arrived, Shoshana suddenly disap-peared (she had run to the bathroom). I stood with the baby in my arms and turned in despair to a group of soldiers standing some distance away:

"Friends, help me, please." In a moment, all our possessions were carried over the heads of the crowds that had gathered at the doors to the carriage, and then I went after them with the baby, Naftali, and Shoshana, who came running at the last moment.

I experienced many moments of kindness from simple Russians, despite their roughness and sometimes even external rudeness, and I also saw this in daily interactions. For example, in 1965, I traveled from Warsaw to St. Petersburg (then Leningrad) to the state archives, searching for archival material for my PhD thesis concerning the development of industry in Warsaw in the nineteenth century. The living conditions there were harsh. The hotel in which I stayed was in the suburbs. When, early in the morning, I got on a tram bound for the other end of the city, where the archive was located, I saw occurrences just like the one I described above, and perhaps even more touching. The trams of Leningrad were similar to those of Warsaw, meaning that they were absolutely packed inside and out, with people holding on around the carriages like bunches of grapes. At every station on the way, masses of people battled for a place even before the tram pulled up. In this confusion, a woman with a baby struggled to get into the carriage (she needed to be at work at an exact time and before that needed to drop off her baby at the nursery in the factory). She raised the baby and asked, "Please pass him!" The baby was passed from hand to hand by those same people who were themselves pushing others to get on the tram. Inside, someone sitting took him and, in the meantime, others helped the woman to get on. I saw such sights at almost every station.

Such a favor would have been unthinkable among the residents of Warsaw traveling to work in the mornings on the Warsaw trams. I myself, when I traveled one morning to work from Próżna Street to Koszykowa Street with my child, two years old, was pushed out of the tram. Only when we fell and found ourselves between the wheels of the tram did people start to shout and help me to get up.

One day in November 1942, the train finally brought me to the station of Berezniki, in the Perm region (then Molotov), the northern Urals. I asked people how to reach "Magnizavod," the factory to which I was to report. I hoped to find Shoshana and Naftali there. People pointed me toward a bus stop going in the direction of the factory. I stood in the line for the bus, which had just arrived. From the front people alighted, and from the back others boarded the bus. Suddenly, two women who had gotten off the bus stopped by me, looked at me in horror, and said something to me, but in the meantime the people behind me pushed me to get on. From the cries of the women, I only understood one word: "Zemlianka number one." The bus set off and I did not know who they were. According to the horror that I saw in their eyes, I understood that I looked pretty terrible. Indeed, I had suffered from a fever for the entire journey.

I owe my life to these two women, whose names I do not remember.

In the meantime, the bus reached its final stop and all the passengers alighted. So did I. Around me was a massive building site; here and there stood huts or caravans. I was completely exhausted. I needed to find a place to sleep. Between the huts I found the building office of the factory. There I showed them the only document I had. I said that apparently the convoy that I was on from Samarkand had arrived in the meantime, and my sister, who had all the rest of my documents, was among the passengers.

They looked at me and did not understand what I was saying. They saw that I looked like I had just gotten out of the hospital, but no train from Samarkand had arrived. After long searches they found that a freight train, the number of which was identical to that on my document from the hospital, indeed left Samarkand and was somewhere on the way. And thus, I was alone. Shoshana and her son had not arrived.

In the factory they took into consideration that I had just been released from hospital and had not long before returned from the front and gave me light work as a "Tabelshitza." Although I had no idea what that was, they promised me that the next morning, when I would come to work, they would explain the job to me. In the meantime, I filled out the necessary forms. They gave me tickets for the cafeteria, tickets to buy bread, and also a referral to a zemlianka with a few wooden boards. (A zemlianka was a trench built into the earth and covered with a roof of straw.)

At that moment, all that interested me was finding a place to lie down. I simply had no energy left. Thus, I arrived at the zemlianka with great difficulty. I ascended to the third "floor," to the wooden bed I had been given, and stayed there until the next morning.

In the morning, I got up and went to work. As always, on the first day of a new job, I was tense. Would I be up to the job? I still did not know what it meant. Very soon they explained it to me, and a red light went on in my head. My job was to stand guard and check that every worker employed in building the factory arrived at work at exactly the right time and was not late by even five or ten minutes. If someone was late, I was to check the reasons for his absence and write reports. This was one of the "dirtiest" jobs in the Soviet Union of that period (similar, for example, to the cruel law concerning "lazy people and vagrants"). Presumably, my reports, had I written them, would have been thrown in the garbage together with me and my "light" work. I walked around between the zemliankas and visited the workers who did not go to work for only two days. On the third day, fate intervened. More on this later.

I thanked God that Shoshana had not yet arrived and that she would not need to live in this trench with her son. However, I had to wait for her. Two days of work in the factory gave me a chance to get to know the living and working conditions in "Magnizavod" (this was a defense factory, apparently to build planes). These days revealed to me at what human price the Soviet Union managed, in the midst of the war, to rebuild the military industry and pay for the authorities' cruelty in all the years before and during the war. (I did not know anything then about the harsh labor carried out by hundreds of thousands sentenced to forced labor camps, whose bones are scattered in the taiga of Siberia, and in the gulags.)

Here, in the Urals, at a distance of a few kilometers from the city of Berezniki, air industry factories were being built to provide for the needs of the war. In the massive area around this factory, zemliankas were built to provide dwellings for the tens of thousands of workers who volunteered to work there (like me and my family), mainly via the transfer of entire populations, largely from Northern Caucasus and Central Asia. This means that people from tropical or post-tropical climates moved to the cold of the Urals, which in the winter drops to minus 50 degrees or even less. The walls and floors of the dwellings (zemliankas) were earth, without any covering; the "ceiling" was covered with clods of earth. In the zemlianka, on both sides of the walls, were three stories and three columns of wooden boards. Meaning, on one wall there were nine sleeping places. Between each floor and the next there was a narrow passage via which it was possible to climb up to the bed above. In the middle was a small iron oven (teplushka).

This was the winter of 1942–1943, I believe it was December. There, in Northern Urals, the winter was already at its height. When the oven was working, the snow that covered the "roof" started to melt and the water dripped on those sleeping in the uppermost bunks. At night, the oven was off, and the water that built up during the day on the beds and flowed on the clay walls turned to ice. The people living in the zemlianka, who at night were covered with a thin wool blanket, could not sleep in this terrible cold and under ice, but they nonetheless needed to get up in the morning, while all the walls were covered in snow and ice, and run to work.

For the most part it was like this. However, sometimes, after a cold night without sleep, many wanted to warm their bodies. They lit the oven, sat around it, covered in wet blankets and, when I came in to check why they had not come to work, I found the workers sleeping around the oven, and only steps away from them everything was covered in ice. They looked miserable and helpless, just like me. Indeed, I too had passed the night shaking with cold "on the third floor," on my bed. Many of them walked around with fever and various illnesses. I too had a fever. These people did not really have clothing to wear or food to eat. They died there in droves, like flies. Had I written reports on their condition and why they had not come to work, I would have immediately been taken care of by the KGB. My luck was that on the third day of work I fainted and was taken to the sick room.

I do not know how many days I lay in this room unconscious. When I woke up, I found myself in a large, long hut and to my fuzzy consciousness the room had a strong stench, which may be what woke me from my stupor. Before I begin to write about what happened to me, it is worth writing a few words about this institution.

The hut was full of beds filled with patients. Men and women were mixed together, without any divider, around fifty patients or more. Between two rows of beds was a narrow passage. The overcrowding was so great that it was almost impossible to reach a patient; there was no room to pass between the beds. The patients relieved themselves in their beds or, whoever was able, got up and climbed over the other patients to get to the corner of the hut, where there was a container that was emptied once a day. Of course, in such conditions, it is impossible to talk about maintaining even basic hygiene. If there was a nurse or a sanitary assistant there, I do not remember them, and anyway they could do nothing to help. However, I remember the director of this palace that was called "the sick room." He was a head doctor, apparently a refugee from Moldovia. His appearance, once in the morning, aroused panic among the patients. This man knew no mercy. He did not deal with the patients, did not check them, and did not take any interest in their complaints. This was done by his wife, a Jewish doctor, who was forbidden to express her opinion. He pointed at every second or third patient and ordered him to rise and go to work.

His wife, the daily doctor, appeared shocked and fearful. She in fact was merciful, checking the patients, trying to help them and, sometimes, with frightened eyes, asking her director husband to leave a certain patient for another day or two because his condition was severe. In exceptional cases she managed to send a patient to the municipal hospital.

I was in a critical condition. I was weak and had a high fever. The doctor searched for the reason for the fever and weakness, but she did not have the necessary clinical tools. Every day she spent a long time with me; perhaps because of this, "luck" was again on my side. There were a number of reasons for this. Not only did the doctor treated me generously (and this was not without reason), but I also lay in a bed by the entrance to the hut. This was a good place, because at least it was possible to reach me from the entrance and I had some air. For a few days, I lay unconscious or vaguely conscious, I do not remember. Once I saw by my bed two young women, the same ones I had seen at the bus stop outside the train station in Berezniki. I could not talk a lot. With difficulty I asked them only if they knew my sister Shoshana. Maybe they knew whether she and the others had arrived already. They knew Shoshana and me.

These were two sisters who knew me from Bobruisk. They had worked there in the Shveiprom clothing factory, next to the factory in which I worked, and Shoshana had worked with them as a seamstress. They saw us in the cafeteria that was shared by the two factories. Here, on the building site, one of them worked as a postwoman. Every day, she traveled to the train, received the post, and afterward, on a bicycle, she distributed the letters and newspapers to their recipients. Thus, she knew almost everyone in the place, in particular the most important among them, because usually the letters and newspapers were not for the miserable workers. The two sisters had been looking for me since they saw me at the train station. Among others, the postwoman asked the doctor whether she had seen me among the patients, telling her about me and the condition I had been in when she saw me. Thus, I was brought to the doctor's attention, and they were able to find me. The other sister, apparently younger, worked as an assistant in the factory kitchen. Such work in those years of hunger, particularly in a godforsaken place like this, was considered a rare treasure: indeed, both of them had enough food and they were not hungry. During the days I had walked around the site, I had not managed to reach the cafeteria even once. I had not had the strength to eat.

The two sisters, angels from heaven, whose names I did not know and I do not remember, were determined to look after me and help me. I gave them my coupons for the cafeteria and the bread that I received in the factory. They, for their part, brought me hot soup from the kitchen, and because I could not lift my hand to feed myself, they fed me. After a week, I began to eat something. The older sister, the postwoman, was in touch with the doctor and asked her to look after me and ensure they would not send me "home." After a few days, the doctor came to see me with the head doctor, her husband, and was determined to intervene on my behalf. She asked that he leave me for a few more days because I had a high fever. Finally, after a few more days, she asked her husband to transfer me to the municipal hospital, claiming that she suspected I had typhus.

Thus, I arrived in the epidemic ward, this time in the municipal hospital in the city of Berezniki, far from the factory and its building sites, which I never visited again. They shaved my head, put me in a bath, and after cleaning me of all the dirt from the sick room, put me in a clean bed. From all the activity that went on around me, I only remember constantly hearing: "Lift your head up, hold your head up."

When Dr. Yevgenia Meyusayvena checked me for the first time, she realized that I was not sick with typhus but something far more serious and decided to transfer me to the internal medicine ward, in which she was the head doctor. I lay in this ward for many months. Dr. Yevgenia Meyusayvena did not abandon me. She was a Jewish woman who had arrived in the town from the besieged Leningrad (St. Petersburg). (Afterward, I found out that almost half of the residents of this town were evacuees from Leningrad, including the famed Leningrad theater company.)

The conditions in the hospital were harsh, similarly to life throughout the Soviet Union at the time, but the doctors and the staff were, for the most part, devoted and professional. In the hospital they lacked laboratories and the most basic machines, yet they made an effort to give the patients the best possible care. I was carried on a stretcher in the terrible cold for many kilometers for an X-ray of my lungs. Presumably, they obtained the X-ray machine with great effort, and it was not among the best. According to the X-ray, I had TB spread through both lungs. Eventually, as I found out many months later, the diagnosis was mistaken. This was a difficult diagnosis for a young woman of twenty-four years old to receive. During this illness, my teeth started to bleed and wobble. I had scurvy. The doctor ordered me to eat 100 grams of carrots every day to combat this. The rooms were not heated enough, I was covered, like all the patients, with one wool blanket, and at night it was so cold that it was impossible to sleep. Yet, in comparison to the conditions in the building site, it was a paradise.

In the hospital there were no visits. Once or twice the young women from the Magnizavod settlement brought me something to eat.

Once the duty nurse in charge of the patients in our room came to me and turned my bed to face the window. Beyond the window, standing in the snow with one of the women from Magnizavod, I saw Shoshana. She looked at me and cried in despair. I too began to cry. They had finally arrived from their long journey. Three months had passed since I left them at the station in Eris, Kazakhstan. It is impossible to describe how moved I was. I was flooded by hundreds of questions, as well as feelings of concern and warmth. First, I thought, now I will not be alone! I have a family. Shoshana looked healthy. However, to help my family, I had to fight my illness. But in the meantime, I was the one who needed help. I was helpless and my body was battling to live. I was no longer alone in this battle. I was worried and asked her not to go to Magnizavod but to look for somewhere else to live and work in the city.

From here on I must describe how, with quiet courage and sacrifice, my sister Shoshana saved my life. I only found out the full story long months later, in the spring of 1943, when I signed myself out of the hospital on my own responsibility.

Shoshana did not go to work at Magnizavod, far from the city and from me, and did not sleep in the zemlianka there. Rather she asked for and received work in the hospital as a nursing assistant in the pediatric ward. Thus, she could visit me every day. (Subsequently, Shoshana fell in love with working with sick children. At the end of the war, after we returned to Poland, on the way to the Land of Israel with her family, Shoshana worked in a camp for Jewish children, Holocaust survivors, in Germany. She made Aliyah with them in 1946.)

Staff working in a hospital in Russia were eligible to eat in the hospital cafeteria on workdays. Shoshana too received lunch, the value of which was greater than money. She lived with her son in a small room together with two other women, refugees from Poland, who skillfully stole from her the products that she obtained for me with great difficulty. Instead of sending Naftali to primary school, she put him in a kindergarten so that he would be given breakfast and lunch. She did this because her first concern was to save my life, even at the expense of her son's studies (apart from this, they arrived in the middle of the academic year). She obtained coupons for bread for me, and used them to buy onions, carrots, and butter at the market.

This was, as I said, the winter of 1942–1943, our first winter in the Urals and the harshest of the war years. In the town, the water froze at night in the pipes leading to the houses. Therefore, before dawn every morning, workers of the water department heated the pipes by the houses. The apartment in which Shoshana lived had no cooking facilities, so she rose at 5 a.m., when it was still dark, in the bone-freezing cold, and in the street, on the bonfire lit by the municipal workers to warm the water pipes, cooked soup for me. At 6 a.m., after a cold night, a night of fever and high temperature, I received a full pot of hot soup, a fresh onion, and a carrot.

Only someone who experienced life in the Urals, and, God forbid, spent time in the hospital, can really understand the true value of a pot of hop soup in the morning. And still I did not know at what price and in what way this pot was obtained. At first, when I was very sick, Shoshana fed me a few spoons of soup to warm me, leaving the rest for later in the day.

Having been diagnosed as suffering from TB, I lay in a room with other patients suffering from chronic TB. There were two rooms with such patients—one for men and one for women. The veteran patients, those able to walk around, came to my room. I was the youngest of them. They told me that there was a sanitarium for people with TB and that, as a young woman and someone who had come back from the front, I should ask to be sent there. I told Shoshana about this and she saw it as a life raft, not only for me but also, as I understood, for her and Naftali. She brought me paper to write on (which was no easy thing to get hold of).

I wrote a letter to Moscow. I addressed it to none other than Stalin, the merciful Father of the Peoples. What did I write?

Apparently, I poured my heart out. I wrote that I had endured many trials on the front lines in the war, and here I was, in the town of Berezniki in the Urals, about to die from some stupid illness called TB at the age of twenty-four. In the letter I certainly mentioned that there were also more patients like me. The letter was read out to all the patients in both rooms, and everyone authorized it. My sister, with a prayer in her heart, posted it.

Presumably the letter reached Perm (then Molotov), the regional capital of Berezniki and not the addressee, Stalin. After some time, a large medical committee arrived from Perm and checked all the patients with TB, including me and. . . went back again. After a few days, all the TB patients were taken to a sanitarium—all except me and one other, who was in the last stage of his illness and died shortly thereafter. You can understand my disappointment and emotional state. At first, I could not understand why this had happened. According to what criteria did the committee decide to simply leave me there? I asked the nurse taking care of me about this, and she answered me simply:

"In your condition, you won't make it to the nearby station, and the sanitorium is far away. It would be like sentencing you to death."

At least my letter helped twenty other patients.

The doctors condemned me to death. Both my doctor and others in the department visited the room for chronic patients infrequently. However, I did not want to die. After months of high fever and no appetite, one day, when Shoshana brought me a pot of hot soup and all the rest of the luxuries (an onion, a bit of butter, a carrot) and went to work, I ate all the soup in the pot in one go, even after the breakfast I had been given by the hospital. When Shoshana returned after work, she found the pot empty. When I told her that I had eaten all the soup in the morning, she burst into tears. As she cried, she spoke harshly, telling me that I had no idea at what price she had acquired the soup, that she could not do it anymore, and so on.

Shoshana had not wanted to say these words in my presence, but they burst out of her in her great despair, hitting me like lightning on a clear day. I suddenly understood her situation. Suddenly, I saw her once again starving and sacrificing herself and her only child, this time for me. How had I not thought of that until now, how could I be so blind and stupid not to consider the extent of her sacrifice for me? I asked her to be optimistic. I told her that I felt better. Indeed, the fact that I had started to eat meant that my illness was passing, and that I would endeavor to get out of the hospital soon.

After a few days, I got out of bed for the first time and walked around the corridor a bit. The nurse told the doctors, who were shocked. They all came to check me and determined that my body was overcoming the illness. They saw this as a miracle. I told Shoshana about it and this encouraged her.

Now my condition was unclear: every second or third day my fever went down to 35 and in the evening rose to 39–40 degrees. The doctors had no idea why this happened. In between bouts of fever, I walked around and felt relatively well.

Outside, in the meantime, spring had arrived. The snow had melted, the windows were open, allowing the smells of spring and renewal to drift inside. When I walked around the ward, without noticing, I started to help the nurses with their work. After some time, I asked to go home. My doctor, Yevgenia Meyusayvena, did not want to hear of it. I determined with Shoshana that I would sign myself out of the hospital on my own responsibility. And so I did. (I will add here that after a little more than a year, when I was living in Ivanovo-Voznesensk and I got a high fever again, a blood test detected tropical malaria but found no remnant of TB. For a whole year I received Akrikhin [an alternative to quinine] once a day, and the mysterious fever never returned, although I still had ringing in my ears. It is possible, therefore, to determine that the diagnosis by my doctor in the hospital in Berezniki was wrong.)

I moved from the hospital to the crowded apartment in which Shoshana lived with Naftali and two other women. The child had stopped going to kindergarten. He remained at home, and he slept on a table that stood on the side, by the entry door. Shoshana and I again slept together in a narrow bed, as in my childhood, and the other two tenants slept in the other bed. Naftali should have been going to school for some time already. However, the family's frequent relocations due to the war, as well as the living conditions in Urgut, had resulted in him reaching the age of ten without ever attending school.

I had a month of holiday after I left the hospital. From the town, I received coupons for bread and a municipal cafeteria, where I received lunch. This I took home and shared with Naftali (Shoshana was at work and ate there). In the same cafeteria I was offered "light work" as an assistant to the accountant. Their intentions were good. I had served in the army and was exhausted after an extended illness. They offered me work that would include food and enable me to get my lost strength back. However, I rejected the offer, which anyone else in those days would have grabbed with two hands: this generous offer reminded me of the story of Murzyn in the sweet roll bakery in Bobruisk.

In the Urals, and around Berezniki, during the most difficult years of the war, the military defense industry was being built in inhuman conditions. Since I had become ill and was transferred to the hospital, my connection with the building site and its workers had been severed. There was no connection between it and the town due to the long distance and lack of transportation. Thus, I lost all contact with the two sisters who had helped me in my critical first few days in the region. The difficult life of the workers on the building site and the calm life in the town of Berezniki were so different, it was like living on another planet.

Berezniki was a small town. During the war, it became home to refugees fleeing the besieged Leningrad and other occupied cities in the western Soviet Union. Here the Leningrad theater troupe, which was of the same level as the best western European theaters, found refuge. The town made great efforts to make life easier for the refugees. Among other things it allocated plots of uncultivated land, which were plentiful, to anyone who wanted one and could cultivate it, in order to grow potatoes and other vegetables. It is not easy to cultivate such land with a simple spade and one's hands, but many did so. It is worthwhile remembering that even in the big cities in central Russia, which had no fallow lands, the residents grabbed every bit of land by their homes, often at the expense of the pavement, and planted potatoes and vegetables. Thus, people fought hunger and shortages.

We too received a plot of uncultivated land, which the three of us (including Naftali) cultivated, planting bits of potatoes with signs of shoots. A few hours' work and time in the field strengthened us a little and improved our moods.

As I noted, after leaving the hospital, I enjoyed a month of recuperation. In the hospital, they had shaved off all the hair on my head, and it grew slowly, making me look rather comical: the top of my head was covered with curly down. I did not want to cover my head with a scarf, but I was embarrassed to go bare-headed. Using the threads of an old sweater that she unraveled, my wonderful Shoshana knitted me a funny hat that became an inseparable part of my dress for a long time. So that I would not be bored, and to lift my spirits, she brought me a friend. He was a young tailor, an innocent and good-hearted person, a refugee from Łódź. If I am not mistaken, his name was Avraham. He took his role of entertaining me very seriously, but he himself was rather boring, because without meaning to, he fell in love with me. Avraham worked as a tailor for the theater troupe. He was good at his job (he sewed me a suit of clothes from a wool blanket that Shoshana bought in the market). As a worker in the theater, he received free tickets for every show. We used this generously. We saw the best plays, based on the classic Russian works, such as those by Dostoyevsky, Tolstoy, Chekov, Lermontov, and others, performed by the best actors from Leningrad. We always went to the theater the three of us: Shoshana, Avraham, and I (he also benefited, because he enjoyed the shows and without us he would not have gone to see them). The shows finished late, after midnight. This was the season of the white nights of the north—beautiful and unforgettable.

After a month of sick leave, I started to work in the surgical department of the hospital in which I had been hospitalized. I loved the work very much and my patients enjoyed my care. The conditions were highly primitive. It is sufficient to mention that interviews conducted with the arriving patients, the manner of the treatment that the doctors recommended, and even prescriptions for medicines were written on printed papers—pages torn from old books, pamphlets, and journals. The equipment was disinfected in the most primitive manner (boiling water), etc. The staff of doctors and their assistants was limited because the majority had been recruited to the front lines. Despite all this, a massive effort was made to maintain a suitable level of cleanliness and hygiene. There, in the surgical department, I could see the wonders of medicine more than in any other department in the hospital. For example, one night they brought to me a young man bent over with stomach pains. The doctor on duty in the emergency room wrote the diagnosis "hard stomach," meaning, "intestinal blockage." Such a case requires an immediate operation. I alerted the surgeon, who was asleep at home, set up the operating room with all the necessary equipment, and within a short time the young man was on the operating table, with me assisting in the procedure. After the operation, the patient slept soundly. Two days later he was walking around as though reborn.

Such cases and more difficult ones were our daily bread in the surgical ward and left us with a sense of great satisfaction. The work was hard and physically tiring. We, the nurses, worked three shifts. For me, the night shift was especially difficult. There were always a few patients who had undergone complicated proce-dures, and I needed to be on alert. I was perhaps the only one who walked around at night with a torch in my hand, going from bed to bed, room to room, to check the state of the patients. I knew that other nurses rested during the night shift, but I could not do so. Responsibility was in my blood. Therefore, the patients were always pleased when I arrived for work. In praise of the doctors in this hospital, it should be said that they had a very developed sense of duty. They were devoted to their work and, despite the extremely modest means available, endeavored with dedication to save human lives. I miss these doctors and their approach to their patients.

CHAPTER 8
IVANOVO-VOZNESENSK— ESTABLISHING A FAMILY

Reunion with Heniek

Working in the hospital, as I said, gave me great satisfaction. I felt that people needed me and valued my work. I dreamed of studying medicine and becoming a doctor, and the doctors with whom I worked encouraged me in this regard. However, it became clear that my work as a nurse was taking a physical toll on my body. Perhaps not the work itself, but I had simply not completely recovered. I often had a fever, in particular after my night shifts. Sometimes my temperature rose to 40 degrees and within six or seven hours returned to 35 degrees, and the situation became increasingly mysterious. The doctors could not find the source of the problem. Perhaps, they thought, the climate of the Urals was affecting my health. They advised me to change the climate.

It was reasonable advice. However, where should I go? I was not alone, and I could not leave Shoshana and her little boy again. Apart from this, where could I go? How could I live somewhere else, with no means to support myself, sick? In the Soviet Union there was a well-known saying: "Whoever doesn't work, doesn't eat." And I was sick, even though I was still working. Not much was left of the soldier who had arrived in Urgut a year and half previously, who took Shoshana out of the hospital and signed up her family to get out of the dead town, setting off for the unknown. Now I was too weak for new adventures with my only family.

Here, in Berezniki, I had work in the hospital, where I was wanted and loved. The plot of land that we worked in the spring, planting bits of potato and cultivating it, had turned green and blossomed. In another month or two, we would have our own potatoes. This was valuable in the third year of the war with the food situation as it was. Here Shoshana was also successful in her work in the hospital and liked it. How could we again go out into the unknown?

At that time, we talked a lot about Heniek, of course. I had lost touch with him from the moment they took me out of my regiment and put me into the nieblagonadiozhnyie. Since then, two years had passed. Apart from Shoshana, Heniek was the only person close to me in the Soviet Union. I did not know what fate my other friends, spread throughout this country, had met. Had I known, perhaps it would have been easier for me to turn to one of them (just as more than one of them followed me to Simferopol) than to Heniek. Heniek was not just a friend, and I was not just a friend to him. It had been a long time since we had parted in Bobruisk. Indeed, more than three years had passed since then. I had caused him pain, forcing him to leave. Although in our correspondence afterward we reached an understanding and expressed the hope that we would meet again, a lot of things had happened in the meantime. Then I was a young woman of twenty, healthy and blossoming. Now I was sick and tired, I had grown old in my soul more than I had in years.

Apart from all this, I did not know where Heniek was and what was happening to him. Perhaps he had met another woman, perhaps he had erased me from his heart? Perhaps he thought I had been killed somewhere on the front? I thought that it would be only right for him to think this way. Indeed, so many things had changed, each one of us had undergone different experiences that certainly affected our natures and personalities in various ways. It was doubtful whether we would be able to find a common language again. And where was he and what had happened to him?

That was how I understood matters, and I tried to persuade Shoshana that I was correct. I thought we should stay in Berezniki until the end of the war and then return home. That same winter of 1943 broke the German advance, and the Soviet attack began. We knew that the Allies in Europe were striking against the Germans and that the end of this cruel war was in sight.

However, my Shoshana, seeing my health declining, wanted to save me. After going through her various sacks and papers, she found the address of Shmulik, Heniek's brother, who before the war had lived in Saratov, on the Volga River. To this day, I do not know how she got his address. She too could not explain it. She had the idea of moving to Saratov. I was not sure that he was living in Saratov—I had never corresponded with Shmulik at this address. I was hesitant about the idea, because I knew him, and in particular his wife, and I knew they could not be trusted, and I had my own reasons for this. However, Shoshana had her own, secret perspective. She presumed that if Shmulik was still at the address, he would certainly know how to find Heniek. She sent him a telegram asking for Heniek's address. I knew nothing about this telegram.

I was still working at the hospital. Every so often, my temperature soared, and I lay in bed for a day. In "our" plot of land, the potatoes were ripening. My hair was growing, and small curls covered my head. Avraham spent his free hours with us.

One day, Shoshana received a postcard, a piece of blue cardboard, from Ivanovo-Voznesensk. The postcard was from Heniek. I kept it for many years together with our correspondence, which built up over the long years of our life together. I lost it in one of our many moves to a new home, to a new city, and eventually to a new country. I lost the entire package of letters. Yet I remember well how it looked, this piece of cardboard with a Soviet stamp on it, and its contents.

Heniek wrote to Shoshana saying that his brother had told him about the telegram from her, which contained her address. He understood that Shoshana was searching for a trace of Bina (meaning me). Sadly, he informed her that he had been looking for me for two years without success. He also told her that the last letter he had received from me came from somewhere not far from Stalingrad (Volgograd). He assumed that I had fallen in the famous battles for that city (as is known, in Stalingrad the German Sixth Army was broken and the sacrifices for this city became a symbol of the war's turning point). Heniek promised Shoshana that he would not rest until he found me or my grave.

I read these words, written on a bit of cardboard. What could I say? I felt a massive wave of warmth. I was flooded by memories of our innocent years of shared youth and idealism. I burst into bitter tears. To my humiliation, Avraham, the tailor with whom I went to the theater and who had become a friend in our troubles, was at that moment in the room. Seeing me ashamed and crying, he apparently felt uncomfortable—he turned pale and hurried to leave our house.

I felt terribly tired of my difficult life and, first and foremost, as always, I blamed myself for all the trouble. Indeed, I had never forgotten Heniek. On a few occasions in the long nights in the hospital, under the thin blanket, shivering with cold and fever, I thought about Heniek with concern—where had fate taken him? Would the fates bring us together again, and, if so, when? I will not deny that these memories and my longing for him were mixed with bitterness. I did not know whom to blame for this bitterness: him or me. Now it all came back to me with great clarity, in particular the memories from Bobruisk. I felt great shame.

For almost two years, Heniek thought I was no longer among the living, that I had fallen in battle. Presumably, he was not waiting for me; he may have married another woman. It was nice of him to write to Shoshana that he was looking for my grave (there were then no marked graves for the victims of the war). If so, why ruin his peace? All the hesitations resurfaced, in particular, in my current state of sickness and exhaustion. The letter gave me no rest in the coming days and nights. I argued with myself and with Shoshana about a Shakespearean-style question—to write to him or not to write to him?

Eventually, I wrote to Heniek, asking for his forgiveness and telling him that I was alive. I wrote about everything because we were always entirely honest with one another. I wrote that I was very sick, I even exaggerated, and I added that sadly, without my knowledge, Shoshana had reawakened his memories of me. I wrote that I had changed, that I was no longer the young woman who had parted from him three years ago, and that apparently he too had changed. If so, perhaps it was better to remain friends at a distance.

Quickly (of course, in terms of the Soviet postal service during the war) Heniek began to flood me with letters, revealing his feelings and his longing for me over the past three years. He refuted my claim that I could not return to him because I was sick and no longer the same Bina he had known, reminding me of our shared idealism, in the name of which I had sacrificed my health. Therefore, he believed that I had no right to carry the results of this alone. He wanted to share his part in this responsibility and asked me to come to him, to Ivanovo. He was sorry that he could not come to help me (I found out afterward that he had been conscripted into the labor units and due to his attempt to gain release for a few days to come to me he was arrested and imprisoned).

Shoshana used all her powers of persuasion and influence on me. She had always supported Heniek and saw him as the best partner for me. Even in Bobruisk, when I left him and returned to live with my family, and Heniek sat in my home until late at night, she and Moshe, her husband, treated him like a member of the family. Now she believed that the two of us had suffered enough and the time had come to establish a family. She advised me to go to Heniek.

Not without doubts and uncertainties, I decided to go. It was hard for me to leave Shoshana and her little boy. It made it easier knowing that the potatoes in our plot of land were ripening, and therefore the two of them would not go hungry. We decided that I would endeavor to bring them to me as soon as possible in Ivanovo.

I left. I was tense and consumed with curiosity as to what kind of Heniek I would meet, after more than three years apart. Heniek would wait for me at the train station. If he could not be there, he sent me the address of his friend, Brunek Safichai, a Polish Communist. I understood from this that Heniek did not have his own apartment, but I set off toward him with an open heart, full of love.

I do not remember the journey. I reached Ivanovo in the evening. The light of the torches was weak. I looked for Heniek and could not see him. The train station emptied of people. Therefore, I decided to go and look for the address he had given me. The street on which the man lived was small and almost dark and empty of people. However, from afar I saw someone walking toward me with some hesitation. He was of a similar height to Heniek.

Yes, it was Heniek. We fell into each other's arms, embraced, and kissed. The hugs and kisses expressed all the longing and suffering we had experienced. With tension and impatience, he explained to me that he had waited at the train station for two hours: apparently he had been misinformed about the time of the train's arrival. Since then, he had been walking around the street, because he could not go home without me.

Yet he still did not take me "home." Instead, we went to a nearby avenue and sat on a bench. The avenue was quiet. We sat down and he took my hands in his strong ones, just like he had many years ago, when we sat on the little Kościuszko Avenue, close to Pomorska Street in Łódź.

The first thing he did was to take off the wool hat that Shoshana had knitted for me, which until then I had worn constantly. Heniek looked at me and his eyes filled with light and happiness. From my letters, he had thought my condition was much worse, that maybe I was disabled. He even liked my short curls. After that, I stopped wearing the hat. I looked into his blue eyes and saw the Heniek I knew. He had changed a lot: he had become tougher. He had become a man. In his face I saw that life had not been easy. He looked tired and full of worry. He also looked somewhat neglected.

I did not have a place to live. With some degree of embarrassment, Heniek told me that he was still living in the home of a woman; he needed to leave and look for a place for us to live. In the meantime, I would be staying with his friend Brunek for a few days. I was not happy about this, but I accepted it with understanding.

Heniek had worked hard in various places and had also spent a few days in prison; in short, he had led a hard, almost double life. I guessed this before he told me about it (there were never any secrets between us) because the things I saw around me did not arouse excitement but rather deep concern.

While we were sitting on the bench in the avenue, I suddenly noticed that men were walking around and looking at us. Heniek hinted something about these people. My soul went cold. He explained that he had no choice. I told him about my bitter experience in the army, and that only by means of a miracle had I not received a bullet to the head. He found it difficult to hear this story.

After some time, after a few hours of talking and finding each other again, Heniek took me to the home of Brunek Safichai. As soon as I crossed the threshold of his home, which was full of people, and greeted him and the others in Russian, Brunek told me immediately:

"Here, in this house, we speak only Polish. We say 'dzień dobry.'"

I stood confused for a moment, until Heniek came to my aid and introduced me to those present. In this way, I entered Heniek's new life and a unique Polish environment, about which it is worth saying a few words.

Bronisław (Brunek) Safichai was wearing a uniform, the source of which I did not know. Afterward I found out that this was the uniform of Russian prison directors. And here is the story. Brunek Safichai was among the upper echelons of the Polish Communist Party. When Stalin gave the order to eliminate the members of the Central Committee of that Party, who were in Moscow because the party was illegal in Poland, Brunek was incarcerated in a Polish prison in Lvov, where he had been for some years. In September 1939, when the Germans invaded Western Poland, the Soviet army conquered the eastern territories of the country, including the city of Lvov. The prisoners in the Lvov prison were released, and Brunek, the veteran prisoner, was appointed to manage that same prison, which was filled with new prisoners. With the German invasion of the Soviet Union, Lvov was one of the first cities conquered. Brunek managed to escape, arrived in Russia, and settled in Ivanovo. Thus, he had the uniform of a prison director, and he wore it until the end of his life (he died in Moscow close to the liberation of Poland). This man was very sick. He had bone TB and he needed help. Thanks to the endeavors of Wanda Wasilewska, he had some privileges. Among other things, he had a nice apartment and a woman to look after him, and apparently also a nice pension. This apartment served as a refuge for any Polish refugee or activist who came to the city.

That first evening, I met in his home a young woman with a penetrating and subversive look, Genia. I found out afterward that she was also dangerous. In Ivanovo there was a large Polish community (and among it also former Jewish Communists, who would later be part of the leadership core of the Polish People's Republic [PPR], with Stalin's blessing). They seemed highly suspicious, although this was concealed under the cloak of Polish manners.

In the suburbs of this city, there was an extremely well-kept international children's home situated in an expansive garden. This was a children's home for the activists of the Communist movement in various European countries. There, among others, were the children of Dolores Ibárruri, the legendary heroine of the Spanish civil war and leader of the Communist Party in that country; the children of Bolesław Bierut, the first president of the Polish People's Republic, and Małgorzata Fornalska, his wife and the leader of the Polish Party, who was murdered by the Gestapo. They were accompanied by their grandmother, who was considered the grandmother of the revolution (from 1905). Also in this home were the children of leaders of the French Communist Party, Maurice Thorez, the children of the Italian Palmiro Togliatti, of the Czech Gottwald, and others. Szymon Zachariasz, the well-known Communist who was active on the Jewish streets in Poland and was a member of the party's Central Committee, worked in this children's home as stockkeeper, and his wife Hanka taught the school-aged children. There was a large group of Poles there, not all of whom I knew. Some of them, among them Szymon Zachariasz and Brunek Safichai, were later called to Moscow.

This was the turning point of 1943–1944, when the Soviet army advanced to the borders of Poland. To conquer that country, or to liberate it from the German occupation, Stalin needed Poles and Jews from Poland who were faithful to the Soviet regime. In the months of March–June 1943, the Central Committee of the ZPP (Union of Polish Patriots) was established, which I already mentioned. This organization founded branches in every location with a concentration of Polish and Jewish refugees. At the encouragement of Stalin, a Polish military unit named after Tadeusz Kościuszko, the famous freedom fighter from the end of the eighteenth century, was established on the soil of the Soviet Union. It was commanded by General Sigmund Berling, and it fought in the battles over Lenino and alongside the Soviet army for the liberation of Poland.

These were days of warm hope and expectation. There were hopes that a liberated, Socialist Poland would emerge that differed from the Soviet Union, and that we would return to Poland, to our relatives and families. Our evening gatherings at the branch of the ZPP offered us warmth. It became almost our second home. There were active arguments about what the new Poland would look like. I should add that almost all the leadership of this organization were Jews, refugees from Poland (in the region, in the towns and villages of the area, lived Poles who had been transferred from the eastern territory of Poland that was occupied by the Soviet Union in 1939). In Ivanovo, among the Poles who visited this branch, was a local man of Polish descent, a professor of physics named Stradomski, who came there to enjoy the Polish-Jewish language[4] and atmosphere but did not intend to move to Poland.

Thus, this group and its activities became part of both our personal and social lives. It made my acclimatization in Ivanovo easier. Ivanovo-Voznesensk was a regional capital in European Russia, with a population of around 30,000 residents. It was a well-known center of the textile industry and the manufacture of machinery for this industry. Also located in the city was a scientific institution that served the textile industry. However, everything was on a small scale. The city itself was gray in its external appearance and a cultural desert in comparison to Berezniki.

---

4 Polish with a heavy Yiddish accent and occasional Yiddish words.

The only vibrant and lively institution in the city was in fact the center of the Polish organization. I think that the atmosphere there and our active participation within it helped us, Heniek and I, to come together again and to build our shared life. Years of separation, during which each one of us underwent and experienced different things, had left their mark. Each one of us had grown up differently, and the years had changed our personalities and ambitions in different ways. For me this was an intensive year. I met new people and became acquainted with the new surroundings; I went to interesting meetings at which visions of the new Poland and a new shared life were woven.

We rented a room from a woman of Polish origin, who lived with her son. (Later, I found out that her husband had been sent to a Soviet forced labor camp in the 1930s and all traces of him had been lost). The woman never mentioned her husband and what happened to him in our presence.) Thus began our life together. Quickly Heniek began working at the ZPP as an instructor, and immediately after my arrival I was given work in the internal medicine ward at the local hospital. Both of us worked hard, and the lack of basic products did not make life easy. I did not feel hungry, because first of all I was not a big eater and second of all the nurses in the hospital, and I among them, received lunch. However, Heniek, apparently, would have eaten a lot more, given the possibility.

In November, when Shoshana and Naftali arrived, we lived together for some time in the same room. Shoshana began to work as a seamstress. Then a new dish appeared on our table, a recipe that Shoshana learned from the other women she worked with. Potatoes were very expensive, and it was possible to buy only their peels on the black market. After cleaning and cooking them, Shoshana added to these peels egg powder that we received on a monthly ration (sent by America in the form of humanitarian aid, and we called these "Uncle Sam's balls"). Together, she fried them. In those days we could eat even this.

A New Family Member—Wituś

I became pregnant. How was it possible to bring a child into the world in such conditions? What could I offer him? How and where would we raise him? We decided that I would have an abortion. I was working in the hospital, so I asked one of the nurses for advice. The head nurse, who was in her private life also a midwife, agreed to do it, but beforehand she wanted to see my partner and talk about it together. We were determined to meet in her home. She was an honest woman with a good heart. When she saw us holding hands and Heniek's eyes full of love, she looked at us for a long while and decided not to perform the abortion. She justified her decision, telling us that aborting a first pregnancy was likely to have a bad effect on me. She added that, in her experience, economic and material conditions do not have to be a deciding factor, that the war would end, and the conditions would change. Finally, she foresaw that our children would be beautiful and intelligent. She encouraged me to continue with the pregnancy. Shoshana was also against the idea of an abortion. They persuaded us.

We moved to another apartment. There were two reasons for this. First, we had decided not to have an abortion. Two families in a crowded, small room left no room for privacy. Second, Heniek was not enthusiastic from the beginning about the idea of living with Shoshana (he was a bit jealous of the close connection between us). Shoshana and her son remained in the room we had lived in until then, and we rented a room with an older woman in a beautiful wooden house that had a spacious yard containing a few trees. Our room was also spacious, with a separate entrance. It had a large Russian oven, and in the yard was a pile of wood for heating in the winter.

I experienced the singular thing that is a first pregnancy, carrying a living being inside me for nine months. Only mothers that have been blessed with this experience, which, although it involves suffering and pain, is a singular event, can understand it. Heniek dreamed that we would have a son with blue eyes, pale, etc. Exactly such a son was born to us. However, when he finally arrived, Heniek had to wait some time and contribute a lot.

My Victor (Witek, Wituś) was born in Ivanovo-Voznesensk on August 4, 1944, around two weeks after the Polish people's government in Lublin published its manifesto (July 22 of the same year). In honor of this he was given the name Victor. He was born with jaundice. He was entirely yellow, and he was the ugliest baby among all the infants that they brought to the mothers to be nursed. He had such a large nose (the length of my nose and the width of his father's). The new mothers in my room pitied me and comforted me, saying that an ugly baby will become a handsome young man. My baby showed signs of a great desire to live. From the first moment that they brought him to me, I apparently had too little milk for him and he bit my nipples. I got an infection in one breast and a massive ulcer in the milk glands accompanied by a 40-degree fever. However, until they discovered the infection, I nursed my baby, despite the pain, and it may be that this was why he became sick with dysentery. I will not describe how and with what inner strength a mother can fight for the life of her baby, in conditions of war and hunger. I will only say that for the first three months of his life, he was dying. On a few occasions, I sneaked him out of the hospital for babies (because dysentery is infectious and therefore according to the Soviet law it was forbidden to keep him at home).

At home too, the conditions were unsuitable and there was no peace. I had a bloated breast full of puss, was in terrible pain, and suffered from a fever. The baby was dying, and I had to watch over him day and night. My husband had no idea what to do about all this. You could say that he stopped functioning. It is necessary to remember the conditions then: diapers were made from all kinds of rags and old sheets that acquaintances brought to me. We had to wash, boil, and dry them. All this was done in one room, with a baby and a sick woman suffering from high fever. Although we had one big pot especially for boiling the diapers and hot water for washing the baby, all this was done on a primus. Every evening we went through the same ritual: heating water to wash the child, washing and boiling diapers, and afterward ensuring that they would dry around the primus.

In addition, we had to make food not only for us but also to obtain mother's milk for the sick baby, and at night we took turns next to his cot. As a result of all this, Heniek broke. He became so weak and sleep deprived that when he returned from work and sat down to eat lunch or dinner, he fell asleep at the table. Despite my pain and high fever, and perhaps because of the latter, I was in a constant state of tension that forced me to function. However, this did not happen to Heniek. Perhaps I did not understand then what he went through. Both of us were irritable, we fought and quarreled; I was most irritable, like flammable material ready to explode any moment. All this caused Heniek to search for refuge outside our home. The dying baby had reached the age of six weeks when Heniek came home and announced that he had enlisted in the Polish army and was going to fight for the liberation of Poland. I was not surprised.

A day before this Shoshana had come to visit. She brought me a bag that she sewed from material and filled with hot salt to put on my bloated breast. All that day, I applied the hot salt, and the puss began to collect at one point. In the evening, the puss burst out in a jet, filling a large bowl. I fainted and Heniek looked after me. Afterward, I felt much better and my fever began to decline. The next night I accompanied him to the train bound for Moscow. From there he would join the army unit, which was then in Lublin.

It is not nice to admit it, but I felt a certain degree of relief, emotional peace with Heniek's departure. Perhaps because in conditions of crisis each one of us chose radically different behavior and reactions, living together became unbearable. It was good that he went, even though I was left alone with a sick baby, without a penny, with a landlady who wanted to get rid of her tenants and refused to give us wood for heating, and I did not know how and when I would return to work after my maternity leave, etc.

Apart from all this, there was a problem with milk for the baby. I could not nurse him myself, but the doctors ordered me to find him mother's milk. In the hospital they let him nurse from another mother who nursed her baby, but in the hospital he was dying and neglected. Therefore, I took him out a few times in secret and I found a woman, the mother of a baby, who had enough milk for my baby too. I paid her money for one cup of this milk and gave her all my monthly coupons for bread. I thought that if I could not nurse my baby, I did not need bread. As long as Heniek was at home, he brought the milk from this woman, when he came home from work. However, after he left, I went to bring the milk myself for the first time. I prepared, as I did every day, a sterile bottle, and, with the baby in my arms, I went to get the milk. The woman lived on the first floor, to which one ascended via wooden steps. It was September, a hot day. The one-room apartment was crowded: I found a few dirty children in a home full of dirt. On the table stood a cup of milk, uncovered, with flies walking around it inside and out. This was the cup of milk for my baby. Without saying a word, I transferred the milk from the cup to the bottle and left. In my great anger and emotional turmoil, I fell down all the stairs with the baby in my arms. Fortunately, I was not seriously hurt. I threw away the bottle with all the milk and the matter was finished. Now I had another problem—what to give the sick baby.

Shoshana, as always, came to my aid. She and Naftali came to live with me and together we tried to deal with the situation. The baby could not digest even the milk of that woman. After every spoonful, he was bent over in pain and immediately spat out onto the cloth diaper bits of curdled milk. So we began to give him normal milk diluted in water. The result was the same.

One day, I received a package from Moscow: a package of things for the baby, beautiful things. It is a shame I did not have a camera and could not take a photograph of them. Among them were warm satin vests, a warm sleeping bag in light blue, and a package of diapers the likes of which I had never seen: they were not throwaway diapers, but they were easy to wash and dry, made from a special, gentle fabric. However, they still needed boiling. Who sent the package? Here is a little story.

When I was in the eighth or ninth month of my pregnancy, one day a pregnant woman, around the final month of her pregnancy, came to the branch of the ZPP. She was a beautiful woman, blonde and tall. I do not remember her name. She came with references from important people in Moscow who asked us to help her in any way we could. She presented herself as the wife of General Sokorski, who was the deputy of General Berling, the commander of the Polish army. He was politruk in the headquarters and the pregnant woman was his secretary and lover (in addition to his wife, who later divorced him). In short, General Sokorski was very worried about this woman and sent her packages of luxuries. She gave birth to a daughter a few days after I gave birth to Victor. Some of the people I had met in Ivanovo, including Brunek Safichai, Szymon Zachariasz, and others, were by this time in Moscow. Brunek apparently meddled in all the matters of the modest economy under the Polish government that was consolidating. He also knew that I was due to give birth. When he heard that a package of gifts was to be sent for Sokorski's newborn baby, he apparently ensured that I too would get the same. I discovered that on the same day this woman got a similar package, in pink, for her daughter. I had an opportunity to get to know Mr. Sokorski when he came to Ivanovo to visit his daughter and take them both back to Moscow. In honor of the event and their departure, he organized a party for all the activists in the organization. In Poland, after the war, he played various important roles in the leadership echelons. In the 1960s he was chairman and acting director of the Polish state radio committee. He was known to be a womanizer. Every few years he changed wives, without feeling responsible for the children that he left to each one of them.

And thus, my baby was dressed like a prince, but inside this clothing he was miserable and dying. A Russian biologist saved us. I already mentioned that Professor Stradomski, a local physicist of Polish descent, often came to the ZPP. He became friends with us and often invited us to his home. When he discovered my despair, he arranged for me to visit his friend, a professor of biology, saying that if the doctors could not help, perhaps he would be able to do so. I went to him (I do not remember his name). He placed my baby on the palm of his hand, walked around with him, and I saw the end. He was a creature no longer of this world: small, old, his skin was like the peel of an apple from last year. He no longer cried, just made a twisted expression with his face and let out a soft wail, his small head dropping from one side of the hand and his legs from the other. The professor looked enchanted by his appearance. He told me: this creature has almost no life left in him. All his intestines inside are covered with small ulcers and wounds and every spoonful of milk or water causes him terrible pain. There is no chance that he will live. It is possible to take a risk and try something that may perhaps reduce his suffering and maybe heal his wounds. He advised me to give him a teaspoon of chamomile tea and wash him every day in chamomile water.

This was my only remaining hope: chamomile. We overcame the difficulties and got hold of large quantities of chamomile flowers. He took the first teaspoonfuls that I gave him and there were no signs of pain on his tiny face. And thus, slowly, he began to drink chamomile tea and we washed him in chamomile. When he started to recover, I began to give him watered down milk. (When after around two years, Heniek and I were walking with little Wituś in Łódź, we met a woman who knew us in Ivanovo. She was shocked to see the beautiful child and half-asked, half-declared, "And the one from Ivanovo, the poor thing, died?")

Kostroma

Winter came. I despaired. We needed to look for a place to live. The landlady would not give us wood for heating from the large supply in the yard, demanding that I pay her for every bit of wood. However, we had no money. After three months of maternity leave and another month taking care of the sick baby, I needed to get back to work. Although my baby, Victor, had begun to recover, and for the first time he was putting on a bit of weight, he still needed to be looked after with great care. I had not received any news or even a letter from Heniek, but apparently some good angel, or good friends, had not forgotten us.

In these difficult days, the Central Committee of the ZPP in Moscow invited me to establish a local branch of the ZPP in the Kostroma region. I was appointed as general secretary; I would be given training for the job and good wishes for the journey. The letter I received indicated that in a few villages in the area of Kinishma, in the Kostroma region, there was a large concentration of Poles exiled from Western Belarus and Lithuania, which had belonged to Poland and were conquered by the Soviets in 1939. Among the other documents accompanying the letter was a referral to the local authorities in Kostroma, asking them to help me find a place to live and take care of the rest of my needs.

I ran to our branch of the ZPP with the documents to ask who had arranged it. No one knew. Only the head of the organization, Mr Levin, who denied that he had anything to do with it, had a bit of a dastardly smile on his face. He counseled me to take the offer and go to Kostroma. (Some eight years later, as a reporter, I met him in Kielce, where he was secretary for party propaganda in the region.) We decided, Shoshana and I, to take the offer.

In December 1944, we once again packed up our few belongings, which were now more complicated because of my baby and the things he needed, and left for Kostroma. (I already described how we got on the train in Ivanovo.) The Kostroma oblast lies north of the Ivanovo-Voznesensk oblast. The city is located on the eastern bank of the upper Volga. This was a typical central Russian city of that period with around 150,000 residents. Most of the buildings were one-story wooden houses and only in the center of the city were there stone buildings of two or three stories. It was a sleepy, calm city, although there were a few small factories making textiles, shoes, and more. It was also considered a port city on the Volga. In the war years there were around 150 Jewish refugees from Poland and a few Polish families in the city. However, there were rather large concentrations of Poles who had been evacuated, as I mentioned, living in the villages in the area of Kinishma, and their freedom of movement was restricted. Their civil status scared me a little: I feared that they would not accept me with the trust needed for my work.

In Kostroma we were given one room in a shared apartment and wood for heating. A small salary was sent every month from the Central Committee of the ZPP in Moscow. The small room had once, perhaps before the revolution, been part of an apartment with three rooms, a kitchen, and a bathroom. Each room had its own entrance from the corridor. At that time, a different family lived in each room and we shared the kitchen and bathroom. The kitchen had a Russian oven on the wall that required a lot of work and wood to operate it; however, it heated our room. The only furniture we received from the municipality were two iron beds with straw mattresses, a small table, and two chairs. Anyway, there was no room for any more furniture. Shoshana found a box that we turned into a cupboard for kitchen utensils, placing it next to the door. Around it we hung a colored curtain that hid its contents, and above it stood a primus on which we cooked.

After a few days in Kostroma, I received a list of the villages in which there were concentrations of Poles. I sent invitations to a general meeting, and, with the help of the local authorities, I organized a meeting of Poles in Kinishma. In order to arrange such a meeting, I needed authorizations from all the local institutions. I had to ask them to allow people to travel from the villages for the meeting. Having no other choice, the meeting took place in the presence of representatives of all the official institutions: the local municipality, the KGB, the ruling party. I was afraid of this meeting. The Poles living in the region had been uprooted from the areas of former Eastern Poland, deported from their homes and lands, and transferred to forests and villages in this area. Some of them were former landowners from aristocratic dynasties, some of them former adjutants, and others simple peasants. They were for the most part anti-Semites. I, a Jewess, came as the emissary of the ZPP to this community, hoping to arouse in them patriotic feelings in light of the great hour that was approaching.

I was not received with applause. The meeting proceeded in a matter-of-fact fashion. A committee was chosen for the Kostroma oblast branch of the ZPP: the chairman was Franciszek Cybulski and I served as general secretary. We established local committees in Kinishma and a few additional villages. Chairman Cybulski, a former landowner from the Białystok area, barely tolerated me. The Polish exiles had a lot of school-age children who had never studied in school. The issue was raised at this meeting and I promised that, together with Chairman Cybulski, I would endeavor to do something about it. Indeed, I made every possible effort: I ran from office to office, contacting every institution, from the KGB and up to Moscow, and I received the necessary permissions and even school books in Polish. The teachers were chosen meticulously. We opened two Polish-language elementary schools, a children's home, and alongside them a dormitory for the children from the villages. Their upkeep, uniform, etc., were funded by Polish elements in the Soviet Union.

In 1945, we opened the school year with a great celebration in the two elementary schools, attended by all the "important" people of Kinishma and representatives from Kostroma. There was a lot of vodka. The secretary of the local party presented me with a large cup full of vodka and ordered me and Cybulski to drink a toast to the Soviet regime (za sovietskuiu vlast), saying, "Let's see how much you love us. Drink up the entire glass!"

I do not know whether Cybulski drank the entire glass. All eyes were on me, because I never drank vodka; even in the army, the soldiers did not manage to force me to do so. Yet here, on this occasion, I drank the entire glass, and afterward they hoisted me up into the air a few times. I felt terrible. Finally, I ran outside and vomited.

Around the same time that I arranged the schools, a young man whom I knew from the ZPP in Ivanovo, Yosef (Jozef) Levental, arrived (after the war he changed his name to Jezierski and became secretary of the Polish United Workers' Party [PZPR], in Mokotów, Warsaw). He had completed his studies in high school and had a teaching certificate. For some time, he lived with us in our crowded room and slept on a bed of straw on the floor (together with Heniek's brother, who came back from the army wounded). After consulting with Chairman Cybulski, I appointed him as director of one of the two schools in Kinishma. Yosef Leventhal moved to Kinishma and with him we also sent Shoshana's son, Naftali, who was already ten years old. There, finally, the child started going to school.

I visited the schools as well as the local branches of the ZPP many times. Despite the not-particularly friendly relations between us, I felt the Poles were grateful. They were very happy that their children were learning in Polish schools, at a suitable level, and I too felt satisfied with my work, because I saw its fruits, at least in the schools and the children's progress. The end of the first school year (in seven classes) was festive. The children staged performances (I had a lot of pictures of the children's performances in honor of the end of the school year in these two schools).

In the meantime, Wituś, my son, began to develop and became a normal child. Naftali, ten years old, looked after him when Shoshana and I worked (until Naftali was sent to school in Kinishma). Every so often. I came home to feed the child and then I took him out in his pram, in summer, and in winter wrapped him in a down blanket, and Naftali would watch over him. However, Naftali, himself a child, wanted to play. Older street children and small-time thieves followed him. They asked him to play football and, as they did so, they drew out of him the information that I received money from Moscow on a certain day every month. He led them to the apartment, and they learned how to go in and get out of it. Apart from the entry door to the entire house, which was closed from within, the door to the room in which we lived had no lock and was only locked using a hook that we added, and so it was easy to open it. At night we tied it from the inside with a sock.

If my memory is not mistaken, more than twenty people worked in the branches of the ZPP in the Kostroma region and its institutions: teachers, managers of the dormitories and the branches, including me. They received a salary that was paid from the money sent to me by the center in Moscow. This was a respectable sum. The money reached me on a certain day and the next day Cybulski came and took the entire sum for himself and the rest of the workers and teachers. This money arrived at my home every month and remained with me for one night. Once, on that night, while the money was in my possession, I was woken by a sound of glass breaking and something falling. I sat up in bed and lit the night light. I saw the fingers of a hand trying to take off the sock that held the door closed. The package of money was lying on the table, only one step from the door. I shouted out, "Who's there?"

Shoshana and Mundek, Heniek's brother, woke up. The hand that was behind the door disappeared. After a few minutes, we got up to investigate. The window in the kitchen was broken, our washing things, which stood on a bench under the window, had fallen, and the intruder had disappeared through the entrance door, which was now open. Naftali admitted that he told his gang about the money. (This same child, the son of my sister Shoshana, who died in 1993, who started studying school only at the age of ten and afterward had another two-year break, until his family immigrated to Israel, this Naftali is an engineer, a retired lieutenant colonel in the Israeli Navy, and father of two daughters.)

A lot of Jewish refugees and a few Poles lived in Kostroma. Upon my arrival, I established in the city an official branch of the organization, and we held cultural activities, meetings, etc. Every so often we received packages of used clothes from the Polish community in America, which the regional committee distributed. Mine was the only address used by the center in Moscow. Therefore, apart from letters I also received newspapers and other printed materials in Polish.

At the beginning of April 1945, I received in the post a small pamphlet written by the historian Berl Mark. The title announced the destruction of Polish Jewry. This was the first information that reached us about the crimes the Nazis had committed against the Jews in Poland. We sat next to our small table, Shoshana, Yosef Levental, who had come for a short visit from Kinishma that day (he was, as I mentioned, the principal of a school), and I, and I began to read it out aloud. The hairs on my head stood on end, I felt a lump in my throat, and I could not continue reading. Yosef took the pamphlet from me and continued reading. Yet, after a few minutes, he too went quiet. Shoshana tried to go on. Thus, we read the terrible document in its entirety. From beginning to end. Our brains did not want to grasp the content of the document, our minds could not absorb it, and our hearts did not want to accept it. I knew this Professor Berl Mark. It was impossible not to believe what he said. It is difficult to describe the terrible feeling that did not leave us for even a second. After the first reading, each one of us read it through again, in silence, and again and again, until we absorbed its full content. I carry its content with me to this day.

I called a general meeting of the Polish refugees in Kostroma, most of whom were Jewish, and presented to them the content of the pamphlet. It is not necessary to describe the reactions of those present. Despite the terrible facts that screamed out from every single word and page of the pamphlet, it was impossible to grasp the size of the catastrophe. Subsequently, we lived under the shadow of the murder of our nation, yet in the hope that perhaps the historian Mark was exaggerating, perhaps at least part of our family managed to survive. After Poland was liberated from the Nazi murderers, I sent the local administration in Końskie a request for information about my family. The response I received informed me officially that my family had been sent, together with all the Jews of Końskie, to the extermination camp of Treblinka in November 1942 and no one had returned.

Since moving from Ivanovo to live in Kostroma, I had had no contact with Heniek. When he left us, our son was dying and I was sick. I must admit that I did not make any effort and I did not look for this connection, because I was angry with him for leaving us in such a terrible state. At some moments I thought in my heart that his behavior in the first weeks after the birth and the situation in which he left us were evidence of his irresponsibility. Is there a better test to assess the nature of a man as a father and as a friend for life? I thought about not returning to him at all. However, I could not withstand this challenge. I was afraid of loneliness, and mainly I was afraid of leaving my son without a father. And what would I tell him if he would ask me, when he grew up, why I had done this? Was my judgment justified considering the inhuman conditions in which we were living then? Did I act correctly, did I try to understand his situation?

In hindsight, after many years of life together, I can say that since then Heniek, of blessed memory, on more than one occasion withstood difficult tests and always did everything in his power for our family. I too was not always in the right. More than once I blamed myself for demanding too much of those around me, but I held myself to the same standards.

At the beginning of March 1945, I was asked to go to Moscow to visit the Central Committee of the ZPP. For the first time in my life, I visited the capital of the Soviet Union. I do not remember much about the visit, apart from the atmosphere I encountered at the train station, on the streets, everywhere I went. This was the year of the Soviet Union's victory over Nazi Germany (at least on the eastern front). The Soviet army had liberated Poland and already stood on German soil. We were all gripped by euphoria mixed with fear. We did not know what and who was waiting for us there. And there was also happiness that soon we would return home (we did not know then that we would wait another year before returning). At the train station in Moscow, I felt an atmosphere of joy mingled with sadness: masses of people lay on the floor in the terminal, everywhere, many returning soldiers, disabled and wounded, meeting their loved ones, tears and rejoicing mixed together. I felt the same tension and uncertainty in the Moscow metro. The metro, which I saw for the first time, made a significant impression on me: the gleaming marble, the wide spaces, the large wall paintings and statues in every station—it is difficult to describe this impression. What amazed me most was that despite the masses of people I saw in every metro station, the stations were sparkling clean.

I felt that same Reisenfieber (ger: travel fever) and tension that gripped us most acutely in the building that housed the ZPP. Some of the Polish activists had already been sent to Poland to fill various key positions. In the long corridor, I met Szymon Zachariasz. He grabbed me by the hand and took me to his office. I felt something, as though he was uncomfortable with me, but I did not know the reason for this. He began to make excuses, claiming that he did not know my address and could not send me the pile of letters from Heniek that had accumulated, asking for some information about me (in the second or third room in that corridor was all the information, including my address). I felt bad for Heniek. I ignored Zachariasz completely.

From the letters I understood that Heniek thought our son would not survive. Therefore, after returning from Moscow, the first thing I did was to take a photograph of our Wituś, then eight months old, and with pride I sent the picture to Heniek, accompanied by a letter. This is the first and only photograph of Witek in the Soviet Union and to this day it remains in the family album. We soon received a letter from Heniek with some important pieces of information. On one of his visits to the ruins of the Łódź Ghetto, he met Avraham Rosenfarb, my cousin, who had also arrived with the army, and he took him to meet Moshe, our oldest brother on my mother's side. He was the only one who survived Auschwitz and the death march in which he lost our brother David, sick with typhus, watching as, before his eyes, the Germans threw him to the side of the road. He also lost in Auschwitz his wife and daughter, my sister-in-law Yitche, whom we all loved, and my niece Rita (named after our mother, of blessed memory, Sara Rivka). Moshe planned to immigrate to the Land of Israel. When he found out that we, meaning Shoshana's family and I, were in Russia and intending to return, he decided to remain in Łódź until we arrived.

I then started receiving regular letters from Heniek, learning, among other things, that he was among the first to arrive in Łódź from Lublin, tasked with opening a censor's office in Łódź (in nicer words it was called: Centralne Biuro Kontroli Prasy, Kultury I Widowisk—The Central Office for Controlling Press,

Culture and Entertainment). All the head offices were first opened in Łódź because Warsaw was still in ruins.

For my son's first birthday, I arranged a party typical of the impoverished in the wartime Soviet Union. Shoshana obtained a carp and we cooked it according to the Polish-Jewish recipe. I invited, among others, the chairman of the organization, Cybulski. There was not a lot of vodka. I honored him, as was customary in our traditional Jewish home, in which the head of the family or a very important guest receives the best, with the head of the fish. Cybulski did not touch it and did not forgive me for my ignorance of Polish tradition and my bad manners.

In the meantime, summer passed, and the Russian winter of 1945 approached its end. I divided my time between the house and child, on the one hand, and work and the activities of the organization on the other. Shoshana stood constantly and bravely at my side. The repatriation to Poland approached. Yet before this, Heniek had a surprise for us. One day in 1946, Heniek appeared in our home in Kostroma. Shoshana and I were at work. In the courtyard stood a pram in which Wituś was sleeping and some way away Naftali was playing with a ball. Heniek recognized Naftali but not his son. Naftali pointed out his son. They told me, when I returned, that the child woke up and did not want anything to do with this strange man, having no idea who he was.

I met a different Heniek. Before me stood an elegant, polished man, smiling, with a strange smell, the smell of Poland and something else, hidden, which only a woman can detect. However, I kept that secret. He spent two weeks with us, and his son rejected him. He did not want his father to hold him or kiss him. Between them a secret jealousy (I think unconscious) began to develop, as they competed over me. The baby was a year and a few months old, already running around the house and yard, and he slept in my bed at night, for two reasons; first he did not have his own bed and there was no room for a bed in the crowded room. Second, in the freezing winter of this area, even in our apartment, it was cold at night, and I warmed my child with my body, which he loved. When Heniek came I had no choice. He took the place in my bed and the child had to sleep in his pram. He did not want to recognize that someone else had taken his place at my side. I think that in our first years in Poland the competition between the two men—father and child—continued and there was some discomfort in this regard. Over the years, my son became very attached to his father.

From Heniek's stories, we found out, among other things, that he was among the first to visit Majdanek, next to Lublin, the famous extermination camp that the Nazis had established. The furnaces for burning the bodies of the Jews were still hot, surrounded by piles of corpses that they had not managed to burn. He told us other horrifying things that he saw there and that in a short time I would see for myself. He told us about the destruction of Łódź Jewry, about his feelings as he walked, almost daily, through the ruins of the ghetto. Of his large family, no one remained apart from two brothers who had managed to escape to the Soviet Union: Shmulik and Mundek.

A short time after the war, Shmulik left for the Land of Israel, and Mundek, Heniek's little brother, who was with us for a while in Kostroma, remained in Warsaw even after we immigrated to Israel in 1968. Heniek and Mundek are no longer alive. Heniek died on June 29, 1997, and was buried in the cemetery in Herzliya. Mundek, who died tragically, was buried in Warsaw in the Jewish cemetery. A few words in his memory:

Mundek was Heniek's little brother and people foresaw for him a promising future. When we left for Russia, I did not go to say goodbye to Heniek's family because I had not been introduced to them as his bride. Therefore, although I knew all the sons of the Garncarski family (I worked with them for some time, when I was employed by their brother, Alter), I had almost no contact with Shmulik and I did not even know that Mundek was at the time in the Soviet Union. One day, a short while after Heniek joined the Polish army and left, when I was already in Kostroma, Mundek showed up wounded. I discovered that he had been on the front with the Red Army, was wounded in his arm, and after he was released from the military hospital, not completely healthy, he decided to come to us. He traveled to Ivanovo because he thought his brother was there. When he found out that Heniek was in the Polish army and I had moved to Kostroma, he came to be with me. Thus, he showed up on my doorstep. The wound on his arm never healed. He suffered from a chronic infection in the broken bone. He lived with us, in the room that I shared with my baby and Shoshana and her son. Despite the difficulty and crowding, we managed somehow. He slept in a corner on the floor on a mattress of straw (often with another visitor such as Yosek Levental-Jezierski). Together, we returned to Poland.

Mundek registered for the university in Łódź, where he studied mathematics. However, after two years, he left his studies because his promising talents as a poet and excellent writer were discovered (according to the opinion of one of the best Polish poets—the famous Jew Julian Tuwim, who greatly esteemed Mundek's poetry). Yet, Mundek did not know how to get by in life and it was hard to get along with him. When we moved to live in Warsaw, he again lived with us on Rakowiecka Street, in a small room that was intended for servants in our three-room apartment. After quite some time, he went to live with his girlfriend.

From this relationship he had a daughter (Ursula, today a doctor living in Ramat Gan). Mundek's wife left him when their daughter was fourteen years old, and the two women left for Israel. He remained in Poland. He wrote in Polish and worked as an editor on the cultural and literary section of the weekly *Po prostu*. He married again, this time a Polish woman, who also bore him a daughter, Miriam, and this woman too left him. He tried to return to his first wife and move to Israel. Mundek came to Israel as a tourist, but his ex-wife was not willing to have him and had complete control over his daughter. He returned to Poland. Due to the wound to his right hand and the lack of suitable treatment, it was likely his hand would have to be amputated. Alone, neglected, and sick, he reached the end of his emotional journey and killed himself. He was in his fifties.

In August 1993, when we were in Poland, we visited his grave in the Jewish cemetery in Warsaw. For a long time, we searched for his grave. The grave was neglected, the tombstone concealed by weeds.

If I already mentioned our visit to Poland in the summer of 1993, it is worthwhile taking this opportunity to recount some impressions from that visit. I myself was in Poland before that, in 1988, researching and searching for materials in the archives in Warsaw, Lublin, Łódź, Krakow, and other cities. However, in that summer of 1993, I traveled with Heniek, helping him to realize his wish: to visit for the last time the town in which he was born. For him this was the first time that he had returned to Poland after leaving in 1968. He was already very sick. Apart from severe heart disease, he had Parkinson's and an advanced state of cognitive degeneration. He felt that something was happening to his mind. We still did not know the truth about his condition. In fact, he had the most inhumane of illnesses, Alzheimer's. Before the fog consumed his brain entirely, he expressed his wish to visit the town of his birth and childhood, Przyrów, next to Częstochowa. So, we set out.

In Warsaw we spent a few days with our only friends remaining in Poland, Zenon and Tamara Kasztański, of blessed memory, and we traveled by train to Częstochowa. There, when we got off the train, we were met by a storm: howling winds and pouring rain. Heniek stood there, unable to breathe or move. There was no taxi in the city or any other vehicle. I was almost helpless. I did not know where the hotel was. With a heavy suitcase in one hand and with the other using my coat to shield Heniek against the wind, I somehow got him to the hotel, which was, it turned out, not far from the train station. This was in fact an Orbis hotel, one of the chains of hotels in Poland known for their good service. There we spent the night. We rose early the next morning. It was a beautiful day, sunny and refreshing. After a rich and good breakfast, we set out by bus for Przyrów, near Częstochowa.

The bus stopped in a square next to an inn that was closed. According to Heniek's memory, here once stood the market and around it lived all the town's Jews, around thirty families in total. Here, in a radius of a few dozen meters, was once concentrated the social and spiritual life of the small Jewish community. Not one living Jew remained there. Now there was a bus stop, an inn (closed), and opposite it, on the other side of the square (which was once the market), we found a small avenue planted with trees and flowers, a few benches, and in the middle a monument to the war heroes (I will come back to this monument later).

Przyrów is a tiny, sleepy town that lies among forests. We saw almost no one. Two intersecting roads make up the entire town. The only heavy and impressive building in this town, which towers over all the surroundings, is the Catholic church. We walked around the street. Heniek wandered off deep in thought, as though I was not there. He dreamed of the days of his childhood, wrapped up in memories. Once they had a sawmill, where he played and fought with the Polish children on piles of sawdust, and afterward they jumped into the river that ran past the mill. However, he did not know where it was, and he could not find the river.

Suddenly, Heniek became agitated and impatient. His attention turned to a complex structure with a large yard. He began to survey it, walking around and around, and then he remembered that once it had contained the synagogue, study house, and mikveh. The only evidence of all this were the stone steps in the yard, now broken and leading nowhere. Once these steps led to the synagogue gallery, where the women prayed; there in the corner of the yard it was possible to discern the remnants of the mikveh. My Heniek stood there as though in a daydream. He saw pictures that only he remembered. This place remained holy in his soul. I saw tears in his eyes, something that never happened. I stood next to him in silence. A truck approached and some people got off. They saw us, strangers, and apparently understood why we were there and what we were looking at. They approached us and demanded that we leave immediately. We left the yard. On the front of this building was a sign saying: "Państwowe Zakłady Mleczarskie I Rozlewnia Mleka." The Jewish synagogue had become a state factory for processing milk products.

Again, we walked around the street between the rows of one-story wooden houses that looked like something from a fairy tale. Heniek searched for the home in which he was born and raised. It seemed that he found it, but we did not approach. In a Yiddish poem that he did not manage to finish, he describes the life of this Jewish town, the customs and the festivals that remained in his memory. Everything is seen through the mystical veil that enveloped a religious Jewish child raised in a tiny town, almost all the Jewish residents of which were members of one family.

Next to what was once the synagogue, almost opposite the church (all the town was built around the church), was a patch of green grass and at its edge, on the edge of the street, stood a cross with a small prayer house, decorated with flowers (chapel). Heniek remembered this cross and he gazed beyond the patch of grass. There stood a house. He murmured something quietly, as though battling with the flashes of memory. Quietly he said, "That was the rabbi's house. From here the funerals set off. Where is the cemetery?"

We started to search for the Jewish cemetery. Heniek could not remember the way. We followed the road behind the town.

Heniek saw a woman at some distance in a field and ran to her to ask her. In the meantime, on the other side of the road, I found a hostel or café. I called Heniek back, and we went inside to ask. We found a small place, sparkling clean and intimate, in which the owner, a nice, middle-aged woman, welcomed us. There was no one in the café apart from her. It was not hard to identify us as Jews from another country. The owner served us aromatic coffee and sandwiches, and we asked that she sit with us because we had some questions. She did so willingly. We asked, of course, about the Jewish cemetery that should be somewhere around there.

The woman led us to a young patch of forest. On this hill, she told us, was the Jewish cemetery. Among the young trees there were still remnants of graves, under our feet we felt mounds, but no tombstone or even a shred of a tombstone remained. The woman told us a story that we found hard to believe, but it was verified by what we saw with our eyes. This small Jewish cemetery lay on a hill on the edge of a thick forest. A few rows of trees separated it from the road. These trees ostensibly hid it from unwanted eyes. The Germans did not notice its existence; however, the local residents knew about it. The Germans deported all the Jews of Przyrów to another ghetto and from there to an extermination camp. Only the Jewish cemetery remained.

After the war, in the 1950s, the local council decided to establish a monument to local heroes of the last war (we saw it from a distance on part of the former market). Then they remembered the tombstones in the Jewish cemetery, which could be used to build the base of the memorial. And so it was. The woman told us that in order to remove the Hebrew characters engraved on the tombstones and fit them to one size, they brought in special machines. The noise of these machines was heard by the entire town for a few weeks. The tracks made by the teeth of these machines could still be seen on the paving stones, she added.

We left the woman and returned to the town to look closely at the monument in what was once the market square. It was still early morning and no one bothered us when we examined the strange stones at the base of the monument. The machines had left deep, circular marks on the stones. However, the machine did not manage to reach the edges and remove everything. Therefore, it was still possible to discern, here and there, on the margins of some paving stones, Hebrew characters. We sat by these stones, photographed them, and thought that the residents of Przyrów had made themselves a monument out of vandalism, to their eternal shame. It also testifies to their intentions in this memorial and their attitude toward the tragic genocide of the Jews of Poland.

I have run forward to my memories of the more recent past and our journey to the hometown of my husband, of blessed memory, the father of my children, who was my close friend and partner for nearly sixty years.

PART 3

The Polish People's Republic

CHAPTER 9
THE RETURN TO POLAND

Łódź

The day of repatriation to Poland was approaching. We had received no news from Moshe, Shoshana's husband, since his conscription into the labor battalions in Urgut. He did not have our address and we did not know where he was. We thought that he was likely to arrive in Poland with the refugees from wherever he was. We received information that all those recruited into the labor battalions had already been released, therefore we decided not to wait until he would find us.

The return of Polish citizens in the Kostroma region was well organized and took place in March 1946. Although I could have traveled with my family on a regular train and in more comfortable conditions, I preferred to stay with everyone in a special freight train. I must admit with sadness that as soon as we got into the wagons, we could sense what awaited us in Poland. There, at the train station in Kostroma, Mr. Cybulski, the chairman of the ZPP (Union of Polish Patriots), who until then had somehow cooperated with me—indeed, without me would not have been able to do anything—now felt free of the Soviet regime and took responsibility for the evacuation. As far as he was concerned, I no longer existed. As the people were getting on the train, he conducted a selection: separating Jews and Poles and placing them in different wagons. In our wagon there were a few Polish families. He removed them almost forcefully and transferred them to another wagon.

As long as I believed in Socialist principles and that Poland could be different from the Soviet Union, I endeavored to find justifications for this kind of phenomenon. I explained to myself that his acts were an exception, that those Poles were mainly landowners from Eastern Poland, the enemies of Socialism and anti-Semites. They had been forced to go to the Soviet Union, and therefore they treated us as supporters of the Soviet regime. I only learned how wrong I was, how I had failed to understand the Polish soul, during the instructive years of the 1950s and especially the 1960s. A great many of the Poles traveling with us got off at various stations on the way. We continued on to Warsaw.

The train tracks terminated at the station "Warsaw East" in Praga. Around this station everything was destroyed. From here, each one of the returnees on the train had to make his own way. My role as secretary of the ZPP was over. Since then, even though every job I ever took was in one way or another public, I never again worked for the state or the mechanism of the regime.

In Warsaw we were welcomed by an unusually strong, stormy wind. Garbage cans, parts of rafters, broken bricks, bits of concrete, telephone or electricity wires all flew through the air. At the station there was no taxi or other means of transport. No one waited for us. We left the suitcases and belongings for safekeeping at the station, because we needed to go on foot over the Vistula, to the central station. The storm made this walk dangerous and long. Our small family set off: I, my son Witek, one year and eight months old, Shoshana, Naftali, eleven years old, and Mundek, Heniek's brother, who held the baby to his chest under his coat. So we walked.

In all my years at the front I had never seen anything like what I saw in Warsaw. The beautiful prewar city, which was home to one million residents, among them around 400,000 Jews, lay in ruins. The largest concentration of Jews in Europe was burned and destroyed during the ghetto uprising, an uprising that became a symbol of the Jewish battle for humanity. Later together with others, I participated in removing the ruins of the ghetto, I would follow the rebirth of Warsaw and its reconstruction and even fall in love with this city.

As we walked then, in the spring of 1946, we saw almost no undamaged buildings. Here and there, the skeletons of tall, burned buildings stood out. Sometimes, within the ruins, it was possible to see a lamp or light, a sign of life; here and there we saw people digging in the ruins, looking perhaps for belongings, signs of life, a reminder of their loved ones.

Battling with the raging storm, we eventually arrived at the central station, which was also half ruined. We traveled to Łódź. There, at the station Łódź Fabryczna, the survivors of our family welcomed us: Heniek, Moshe, Shoshana's husband, who had been released from his unit in Russia and returned to Łódź before us, and our brother Moshe, liberated from the concentration camp of Buchenwald.

The city of Łódź was almost untouched. Only the northern part, where the Jewish Ghetto had been, was totally destroyed, and even there the ruins had been removed. Of all the Jews that filled the ghetto, only a few survived. Our hearts ached for our murdered loved ones. The two husbands had arranged apartments for their families; Shoshana, her husband, and Naftali went to live on Północna Street, on the border of the destroyed ghetto, in the temporary home of our brother Moshe. They planned to leave for the Land of Israel (before doing so, they were forced to spend time in a transfer camp in Germany). My Heniek had secured for us the most splendid apartment on Narutowicza Street.

When we entered the apartment, I felt like we were in a luxurious hotel, at a temporary stop. This feeling of ephemerality, of not belonging in this apartment, accompanied me the entire two years that we lived in Łódź. Quickly, it became clear to me that the entire house was under heavy guard. This was a building in which select workers of the Polish Ministry of Interior (MSW) were given apartments. Heniek had received an apartment in this building because he was a senior worker in the censorship, which was part of the MSW.

Our apartment was on the second floor, and above it was the home of Mieczysław Moczar (I'll come back to him later), then director of the MSW in Łódź and the region. It had five rooms, but we had to share them with another family, Poles; the husband worked for Moczar. This family, Bogdański, had one son aged eighteen. They had a separate entrance from the small, shared corridor. However, when the husband came home drunk late at night, he went straight through our entrance to avoid waking his wife and causing scenes.

I should describe our home, which was in fact only two rooms and a shared kitchen. The shared entrance through a small and nicely decorated corridor led to a spacious lobby, in which a beautiful crystal chandelier hung from the ceiling and an expensive carpet covered the parquet floor. One of the walls in this hall was almost entirely covered by a glass sliding door that led to a well-lit guest room that was furnished in good taste with black furniture. In two corners stood small bronze-topped tables decorated with artistic drawings in the Eastern style and next to them were matching chairs. (The customs officials in Poland did not allow us to take one table top out of the country and confiscated it as a "national art property" that they took for themselves. The second table I gave as a gift to Dorka Francuz who lives in Jerusalem, and to this day it decorates their guest room.) In the middle of the large guest room stood a round table and green armchairs. A separate entrance led to the bedroom, which was also large and furnished. In these two rooms there were, of course, beautiful rugs. I will not describe all the crystal and other pieces of art, or the kitchen, in which each family had its own cupboard, or the separate toilet and bathroom for each family.

After the living conditions in Ivanovo and Kostroma, when we lived at least four people, and most of the time five, crowded into a room that was around a quarter of the size of the hall I described above, I could not feel at home in this apartment. The entire time we lived there, I saw it as a temporary apartment, as though we were living in a luxurious hotel. There was another reason that I felt uncomfortable and strange in this elegant apartment. I found out that before the war it had belonged to a rich Jewish family, all members of which perished in Auschwitz. After the family was moved to the Łódź Ghetto, the Germans requisitioned the house. It seemed to me that not only the furniture belonged to the owners but also all the kitchen utensils and the remainder of the apartment's contents.

In the meantime, I was forced to part from my family, with all the pain this entailed: my brother Moshe and mainly Shoshana and her family, to whom I was so attached. They left for Germany and planned to immigrate to the Land of Israel. We, meaning Heniek and I, decided to remain in Poland. This decision, among other things, resulted from our belief that the new regime would be better and more just than prewar Poland, and also more just than the Soviet Union. However, at least for me, the main reason was rooted deeper in my heart. I felt more connected to Poland than the distant Land of Israel. The graves of my ancestors and the dust of those murdered and burned in Hitler's extermination camps were in Poland; this was the country of my birth. In Poland I had known great poverty and also moments of happiness; there, the Polish soil, my Polish-Jewish cultural tradition was molded. Jews had lived in Poland for more than 1,000 years and their history was interwoven with that of the country. I felt that I had a full right to see Poland as my homeland. Thus, my emotional turmoil was even more pronounced when, twenty-two years later, I decided to leave Poland forever with my family.

Heniek, as I noted, worked for the censor. These were difficult days. His salary was tiny. The rations of food products we received were also minuscule. I looked for work that would enable me to watch closely over my child. Witek was only one year and eight months old when I took him to a kindergarten that accepted children of three years and older. The director of the kindergarten, who later became a close friend, Wanda Koszutska, agreed to take my child on the condition I would also work there as a nurse. I agreed immediately. This kindergarten took children of workers in the state textile factory, which before the war had belonged to an industrialist of German origin, Birman (he and his family were executed by the Nazis because they did not want to collaborate and be recognized as Volksdeutsche), and the children of workers in the Ministry of Public Security. The children of the textile workers usually suffered from malnutrition, anemia, and neglect. In contrast, the children of the workers at the Ministry of Public Security were usually in a better state. Most of our attention was devoted to the first group, in terms of nutrition and in other respects. The kindergarten was located in a large and beautiful villa, full of light and sparkling clean, which had belonged to the Birman family, in the midst of a beautiful garden. The director, Wanda Koszutska, lived with her two children and adopted son on the second floor of that villa.

Mrs. Koszutska was the daughter of a well-known family that had risen to prominence at the end of the nineteenth century. Her father, an eye doctor in Kalisz who treated patients free of charge, fought for the freedom of Poland and belonged to the left wing of the Polish Socialist Party. This family, two daughters and three sons, together with their parents, were known as exemplary symbols of morality and humanity. Wanda suffered a difficult fate: a skin disease ruined her beautiful and noble face, leaving her scarred, and her husband abandoned her with two small children, Ja and Małgosia. Despite the difficulties of the war, this brave woman found a Jewish child somewhere in the forests while fleeing from the Germans and raised him. He also helped her and her children, being already eight years old. He remained with her after the war, even though his relatives from America wanted to take him there. When I knew him, he was around fourteen years old. Today he is the famous Professor Feliks Tych, Director of the Jewish Historical Institute in Warsaw.

I worked in this kindergarten for almost a year. There, as in my work in the hospital afterward, I came face to face with human tragedies, the aching remnant of the Jews left after the Holocaust. One pleasant young woman brought her little daughter, around four years old, to the kindergarten every morning. The child tried to slip out of her mother's grasp, struggling, cursing her, and shouting, "You Zhid (Jew), I hate you, you're not my mother." The woman, crying, told me her story. She gave her baby to a Polish family in a village and left them all her belongings in return for saving her baby. Her husband died in Auschwitz, but she survived. She returned to take her child, but the child did not recognize her biological mother, and there, in the village, she had learned to hate Jews. The woman told me that at home the situation was even worse: the child ran away and did not want to be near her.

This was one of many similar stories. In one it was a monastery, in another a baby thrown from the freight wagon on the way to Majdanek or Auschwitz, and someone collected and adopted the child. Although one of the biological parents survived and found him, after great efforts, the child was already four years old. The parent went through hell; he was broken, had grown old in the bunker or camp, and suddenly he showed up and wanted his child. The child did not recognize him and did not want to go with him.

The director of the kindergarten, Mrs. Wanda, looked after these children with special care. She decided to try to take the children, most of them from impoverished families, for a winter holiday in the mountains, together with the staff. I went with her to Warsaw to try to realize the project. We managed to receive all the necessary authorizations and the funding we needed. In February 1947, we set out for Żegiestów in the Carpathian Mountains, a mountainous and pleasant place, with all the children, among them my son Witek, a few mothers, and also a doctor. The views, the mountain air, and the snow made the three weeks' holiday very enjoyable and also strengthened the children's health.

When my son could remain in the kindergarten without me, I went to work in a hospital that was run by the Interior Security Ministry in Łódź, on Północna Street. I worked in the internal medicine ward, which was headed by a cardiologist of international fame, Professor Jochwetz. At the same time, I signed up for evening school in order to finally complete my matriculation certificate. I was lacking one academic year. Professor Jochwetz advised me to sign up for medical studies at the university. He foresaw for me a scientific career in the medical field. I had long dreamed of studying medicine. Even in the Soviet Union, after I was released from the hospital, I wrote to the medical academy in Moscow asking to study there, but I did not even get an answer. And so, in 1947, I registered for the faculty of medicine at Łódź University and was accepted, together with Dorka Żorek-Francuz (about her below). Despite my ambitions and dreams of being a doctor, I did not even get to the first day of studies. The hand of fate decreed that only after another decade I would become. . . a historian.

Pediatrician Dorka Francuz was five or six years younger than me. She was related to me (my sister-in-law Chava, of blessed memory, David's wife, was Dorka's aunt). A warm relationship developed between us, and I think that it continues, even though we rarely meet. We first met in my youth, when I worked for David, my brother. One day, a child of ten or eleven from the town of Zduńska Wola came to visit her aunt, Chava. The child looked hungry and poor. She remained with the family and naturally became attached to me. For some time, she saw me as close to her. I, as you will remember, did not spend long with David before I was fired. Dorka, a child herself, took my place looking after their child, my brother's son Naftali, who was then four or five years old.

Together with all my family and her family, she was taken to the Łódź Ghetto. She was among the fighters in the ghetto resistance and together with all the Jews was sent to Auschwitz. She was the only one to survive. The armies of the Soviet Union found her in a labor camp in Germany, dying of typhus, with a high fever, unconscious. However, she murmured that she wanted only a Soviet doctor, because she wanted to go to Russia to look for me and refused to see any other doctors. They brought her a Russian doctor, and she was transferred to the Soviet military hospital and with it to Russia. With all that she had gone through in the extermination camp, she was lucky that in Russia they did not send her to a Soviet forced labor camp. She returned to Poland and found me in Łódź. I was the only relative remaining from all the family. She lived with us and began to study medicine. When we moved to Warsaw, Dorka moved to student dormitories. There she met her future husband, Heniek Francuz, also a survivor of a German concentration camp. Heniek studied economics. For a certain period, until they were given an apartment, they lived with us in Warsaw. In 1956, they immigrated to Israel, and they live in Jerusalem.

Why did I not become a doctor?

In the spring of 1948, Heniek, my husband, was transferred to the central censor's office in Warsaw and he demanded that we move to the capital city. Apart from this, there were other difficulties: he could not provide for the family alone, and during medical studies, which take six years, it is impossible to work and make a living. Apart from that, Heniek did not like my ambition to study. It turns out that I too needed to "mature," to become more independent, and to stand up for my desire to realize my ambitions. There was another reason.

On the first day of studies at Łódź University, I was at home with my son (Heniek was already in Warsaw). Witek had a 40-degree fever, he began to shake and fall into fits. I was worried and called a doctor. So, I could not go to the first day of studies. I did not become a doctor.

Warsaw, Próżna Street

So, instead of studying medicine, I moved with my family to Warsaw. It was the summer of 1948. In the ruined Warsaw, there was a serious housing problem. The new ruling authorities continued to expand their power. This was Władysław Gomułka's first period as the first secretary of the ruling party, Polska Zjednoczona Partia Robotnicza (PZPR), The Polish United Workers' Party, and as almost the sole ruler in Poland. Among other things, all existing houses and those under construction were nationalized. This meant that one could only obtain a place to live via one's workplace. Due to the lack of apartments and according to the perception of the leader of the party—who once said that a room of eight square meters and one lamp are sufficient for the proletariat—to this day the buildings constructed or renovated bear the signs of that period. The first apartment we received there was an example of this.

We were given an apartment on Próżna Street, a small lane that links between the main street Marszałkowska and Grzybowski Square, not far from the Saski Garden. The entire street had been destroyed. Only the skeletons of the external walls remained. Beyond these walls, everything was being rebuilt and temporary additions were constructed. Our apartment was on the fourth floor in a crowded "well" courtyard, meaning it was closed in on all four sides with buildings of a similar height and had only one entrance gate.

Our apartment had two rooms with all modern "conveniences"—a kitchen and even a corner for a servant (which we did not have). The size of the entire apartment was 35 square meters. The tiny rooms, which did not even meet Gomułka's standards, had a certain "advantage." When we sat in the dining room (which was also the living room), without getting up it was possible to reach out a hand and take something from the kitchen and just to turn around in the chair and jump straight into the bed in the bedroom, all of which was taken up by narrow sofa (there was no room for a double bed), and in the corner was the child's bed, leaving no space whatsoever. There was also a balcony without a railing. It was dangerous to open the door to the balcony because of Witek. At the same time, the neighbor who came home late at night drunk could get into his apartment via our balcony when his wife would not open the door.

I said that this was an apartment with all modern "conveniences." Yes, it had a toilet and a shower that could be used only in the summer. They were stifling because they were made from boards and tin and had been fixed to the building from the outside. In the winter it was not possible to use the toilet because the water inside froze. The child, now four years old, alert, and full of life, had no space and constantly bumped into a door or a piece of furniture (we left some of our furniture in Łódź, and the rest we divided between friends, because this apartment was too crowded for it). This apartment was dangerous for my son.

I describe this apartment in detail because numerous families lived in ones similar to it. Likewise, it gives an idea of the housing problem in Warsaw. Mainly, it emphasizes that the living quarters that were then common in Warsaw accorded with Gomułka's ideas of what was suitable for the "working class." When he returned to power again in the 1950s, a worker's settlement (osiedle robotnicze) was built behind Saska Kępa in Praga. All the new apartments had 3 rooms and were 40 square meters in size.

We lived on Próżna Street for around a year before moving to Rakowiecka Street. This building had survived the war almost unharmed and the apartments in it were "old style." Our apartment was on the second floor, large and beautiful. It had three large rooms, a large kitchen (in which I studied and worked at nights), and a room for a servant. However, one room was given to strangers, who changed every so often, and in the small "servant's" room, which had one window, Mundek, Heniek's brother, resided for a certain period. This apartment belonged to the office of the censor, where my husband worked. Thus, all the residents of the third room worked for the censor too. At first a nice, quiet young woman lived there, afterward she brought her mother to live with her, and then it was less quiet. When the young woman married and left, Dorka and Heniek Francuz, my relatives, moved in, with a large dog, a German shepherd, whom I loved. When they left for Israel in 1956, two young women were sent to live with us, Zosia and Dorka. Both were very intelligent, and I loved the conversations with them. By contrast, Heniek could not bear them. Zosia, who worked for the censor, spoiled Dorka, who worked at the large publishing house Książka i Wiedza and had asthma. Zosia left for Israel in the 1950s and Dorka, sick and restless, started to argue with Heniek. A year before we left for Israel, she moved into a new worker's building in Praga.

In Warsaw I started to work in a clinic that belonged to the MSW as a practical nurse (siostra zabiegowa, a nurse authorized to give infusions and injections into the veins). The clinic was on Koszykowa Street and every morning I traveled by tram with Witek, my son, to the kindergarten and then continued on to work (I already described the experience of taking the tram in the mornings in Warsaw). When the hospital that was run by that same ministry was built in the suburb of the city, on Wołowska Street, I moved to work there, in an outpatient clinic, in the same role. I would have gotten lost there, had my friends not helped me to get out of there, because I got involved in matters that should not be discussed or made public. I was a member of the party cell of workers in this hospital, and every so often there were party meetings. I did not then know a lot about the MSW and what it did. Nurses came to me and told me about their work and how they were treated by the wives of men in high positions. These women knew how to use the services of the nurses from the hospital, my friends. When the wife of such a functionary had a baby, three nurses in three shifts were at her service for an unlimited period. When the child or woman got sick, not to mention the husband himself, nurses were sent from the hospital to their home. The way the nurse was treated was unbearable: she was sent to eat in the kitchen together with the servant, but they treated her even worse than a servant. She was given instructions in a most humiliating fashion. Not only the nurses sent to the houses of the "important people"—who were often of a much lower professional level than the nurses, not to mention their wives—suffered, but also the nurses who remained in the wards and had to take on the extra burden.

I was not sent to do such jobs, perhaps because I had a sharp tongue, was proud, and could not bear such humiliation. On more than one occasion I was sent to the deputy minister, who was later known for his cruelty, to give him an injection and apply a cupping glass. It was possible to say that this was in the framework of my role as a practical nurse, and I did not complain. However, the nurses that served the wives of the senior workers at the MSW came to me and cried bitterly.

In the hospital, I got to know a laboratory worker, Maryna Arasimowicz, of blessed memory, who later was my closest friend and greatly influenced the rest of my life. As a member of the party, she went together with me to one of the meetings of the party cell in the hospital. These meetings were usually closed, meaning only party members participated in them. In this forum, so I thought, I could speak freely. . . and I took the opportunity to voice a litany of complaints, relating how the "important people" treated the nurses. My speech was followed by complete silence. A break was announced.

People from the MSW attended that same meeting. I knew one of them. This was Kratko, who was injured in the war, losing a hand. (His brother, Zalman Kratko, of blessed memory, was active in the professional associations in Warsaw. I got to know him many years later, and for a little while we worked together in the Institute for the Study of the Diaspora at Tel Aviv University. He died a few years after moving to Israel.) During the break, this Kratko took me aside, I do not remember his first name, leading me by the hand from the meeting room. He spoke to me in a very friendly manner. First of all, he hinted that this speech was likely to bring trouble down on my head and asked me why I had spoken. Afterward, he tried to justify the way the members of the government acted: they labored day and night and had no time to look after familial matters, etc. Finally, he admitted that control and power corrupt: this is the nature of human beings.

I could not agree with him. So too, when I told her about my conversation with Kratko, Maryna Arasimowicz was also worried about my fate. After a short time, Maryna disappeared. She stopped working in the hospital.

I found out that another institution helped her get out of the hospital. She soon visited me at home, and from then on we became soul sisters. I owe the change in my life that followed this meeting to her and her group of friends. We worked together for almost ten years.

She came to my home and asked me whether I would be willing to change my career and try to write articles. I told her that apart from writing for the "wall newspaper" at school or in a factory, and stories in my notebook and diary, I had not written anything. She responded to me with a Polish folk saying: nie święci garnki lepią (you can learn anything with a bit of practice). She too was no journalist. She told me that she nevertheless saw this work as a calling and thought that I was suited to it. Indeed, we both believed in principles and social justice. We talked about it and we parted. A few days later I was called to a meeting at "the holy of holies"— the building of the Central Committee of the United Worker's Party (KC PZPR), the ruling party—with comrade Matatiyahu Oks (a strange surname, in Yiddish and German it means "ox"). Before me there was no ox. He was a small man, very thin, the complete opposite of his name: a worried man who spoke quietly and warmly. He was the director of the organizational department in the Central Committee.

Then, at the beginning of 1949, life was still rather modest, and people still had great hopes. The building of the Central Committee was pleasant but not big (compared to the building constructed for this purpose in the 1950s on the corner of Jerozolimskie Avenue and Nowy wiat Street). The old building had served the Nazis during the war as the offices of the occupying authorities. It was located in a beautiful place, on the corner of Belwederska and Dolina Słu ewiecka. Comrade Oks asked me a few general questions and I had to tell him a bit about myself, about my family, and so on. Finally, he told me that they wanted to produce a party journal to fight against bureaucracy and negative phenomena within the party, and they wanted me to join its team.

The idea of starting an entirely new profession caused me great fear and I talked about this openly. I had no formal education for this. During the conversation, a handsome man walked in. He was dark skinned with sharp and penetrating eyes. Afterward, I got to know him closely. This was Artur Starewicz, head of the journalists and media office in the propaganda department. This department controlled all media, information, literature, and culture and creativity. Starewicz, a sharp man, later became a member of the

Central Committee and a member of its "ideological committee" and later also one of the secretaries of the Central Committee.[5]

Thus, I took my first steps as a journalist for the journal *Życie Partii* (Party Life). Before this, I had to leave my job in the hospital run by the MSW, and I learned that doing so was not an easy feat. Only the intervention of Comrade Oks helped. When I came to the MSW to present the document testifying that I had no obligation to any department, the official looked at me and said, "Here people don't quit of their own free will. We fire them, and then we send them to where they get sent."

Yet, the next day, nevertheless, I received the authorization that "I had moved to another workplace."

Hania

In the meantime, in December 1949, I conceived again. It was a difficult pregnancy. I was immersed in a new job and working hard. However, I never thought about terminating the pregnancy, mainly because two years earlier I had been forced to have an abortion, even though I really wanted a baby girl. Then Heniek was busy with the move to Warsaw, the conditions were difficult, and I had agreed to the abortion. This time I would not do so. I wanted a baby girl, despite the doctor's warnings that the pregnancy could leave me deaf (I suffered from blood clots in my nose). On September 10, 1950, my daughter, Hania, was born.

After three months of maternity leave, during which I enjoyed every hour and every day looking after the baby, I had to go back to a job that demanded from me complete devotion. Heniek was by this time working as a journalist for the Polish Radio and he too worked hard. We needed to employ a maid, and for a short time, also a nursemaid for the baby.

---

5 On his political views and acts, which were not always in the spirit of the leadership, see Mieczysław Rakowski, *Dzienniki Polityczne 1967-1968* (Warsaw 1999).

In the coming months, the baby developed normally. Of course, she demanded a lot of time and attention. However, dealing with her, following her development—this is the most beautiful period of motherhood. Sadly, I missed it to a great extent and on more than one occasion I felt guilty, especially vis-à-vis Hania. We went through quite a significant crisis with her.

Also, my son needed special attention following the baby's appearance in our lives. Until now I had devoted my entire heart to him. After Hania was born, I gave her most of my time. That same month, Witek, who was six years older than her, started first grade. He was a year ahead of other children (according to the recommendations of the pedagogues and kindergarten director). It was not easy for him to sit at his desk for a whole hour, especially because he could already read, although he did not know how to write (I did not want to teach him too early, but he learned to read the printed letters by himself, I do not know how).

I devoted my lunch break to the children. The newspaper did not require us to work from the office. Output was important: we needed to produce high quality articles. A car with a driver was always at our disposal to take us to and from work. Thanks to this, I spent around three hours every day with the children (when I did not need to leave the city). Usually, the children had already had lunch. However, we had a ritual that when I came home, I took Hania on my knees and Wituś stood near me on the other side, and I ate lunch together with them (Hania in particular enjoyed this). It became a ritual. Afterward, I put Hania to sleep and sat with Wituś, who did his homework quietly. When Heniek returned from work at around five in the afternoon, we changed shifts: I went back to work and Heniek was with the children, mainly Hania.

In the evening, when I came back from work, there was an hour of fun washing the baby, which her brother Witek helped with from the first days of her life. These hours of bathing the children and putting them to bed were the ones I treasured most.

After all this, and after dinner with Heniek, when he went to sleep, I sat down in the spacious kitchen and worked on an article or studied into the night. Thus, our life continued in the first months of the spring. Our daughter developed normally, was healthy and mischievous, but I was exhausted.

In the summer we decided to rent an apartment in Świder, a holiday village near Warsaw. We found a registered nurse (with references) and took her and Hania to Świder. Witek was in first grade. One of us, Heniek or I, visited once in the middle of the week to see what was happening with our daughter, and at weekends we all went there, and the nurse had a vacation. From the first weeks in Świder something started to eat at my heart. It seemed to me that my child was not developing properly. After another two weeks, I was very worried. Hania was already seven months old. She was growing too fat and was very suntanned, but she was not moving. She did not know how to sit up or move and only lay in the pram or in her cot. I saw a clear regression in her development. I was beset by terrible fear. I asked the certified nurse why my daughter was so suntanned, and she did not know what to say. On the spot I fired her, I took my Hania home and asked the pediatrician to check her.

The doctor, Dr. Fidler, was a unique character. She was very motherly and authoritative. A heavy and large-proportioned woman of around sixty, she had a way with children. Her husband, Franciszek Fidler, one of the members of the Central Committee of the Communist Party in Poland before the war, was an almost legendary figure. When all his fellows in Moscow were killed in the 1930s on Stalin's orders, Fidler was in Paris at the order of the Comintern. He did not respond when he was called to Moscow, and thus he survived, the only one among the members of the Central Committee to remain alive. Dr. Fidler cared for the children of the highest level of the party echelons and associated institutions. The people who inhabited these echelons had special rights (in the first period, when there were great shortages, they had special shops known as "behind the yellow curtains," a separate medical system, and so on). For a certain period, when Heniek worked for the censor and later when I worked as a journalist at *Trybuna Ludu*, my family enjoyed some of these benefits. Thanks to this, Dr. Fidler took care of my children. She checked Hania and declared that there was nothing to be done. The child would remain undeveloped. She also tried to comfort me by telling me how successful my son was.

It is superfluous to say how I felt. Nevertheless, I thought, until a month previously, maybe six weeks, she had developed normally. It was not possible that the situation was irreversible. We looked for a specialist and made an appointment with Professor Bogdanowicz, the authority on children's illness. He determined, first of all, that the damage was not genetic but motoric. Too much sun had caused the fontanel on her head to close too early, but the skull was still stable and therefore it was not too late to return her to normal development. It would require a lot of patience and hard work. He gave me a prescription for medicine and advice on how to treat her properly.

I took three months unpaid leave to devote all my time to Hania. This was 1951. Genia Łozińska, my boss, arranged for me to spend a month with the child in Zakopane, in the mountains. I worked hard with her.

Hania was already a year and two months old and still not talking. However, after a short time, she started to chatter. She sat up in her bed and taught herself how to say certain words that were hard for her. She repeated words infinite times, until she got them right.

When he saw her a few months later, Professor Bogdanowicz shook my hand and said, "You did a good job." He promised me that she would be very intelligent. Since then, she has developed normally.

However, something from her infancy remained for a protracted time. She did not move easily or quickly like other children in the kindergarten. Apart from that, when she was around three, I saw that her beautiful little legs had started to look like X. An orthopedist gave her special shoes that she had to wear all the time. In Warsaw, the children's kindergartens and schools had shiny, polished parquet floors. Upon arrival, the children removed their shoes and put on gym shoes. Hania was forbidden to take off her shoes. Therefore, I made her thick fabric coverings to put over her shoes. This added to her discomfort and tension, but after two years her legs were straight and beautiful. However, she was left with quite a few complexes.

Hania was the opposite of Witek as a child. Witek acknowledged all the "social" rules without asking questions. He was a good and easy child, always ready to help. By contrast, Hania was more difficult, and I did not manage to guide her, to direct her. She was a non conformist (this too was the opposite of Victor) and stubborn from an early age.

Hania was a very sensitive child, unsure of herself, in no small part due to the certain "heaviness" that I mentioned but also, to no small extent, because of her brother, Witek, although it was not his fault. I did not have the brains to praise Hania when she deserved it and spoil her more, and she, apparently, needed it a lot.

I write these words with great pain. Man's success in the eyes of others is selective and has many faces. My two children are intelligent, each one of them in their own field. Victor went to the sciences and technology; Hania is a clear humanist and a walking encyclopedia with knowledge in many fields.

Although Hania was a daddy's girl, she missed me and longed to be pampered by me. Once, when she was eight or ten, she told me that she loved to see me in my dressing gown. This was without a doubt an expression of longing for a "normal" mother.

As a child, Hania was often ill. She loved to be sick and lie in bed because then she would not need to go to kindergarten or school. She also loved to be ill because from her infancy she loved legends and books. When she still did not know how to read, she loved to lie in bed and ask, "Read to me (using her special word for this—czytuś)." I, or Heniek, whoever was home at the time, read her fairy tales and stories (I did this with great desire, because both of us loved, and love to this day, legends and fantasy tales). Afterward, she swallowed books with great enthusiasm.

While the children were small, every year, in the summer holiday, we took them for a family holiday. Sometimes, to make the holiday last longer, I went with them first and Heniek joined us two weeks later; in the coming two weeks, we were all together. Afterward, I went back to work and Heniek stayed with them for another two weeks. Usually, we went to the mountains and once or twice to the north, to the Baltic Sea, renting an apartment from locals.

Once, when Hania was four or five, we went to Żegiestów or to Polanice, to the mountains. There we rented an apartment from farmers. In the bedroom there was a picture of the Virgin Mary on the wall. I put Hania to bed and then left the room. When Heniek went in to give her a good-night kiss, he opened the door and signaled to me to come to see something. I saw Hania on her knees and praying to the picture. We asked her where she learned to do this. She saw it in church, which she once attended with Mrs. Bronia (our housekeeper, an honest, good-hearted older woman), and she liked the idea a lot. When we explained to her that we are Jews, and Jews believe in a different god, and pray differently, she was not persuaded. However, Hania, as I said, loved stories and legends. So, the next day, Heniek related legends about the gods of ancient Greece, of the east, and all kinds of folk and religious stories, and with the right explanations she understood that people also prayed to other gods, not just the Virgin Mary. We were not religious, so it was hard to understand that our Hania not only stopped praying but over time became a complete atheist. Now she knows a lot more than I do about different religions and their histories.

My daughter's health problems did not stop. On one of the holidays, as always, friends came to our home with their children. Hania was then seven. The children played in the spacious children's room, and we, the adults, sat in the other room, arguing—as was usual in those days—about the politics of the ruling authorities, about anti-Semitism. Sometimes we sang together songs from our youth. At some point, Witek came to me and whispered, "Mama, come to our room." I went. The children were playing "Chinese whispers." One whispers a word in the ear of his neighbor, and that one whispers it in the ear of the next child. When Hania's turn came, she started to shout, "What? What?" loudly and got angry. It was clear that she could not hear. I arranged for them, together with Witek, another game, I played with them a bit, and I waited until the guests left. Then we began a battle to save her hearing, which lasted around two years.

A few months before this she had had mumps, the children's disease. Ostensibly, it was not a big deal. I did not know that this illness could be dangerous. I found out that in rare cases it caused meningitis without any symptoms. This in turn harmed the hearing nerve in girls, and in boys could cause fertility issues. It is not necessary to say that as soon as we discovered that Hania could not hear in her left ear, we did not rest. We visited every ENT specialist in Poland, seeking advice. They all expressed the same opinion: this was a rare case. It was irreparable because the auditory nerve had been compromised. Yet, nevertheless, we wanted the opinion of world experts. We sent copies of the hearing tests together with the opinions of the Polish doctors to experts abroad. We received a response from two countries—Austria and Israel. In the latter, my sisters found an expert who wanted to see her. We received from both countries invitations to visit with our daughter. My friend, Alexander Szurek (to whom I will return later), was in Vienna and invited us to visit him. This time, Heniek wanted to go with Hania. He wanted to visit Israel.

All this certainly affected her life and her character. Today she is vulnerable with regard to health issues. Her teenage years were a special time. We experienced them differently from Victor's teenage years. Witek and his friends were wild, so much so that I wanted to pull him out of the school he attended. By contrast, Hania became introverted, closed, met with a select few friends, and mainly spent her time after school reading books. She spent hours at the university library, where she found books that interested her. After the short period of changing proportions that usually happens when moving from childhood to womanhood, she became a beautiful and interesting young woman.

Life as a Journalist

As I mentioned, I started work in the editorial team of the party journal, Party Life. The entire editorial team was made up of three women: Genia Łozińska, the editor-in-chief, Maryna Arasimowicz, and me. This was not only the beginning of my career as a journalist but also the beginning of this journal.

I was accepted for a trial period as an investigative journalist. After my first trip to a certain city to check some matter, I returned with my notes, and then the three of us sat together and I reported on what I had seen and found. Łozińska was impressed and asked me to write everything as I had told it. Wonderful. However, I found writing very difficult. I sat for days and nights on my first articles (and not only the first ones). It didn't work. The things that I wrote had to go through Maryna's hands, and she almost completely rewrote them. This is how it was the first time and quite a few times after that. I ate myself up and wanted to quit. After around two months of working there, I talked to Genia Łozińska, the editor, about this. She would not hear of me quitting. "After six months," she answered me, "if you don't succeed, then you can quit." She was certain that I would be a good journalist. So, I battled with myself and with the material I brought for a good few months. With never-ending patience, Maryna Arasimowicz and Genia Łozińska taught me to write my stories on paper. These were my first steps as a journalist.

Our journal stopped appearing after around a year (in the meantime, I gave birth to Hania), and after my maternity leave, I joined Genia Łozińska and Maryna, who in the meantime had moved to *Trybuna Ludu*, then Poland's central daily and the mouthpiece of the ruling party. The newspaper established a section devoted to the life of the party, PZPR. There was already a large team. In addition to Genia and Maryna, who returned from exile in France, there were a few more exiles who had also spent time in France and a few veteran journalists of the newspaper who moved to our section. Although I was the only one who came from a different background and the youngest in this warm and interesting group, they became my good friends. Genia Łozińska continued to head the department and accompanied me for a good few years in my work as a journalist. Around the same time, Heniek also left the censor's office and moved to work at the Polish Radio as a journalist.

I worked at Trybuna Ludu in the years 1950–1956, really until 1958. In truth, from 1956 onward, I had an informal connection with the newspaper, because I was working towards a different goal. In 1953, I became a student.

I divided my time between the house and children, on the one hand, and, on the other, work that involved "short trips" of four to five days to investigate stories in various Polish cities and towns. It was not easy. Over time, I became a professional journalist and every article I wrote took up half a page in the analytical part of the paper. I worked hard, days and nights, on every one of my articles. Journalist and writer Roman Juryś once said to me—when I told him about my difficulties writing articles—that there was a drop of blood from his heart in every article that he wrote. So too, my writing caused me a great deal of suffering and pain. It was not easy to be a journalist in the People's Poland. Every word carried weight, and I was responsible for it. There was not only an official censor but also the internal censorship, no less strict, of the editors, and of every journalist who wanted to keep working. The gap continually grew between what I saw and discovered and wanted to report to the public, on the one hand, and what I could publish, on the other. This dilemma, one felt by every journalist who cares, reflected to a great extent the Polish socio political system. It was seven times harder for me. I dealt mainly with social and party problems. I was not built for compromises in fundamental matters. I could not stay quiet or close my eyes and ignore things that, as I understood it, negatively affected the morals with which I identified.

Journalism cultivated within me certain qualities: responsibility for the written word and an ability to listen with patience to whatever a person has to say and try to understand him. By contrast, I was never successful at public appearances. I have a command of the written word but not its spoken counterpart. When I lectured to students at Beit Berl college, and afterward at Tel Aviv University, I prepared for every lecture and wrote it, and afterward I prepared the main points, and only then was I sure of myself.

My work as a journalist was difficult and entailed great responsibility. Today an investigative journalist has access to various sources of information regarding every question; all the sources are open to them. At that time in Poland, there were not many journalists like me, people who traveled to a city or a region for a week and sometimes returned for another week to conduct dozens of interviews. My presence was often unwanted, in particular by the local bosses, who did not want me going through their affairs, looking for reports and documents, and finding the answers I was looking for. And if an article dared to criticize a party secretary in the Kielce region, for example, a semi-illiterate man in a position of authority, it would end up straight on the desk of the official responsible for this region and the head of the department in the Central Committee of the party, causing problems. They would start investigating. However, they would not investigate the facts and their sources, but rather to what extent the article could harm the position of the secretary or his close associates higher in the hierarchy.

I was troubled by the humiliating way in which people who encountered difficulties in the bureaucratic machinery of the regime were treated. The cruelty and ignorance of the rulers, who terrorized the people under their command, angered me. It is important to remember that the local committee (urban, regional, or district), and in reality the party secretary at its head, were all-powerful and responsible for all areas of life. If, for example, I managed to locate a clique in a large factory in the city of Wrocław, which was headed by leader of the party committee in the factory who systematically cheated the workers, stealing from them what they deserved to get, I first had to conduct dozens of conversations with the workers and the technical staff in almost underground conditions, because the workers were afraid to speak to me openly. I was not allowed to interview the workers in the factory offices. After an exchange of harsh words with the management, I was permitted to talk to them only in the half-destroyed bathroom, while outside stood a long line of workers who wanted to talk to me. The factory management placed before me obstacles so that I would not be able to get to the relevant documents. Only thanks to the involvement of the editor-in-chief of *Trybuna Ludu* (then Leon Kasman, who was serving in this role on behalf of the party) was I able to find the relevant material.

I must mention here two episodes in which I was involved that damaged my health and led me eventually to distance myself from journalism. These episodes demonstrate the situation in which Polish journalists who tried to fight evil found themselves.

Party propaganda under pressure from the Soviet advisors advanced the idea of collectivizing agriculture. Thus, the branches of the party and the local authorities were under pressure to organize agricultural cooperatives in villages (Spółdzielnie produkcyjne), similarly to the kolkhozes in the Soviet Union. The propaganda included all the media and party branches, and in the field, apparently, the local mechanisms were active in various ways, ostensibly competing to see which would establish kolkhozes more quickly. The plans were not successful. The farmers did not hurry to hand over their lands and their animals to some unknown body.

In early spring 1956, there was a meeting of the executive committee of the Central Committee of the party. Leon Kasman, the editor of the *Trybuna*, was a member of this committee. At the meeting, they talked about the collectivization of agriculture, and, among other things, the successes and achievements in the Lublin region, in particular the district of Hrubieszów. The members turned to Kasman and requested that his newspaper cover the popularization of the methods that led to such great success there. The next day, at a meeting of the editorial team, the idea was born that I would go to Lublin to investigate. I was not an expert in agriculture, so I asked that Mariańska, my colleague on the section, a journalist at the start of her career who was raised in a village, join me (in retrospect, it seems to me that editor-in-chief Kasman chose me, rather not Ruschitz, the agricultural expert, because he already smelled something fishy in this race for collectivization and trusted my sense of smell). We set off.

In Lublin, at a meeting with the regional party secretary and the official responsible for the district of Hrubieszów, we received information about the district and the great achievements in the field of collectivization, which already encompassed around 80 percent of the agriculture in the district. The district secretary tried to persuade us how important it was to publicize the excellent achievements, which would serve as an example to the entire country (and would certainly give him glory). Afterward, we received a detailed and extensive survey from the official responsible for this district. He advised us to talk to the regional secretary, Comrade Ney, the man who had worked wonders.

Encouraged, we left for Hrubieszów. This is an agricultural tract of land, full of forests and orchards, lying at the foot of the Carpathian Mountains, a magical place; the beauty of the landscape is breathtaking. It was spring. The trees blossomed in all shades of colors and the smells were intoxicating. We set out, at the recommendation of the district official, for the local Party Committee. There Comrade Ney awaited us. He lectured us for a few hours, using a prepared lecture in which he described the development of the kolkhozes and how they were flourishing. His lecture included all the necessary material for writing a series of articles on the beauty of collectivization. Mariańska, who accompanied me, was new to journalism. She was sure that we had everything we needed. We could go home and write our articles.

Indeed, it seemed that in Hrubieszów the experiment in collective farming was likely to succeed because the area had a certain historical tradition of shared village life. The lands had in the past belonged to Stanisław Staszic, a well-known reformer who lived at the end of the eighteenth century and beginning of the nineteenth century. In the framework of his reforms, he established in 1816 an "agricultural society," Fundacja, which gave farmers on his land permission to establish joint farms, and thus they were also released from their vassalage.

Ney's lecture was persuasive. Yet I wanted to see what a kolkhoz (which in Poland was called "spółdzielnia produkcyjna") looked like. I asked for a vehicle to travel to one or two kolkhozes and see how they looked. Comrade Ney was surprised. Why go to the villages? That was not comfortable. He had given us all that we needed for the article. Did I doubt his words? The more he tried to persuade me that it was not necessary to visit a village, the more my distrust grew, accompanied by a sense that something was wrong. Finally, he agreed and said that he had a meeting at a collective farm later that day, and we could accompany him there. We agreed.

We found ourselves in a dingy, dark room with worn-looking walls. In place of electric light, a sooty oil lamp stood on the table. There were a few long benches, on which sat 10–15 quiet and angry people. Mariańska and I sat down on one of the benches together with the farmers. This meeting was supposed to be an annual summary of the cooperative's achievements and a survey of the farm's situation. Mainly Ney spoke, telling those present the same story he had sold to us. The head of the kolkhoz appeared too, reading something from the paper that no one understood. Everyone was quiet. At a certain moment I felt someone grasp my hand and put a note in it. I held the note tight. When we went back to the dormitory next to the party headquarters, we read the note. The man asked us to come the next day without additional witnesses. We decided to go back there to talk to the people openly.

Ney did not want to give us a vehicle to visit the villages (although he was required to do so) and there were no taxis in the town. We decided to walk, and on the way, we would ask people about the village we had visited. We did not have to go very far. As soon as we left the town and approached a road leading between the forests, someone came toward us and asked us to follow him to a thicket of bushes and vegetation where people were waiting for us. Among these bushes we found a lot of people. They asked to talk to us. We accepted the invitation, went deeper into the forest, and here we found ourselves among masses of farmers and women sitting and waiting for us. A rumor about representatives of a newspaper from Warsaw had spread through the villages at lightning speed, awakening among the residents a spark of hope. We sat down in the forest and listened and recorded the farmers' stories. In the following days we visited a few villages and the houses of farmers.

What we saw and heard forced me to return to Warsaw and consult with the editorial team.

In the meantime, the editor-in-chief Leon Kasman had been replaced by Władysław Matwin (these were the frenzied days of October 1956, to which I will return elsewhere). Factions had already emerged within the party. There began a wave of personnel changes in the highest echelons and one of the victims was Kasman, the editor of *Trybuna*. Matwin was known as a brave man, a supporter of reforms. I asked Genia Łozińska, as the head of our section, to report to the editor-in-chief about what we had seen in Hrubieszów and she asked Matwin for an urgent meeting. He invited us immediately. I was holding in my hands "explosive criminal material."

Matwin had almost no idea who I was. We had met perhaps once or twice, but he had apparently read my articles before joining the editorial team, when he was party secretary in some region (I don't remember which). After hearing my report, he put at our disposal an editorial car, unlimited time, and gave us his blessing, saying that we were not alone, and the editorial team would support us.

We, Mariańska and I, spent another two weeks in the villages of the Hrubieszów district (visiting our families on weekends). The cry of this beautiful area was not heard on the surface. Ney, who ruled the residents and their lands, had destroyed their lives. He was in complete control of the area as local party head, head of the Ministry of Public Security (Bezpieka), and also director of the local regional authority.

His system was simple in its cruelty: anyone who did not want to give his last cow to the "cooperative" or to surrender his plot of land was sent to prison. The roof and the doors of his home were destroyed, a special guard visited his home day and night, destroying what was left of his home and property and setting fire to his threshing floor. This did not happen all at once, but gradually, slowly, until the women left at home were gripped by madness and their husbands sent to prison. We saw partially destroyed houses, without roofs and doors, their windows broken. We saw a woman sitting in the corner of the kitchen of a destroyed house; all they had left her was a tin mug and a kettle. There was madness in her eyes. We were told about people tortured in the basement of the Bezpieka, which was under Ney's command, etc.

We looked for protocols of the Executive Committee of the local party regarding these activities. We found some evidence, albeit not a lot. Yet, in fact, it was very relevant.

I came home in a terrible mood. I knew that I could not publicize the entirety of this terrible crime. I had to choose the less harsh facts. For example, about people who were previously party members, even active in the left-wing Gwardia Ludowa, during the war, and now had been thrown out of the party, arrested, and their families destroyed, all this because they refused to hand over their last cow (from the protocols of the local Party Committee meeting). I could not write even a quarter of all that I had seen and heard. I submitted a detailed report of all that we had seen and heard to Matwin, my boss, signed by myself and Mariańska.

Only two articles about the episode in Hrubieszów were published. After the publication of the articles, the expected reaction ensued: committees started to investigate the episodes in Hrubieszów. The local Party Committee in Lublin concluded that everything in the articles was invented: it was all the fruit of the journalists' imaginations.

Matwin was not ready to concede. The Central Party Committee dispatched a commission to investigate the facts. It too reached the same conclusion: the articles were lies. Then we were called to the Central Party Committee—Matwin, Łozińska, and I. The Committee demanded that Matwin print a refutation on the first page, in a prominent place, and also "draw conclusions" about Mariańska (who was completely innocent, I dragged her along) and me. Matwin revealed himself to be a stubborn warrior, ready to endanger himself: he trusted his workers and was sure that the facts we had uncovered were the truth. Apart from that, apparently his experience and common sense told him that there was a reason to fight. He demanded that another commission be sent—this time a joint one made up of people from the Central Committee and editorial team of the Trybuna. After heated debates, they agreed. The manager of complaints and letters to the editor (I don't remember her name), a Jewish woman sensitive to injustice, was sent on behalf of the editorial staff, together with Ruschitz, the agricultural correspondent. Mariańska and I went along as the guilty parties, but we were not allowed to take part in the committee's investigations. We sat in the dormitory and waited.

After the first day of the committee's investigations, in the evening, our friends at the editorial staff returned and told us that it was not necessary to change even one comma in the articles. Indeed, the situation was far more terrible. In the coming days, she and Ruschitz turned all the conclusions of the previous commission on their heads. The representatives of the Central Committee were silent. I was saved for the umpteenth time. What was done to the guilty parties, meaning, what the Central Committee and mainly the justice institutions concluded regarding the criminal Ney—that was not my jurisdiction.

I did not hear a thing about what happened afterward in Hrubieszów. However, I believe that in some small way I influenced an extensive publication that appeared a few weeks later detailing the decision of the plenary meeting of the party's Central Committee about "mistakes and distortions" with regard to collectivization in the region of Koszalin. As I found out, the "mistakes" in Koszalin were far less serious than those in Hrubieszów. It seemed to me that since then the propaganda for the collectivization of agriculture was abandoned. This was in 1956, the year of political and economic crisis and the personnel changes in the party's highest echelons.

The Hrubieszów episode is one of many that I went through in the People's Republic of Poland.

I will briefly mention another episode, which dictated that I finish for good with journalism in Poland.

I believe it was in 1957. The head of the office for complaints and letters to the editor asked me to investigate a complaint from an engineer named Zapałowski. He lived in Warsaw. I invited him to the editorial offices for a conversation. He was a serious, forty-year-old man, tired of life. He had a story similar to that of hundreds and thousands of Poles wandering Poland and who knows how many thousands in prisons in Poland or Russia. It made the life of this man miserable. Zapałowski was an engineer, a profession in high demand. He easily got work. However, as soon as the authorities found out he was working, he was fired. His family lived in poverty and despair. What was his crime?

Almost a dozen years after the war, he carried the stigma of his wartime past. During the Nazi occupation of Poland, he fought in the Jewish underground, Armia Krajowa (AK), which was under the authority of the Polish government-in-exile in London. The Soviet Union, due to its interests in the future of Poland, opposed this government. Apart from the AK, another underground was active in occupied Poland, Gwardia Ludowa (GL), which received help from the Soviet Union, building an infrastructure for the People's Poland.

I knew the story of the war between the AK and GL—the two underground forces fighting the Germans. I also knew about the war against the AK and the persecution of its members by the security forces of Poland (and behind them Soviet Russia). I knew that I was going to hit my head against a brick wall. However, I saw Zapałowski as a symbol of a painful and much wider issue, which encompassed all the members of the AK and others who in the past had been members of organizations that did not wave the red flag.

I will not recount all the details of the battle I waged on behalf of this engineer, running from one factory to another—from each one I received a letter stating their excellent opinion of the man. I will not describe the meetings with the local committees of Warsaw and a few meetings of the Party Municipal Committee attended by a representative of the security forces. Finally, I published an article entitled, "The Question of Engineer Zapałowski" (Sprawa inżyniera Zapałowskiego).

This article caused a commotion in Poland and was even quoted on the Polish-language radio station "Free Europe," the most popular station in Poland (even though listening to it was illegal). The subject touched on one of the most "reeking" aspects of the regime. I will not relate how many times I was called to the Municipal and Central Party committees. However, Engineer Zapałowski finally got a permanent job and could breathe freely. "The Question of Engineer Zapałowski" continued onward, only its heroes changed, as did the names of those who visited my home looking for help a long time after I had already left *Trybuna Ludu*. This was testimony to the fact that my fight was, for the most part, "a fight against windmills" (like Cervantes's Don Quixote). Meaning, I could sometimes help individuals, sometimes cause the leaders of the regime to think again, but my article and my war could not change anything fundamental and could not change the treatment of former AK members. I will only note that from the beginning of the 1960s, when Mieczysław Moczar became the head of the investigative department at the MSW and later the minister, when he gained strength and served as head of the organization of war veterans, he accepted into his service not only members of the former AK but also people from the extreme nationalist and anti-Semitic sect that was active during the war and after it against the Communist regime.

Pretty quickly I understood that the government, the Sejm, the municipal authorities—all these were fictions, or a tool to carry out the instructions of the true rulers, according to their moods and whims: the chief secretary of the Central Committee, his politburo, and the mechanism of the Party that ruled the country. Sometimes the power of the head of the Ministry of Public Security (the Bezpieka) increased, and in important matters, Moscow's power.

I must emphasize that writing about social phenomena of that period suited my sense of social justice and accorded, or so I thought for a certain time, with the idea of the party I had joined. There were others who shared this belief: usually, my friends at the party section of the paper and also the editor-in-chief. Therefore, despite all the suffering I endured, I always received the full back up of the editorial team. I must emphasize that my socio political views also changed as my journalistic experience increased. With increasing frequency, I encountered in the field phenomena that contradicted my concept of the role of the ruling party, contradicted the elementary principle of democracy, even of "centralized" democracy (according to Lenin's teachings).

I would not have survived with relative freedom without my friends at the editorial staff and the decisive opinions of its heads. Matwin, like Kasman and Genia Łozińska, saw journalism as a tool to fight evil.[6] When my political status became shaky, and it seemed likely that I would be fired, my friends at the editorial team also helped me get a scholarship to study. Therefore, I must mention some of my friends from the *Trybuna Ludu* who saved me more than once from difficult situations, at least those closest to me—Maryna Arasimowicz, Genia Łozińska, Alexander Szurek, and Ela Mink.

---

6 Matwin served for a relatively short time as the editor of *Trybuna Ludu*. From there, I believe he went to the Central Committee of the PZPR, and afterward to an institution for training cadres. In the stormy days of 1968, he was fired from his job and the party. He was not a Jew.

Maryna Arasimowicz was older than me. She was maybe in her forties or even fifties. She was severe with herself and with others, an uncompromising idealist. Always ready to help others, she was also highly critical of acts and opinions with which she did not agree. She helped me a lot but also criticized me sharply when I did something that was wrong in her eyes. She was my closest friend.

Maryna was married to a Polish Communist and had two daughters: Marta and Irena. She was a very beautiful woman, blonde with gray eyes, but the signs of a hard life were evident (her blonde hair was almost gray already). Her relationship with her husband was, as I discovered, miserable. She did not tell anyone about her private life. I often visited her at home and our children played together. When I went away for work, she was in close contact with my husband, Heniek, and my children. However, I rarely met her husband. I knew only that he did not have permanent work. Once, she came to my house and, during our conversation, told me that she was going to get divorced. I was shocked. I had not known to what extent she had suffered and borne the pain for so many years. Her Polish husband was a Communist and a great and dangerous anti-Semite. As a Jew living in occupied Paris, Maryna battled for her life and the lives of her daughters. However, her husband tried to turn her over to the Nazis. To her good fortune, he failed: the underground organization in which she was active found out, and its members threatened him, telling him that this would mean the end for him too. She was silent for years, until the girls grew up and could understand. She revealed to them that she was Jewish as the wave of anti-Semitism was beginning during the events of 1956 (on this below). At the same time, their father revealed his hostility toward Jews. This was the breaking point. The girls asked their mother the necessary questions. She had waited for this moment for years. With their agreement, she divorced him and returned to her maiden name, a typically Jewish name, Finkielkraut, and the girls, demonstrating their solidarity with her, adopted this name and cut off all contact with their father. At that time in Poland this was a very brave act.

My relationship with Maryna and her daughters continued many years after I left the *Trybuna*. Her opinion was very important to me and I valued her wisdom. At the beginning of the 1960s, I wrote my first book, *Fortuna kołem się toczy* (Fortune Is Fickle) based on my master's thesis, which was published by a popular science publisher in 1965. Its hero was Jan Bloch, "the king of the railroad" that was built in the kingdom of Poland and Russia in the nineteenth century. I researched the process of constructing and operating the train line between Warsaw and Łódź Fabryczna. This study was based on extensive archival research that included the annual reports of the stock company established and headed by Bloch. And so, I discovered exploitation and embezzlement. Although I tried to depict my hero as an outstanding man, unique in his generation, a scientist, a realist, a man of peace with a warm Jewish heart, even though he converted when he was fourteen years old, apparently the account was less positive than I had hoped.

I asked Maryna to be the first person to read the manuscript before giving it to the publisher. She did not like my discoveries of exploitation and so on. She thought that the story was not balanced and that Bloch was depicted too negatively. Years later, I understood she was right. To this day I miss her wise, critical opinion. Maryna filled, to a certain extent, the empty space left by Shoshana when the latter went to Israel. Maryna died around a year after we moved to Israel. Her daughters, I believe, left for Scandinavian countries, and I lost contact with them.

Almost everyone in this Parisian group suffered problems and personal tragedies.

Genia Łozińska, who established the monthly Party Life and afterward headed the party section at *Trybuna Ludu*, was a unique character. A knowledgeable, intelligent, and wise woman, severe but with a heart of gold, she was a talented pedagogue and psychologist. She and Maryna Arasimowicz made a journalist out of me. She belonged to the "hard" Communists. Lenin was her guide. As happens to many such people, after the disappointment of 1956, she was the first to speak out against Stalinism and all the ideology that she had believed in so fervently. However, she always remained a firm believer in human rights and social justice. In the drawer of her desk was a thick book full of quotes from Lenin's writings. Every article that left Genia's office for print was accompanied, above the title and name of the author, with a quote from Lenin's writings that suited the topic. Yet, when she saw acts of injustice, she would fight to the end. I will give one example that demonstrates Genia's character.

Bernard Sztetler was our close friend, a journalist working in the next room, in the foreign section. We all loved him. His wife's brother, who was of a high yet not particularly flattering status (head of the department for investigation of political prisoners) in the Ministry of Public Security (where he took the name Światło), fled Poland during the wave of strikes and the continuous protests that ensued when the dirt about the upper echelons was made public. He apparently feared for his life. The episode aroused a great commotion in Poland and outside it, because he knew a lot of secrets and could cause damage to the Polish regime. No one justified his actions. We did not know him, although when, immediately after his flight, his family was arrested, including Brunek Sztetler, who was placed under house arrest, the matter angered us. Brunek had no connection to his brother-in-law. His wife had just had a baby and was sick. Although no one was allowed to visit them, the authorities could not prevent the car of *Trybuna Ludu*, the central mouthpiece of the party, from approaching their home. And thus, at the initiative of Genia Lozińska, and accompanied by cars of the secret police, we visited his family every day as a sign of protest, watched by the agents of the secret police, and brought the couple what they needed. Genia was exceptionally brave when she went out to fight for the innocence of Brunek Sztetler and his wife. Sadly, the family was sent somewhere isolated, in terrible conditions. Once the internal politics thawed to a certain degree, the family returned to Warsaw and Brunek to his work.

After I left the *Trybuna*, I lost contact with them. In the 1960s, they left for Israel. We lived in Jerusalem then and did not know what had happened to them. Only after some time did I find out that Brunek had begun to work at a well-known advertising agency, but soon after he discovered that he had cancer and died. His two daughters live in Bat Yam with their families.

Genia Łozińska was divorced, with a son, Marcel. Her former husband, Roman, was a party theoretician, editor of the theoretical monthly *Nowe Drogi*. Marcel Łoziński was very talented. To the best of my knowledge, he is now involved in cinema in Poland.

All the "Parisians" that I knew were intelligent, fantastic people. They all arrived from Paris, where they had been in political exile, forced to leave Poland because they were persecuted as Communists. There, in France, they all participated in the underground war against the Nazis. One of them was Alexander Szurek. During the civil war in Spain, he served in the international battalion. He was the adjutant of General Swierczewski in the Polish unit named after Jan Dąbrowski.[7] Szurek was wounded in Spain and lost an eye. He avoided the fate of his fellow warriors in Spain, who were persecuted by Stalin. Many of them were arrested and murdered. General Swierczewski himself was murdered "accidentally." Szurek was saved because in the same year as these persecutions he was serving in the Polish embassy in Austria (my husband visited him with Hania and he arranged for my daughter to see

---

7 One of the great generals of Poland at the end of the eighteenth century, a hero of the Kościuszko uprising of 1795, who afterward established a Polish regiment in Italy that fought alongside Napoleon's forces and participated in liberating a significant part of Poland.

an expert physician) and those above him did not hurry to return him home or to follow Stalin's orders. Szurek was a wonderful and good-hearted man. For a while he tried his hand as a journalist at *Trybuna Ludu*, in our section. He did not really succeed and went to work in the Foreign Ministry. However, the friendship between us remained, as with all the group.

There were another two former "Parisian" women: one of them took on the underground name "Foka" while she was in Paris, and we called her "Foczka" due to her coat (it was made of seal fur). Always elegant, always full of life, always ready to help others, Foczka was a divorcee. Her former husband, a Pole, served as Minister of Agriculture (or perhaps in another ministry, I don't remember). They did not have children. The other was Ela Mink. She had feelings of inferiority, perhaps because of her difficult home life. Although, as I already mentioned, we never spoke about these things, there was an evident coldness between the couple. Her only son was a little younger than my son, and when she went out in the field and I remained, he often stayed with us.

Among the many documents I have saved, there are some that today arouse my wonder. One of them testifies that in the years 1950–1958 I worked as a journalist at *Trybuna Ludu* and the other (from May 19, 1960) signed by Richard Gradowski, the proctor of the high school for social sciences (Wyższa Szkoła Nauk Społecznych in Warsaw), determines that I studied history and sociology in the years 1953–1958 and that I was now continuing my studies to master's level (which I finished in 1961).

How did I, a mother of two, among them a baby born in 1950, manage to work at a daily newspaper, including investigative trips, to study, and to be also a wife and mother? I don't remember all these days and all the crises I went through on the way. Around

1952, I found myself in a small, special hospital, which was then on Jerozolimskie Avenue, after doctors decided that my physical exhaustion had reached a red line and I needed to choose between a coffin and the crazy life of work, studies, and children. It was not necessary to order me a coffin and I did not change my lifestyle. After a short rest, I went back to normal.

But I must emphasize that without Heniek, his patience and his great sacrifice, I would not have been able to work as an investigative journalist and to study. It was not easy for either of us. Certainly, it was not easy for Heniek. I have to admit that in hindsight, his love and devotion to our family gave him the energy to put up with me, my frequent absences from home, my late nights immersed in work and studies.

Without his patience, tolerance, and great help, I would not have been able to do it all. Heniek shared the chores at home, cared for the children when I disappeared for days and nights. Even the crises along the way were resolved in good spirits.

CHAPTER 10
THE LAST DECADE IN POLAND

In 1958, I completed my studies. Together with them, I also completed my obligations to the *Trybuna Ludu* (during the period of the scholarship, I was required to submit at least two articles per month, including collecting material in the field, sometimes also a feature or a lead article). I did not think about going back to working as a journalist full time. There were a few reasons for this. One of them, the main one, was that I was tired of the constant battles. I understood that journalism in the existing regime was not free and it did not have the power to change anything. The second reason, apart from family problems (to which I will return later), was that I had the opportunity to realize my dream and study for a master's degree (which I received in the spring of 1961) and to pursue a scientific career, without politics. Therefore, I chose a route that was by no means simple and which today is so rare—economic and social history (I researched this field in the thesis for my master's degree).

In the meantime, I needed to work. Unlike my fellow students, I did not receive a referral to a workplace upon completing my studies, and for a certain period I was unemployed. There were, ostensibly, reasons for this. In this period, I went through slow and fundamental processes of sobering up and reflection.

I must explain by going back a few years.

In the spring of 1953, I was on a two-week holiday after being sick, somewhere in the Carpathian Mountains. On one of the first days, I heard on the morning news about Stalin's death. I was beset by a feeling of fear and panic. Immediately, I left the magical holiday resort and went back to Warsaw to be with my friends and family during this time of "great mourning." I cried together with them. The memory of those days reminds me that I still believed Stalin and the Soviet Union were positive things in a cruel world.

However, as an investigative journalist checking facts in the field (I spent at least a few days in almost all the towns and cities in Poland investigating something), I knew what the residents thought and, even more, learned about the actions of the small leaders, the tyrants. At the same time, my studies helped me sober up. Within their framework, among other things, I studied with great thoroughness the fathers of Marxism, from the first thinkers of utopian Socialism to Hegel, Marx, Engels, Lenin, and Stalin. I saw in the teachings of Marx and Engels a complete philosophical system, albeit to a certain extent eclectic, but rational, interesting. Despite this, their social and economic vision did not withstand the test of history. Friedrich Engels understood this at the end of his days. Moreover, he warned the Socialist-revolutionary world about transferring the focus of the social revolutionary movement from developed and liberal Western Europe to Russia, which was weak socially and economically. He saw this as a disaster that was likely to distort the entire Communist idea. How right he was!

Thirty-something volumes of Lenin's writings, translated into Polish with literal punctiliousness, as though they were holy books, were published in Poland. When I read his many articles and essays during my studies, seeing the rude, condescending, polemical style that he used to argue with his ideological opponents, I was amazed at my inflexibility, that I was unable to understand and properly value Lenin's teachings. I simply did not know whether to laugh or cry. How was this man able to inspire the masses, cause a division in the international Social Democratic movement, and the rest of the things he did?

I see the teachings of Lenin, the leader of the October Revolution, about the "dictatorship of the proletariat" and "centralized democracy" as a source of all the evil in the Soviet regime. He was responsible to a great extent for the rise of Stalin and his actions, although, perhaps, he no longer had the power to stop this process.

For me, the speech given by Khrushchev at the twentieth summit of the Soviet Communist Party at the beginning of 1956 was the breaking point. The summit was attended by party leaders and heads of states from the Communist bloc, among them Bolesław Bierut, the first president of the Polish People's Republic, who returned in a coffin from Moscow. A few days after the summit ended, I was chosen to join the guard of honor standing by his open coffin in the party house on the corner of Jerozolimskie Avenue and Krucza Street. I stood there with very mixed feelings. I liked the man. He was, apparently, unable to return to Poland alive after the terrible revelations of the acts committed by Stalin and his close associates and pretend to know nothing. He must have been involved in some things, like in the war against the former AK members, the warriors who fought in the civil war in Spain, remaining silent about the "Katyn massacre," in which thousands of Polish officers were murdered in 1939 after falling prisoner to the Red Army, and afterward their mass grave was found, and more like this.

As I stood with the guard of honor next to Beirut's open coffin, I still did not know the content of Khrushchev's speech at the twentieth summit. That arrived later. However, I saw a long line of people on the street, all waiting to pay their last respects to the president of Poland. I stood and listened to the whispers. A lot of people wanted to see what he looked like, because a rumor spread that he had been poisoned in Moscow (perhaps he killed himself there?). The official statement said that he caught pneumonia and died. No one believed it. Many men, women, and children went past the coffin and whispered: "They killed him" (meaning the leaders at the Kremlin in Moscow).

It is strange: Klement Gottwald (1896–1953), president and leader of Czechoslovakia, also returned from that summit in Moscow in a coffin.

After a short time, at the end of March 1956, there was a full meeting of the Central Committee of the PZPR to discuss the ramifications of Khrushchev's revelations. At this meeting, a new-old leader was chosen for Poland, Władysław Gomułka, who in 1948 had been removed from power and classified as an unwanted person, even spending a certain period under house arrest. Now he was completely rehabilitated. In discussions of Khrushchev's revelations, fundamental differences of opinion became evident, as a result of which sects emerged in the wider party leadership. These subsequently accompanied the life of the party and state until the end of the Communist regime, although the sects changed and developed.

At that same meeting, it was decided, among other things, that the content of Khrushchev's speech at the twentieth summit of the Soviet Communist Party would be shared with only a limited circle of active members of the party and leadership. The speech was printed as a classified booklet (meaning there were a set number of copies; a person signed that he received a booklet with a certain number and was obligated to return the same one with the same number). Following the meeting, I was among those who received a booklet. On the way home, I walked along unable to see or hear anything; I did not know what to do with myself. This continued until I fell on the tram track not far from home and got a shock.

Days and nights I reflected on my life since I first encountered the Communist movement, asking myself, "Where was I?" Was I in some way guilty of this chaos filled with blood and suffering? Why had I not heard or did not want to know how the peoples of the Soviet Union lived?

In the coming days, I attended meetings of the party organizations in various places—the university, various higher education institutions, the Institute for Sociology and History. Young people stood up at these meetings and related how the KGB took their parents and they never saw them again. I remember in particular the stories of Dr. Władysław Krajewski, the grandson of Adolf Warszawski-Warski, and the historian Dr. Jan Kancewicz, the nephew of Max Horwitz-Walecki. They were among the prominent leaders of the Central Committee of the Polish Communist Party (KPP) and, together with their families and all the leadership of the KPP, they traveled to Moscow at the end of the 1920s. They were murdered there. Their children and grandchildren, among them the two I mentioned, were taken to Soviet orphanages.

The small children of these families, like Dr. Krajewski, were raised in orphanages in Russia and believed that their parents were traitors and agents of Anglo-American imperialism.

These were very emotional meetings. It is strange but I wanted to attend every single meeting and hear and feel the pain of those telling difficult and similar stories. Madness, a kind of masochism, took hold of me. The pain I felt then was a fundamental turning point in my life. I should add that I was not the only one to go through emotional turmoil at this time; many suffered similar crises.

I mentioned that after the plenary meeting of the Central Committee of the Polish United Workers' Party (PZPR), divisions emerged in the party. It is hard to say that these were consolidated divisions, but without doubt there was some kind of line dividing between groups. Over the years, this line widened, and the groups consolidated into camps. With the return of Gomułka to power, he of course instituted widespread personnel changes, seeking to get rid of the old guard.

Interestingly, many of that old guard now belonged to the faction of the party that demanded significant structural reforms (these were known as the "soft" group or "Puławianie"—after the name of the street on which most of them lived, Puławska Street), as opposed to the "radical" stream, or "Natolin"—they held their meetings in Natolin—who were suspicious of any kind of reform. Without going into details of the internal fights, which changed over the coming years, as did the names of the prominent figures in the factions, it is worth noting that since Khrushchev's revelations, two parallel phenomena emerged side by side in Poland: on the one hand the social ferment demanding change, freedom of expression, democracy, and less dependence on the Soviet Union intensified. It was headed, as always, by the intelligentsia: writers, artists, scientists, and students, including quite a few of the old party guard. In these circles there were many Jews (the KOR, "the committee for defense of the workers," and later the Solidarność movement that put an end to the old regime, was born from them). On the other hand, the opposing camp gained power. The ranks of the party and the ruling mechanisms recruited dubious elements. They controlled the security forces, meaning the army, and the interior and foreign ministries, and quickly embarked on a battle against the ostensible revisionists and servants of imperialism, which was mainly intended against Jews. Among the members of the Natolin stream were people such as Władysław Kruczek, Zenon Nowak, Kazimierz Mijal, and Mieczysław Moczar, and others who sought to gain control of power and the government by releasing a wave of anti-Semitism. They were in constant contact with Soviet advisors in Poland, and via the Soviet consulate passed on false reports, according to which, for example, the Jews and revisionists intended to sever the relations between Poland and the Soviet Union.

In the speech he gave upon taking office, Gomułka promised more independence, less reliance on the Soviet Union (Khrushchev did not let that pass in silence), and democratization. The enthusiasm among the people was incredible. Had he really wanted to implement even part of his promises, Gomułka could have made changes. It is possible to say that over a few months (March–October) there was a certain degree of political and civil thawing (which I also enjoyed, because they opened some of the archives that had previously been sealed). Yet Gomułka did not mean it. He was by nature a dictator, a harsh man, and, it seems, enjoyed the anti-Jewish atmosphere, drawing close to him people who built their personal careers based on it, such as Mieczysław Moczar, who became his right-hand man. (This Mieczysław Moczar, whose life story was different, as we know, was in fact of Ukrainian and Provo Slav origin and had a different name.) A lot has been written about those days and about Moczar.

In short, 1956 was a year of social ferment in Poland—strikes in large factories, in particular the port of Gdansk, in Łódź, and in Warsaw, accompanied by stormy street protests. I too attended a few of them. The ferment reached a peak in October, when Khrushchev came "secretly" to Warsaw and his tanks surrounded the capital city. After an exchange of harsh words with Gomułka, and considering that the events were likely to turn into a general uprising against the Soviet Union and the existing regime, they reached a compromise. Konstantin Rokossovsky, the Soviet Marshall, who served as Poland's defense minister, was forced to leave accompanied by protests, calls of disdain, and stones thrown at the wagon in which he sat.

⚏

In 1958, after finishing my studies, I found it difficult to find an appropriate job. In Communist Poland, unemployment was not recognized and there was no concept of unemployment benefit. After studying, a graduate was referred to a workplace, with official appointment to a certain role. I left my studies without such a refer-ral. It may be that the newspaper *Trybuna Ludu*, which belonged to the workers' cooperative Prasa (journalism), was instructed not to renew my work contract. To be unemployed—this was a new state for me. It was not nice, but perhaps it was necessary in order for me to recognize the facts.

How long was I unemployed? Apparently, a long time, not taking into account temporary work. For a certain period, maybe a year, I was employed by Hersh Smolar, the editor-in-chief of the Yiddish newspaper *Folks Shtime*, editing a Polish-language weekly supplement. When this contract ended, I was again with-out work.

I had nowhere to turn. Friends and acquaintances who had studied together with me were working in various places. Some of them worked in the party's Central Committee, but I did not want to approach them. Among them was a friend with whom another student and I had studied together almost every day for long hours. This was Andrzej Bril. When I bumped into him and told him that I was unemployed, I felt that he wanted to get rid of me as quickly as possible. He did not want to be seen in my company. Also my good friend Hania Kitlińska could not help me. Thus, I discovered that I was on a "blacklist," meaning that I was not loyal enough (as in the Red Army many years before). However, other friends, those who were not so close to me, were not afraid to offer help.

Among the documents that I have kept is a certificate signed by the Rector of the Higher School for Social Sciences (WSNS) on May 19, 1960, informing me that I had completed my studies and was continuing to study for a master's degree: "Because the stu-dent (name) is moving to work at 'the Society for the Development of the Western Territories,' it requested to "preserve the continuity of her work for the purposes of tenure." This document notes that I had finished my studies in 1958 and it seeks to maintain conti-nuity of my work to 1960, meaning that I was without permanent work for two years. Why did the Rector suddenly ask this society to take my situation into consideration?

Once, apparently in the spring of 1960, I met on the street an acquaintance of mine, Nazarewicz, one of my friends from my studies. When I told him that I was unemployed, he did not run away, did not promise anything, but invited me to a nearby café. While we walked, I discovered that he worked in a department at the party's Central Committee. By the way, he was a Jew, like Bril, but he was much more intelligent than him. He was also not a coward and had pleasant manners. We said farewell (to this day I do not know what happened to him). After a few days, I received a phone call from him. He suggested that in the meantime I approach a certain society. This institution, which was among the institutions under his supervision, was the "Society for the Development of the Western Territories" annexed to Poland after the war, Towarzystwo Rozwoju Ziem Zachodnich.

At the same time, in a strange coincidence, I received a letter signed by the Rector of the WSNS. Apparently Nazarewicz, my friend from my studies, had not forgotten me and took care of my case thoroughly. He was also apparently the one to take care of the WSNS. All kinds of people worked in the Society for the Development of the Western Territories. Most were anti-Semitic, largely from the Poznań region. However, funnily, they were afraid of me, because they thought I had been sent to monitor them. I did not try to correct their mistake. Ostensibly, I worked in a rather rich library (I say ostensibly, because no one did anything). Sometimes we took trips to the western territories to search for a connection to the nation on the banks of the River Oder. A few dozen people (as well as the workers at the branches, of whom apparently there were hundreds) who could not get work anywhere else found there Synekura (a good position with no real content). I was busy looking for archival material about Jan Bloch at the time, and I finished my master's thesis. After receiving my MA, I began the process of progressing to a doctorate.

After two years, in 1963, I moved to a much more interesting job in the First Department of the Polish Academy of Sciences (Polska Akademia Nauk, PAN), which supervised all the humanities and social sciences institutions. The PAN and its departments are housed in "Pałac Kultury i Nauki" (Palace of Culture and Science—Stalin's gift to Warsaw, hated by its residents). The First Department occupied the twenty-first floor of this palace. The manager of the First Department was Stefan Żółkiewski, a professor of literature. He was a wonderful man, so fat that a special enormous chair was made for him. In these terrible years, he underwent an intellectual and ideological metamorphosis. He had two replacements: Professor Aleksander Zawadzki, an expert on international law, careful in his public expressions but an honest and good-hearted man, and Professor Tadeusz Cieślak, a historian, who rose in rank on the wave of anti-Semitism. He was responsible for personnel in the department and the scientific institutes it oversaw. Later, he also served as branch secretary of the party in the PAN. This was my last workplace in Poland.

As a senior assistant, I coordinated and adapted research programs for all the scientific institutes that this department oversaw. In carrying out my duties (every year I prepared a booklet on the topic), I was constantly in contact with the highest scholarly echelons in the fields of humanities and social sciences (the Institute of History and Sociology, the Institute for Linguistics, the Institute of Literature, etc.). I often also joined meetings of the highest authority of the PAN, presided over by the president, Professor Henryk Jan Jabłoński (at the end of the 1960s, he served as minister of culture and science). There, I witnessed fervent discussions regarding the future of the humanities in Poland. I will not forget the concern expressed by the oldest of the professors (Tadeusz Kotarbiński), who despaired over the lack of the study of ancient Greek and also complained that the study of Latin was far from satisfactory (what would he have thought of the state of humanities today?).

Visits to Israel

I did not have contact with my family in Israel for a long time. In the summer of 1956, as part of my studies, I often visited the university library on Nowy Świat Street. One day, on my way home, I ran into my acquaintance Mrs. Kowalski. She was among the veterans and activists of the Polish Communist Party (her husband was murdered in Soviet Russia and the president, Bolesław Bierut, managed to get her out of there after the war). I was surprised that she was so happy to see me. She pulled me to the gate of a nearby building and spoke to me harshly, reprimanding me for failing to try to contact my family in Israel. I did not understand what she was getting at, I did not even know she was Jewish. However, I immediately caught my mistake and asked her:

"And you, have you tried to make contact with your family?"

Instead of answering my question, she took from her bag a picture of my sister Esther, whom I had not seen for eighteen years, with her family, which I had never met. I do not need to describe the storm of emotions I felt and my embarrassment. I looked at her in wonder.

The situation was absurd and impossible to grasp. While I was in the Soviet Union in the war, I corresponded with Esther constantly, I received from her letters, and via the JOINT, I also received from her a few packages of clothes. People did not want to believe it, but this was the truth. In one of the packages was a gray woolen blanket, from which the tailor Avraham made me a decent suit of clothes while I was in Berezniki. After the war, in Poland, I was in touch with my sisters, Esther and Shoshana (the latter immigrated to Israel in 1948), until the start of the 1950s. Yet the show trials of 1952–1953 involving Jewish doctors in Moscow and Zionists and "cosmopolitans" in all the countries of the Soviet bloc, and the persecution of people who had any contact whatsoever with the West, in particular Israel, paralyzed everyone, including me. The connection with my family was severed.

Now, on Nowy Świat Street, Mrs. Kowalski told me about her visit to Israel. I found out that this woman, who was very close to the leadership of the ruling party—I had no idea what she did exactly, but she certainly knew which way the political winds were blowing—was the first to know about a thaw in the political attitude toward Israel and the possibility of visiting the country. Without telling anyone, she was also the first Pole to visit Israel. Kowalski's visit made echoes here in Israel. The sensation was loaded with strong feelings, and in the first two weeks of her time in Israel, as she told me, masses of people whose relatives had remained in Poland crowded around her, seeking to discover their fate. Kowalski told me: It was already evening, and the people had dispersed. One small woman remained sitting in the corner of the sofa, crying quietly. Kowalski approached her and asked why she was crying and what she was doing there.

This was my sister Esther. She explained that she had been waiting for many hours and now it was so late, but she was afraid to ask about my fate. Perhaps I was no longer among the living or maybe she did not know me at all. When Kowalski heard she was talking about me, she burst out laughing. "You are Bina's sister? I don't know just her, but also her children. We meet almost every day for lunch together." I saw her in a restaurant on Bagatela Street, where I ate lunch, frequently together with my children. I did not have time to cook, and I used this restaurant, which was ostensibly for the higher ups, meaning it was good and cheap (indeed, I worked at a newspaper run by the Central Party Committee). Sometimes, my son Witek went there to bring home meals for the entire family, and we had a special set of dishes for this. This Kowalski, when she saw me there, always sat next to my table to talk to me. She could, therefore, tell my sister everything she knew about my family.

The meeting with Kowalski was, for me, a refreshing gust of wind from another world. She told me about her impressions of Israel and added that the separation of Polish citizens from the

West had caused terrible damage to Poland's image in the world; she told me about the country and its people. Clearly, I immediately wrote to Esther and Shoshana, and I asked after Moshe, my oldest brother, and his family. I started to take steps to obtain permission to visit Israel with my children.

We traveled at the beginning of August in that same year, 1956. We flew to Zurich and stayed there for eight hours. I took my children for a short walk in the beautiful city, and from there we flew to Israel. Hania was then six, graceful and full of life, and Witek, twelve, was dressed in a white shirt with a red necktie of the Scouts. I dressed him like this to show off, and so we arrived on the El Al plane in Lod.

Our arrival aroused great curiosity as soon as we landed, especially the children, and Witek with his red kerchief. The family was waiting for us. Amidst all the hugs and tears, I did not notice that the journalists saw my Witek as something special and ran up to talk to him. Not only did I receive a shock from my meeting with the "rotten West," full of doubts and suspicions, but I was also angry at the journalists: they did not understand that an interview with my son was likely to cause my family suffering.

We all went to Haifa, where our small family resided. The Hadary family, Esther, Shlomo, and their two sons, lived on Allenby Street, in a large house, formerly owned by Arabs that was now divided between the two families. The neighboring family was Armenian, and the two families were very friendly. This was the period of austerity and my entire family lived modestly and in poverty. This was especially true of Esther's family. I did not grasp then how much they endeavored to give us the feeling that all was well.

Esther shyly asked if we liked tomatoes. Certainly, we did. In Poland we only had tomatoes in the summer, and they were relatively expensive. She was happy about this, and we ate bread with tomatoes and salads in evenings and mornings.

Esther and Shlomo worked a lot. They told me about their life on the kibbutz—they had been among its founders—about the hard work, about the poverty, and Esther's illness. They left the kibbutz because she did not want to be a burden, endeavoring to build their life anew. Shlomo, a handsome man, with gray eyes and a blonde forelock then fashionable in Israel, dressed in an open-necked white shirt, did not look like a Polish Jew. He was a typical Israeli, like the ones you see in pictures of those years, the generation that established and built the state. It was impossible not to love him. In addition to this he was a wise man. He returned from the war (he fought in the Israeli unit of the British army) with many medals, and he was also decorated in the War of Independence. He was offered tempting state jobs, but he rejected all of them and chose to be a simple worker. He arranged a group of people like him and together they worked in construction (so I believe). Dubi, their oldest son, today a psychologist, was two years younger than Witek. Then we thought that he would be a musician because he already played the violin beautifully. Gideon, the younger son, was six, Hania's age. Today he is also a psychologist, living with his family in London. The children did not understand one another, but somehow they found a shared language in games, in particular Gidi and Hania.

Esther and Shoshana argued over who had the greater right to host us. I had to stop the argument and maintain the peace between my sisters. In truth, being with Esther's family was a special experience. Shlomo, who I had only just met, was an interesting and unique character (I knew Shoshana's Moshe from Poland and I felt at home with them). Friends from the kibbutz, all from Poland, came to visit Esther and Shlomo and spoke freely in Polish or Yiddish. It was interesting to hear their stories about life in the kibbutz. I found in Shlomo an understanding friend, even more than Esther, because she, so it seemed to me, felt somewhat hurt, or felt sadness that we had not managed to be more open in our childhood. I was not the only one who retained complexes from childhood; Esther too was full of them. In addition, I felt that Esther was trying hard to create a closeness between us. Yet, every so often, without meaning to, she repeated what she used to say to me when we were children: "What do you know, did you read the Bible?" Immediately, she would regain her composure and we laughed together. For hours upon hours, after the children went to sleep, we sat and remembered our miserable childhood. I loved her very much.

With Shoshana and Moshe, I felt, as I said, at home. I loved being with them. Naftali, who left Poland when he was thirteen years old, was now an officer in the IDF. Tall and handsome, with a moustache, he looked like Shoshana but was always happy like his father, Moshe. He was then dating a beautiful girl, with whom I could not talk due to the language gap (they married, Shoshana was happy, but after a while they divorced). Naftali still remembered Polish. To this day, when he calls me, he asks me how I am in Polish. His father, Moshe, fell in love with my children, in particular Witek, and Shoshana, who all her life had longed for a daughter, spoiled Hania. This pampering and her happiness radiate from the pictures that eternalized these moments. Together with my two sisters and their children, we enjoyed many hours at the beach, ate sabras, and endeavored to eternalize in our memories of this happy time together. I never thought that twelve years later we would become permanent residents of Israel.

Of course, we visited our brother Moshe a few times. In his home, the atmosphere was totally different. As I already related, even before the war there was a distance between us. The relationship between us was not like my relationship with Shoshana. This was due to the age difference, because we did not grow up together, and also because of the relations between Moshe and my father, his stepfather. However, before the war, his wife, Yitche, a warm and wise woman, brought us closer together. She perished, together with their daughter Rita (Rivka) in Auschwitz. After Auschwitz, Moshe was a different man. So too his second wife, Hannah, she was also a survivor of Auschwitz, and whom I had not met before, was different. Moshe became more religious, his home was very traditional, his small daughter, a beautiful girl, Sara-Ahuva, looked at us as though we came from a strange world. Moshe, who left Poland in 1946, thought that his homeland was a dark and terrible place. He had to check our shoes, to see whether they were made from real leather (in Israel, the soles were no longer made of leather, while in Poland, an agricultural country, there was no lack of leather for shoes and soles). He felt our clothes and was surprised to find us not badly dressed. They had a clothes shop on Jaffa Street. Moshe told me a lot about Auschwitz, about what he endured there, about the death march, about the tragic death of David, only weeks before the liberation. If I am not mistaken, we ate with his family a festive meal on Rosh Hashanah, which that year was at the end of August. We received a few gifts from his family and from him.

It is worthwhile relating one of our experiences during the visit to Israel in 1956.

Esther, the proud Zionist and patriotic Israeli, wanted to enchant me with one of the national achievements. She organized for us (presumably with Shoshana's financial help) a trip to Jerusalem. We traveled to Jerusalem by train, Esther, our four children, and I. The city itself truly enchanted me (later we would live there; I love life there and with great sadness moved to Tel Aviv and Holon). There was a heavy khamsin and we ran from one shady place to another, visiting Mt. Zion, which then was the border with Jordan. From afar, down below, we saw the Western Wall. (The Jews praying in Poland always turned east, to this wall, the ancient remnant of the Temple. It is interesting, in Polish it is called the Wailing Wall—Ściana Placzu.) There, on the mountain, I saw a world that I had almost forgotten. I saw the grave of King David and the memorial to the Jewish communities destroyed by the Nazis (which, after the establishment of Yad Vashem, was moved to a new location), and more. In the midst of everything, I suddenly heard a tune that paralyzed me. This was my father's melody, the tune that accompanied his Talmud study on Sabbaths and early on Sunday mornings, the tune that accompanied me everywhere. Esther came close, embraced me, and together we stood and listened. Both of us, without noticing, had tears streaming down our faces. A scholarly man saw us and came out to ask what the matter was. Esther told him our story. The man was moved and accompanied us to the local synagogue. He spoke to me in Yiddish, and turned to Witek in fluent Polish:

"In Poland, where you live, are there people dressed like this?" he asked, meaning a kaftan and shtreimel. My son, a total goy, answered, "We don't have such a fashion."

"Du herst? Oy vey, they don't have such a fashion."

I felt uncomfortable. However, this Jew was not shocked. Cheerfully and with great patience, he explained to him the meaning of this dress. He then also became our guide.

Esther wanted to show us the new building of the Knesset that had been built not long before, in particular the paintings by Chagall and the revolving doors, an impressive technological innovation. I did not want to hurt her patriotic pride. (In Warsaw this was already nothing new. Also, some banks in prewar Łódź had revolving doors. However, we then had no reason to go to banks.) It was getting late, and the children were tired. After a meal in a restaurant, she took us to a modest hotel, where we spent the night, and the next day we went to see the new Knesset. Sadly, it was closed. We went back to Haifa.

Before leaving Israel and parting with my family, I had a long and interesting conversation, actually my last one, with Shlomo (he died three years later, in 1959, in his fifties). I, who saw my home as being in Poland and not in Israel, promised to remain in constant contact with them; perhaps I would have another opportunity to come to visit them. However, Shlomo, as though he foresaw the future, said to me:

"Don't be so sure. Days of darkness may come upon you, and you will be in distress. Establish a code, so that you can give us a sign of life."

How right he was! How sad that he did not see his vision come true.

The time came to part. The suitcases were heavier because of all the presents we got. The parting from my dear ones was, as expected, full of tears.

I left my family and Israel with very mixed feelings. When we left Poland, there was a feeling in the air that the authorities were implementing a policy of anti-Semitism under the guise of a change of the guard. While in Israel, the emphasis on Jewish patriotism, which bordered on extreme nationalism, grated on me.

At the airport in Okęcie, just outside Warsaw, Heniek and Szlamek were waiting for us. After embraces, I breathed freely and said, "What a great feeling to come home."

The two men looked at one another and did not understand. However, on the way home from the airport they told me that in Cracow a young Jewish woman had killed herself after she was fired from her job because of her religion. They told me that many of our friends had been fired for the same reason; that in the entire country Jews were being persecuted. All this within the month I had spent in Israel! This information was like a jug of cold water on my pounding head.

Since then, at home and among our circle of friends, we argued about our place and our future. This became even more pronounced after October 1956, after the night that Warsaw was besieged by Soviet tanks and our friend Józek Jezierski found refuge with us, fearing that on the "night of the long knives" conducted by the Public Security Ministry, he would be arrested or killed. He was the secretary of the branch of the party in Mokotów, one of the areas of Warsaw. The next day I also participated in a demonstration. Józek was fired from his job.

The atmosphere at home was tense. Heniek did not know what to do. He was a Communist. As long as he believed that a society was being built according to his beliefs, he saw his place in Poland. However, now they did not want us. He started to wonder where his real place was and talked about leaving and immigrating to Israel. Finally, after harsh arguments, it was decided at the beginning of 1957 that we would submit a request to immigrate to Israel. Quite a few of our acquaintances had done so (among them Dorka and Heniek Francuz, Manes Zonszajn with his son Lazar, and others). Even though I knew that the act of submitting the request obligated us, I ate myself up, I could not rest, I was sorry that I had agreed to this step. However, after three months, we received a negative reply from the MSW: they would not allow us to leave Poland. To a certain extent I was pleased, I thought mainly about my children and my plans. I would now be able to achieve my goals and I had time to think.

Heniek never mentioned the idea of emigrating again. However, when Hania's hearing problem, which I talked about before, became evident, we wanted to consult with experts out-side Poland. When we received an invitation to consult doctors in Vienna and Israel, Heniek wanted to take the opportunity and visit Israel via Vienna.

In summer 1958, Hania and Heniek left to see experts outside Poland, who supported those in Poland. (Over time, Hania got used to this issue and her healthy ear took on the role of the dam-aged one. Hania's hearing is especially sharp.) Heniek and Hania stayed in Israel for a few months, not only because of her illness. In the depths of his heart, Heniek was apparently ready to stay. Thinking back, I do not believe that he would have committed an illegal act (fleeing Poland). However, another event sped up his decision to return to Poland.

As I already noted, Heniek worked as a journalist at Polish Radio. Ostensibly as a trick, although in complete seriousness, while he was in Israel, Heniek was chosen to serve as Secretary of the Polskie Radio Party branch. They called me and asked me to inform Heniek of this. I wrote to him, and he hurried home. I am not sure but the hand of the Polish ambassador in Israel may have been involved in this (if I am not mistaken, his name was Bida). He knew my husband from their army days in Lublin and afterward when he was head of the censorship. Heniek told me, after he came back, that he met him a few times, and he even suspected that embassy personnel were following him. There was another reason for his return: his wife and son. He felt that he could not tear his family in two, and he returned to Poland feeling uncertain about Israel. There was no more talk about leaving for Israel.

The Six Day War in Poland—Exodus

Over the coming decade we did not talk about leaving. These were ten intensive and important years in our lives. Witek studied in the Warsaw Polytechnic and in 1968 received an MA. Hania finished high school in the same year with a matriculation certificate. Heniek worked at the radio and finished his master's degree in sociology. In 1963, I embarked on a doctorate and invested all my efforts in research. That same year, I succeeded in traveling to the Soviet Union, to the archives in Leningrad (St. Petersburg) and Moscow, where I found an abundance of material on the development of industry in Warsaw's Wola quarter in the nineteenth century, which was the topic of my PhD dissertation. The Wola quarter was also the Jewish quarter at that time, and later, during the Holocaust, the Warsaw Ghetto uprising took place there. In my searches in the state archive in St. Petersburg, in the Saltykov-Shchedrin State Public Library in Moscow, I noticed that most of the stock companies and most of the workshops established and active in nineteenth-century Warsaw were owned by Jews and concentrated in Wola. I noted then to myself the statistics of the Jewish industrialists not only from the Wola area, and I thought that there is perhaps reason to go back and study the topic (without knowing that I would finish it a few years later in Jerusalem).

In those years it seemed that our lives were stable yet intensive. Materially, we belonged to the middle class, the intelligentsia. I worked in a prestigious place, the Academy for Humanities and Social Sciences, and Heniek—in a no less important place—the state radio. Hania registered and was accepted to study at university, and Witek began to work in his profession. At home we did not talk about leaving. Even if we knew that someone, even one of our friends, was leaving Poland, it was as though it did not affect us.

Indeed, there were arguments and disagreements at home regarding the political situation in the country. While Heniek, who worked at the state radio, endeavored to accept the policy as it was, I was "on the fighting opposition." In these arguments, Witek stood at the side and did not want to get embroiled in politics, saying: "Mother opens the Szczekaczka (barker)"—so they called the radio station "Free Europe," the Polish Radio in Western Europe for Polish audiences, which was the most popular in the 1960s, because faith in the official media had significantly declined. The graffiti on the walls of the streets shouted out "Prasa Kłamie"—"the media lies."

I should add that the stability was deceptive. In the high echelons of Gomułka's autocratic leadership there were slow but dramatic changes: people aligned with Moczar and Kazimierz Witaszewski (whom they called Kazio gazrurka, "Kazio gas pipe," because he suggested beating the protestors and striking workers in Łódź with rubber pipes) entered the mechanisms of the party and the regime. The first was already at the head of the Ministry of Public Security (Bezpieka) and the other served as head of the administration of the Central Party Committee. And these figures and their associates amassed power. In his speech to the plenary session of the thirteenth party summit (July 1963), Gomułka adopted a line opposing the intelligentsia and scientists. Persecutions and many arrests began. Thirty-four of the most prominent writers and scientists signed a protest against the persecution of the creative intelligentsia and made a big noise in Poland and outside. Despite everything, the political clubs were still active in Poland, and it was impossible to silence the desire for freedom. Jewish young people were also involved in these clubs and in the demonstrations and student activities. The names of these Jews became an example of the "Jewish conspiracy," which the newspapers constantly discussed. Moczar's people prepared for a decisive war against the left.

It would be too simplified and inaccurate if I defined the events of 1967–1968 only as an anti-Semitic crusade conducted by Gomułka, Moczar, and the "radical" Communists. The problem was much deeper. A brutal fight for the control of the state was underway between different groups. This was also a battle over the extent of Poland's independence or the extent of loyalty to the "big brother," the Soviet Union. The Jews and the anti-Semites were only a tool in the game, used by those groups. The victims of the persecutions were Professor Adam Schaff, Professor Baczko—Jews—and Professor Leszek Kołakowski, Professor Stefan Żółkiewski—non-Jews; Michnik, Jew, and Kuroń, Modzelewski, non-Jews, and others. However, the media was constantly striking against Jews.

⊱⊰

From the end of May 1967, the media outlets in Poland were full of news about the tension in the Middle East. The speeches given by Egypt's leader, Nasser, concerning Zionist aggression in the region, were quoted at length. At the end of June, Egypt closed the Straits of Tiran, a step that prevented the movement of Israel's ships, and, on June 5, as is known, the Six Day War between Israel and its three Arab neighbors, Egypt, Syria, and Jordan, broke out. After three days, the advisors of the political committee of the countries belonging to the Warsaw Pact (Układu Warszawskiego) met in Moscow. They decided to sever diplomatic relations with Israel and embark on propaganda against Zionism and the State of Israel. This decision was obligatory for all countries in the eastern bloc.

The events of 1967–68 were a turning point in my life and the life of my family, and they were accompanied by significant shocks. Therefore, I want to mention them from a personal and very private perspective. I want to put down on paper the feelings, the atmosphere around me and in our home, and the personal experiences of a Jewess, a former Communist, who despite everything felt very connected to Poland, the land of her birth and the soil in which her forefathers and loved ones are buried. It seems to me that I would not be mistaken if I said that my personal experiences in those days were the same as those of most Jews still living in Poland.

From the moment that the war broke out, Poland blindly supported the Soviet Union and its policy in the Middle East. In this Polish imitation of the Soviet Union, Israel's actions seemed like "imperialist madness." It was assumed that it would fall like a ripe fruit into the hands of the interested parties. Against this background it is necessary to understand the statements made by Gomułka in his speech at the Congress of Trade Unions of Poland: he pronounced that most Jews are a "fifth column in Poland." In saying this, the Polish ruler sought to initiate an unprecedented anti-Jewish battle and to distract the Polish audience's attention from internal battles, thus destroying the opposition. This speech was followed by a wild witch hunt.

From that moment, I started to talk about leaving Poland. However, it was not easy. I thought that there could be no going back after Gomułka. I could not be a second-class citizen in Poland, my birthplace. In the meantime, in the first days of the war, the radio and the newspapers publicized the dazzling victories of the Arab armies over the IDF. They reported that the regiments of the Egyptian army had conquered Tel Aviv. We were gripped by fear. First and foremost I feared for my relatives living in Israel: two sisters and a brother, a Holocaust survivor, with their families. Heniek's brother Shmulik lived in Tel Aviv with his family. We switched to listening to Free Europe or the BBC (it was necessary to be careful that the radio could not be heard in the street), and these stations gave us completely different information.

I don't remember which day of the war it was. We managed to catch the BBC broadcast as its correspondent gave a report directly from Jerusalem. We could hear the voices and feel the atmosphere. These were the first moments following the occupation of the eastern part of Jerusalem, and the report was broadcast from the Western Wall. In our home at 9 Rakowiecka Street, I heard for the first time the song "Jerusalem of Gold," sung by the soldiers and the impassioned masses. How did I feel? I felt a lump in my throat, while the tears streamed down my face. Heniek also cried. I saw the shade of my father, the shades of masses of Polish Jews murdered and burned in the Nazi extermination camps, who until their last breath raised their eyes eastwards to the Western Wall, to the remnant and symbol of the Temple destroyed two thousand years before, and prayed.

I was not a Zionist. However, after listening to this report, far from the land and the war, I was closer to it emotionally than ever before. Perhaps in particular because of this I felt that the dazzling victory gave Israel an opportunity to reach a peace agreement with its neighbors. I said then (and my son, if he remembers it, can testify to this) that Israel needed to give back all the territories it had taken, apart from Jerusalem and the Western Wall.

It became clear that not only were we listening closely to the receiver and the broadcasts of the BBC; the same was true of almost all Jewish homes.

The Six Day War ended, but in Poland the humiliating and lying campaign against the Jews continued. This necessarily caused a social awakening in many directions with different meanings.

The anti-Zionist, anti-Semitic crusade was relentless. Everyone who had any connection to Judaism or empathy for Israel—even if he was not Jewish—was fired from his job. The authorities listened in at homes and offices. For example, in the editorial team of the journal *Przyjaciółka* (Girlfriend, a journal for women) there was a small party the day after Israel's victory. Among the workers were one or two Jews, and the entire team was interrogated by the Ministry of Public Security (UB); an officer who referred positively to IDF officers was fired from the army and stripped of his rank and rights, etc.

Also, many Poles listened to the BBC and Free Europe. They derived a lot of pleasure from Israel's victory over the Arab states. There were good reasons for this, as many Poles explained to me. First, they hated Soviet Russia, therefore they were happy that the vast amounts of Soviet weapons provided to Nasser's Egypt and Syria proved to be outdated and inefficient, and most fell into the hands of the IDF. Second, the Poles boasted suddenly about the bravery of our soldiers and the IDF officers, many of whom were of Polish origin; some of them even trained in the Polish army (to what extent this was true, I do not know). Although Moshe Dayan was a "sabra" and had apparently never even been to Poland, Poles suddenly saw him as a brother and friend; here and there rumors circulated that he had finished the officers' training school in Poland. Apart from this, many of them equipped themselves with maps of the Middle East and noted that only with difficulty could one find tiny Israel among the Arab states. Thus, the authorities' wild anti-Israel crusade, which was so difficult to understand and false, aroused a protest against the blind imitation of the Soviet Union's policy. The evident empathy for Israel among significant parts of the Polish population aroused the anger of the authorities against the Jews. This in turn increased the concern among other Poles regarding the damage that the increasing anti-Semitism was causing to Poland's good name and awakened their conscience.

The anti-Semitic crusade did its job. It brought to light the hatred of the Jews rooted among the Polish masses. Now, the ruling party became a clear and open flag bearer of anti-Semitism. Under this flag, all kinds of dubious elements from all ends of Poland united. In a very short period, the party doubled in numbers.

In 1966, I signed a contract with the publisher Pa stwowe Wydawnictwo Naukowe (Polish Scientific Publishers, PWN) regarding the publication of two studies: one of them was part of my PhD dissertation, and it appeared in the eighth volume of *Warszawa Popowstaniowa* after we left Poland (years later I received a copy of my article sent to me by Professor Jerzy Tomaszewski). The second study that I submitted, and for which I received a lot of money, was never published.

I want to describe this last study and the stages of my research. I agreed to undertake it in cooperation with Ms. Jurkowski, who worked in the historical department of the Warsaw Committee, because the subject was close to the topic of my PhD dissertation. This was a monograph on one of the most famous metal factories in the capital, "Drucianka" (a factory that made wire). In the mid-nineteenth century, it was established by Jews in Praga, Eastern Warsaw. After World War I, the factory passed to the hands of the government and in the period between the two world wars it was owned by the government and became one of the factories in the state defense industry. My role was to study and write the history of this factory from the nineteenth century until the Second World War, and Ms. Jurkowski had to complete the history of the factory in the last twenty years.

All the historical documentation regarding the factory was found in the archive of the Ministry of National Defense, in the military compound in the arsenal in Warsaw. Thus, in May–June 1967, I arrived at the archive, ready to investigate the files containing the documents about that factory. These were the days of great anti-Israel tension before, during, and after the Six Day War

One day, when I arrived, I found it difficult to recognize the spacious entrance hall. The wall opposite the entrance was covered with a massive poster of Moshe Dayan in the uniform of a general, his eye covered with a patch, standing in a puddle full of blood, with blood dripping from his hands. All the rest of the walls were covered with characters in the style of the Nazi Der Stürmer with captions about "Israeli imperialism." The atmosphere in the archive and the behavior towards me began to change (it was not hard to see I was Jewish, and I never denied it or hid my identity). I tried, therefore, to speed up my searches there.

The social tension in Warsaw increased, the guards of Moczar and the police sought victims for their bullying and displays of power, even by using provocations. The grotesque order to take a classic play off the stage brought out the students and their teachers to demonstrate in the streets, not only in Warsaw, but in all university cities. The National Theater staged the play Dziady, based on the drama by Adam Mickiewicz, the well-known national poet of the nineteenth century. The poet wrote it between the 1830s and 1840s and it was mainly aimed against Tsarist Russia's conquest of Poland. Ever since its debut, it was staged repeatedly, almost every year. This time, in March 1968, lists of those who went to see the play were drawn up, the actors were suspected of special intonations in certain dialogues that emphasized the repression of freedom by the Russian Tsarist conquerors, and the audience response was considered a protest against the Soviet Union and even against the Soviet regime. After two shows, the play was taken off the sage. Then the student rebellions began, accompanied by a chain of unprecedented provocations by the police and members of the internal security force, the UB.

In the last few years, especially on the thirtieth anniversary of the events of 1967–1968, many books and studies appeared in Poland, including collections of documents about the events, all emphasizing two factors that enflamed the masses: the brutal anti-Semitism and the provocations by the party and ruling authorities. Therefore, I will not repeat these details. I will only emphasize that I was not on the margins of these occurrences.

As I mentioned, I worked in those years at the PAN and was also a research student writing a PhD dissertation, meaning also a student. The atmosphere in the department of humanities was tense. Most of the academic staff participated in the student strikes in the University of Warsaw as did Professor ółkiewski, head of my department and a full member in the leadership of the PAN. He remained all night with his students in this university (the next day he was thrown out of the party and in response said something contemptuous that was not for the record). His office was full of people coming and going and bringing information about what was happening at all the institutions of higher education in the country. On the twenty-fifth floor in the Palace of Culture and Sciences (my department was on the twenty-third) was the Central Office for planning the scientific research of all branches and institutions of the PAN. I had a professional and personal connection with this office. They usually did not suffer from overwork. For the most part, each one of them dealt with studies or planning, like me, for third or fourth degrees. During this period, they sat constantly by the Radio receiver, which was tuned to the BBC or radio Free Europe, and when they heard about some new event, they phoned me to come up for a cup of coffee. Among them was a woman named Bronisława Bratkowska, a smart woman, with much experience, but almost disabled due to a joint inflammation. She lived with her disabled mother on the outskirts of Warsaw (I believe in Jabłonna). We liked each other.

The police forces and secret agents dressed up as Warsaw workers and burst into the university. They stole from the changing room the IDs of those people whose surnames sounded Jewish. Non-Jewish suspects hunted down the owners of the IDs and hit young men and women, leaving them bloody and beaten. The atmosphere was depressing. For the first time in history, the police broke into an institution of higher learning in Poland. All the institutions for higher education and high schools declared a strike and went out into the streets. There were clashes with the police and the like.

In those crazy days, Pani Bronia (Bronisława Bratkowska) invited me to move with my family to her home because of the hunts conducted by Moczar's bullies (during the Nazi occupation her house had served as a hiding place for several Jews). Moved, I embraced her from the depths of my heart, and I answered that this time I was not helpless. We did not intend to hide in a country that we had until now considered our homeland.

For a long time, I had not attended a meeting of the PAN Party branch, although I still had a membership card. Indeed, I was afraid that should I return it, I would lose my job. However, now I did not care. In those days, accounts were being settled with Jewish members at all meetings of party committees and I wanted to hear from the mouths of the members of the party about what was happening. I went to the meeting of the party in the PAN to hear from them. Professor Tadeusz Cieślak was then acting as secretary of the organization and chair of the meeting. At his side sat Professor Richard Kołodziejczyk, who oversaw my MA thesis and was the secretary of the party in the PAN's Institute of Sociology and History. The meeting was very interesting. A cleaning woman stood up, in her hand a page on which her speech was written. She poured fire and sulfur on the agents of Zionism, such as Professor Bros, the known economist, Professor Baczko, a sociologist well-known throughout Europe, Professor Krajewski, the historian, and the list went on and on. In the hall were members of the academic staff who were party members—professors and doctors and other workers with degrees and without. No one responded. After a long and meaningful silence, one young woman, a treasurer of the organization who worked in the general secretariat of the PAN, was the only one who sharply attacked the anti-Jewish crusade that the "famous thinkers" in the party were conducting. There was no response to her performance either. Perhaps the academic staff saw it as beneath their dignity to answer the cleaning woman's rude speech. But this may also have been an expression of the fear reining in the entire country.

After this meeting, I went to Professor Cieślak and, without emotion, gave him back my membership card. We had a very interesting conversation. I cannot reconstruct it and that would be unnecessary. I will only emphasize that Cieślak, a professor who rose to prominence on the wave of anti-Semitism, spoke openly, without hiding anything, about the fact that Jews had penetrated every nook and cranny of the regime; that they held key positions in Polish scientific institutions, in Polish culture, etc., meaning that Poles had no access to these positions. It was necessary to expose all of them, meaning those who were Catholic but of Jewish descent, and treat them accordingly. There was no measurement other than the Nuremberg laws. I thanked him for this open conversation and said that I now understood my place. He replied:

"Why did you ask me? This doesn't apply to you and your status at work."

Of course. I am not a person who will remain silent if you talk about Nazi racial teachings or bring accusations of being a fifth column. I no longer felt welcome. I left.

The purges of the ruling authorities and their institutions still did not touch us directly. It is hard to explain why Heniek still worked at the Polish Radio (the Polish team was explicitly against the anti-Semitic line and apparently opposed firing Jews), and I, despite the above conversation and the fact that I returned my party membership card, did not hear a single word in the style of Cieślak. Quite the opposite. It seemed that Cieślak still feared dealing openly with his boss, Professor Żółkiewski.

However, my husband and I were homo politicus: from our youth we had been involved in political and social life. It is true that since the mid-1950s, I had not been involved in party, social, or political activities. Yet we experienced what happened in the country, and the events were the topic of fierce debates in our home and our limited circle of friends. In the years 1967–1968, the arguments became more and more stormy and I, in particular, for the first time raised the existential question with all seriousness. We asked ourselves, in light of this talk about a "fifth column" and the Nuremberg laws, and considering the openly aggressive anti-Semitic line adopted by the ruling party and the authorities, even if we were still working—did we, in particular our children, have a future in this country?

This question arose repeatedly in Jewish homes in Poland. I too started to talk about it openly at home.

When, in 1957, we received a negative response to our request to leave for Israel, I was, as I said, even happy about it. I was not yet ready emotionally and mentally to leave Poland. I will not say that since then there was quiet regarding this matter at home. The proof of this was Heniek's five months in Israel with Hania in 1958. Since then, as long as I was not sure about it, Heniek remained conspicuously silent on the subject and did not want to talk about it.

Throughout that entire decade, from 1958 on, our lives in Warsaw were intense, and the family situation became more complicated. As I mentioned, in the spring of 1968, during the student strikes and the violent clashes with the police, in which students from the Warsaw Polytechnic were also involved, Witek received his master's degree (the police also visited our home to check in case Victor was involved in the strikes, but our son, in contrast to his parents, did not want to hear about politics and stood on the sidelines). That same spring, Hania finished high school and was accepted to study in the department of Art History at Warsaw University. We too, Heniek and I, were immersed in our degrees.

It was important to me that my children be able, wherever they might be and when the time comes, to continue toward their goals. I urged Heniek to make a decision. He did not want to hear about it. In one of our arguments, he told me that he would not do anything, because I was likely to regret it again. He did not want to assume the responsibility, since he worked in a state institution, etc.

I too worked in a state institution. Yet this time, despite my unending devotion to this country, which I loved and considered my homeland, I knew that I had to make the difficult decision. I did not want to hear about Cieślak's Nuremberg laws. I certainly did not want to be offered a hiding place by my friend Bronia, with all her good intentions. It was necessary to leave Poland. However, I waited to hear Victor's opinion.

Until now I have not mentioned the positions and experiences of our children, who were no longer children but young people. Without the agreement of our children, mainly Witek, who was six years older than Hania, we could not take such a fateful decision.

So, Hania, who all her life was drawn to literature and art, to Polish culture in its widest sense, and apparently to this day feels a strong connection to it, walked around dejected and silent. Although she sometimes suffered from anti-Semitism at school— more than Witek, her brother, because she looked like me—it was difficult for her to leave. And Witek? Witek had a Polish girlfriend,

Mirka, and his friends were mostly Poles. In the meantime, he was silent. So too, Heniek was silent. In March 1968, only I was vocal about the possibility of leaving for Israel, because the remnants of our family were there. One of Witek's friends was called Andrzej. The two had studied together from first grade until their master's degrees in the Warsaw Polytechnic. They were best friends. Andrzej's parents, who were in Vienna, once invited Witek (I think it was in 1966) together with their son to spend the summer vacation in Austria. I think that Andrzej's family influenced Witek's decision to a certain extent, because they also helped us. (I will not go into detail about this interesting family. Maybe one day Witek or Andrzej will write about them.) They are both here in Israel and remain good friends.

One day, Witek came home and said that he understood it was necessary to leave Poland (it was the end of June). The next day, I went to the Norwegian consulate, which dealt with emigration from Poland (together with the Jewish Agency, because Poland had severed relations with Israel). I registered my family and received the necessary papers and instructions about the next steps. There was no going back. Whoever went into this consulate was photographed by secret agents of the Polish MSW and was "burned."

I did it. I decided our fate. The next day, we presented the necessary papers with a request to emigrate and leave for Israel. The next stage was to tell our workplaces: Heniek, the radio; I, the First Department at the PAN; and Witek his new workplace. (When Witek informed his bosses that he was intending to leave Poland, they were shocked. They had no idea that he was Jewish.)

When Heniek told his workplace of our decision, he acted with great honesty: he refused the offer to continue working until he would receive permission to leave. Instead, he resigned on the spot, giving up his three months' pay and unemployment money according to the law. It is necessary to understand his feelings. He felt that he himself was responsible for the step we had taken. This was a matter of principle for him: to a certain extent, he saw it as wrong that Jews should take key positions in Poland, and he thought that to a certain degree it was possible to expect responses like those that were now current in Poland. With his decision to leave for Israel, he was abandoning Communist ideology. Staying in Poland was connected with this ideology. In addition, as it became clear to us both, he was beginning to seek a return to the national roots from which he had cut himself off in his youth.

In this regard, Heniek and I disagreed. For me, the decision to leave Poland was a result of the Polish government's policy, the persecution of Jews. In addition, I had long ago lost my faith in Communism, and I had never felt severed from my Jewish roots. True, I did not miss religious tradition. I considered Poland, as I have already emphasized, my homeland, without connection to one ideology or another and without reference to whether or not someone wanted me in this land. Therefore, I now saw myself as politically persecuted, forced to leave. This was reflected in how I dealt with Professor Cieślak (who was in charge of personnel in the humanities department of the PAN), when I informed him of our decision to leave. He received my resignation but had to take into account my right to three months' pay. He instructed me to take the compensation and leave work. (At least my salary helped us get through the months of waiting.)

So began days and months of waiting and expectation. This was a new status that we had not known before. Suddenly, people who had previously been distant acquaintances came to visit us. They were in a similar state. They became closer to us than ever. Every day brought something new, news of processes, of how winds were blowing, of how the customs people behaved, what was permitted and what was forbidden—all this arrived daily in our home. In our limited group of friends, we were the first to submit a request to emigrate, although most of them were already unemployed.

On the streets of Warsaw, we met people who until recently had held important positions, among them older people who were theorists, veterans of the Communist Party, like Leon Kasman, the former editor-in-chief of *Trybuna Ludu,* now forced into early retirement; Leon Finkelstein, formerly the editor-in-chief of the academic journal *Nowe Drogi,* now unemployed; and many others. They walked the streets of Warsaw, heads down, eyes dull. Many of them had devoted their lives to the ideology they believed in, and sat for many years in prisons. They could no longer help themselves, and they could not even emigrate. There were the ones who decided to wait. When they heard we were waiting to leave Poland, they gave us their blessing.

In the meantime, we began to live like potential emigrants. Every day we received news—who had obtained a permit and who was still waiting. Who had possessions, documents confiscated when their belongings were checked, etc. We worked according to this information. First of all, we had to prepare an official permit, signed by a notary, for all the birth certificates and other documents, and also the documents connected to our workplaces in the entire postwar period, and documents concerning our academic degrees. Every evening, trains full of Jews departed from the Gdański train station on the Warsaw-Vienna line, carrying entire families, among them our acquaintances. The platform was crowded with masses of people accompanying them. The excitement was enormous. There was also sadness. Despite the destruction and the tragedy that had beset the Jews of Poland, these people had believed in and decided to tie their fate to this country. The great majority of those leaving were members of the Polish-Jewish intelligentsia—writers, scientists, doctors, journalists, engineers, now spread through various countries in Europe, America, and Israel. They were accompanied by friends, not only Jews, also many Poles, on whose faces the pain and feelings of guilt were evident. There were fellow students who came to part from their friends, children and young people; there were students who took leave of their friends who only days before had participated in strikes in the university, protesting shoulder to shoulder. Each one brought flowers or some other memento to give to their friends who were setting out on a journey into the unknown.

And here in one of the windows was the beautiful white-haired head of the Yiddish poet Binem Heller. Outside, by the window, a large crowd accompanied him. They shook the hand of this poet, who had tears in his eyes. Binem Heller arrived in Israel and lived for a while in Jerusalem. Apparently, he did not manage to acclimatize in Israel. After a short time, he left and settled in Germany. There too he did not feel at home, and not long afterward he killed himself.

These were unforgettable evenings and hours at the train station.

In those same days, Henia (Henryka) Kitlińska came to my home worried and emotional, telling me that for the good of our children we needed to leave Poland. When I told her that we had already decided to do so and were waiting for permission, she embraced me and burst into tears. She told me that because she was involved with and close to party activists, in particular the younger among them, she knew how the wind was blowing and what was likely to happen. Therefore, she came, with great sadness, to this conclusion.

I would like to add a few words in memory of Henia Kitlińska. I met her while I was preparing for my matriculation exams, which I finally took as an external student at the beginning of the 1950s. Henia was much younger than me, married and a mother of two. The couple were "Apparatchiks," meaning workers in the mechanism of the ruling party. She was not so punctilious about her studies, and all she wanted was to get a matriculation certificate, to go up the career ladder. Although my aims were different, for some reason we became good friends. I was good at mathematics and Henia learned how to copy from me in secret during math tests (the result was interesting: my exam paper was not clean, because here and there I made a mistake and fixed it, and Henia's had clean answers, so she got a higher grade than me, and she thought that this was completely fine). Afterward, we studied together history and sociology. (With someone else named Bril, whom I already mentioned. They, in particular Henia, liked to study together with me in my home. She loved the cakes I made for the Sabbath.)

Our relationship continued after our studies. During the events of 1967–1968, she often visited us to support us with us and to offer words of encouragement. I want to believe that her recommendation that we needed to leave Poland was the result of honest and good intentions. Sometime after we left Poland, I found out that the couple had moved to Cracow. Her husband received a job as one of the secretaries of the regional Party Committee, and she was appointed his mentor. When, after twenty years, in 1988, I returned to Poland for the first time for archival research, this time as an Israeli historian studying topics connected to the history of the Jewish people, I found her phone number and called her. Her oldest son answered me. Henia came to the phone. When I suggested we meet, she asked that I forgive her, but she had no time because the next day they were leaving for Latvia. Her husband had been appointed Polish ambassador there. I do not know why she did this: perhaps she was frightened of ruining or complicating her husband's diplomatic career, or perhaps I no longer interested her. However, on the basis of our acquaintance, I think that she felt a little uncomfortable toward me due to their careers.

At the end of September, Heniek was called to the MSW. At home, I and the children waited nervously: would we receive the permit to leave this time or not? As always when I was tense, I had to do something. So, I baked a cake.

The MSW demanded that we repay the expenses of Victor's studies, a total of 30,000 zlotys. We did not have this sum. After paying it, we would need to sign a document relinquishing our Polish citizenship and then we would get a "travel document," Dokument podróży. Within twelve days of receiving this, we would have to leave Poland. And, furthermore, in that same time and before receiving this degrading document, we would have to present certificates from various institutions and libraries (there was a long list) proving that we had no outstanding debts.

Andrzej's parents loaned us the money—Andrzej was to leave for Israel a short time after us and we would return the money to him there (Witek made the repayments himself; a little later Andrzej's parents also moved to Israel). We had to run from one office to another to receive the necessary permits. Among other things, we had to make an exact and numbered list of all the books we wanted to take with us, a list of the possessions we wanted to take, beginning with the number of chairs, tables, spoons, forks, and knives, and ending with our knickers. The hardest part was the list of books, which was accompanied by conflicting feelings: it was hard to decide to part with half of our library.

We left many things. We gave some of them to our neighbors and others we sold for almost nothing. I felt very bad about this. I felt as though the rabble was lying in wait to take our home and plunder it. This was difficult, it was as though I had been through it before, in a terrifying dream: I saw the ghetto after the Gestapo emptied it of Jews, the rabble falling upon the remains of their possessions and the apartments of those who had fled the Nazis. (This also happened to Shoshana's beautiful home on 20 Pomorska Street.) Now people came looking for bargains: a washing machine, an almost new refrigerator, a desk, etc. We took basic things. We ordered a crate, which was called a lift (all the emigrants ordered these crates from the same carpenter). Half of it was filled with our books, with which we did not want to part. We took a few chairs, a table, a wardrobe that was taken apart, linens, kitchen utensils, among them glassware and, I believe, also crystal dishes for presents, and clothes.

As I said, we did not have gold and silver. We did not even have one rug that was worth taking to another country. Yet we waited for difficult days and hours before we were allowed to get on a train from Warsaw to Vienna. The last episode, which cost me health and nerves, was my encounter with the customs officials. I knew that were I to bribe the officials, they would not even open the crate. However, we were principled people. Most of the time I was the one who stayed with our belongings, facing the customs officials. Heniek was ill for a few days, and afterward he had to run around between the various offices getting permits; the children were busy with farewell parties arranged by their friends; and I had to argue with the customs officials. Because they did not get a bribe, they made my life impossible. Every pair of knickers was checked with meticulous care, the fabric padding of every chair was torn off as though they were looking for gold. They found nothing special to warrant customs payment, so they fell upon my glassware, insisting it was all crystal and I had to pay duty on it. I insisted that I knew how many pieces of crystal I was allowed to take with me. I demanded an expert opinion. They had to agree. The next day two experts came. The glasses and glassware stood on one side (together with a few pieces of crystal). The experts looked at it, looked at me, took a few pieces into their hands and determined: "There's no crystal here."

They confiscated a few things: a small folding table and a felt board, the side of which was engraved with a delicate engraving. I ran to the Ministry of Culture and Arts, but there they also confiscated two large volumes of the Talmud, similar to those that stood on my father's bookshelf, with worn leather binding. Although these were printed in the eighteenth century, it is worth mentioning how they came into our possession. When Witek was a student, he sometimes took the opportunity to work at least a few hours per week. One of his jobs was emptying a cellar full of books that were covered with mold. He knew from my stories about these books and managed to save and bring home the two heavy volumes of the Talmud, which remained in our home (by the way, all the rest of the books were left abandoned). These two suddenly became valuable, the national property of Poland.

Speaking of the books we took with us, they were meticulously checked, not only according to the list we made, but each and every book separately. All the books and journals that had anything to do with politics or the Polish ruling party were confiscated; they took from me one of the two copies of the book I wrote (Fortune is Fickle) based on my MA thesis. Why? Because they wanted to. And this was not enough.

During the months of this exodus of the remnants of Polish Jewry, the emigration authorities placed all kinds of difficulties in the way of those trying to leave. From the moment that we received our "exit permit," we were stateless, with no citizenship whatsoever. Thus, we could be treated according to the will and mood of the person responsible for our departure. It is therefore no wonder that a spontaneous connection was established among the Jewish families about to leave Poland, and ways were found to pass information about every new decree issued by the customs officials to all those affected by it. In this way I found out that the customs officials often confiscated work documents, certificates of academic degrees, awards of honor, etc. I did not care if they took the medals and awards of excellence. However, we could not give up our documents. Believing that this would also happen to me, I made a few copies of these important documents. I put two copies of our documents into two packages, each copy in a separate envelope, and each one carried his own documents. The first envelope was in my bag, and I waited for an opportunity to move it to its final destination: when the customs official was busy looking for gold in the pockets of our trousers and in the chairs, I stood by the open crate and placed in it the envelope containing the documents. Because no personal searches were conducted, but only the suitcases on the train carriage were searched, the other copy also made it safely.

The last episode with the customs officials concerned one of my suitcases. The contents were all handwritten papers, copies of archival documents that I had gathered in Warsaw and mainly in the St. Petersburg and Moscow archives, which I visited in 1965. All these copies and papers were the fruits of my toil for my PhD. The customs people refused to let me take them with me. I decided to fight for this suitcase, because it contained all my hopes and future, wherever fate would send me. I thought about approaching Professor Żółkiewski, the head of the First Department in the PAN, my former boss. However, he was no longer in favor with the authorities, and I did not want to cause him trouble. I went to Professor Sylwester Zawadzki, a known lawyer and Żółkiewski's deputy. Professor Zawadzki knew about my hard work and how valuable this suitcase was to me. He gave me a declaration that this suitcase contained personal notes and there was no reason not to return it to its owner, who was leaving Poland.

This document worked and thanks to it and the contents of the suitcase, in 1971, I received my PhD from The Hebrew University of Jerusalem. However, that is another story. Here I will mention only that my PhD was written in Polish, and my supervisor, Professor Yaakov Talmon, was not only an exceptional personality, a humanist with great knowledge, but also a man who held Polish culture in high esteem. He greatly valued my work. A few years later, I translated it into (poor) Hebrew, and, after language editing, it was published in 1985 by the Diaspora Research Institute at Tel Aviv University, to which I have been connected all these years.

The last event was surprising. A few hours before we left for the train station, we received a notice in the post that the World

Jewish Agency had given each one of our family members five or ten dollars. Twenty or forty dollars was then a respectable amount. However, it was impossible to get it: the banks were closed, and our train would depart in only a few hours. Afterward we found out that we were not the only ones: the Agency sent all the Jews leaving Poland similar amounts, but few managed to redeem them for the same reason.

Vienna—Nighttime Talks

I will pass over the moments of parting from our friends and acquaintances and our children' friends, who came to bid us farewell. I will not recount the tears and the quiet in the last moments before the train whistle blew. We set off. The last check of our belongings took place on the train on Polish soil (at any rate we managed to hide from the investigators our original documents and bring them to Israel).

We got off the train in Vienna. Behind me I left a Polish epic of fifty years. I will not say I was happy. None of us felt happy. The opposite. In particular, the children were withdrawn, sad and quiet. At the train station, the immigrants were received by representatives of the Jewish Agency and the JOINT. It was necessary to decide on the spot with which organization to make contact: those who decided to go straight to Israel were collected and taken to Schönau, a property near Vienna, managed at that time by the Jewish Agency. Those who did not intend to go to Israel were taken to a different place. We, who still had not made a final decision regarding our destination due to Victor's deliberations, as well as a few others who got off the train with us, were sent to live with various families in Vienna. We received a temporary living place with a Jewish family. How can I say this delicately? The living conditions were very, very uncomfortable.

Victor's doubts were understandable. He left in Poland his first love, Mirka. He himself had a unique profession that was in great demand (an engineer in the field, if I say it correctly, of solid state electronics). Even before we left Poland, he sent letters describing his specialty to Sweden and the Phillips Company in Germany. From both these places he received job offers. Hania, our daughter, was eighteen years old and did not feel independent and confident enough to decide on her path.

In contrast to the children we, Heniek and I, decided to go to Israel, each one for his own reasons. Heniek, who in Poland had identified with Zionism and the State of Israel, had begun to learn Hebrew—he had not a second's doubt about what to choose. I, on the other hand, wanted to go there to be with the remainder of my family, my two sisters and my brother and their families, and I also wanted to give our children firm familial and civilian support, so that they would not remain alone in a strange country. There, in Vienna, we had one aim: to persuade Witek to go to Israel. My arguments were rational: he had no citizenship anywhere in the world, only an exit permit from Poland. In any other country, he would be a migrant without identity. By contrast, going to Israel meant that he automatically belonged to a country and a people. If, after some time, he wanted to bring Mirka, he could do so; if he did not acclimatize to Israel, he could leave for wherever he wanted to go with his Israeli passport, and so on.

These conversations went on into the night and the deliberations lasted more than a week. We had no money. We had to decide where to go. In the midst of this, and due to the psychological pressure, we went once to the JOINT. There we found a long line of people. We too stood in this line. After a while, we felt suddenly, all four of us, hurt and humiliated, and we ran away. It became clear that the people there (all Jews from Poland) had been in Vienna for long months and were waiting for some country to agree to take Jewish migrants from Poland. In the meantime, they came every day or every other day to get money from the JOINT. I looked at these people, spoke with a few of them, and knew that we were not built for this. It became clear that we all felt the same.

It seems to me that Witek considered two things when eventually he agreed to go to Israel. One was the feeling of responsibility for the fate of his parents, who, at any rate, were both over fifty and their future in a new country was foggy. The second thing that deterred him apart from the uncertainty was our visit to the office of the JOINT. Our family could not live from charity and handouts.

After this visit, Witek went to talk with the representative of the Jewish Agency, a religious man of Polish origin (his name was Ta-Shma), who told him about his son, an engineer. He told Witek that, without doubt, he would immediately receive a job offer, etc. In some way, they found a common language and the next day we moved to the Schönau property. It was very beautiful and spacious there. We took trips to Vienna; there we celebrated Rosh Hashanah and Yom Kippur. One or two days before Sukkot, we landed in Israel, and immediately we were taken to an ulpan in Nazareth Ilit. We celebrated Sukkot with our family in Israel. A new chapter in our lives had begun.

EPILOGUE

I could fill another long chapter describing our life in Israel and each one of my children's achievements and failures—indeed, it has been over thirty years since we arrived in Israel. I no longer have enough time left for that. Therefore, I will briefly relate the impressions that accompanied me while writing my memories, which I wish to emphasize.

The state welcomed us with open arms. We arrived in Israel between Yom Kippur and Sukkot (we celebrated the festivals, as I mentioned, with my family in Haifa). I do not remember landing, but I do recall our arrival in Nazareth Ilit and our first encounter with the ulpan. We absorbed, first of all, the new and beautiful mountainous landscape. We found ourselves in a beautiful ulpan with a very friendly atmosphere. We stayed in a nice apartment, with three furnished rooms. Here we met a group of immigrants from Poland, whom we got to know gradually. From here on our acclimatization in Israel began.

We had a wonderful teacher, Rivka, our Hebrew teacher. She did not know even one word of Polish and most of us did not know one word of Hebrew. However, from the first day we felt a connection to her. She understood us and helped us a lot. I worried how the children would acclimate, in particular Victor, who, as I noted, had understandable doubts about moving to Israel.

Hania spent the first days like one in shock, almost not present. In the ulpan a group of young people started to get to know each other. I watched their reactions to the new surroundings. On the day we arrived or the day after, Witek came to me, his eyes gleaming, and said that the Hebrew language sounds beautiful; he liked it very much. I was very pleased, and I thought that he would stay in Israel. Indeed, his acclimatization was the quickest and the easiest. He was snatched up by the Technion in Haifa in the first month of our stay in the ulpan. A few months later, he was recruited to the IDF and did his military service during the War of Attrition in Sinai and later fought in the coming wars. The army was at the heart of his absorption and his connection with the country. Victor established a wonderful Israeli family that warms my heart.

Hania's absorption was more difficult. Together with the group of young people from Poland, she was sent to a year-long preparatory program in Haifa and was accepted by The Hebrew University of Jerusalem. She chose to study ancient history and theater. However, the studies were a painful disappointment. The level of the humanities was lower than she expected and the knowledge she had absorbed in Poland was far superior. Eventually, after finishing her studies, she did not want to continue to an MA and finished without a profession. The circle of young people from Poland underwent a crisis and some of them left for various other countries. All this affected her and made it difficult for her to settle in. Likewise, she was always picky in her communication with her surroundings, making her social absorption challenging. Now she is a professional and very talented graphic designer. She is very critical of certain phenomena in our lives and has not stopped longing for European culture. It is not hard to understand her.

The parting from our two children, who suddenly blossomed and left home, was rather hard for us, the parents, and was one of the reasons for a crisis in our relationship in the period of the move.

I took my second homeland into my heart, although over time I learned it is a hard country, full of contradictions, wars, victims and mourning, and the worst of all, a civil war. I sometimes miss the quiet, the green landscapes, the fields that are yellow in the summer and are covered with snow in the winter, the forests of Poland, and the city of my birth. I sometimes miss the wonderful Warsaw theater, the Łazienki Park, in which I walked together with Heniek and the children on free days and holidays. Perhaps these are only longings for a life that we had when we were young and that no longer exists? Two years ago, when I was in Warsaw with my son at my side, we walked again in the park full of beauty and grace, and we remembered those days.

However, I adopted my new homeland into my heart and devoted myself to learning Hebrew. I was prepared to work hard. Thanks to a scholarship from the Jewish Agency for one year (300 lirot per month), I managed to rewrite my doctorate. I had the great privilege of doing so under the supervision of one of the great professors, an international expert, Professor Yaakov Talmon, of blessed memory, a polymath, a modest man with wide horizons, a man of European culture in the best possible sense.

Before reaching Professor Talmon I was helped by a few good people that I got to know here. I want to mention Dr. Arieh Tartkover, who I met after somebody recommended that I call him. He was an academic, a historian and sociologist, who engaged, among other things, if I am not mistaken, in helping academic immigrants acclimate. Dr. Tartkover, a dear man with a massive heart, received me with love, he read my book, which had been published in Poland (an adaptation of my master's thesis) and all the rest of the documents that I brought, and he was the one to work on my behalf so that I would receive a scholarship and be accepted as a research student at The Hebrew University of Jerusalem. Through him I made contact with Professor Talmon. I have no words to describe his behavior and the warm atmosphere at our frequent meetings in his home, where I got to know his wonderful wife and his children.

The scholarship money was modest, as was Heniek's salary for his work at a Yiddish paper, funded at first by the Jewish Agency. During my searches for work and additional funding, I got to know Professor Moshe Mishkinsky, of blessed memory, who then established a workshop (the core of an institute) for the study of Jewish workers' movements in Eastern Europe. He gave me work collecting material from the various Yiddish, Russian, and Polish newspapers and journals published by the workers' movements at the end of the nineteenth century and the beginning of the twentieth century. I greatly enjoyed this work, for which I received the same very small salary that all the students received at the outset. I pinned my hopes on this institute and hoped to improve my salary when I would get my new degree. To my disappointment, the workshop was canceled after the death of Professor Ettinger, who was its patron. A short time after it closed, Professor Mishkinsky moved to Tel Aviv and became the editor of the journal *Gal-Ed*, which is devoted to Polish Jewry. This is one of the publications of the Diaspora Studies Institute that was established at Tel Aviv University. By means of this publication, I too got a foothold in this institute (eighteen editions of the journal have appeared so far and most of them include articles and studies by me).

However, getting work in Israel was no easy feat. Among my papers is a letter from Professor Simonson, then head of the institute and head of the department of Jewish history at Tel Aviv University. The letter rejects my application to work at the university and in the institute he headed. However, despite this, I was nevertheless accepted and worked there for more than thirty years. I should again mention the good people I met, Professor Moshe Mishkinsky, of blessed memory, and mainly, with special warmth, Professor Matityahu Mintz, may he live long. Over time we developed personal and professional relations and today we are almost neighbors. Professor Mintz not only worried about me: thanks to him a small group of historians from Poland were absorbed into the institute, among them Dr. Sabina Levin, Zalman Kratko, of blessed memory, and others, who retired over the years. Thanks to the recommendation of Professor Mintz, I taught at Beit Berl for eight years and afterward at the university.

In Israel I got a lot of satisfaction from my work. Academic advancement was more difficult, or, more exactly, persuading the academic regime of the importance of my field and to recognize the great importance of the history of Polish Jewry for general Jewish and Israeli history. And yet, I also enjoyed small successes. I managed to achieve something and to leave something, perhaps, for coming generations of students and scholars, and I hope that the social and political atmosphere in Israel will change. However, I do not want to recall those difficulties here.

Apart from my connection with professor Mintz and his wife Chayke, whom I esteem very much, I made new friends in the university. Among them I want to mention Professor Emanuel Melzer, also my good friend Sabina Levin, and the special friendship with the person who fixed my bad Hebrew in the first articles I wrote in this language, Dr. Aryeh Gelbard, of blessed memory. Ours was a close friendship. In the difficult days that I endured when my husband was sick, in particular the last months of his life, Aryeh frequently came to take me out of the house, to sit in a café, to spend half an hour in a different atmosphere.

In Israel I endured personal and familial traumas. The most difficult trauma concerned my husband and the father of my children, Heniek, of blessed memory, with whom I shared my life (apart from the war years) for more than sixty years. Heniek received work as a journalist at a Yiddish newspaper. He worked and managed to obtain mastery of modern Yiddish and even return to his Jewish and national roots. However, without reference to his work, a short time after we came to Israel, so it seems to me, he started to change. He underwent changes that I did not understand for a long time. He opposed me continuing my PhD and because of this there was a small crisis in our relations. We got over it. However, from year to year his character and behavior changed and became more and more strange. Over almost twenty years, his mind developed one of the most terrible illnesses known to man, Alzheimer's. His death left us with wounds on our souls for a long time.

I parted gradually from my loved ones: my sisters and oldest brother and their partners, may their memories live forever. I remained alone, the only one of my siblings. However, my small family—my children and my grandchildren—warm me and my heart in my old age. They worry about me. All my gratitude goes to them.

I started writing these memoirs at the end of the previous century, when I reached the age of 83. Now, at the age of 87, my life is apparently reaching its end. I have been writing the story of my life for more than three years, mainly the important chapters. My writing was accompanied by strong feelings. Sometimes my writing flowed as though I was possessed by a demon and I could not stop, but often it was difficult for me. When I described my childhood in the town of Końskie, I lived it once again. I saw images that I had forgotten and relived long ago moments.

In my story there are pages that were written with tears on my face and a lump in my throat. They accompanied me every time I mentioned my mother and father, Esther, Meir, Shoshana. I felt warmth when I described my various friends from my youth and later life. I must mention that in parallel to this collection of memories, I initiated and edited the memorial book for the Jews of Końskie, in which I invested a lot of thought and love. With satisfaction I can say that the book is now being published.

With great excitement and love I described how my children grew and developed and even their worries and fears—all these memories are very dear to me.

Finally, I also want to mention that strong feelings accompanied my thoughts about ideology and my disappointments. Yet, after everything, I do not regret a single thing. All these things enriched my experiences and made me the person I am, and I am happy with myself and the path I took.

March 2004.

INDEX

CREDITS

My deepest gratitude to my dear cousins Professor Goldie Morgentaler of Lethbridge, AB, Canada, Jerzy Cwifeld of Stockholm, Sweden, and Gideon Hadary of London, UK, for their active contribution, encouragement, and unwavering support to this project.

Many thanks to Professor Eliyana Adler of Pennsylvania State University for her encouragement to make these memoirs available to English-speaking readers.

Victor Kadary

Printed in Great Britain
by Amazon